THE
ULTIMATE
ENCYCLOPEDIA
CRICKET
OF

THIS IS A CARLTON BOOK
This edition published in 2006
Copyright © Carlton Books Ltd 1997, 2002, 2003, 2004, 2006

First published in 1997 by
Carlton Books Ltd
20 Mortimer Street
London W1T 3JW

10 9 8 7 6

A CIP catalogue record for this book is available
from the British Library

ISBN 1 84442 184 8

Project Editor: Martin Corteel
Editorial Assistant: Roland Hall
Project Art Direction: Diane Klein
Picture Research: Lorna Ainger
Production: Garry Lewis
Design: Steve Wilson

Printed and bound in Dubai

ACKNOWLEDGEMENTS
All the first-class statistics comply with the Match Guides
issued by the Association of Cricket Statistics. The assistance
of Philip Bailey is acknowledged in the compilation of career
records. The secretarial services of Lyn Steel proved invaluable.
The authors are also grateful for the help rendered by David
Lemmon.

PUBLISHER'S NOTE
The modern world of cricket sees internationals, both one- and
five-day, played all year round. The authors and publishers had
to institute a cut-off date for statistics and records and the end
of the 2005 English season was the obvious choice. However,
notable individual feats in the months following are recorded in
individual biographies where appropriate.

(OPPOSITE) ENGLAND'S HERO *Andrew Flintoff launches another big hit*
(OVERLEAF) SWEEPING BLOW *Michael Vaughan finds the boundary*

THE
ULTIMATE
ENCYCLOPEDIA
CRICKET

of

THE DEFINITIVE ILLUSTRATED GUIDE TO WORLD CRICKET

Peter Arnold & Peter Wynne-Thomas

CARLTON
BOOKS

CONTENTS

ADAM GILCHRIST *Greatest wicketkeeper.*

FOUR BALL *Sehwag strikes out for India.*

INTRODUCTION

This edition of this encyclopedia follows the wonderful Ashes series of 2005, where day after day of exciting cricket produced twists of fortune, cliff-hanger results and the final toppling of the long-time world champions Australia. Public interest had never been higher, with a record 8.4 million television viewers switched on to the last day's play at Trent Bridge. The ECB estimated this enthusiasm could result in an extra £20m a year added to its income. With the new Twenty20 Cup finals day filling the Oval to capacity cricket might almost be called the new football.

However, cricket's appeal is more subtle than the instant excitement of great deeds. It is a unique game which inspires a deep affection in its followers. This love of the game partly comes from its complexity and variety. There are so many angles from which the game can be appreciated and discussed. This in turn has given cricket the best literature of any sport. Such writers as John Arlott, Neville Cardus, C.L.R. James, R.C. Robertson-Glasgow, Alan Ross and Francis Thompson have written memorably about the game. Cricket is, or at least was, a game which goes with an ambience, an atmosphere, an attitude, a way of life, perhaps most commemorated in the phrase "It's not cricket", meaning something which is not in the highest traditions of fairness, sportsmanship and "playing the game". However, as with many things relating to cricket, this phrase may not be all it seems. In quoting it in *Encyclopaedia of Word and Phrase Origins* (Fact on File Publications, New York and Oxford, 1987), Robert Hendrickson suggests that the phrase was possibly first used when villagers of Boxgrove, near Winchester, were prosecuted for playing the game of cricket on a Sunday in 1622, and defended themselves by claiming, "It's not cricket", thus hoping to avoid paying their proper fines for breaking the law. If this were true, then the phrase should not represent an aspiration to the highest levels of behaviour at all but a mean way of avoiding punishment by lying.

The idea that cricket is a byword of honesty and fair play is a comparatively

recent one. Sir Henry Newbolt's poem 'Vitaï Lampada', extolling the sense of honour and bravery which the schoolboy cricketer "bears through life like a torch in flame", having felt his Captain's hand on his shoulder and his orders to "play up! play up! and play the game!" was published only in 1897, during what is now called cricket's "Golden Age".

As the chapter in this book on the origins of cricket relates, cricket had been played for hundreds of years before this, and in the eighteenth century in England was a prime form of betting for high stakes, and no doubt attracted many of the same rogues more usually associated with the equally ancient and aristocratic sport of horse-racing. Bets were struck not only on the outcome of matches but on how many runs individual batsmen would make and attendant bookmakers would change the odds about events as play progressed. Of course this led to bribery, with William Lambert of Surrey, the leading professional all-rounder of his day, being banned from Lord's after allegedly fixing the England v Nottingham match in 1817. And as the chapter on Test cricket in this book describes, two members of the English touring party in Australia in 1881–82 took bribes to lose a match and were denounced when they failed to bribe a third player, who was beaten up for reporting them. A far cry from "playing the game".

In the first half of the twentieth century the idea that people might bet on cricket would have seemed sacrilege to 99 per cent of its followers. Yet with legal restrictions lifted from betting in England in the 1960s, it was not long before bookmakers had offices or tents in the major cricket grounds and even that pillar of the establishment and conservatism, the BBC's *Test Match Special*, began telling listeners the current betting odds as Test match fortunes fluctuated. Ironically it was in 1981, 100 years after the betting scandal in Australia, that the Australian players Dennis Lillee and Rodney Marsh placed bets on England to win the Test at Headingley when the bookmakers were offering odds of 500–1 against. That Lillee and Marsh were playing and collected some very nice winnings was regarded only with amusement by cricket fans. There was rightly no suggestion of any

impropriety on the part of the Australians, only admiration tinged with envy for their good judgement.

Cricket is a game which is ever-changing, usually, according to its fans, for the worse, but, as with the gambling, what is unthinkable one day often becomes the acceptable norm the next. Sunday cricket is an example. The law banning it back in the seventeenth century did not survive long, but it was only during the Second World War that club cricket became common on Sundays in England, and it was not until 1966 that professional cricket was played on a Sunday, and even then it was still illegal to charge for admission. The Sunday League began in 1969, and the first Sunday play in a Test match occurred as late as 1981.

One-day international cricket began in Australia in 1970–71, and there is now so much of it that for space reasons this book has dealt fully only with the apex of it, the four-yearly World Cup.

Cricket fatalists are always claiming that cricket is on its deathbed. One fear is that because of the attractions of more 'instant' diversions there are not enough boys playing it in schools, which anyway lack the equipment and playing fields. Another fear is that the attention span of the average fan in today's rush of a world grows shorter and shorter and will soon be unable to cope with a game which might last for days. And the cricket fan himself is changing, to the annoyance, for example, of the typical MCC member, who likes to sit wearing his bacon-and-egg tie in the womanless pavilion at Lord's and tut at the behaviour of the bare-chested or weirdly dressed in the popular stands, especially those who chant 'England's barmy army', a recent addition to the equally mindless "Mexican wave".

Cricket has always embraced a wide variety of fans and, indeed, players. It was only a few years ago that the announcement of 'F.J. Titmus' as the batsman going out to bat at Lord's was changed as he approached the wicket to 'Titmus, F.J.', he being a professional, not an amateur. He was luckier than the turn of the century professional, who would not have his initials at all on the scorecard, while the amateur would also have the prefix 'Mr'. Thus the England openers against the Australians at the Oval were "Mr. F.S.

Jackson and Hayward". The Australians, being a sort of half-and-half, were allowed their initials but not the 'Mr.', as in M.A. Noble.

It is hoped this book will appeal to the Lords, the Misters, and those whose initials come front or back. As many aspects of the game as possible are covered. Details of the early history of the game are constantly being discovered, and the chapter covering cricket's origins contains the latest research. The spread of cricket around the world is recorded in a summary of the state of the game in those countries where it is at all organized. The Test cricket chapter attempts to give a summary of the sway of fortunes in the series of games between each pair of the ten Test-playing countries. The World Cup, thrillingly won in 1996 by one of the latest entrants to Test cricket, Sri Lanka, is covered by a chapter which describes all eight competitions to date. The players are dealt with in two sections, the larger containing biographies and career figures of almost 200 of the best cricketers in the history of the game. A separate section deals with the legends of the game and gives fuller details of 11 of the giants who have strode the cricket stage, from W.G. Grace to Brian Lara, Sachin Tendulkar and Shane Warne.

There are separate chapters on the famous grounds, on the administration and structure of the game, on the history of the Laws, on equipment, on culture, and on scandals and controversies. There is a short records and statistics section and a chronology, although the book is not meant to be a statistical tome – *Wisden* can supply all the figures – but more one to be read for enjoyment and used as a reminder and reference.

All those casual unsung scorers in club matches all over the world, who each week have to call out "bowler's name?" when the opposition make a bowling change, will be amused to hear of the cry when Glamorgan visited Cambridge University in 1996, and Glamorgan's Test bowler Steve Watkin was unlucky enough to have had his wallet stolen (at Cambridge? It's not cricket). When going out to field he asked a member of the press to cancel his credit cards for him. An enquiry from one of the issuing companies led to a yelled request from the pavilion: "bowler's mother's maiden name?"

THE EARLY HISTORY OF CRICKET

The game of cricket began in the Weald in south-east England. The landed gentry of the area adapted the game, took it to the great public schools and to Oxford and Cambridge Universities. Thence the schoolboys and students took it back to their estates. In Nottinghamshire and Yorkshire in particular the game rapidly gained popularity. Through the army, cricket was introduced across the British Empire.

The search for when and where cricket started has occupied historians since the Reverend James Pycroft made the first attempt at tracing the story of the game in 1851.

A single statement by a witness in a court case in Guildford in 1598 contains the first definite mention of cricket. John Derrick, aged 59, stated that at the time he was a schoolboy at the Free School in Guildford he and his friends played "creckett" on a disputed piece of land in Holy Trinity Parish in Guildford.

Cricket was therefore being played by boys in Guildford around 1550. In 1541 an Act of Parliament aimed at stimulating the practice of archery among the populace banned people from playing and wasting their time on a great list of common games, but cricket was not one of those. Clearly cricket at that point was confined to boys in a relatively small area of south-east England and not worthy of mention.

The second definite mention of the game again comes from the Guildford area, from the hamlet of Wanborough. Here in 1613 a person was hit by another using a "cricket staff". Nine years later an ecclesiastical court in Chichester had before it five youths accused of playing cricket in the churchyard at Boxgrove, a village near Chichester, on a Sunday. In 1624 a coroner's jury at West Hoathly in Sussex listened to a case in which a man accidentally hit and killed a fellow player with a small staff called a "cricket batt". These two men were part of a group playing cricket on Horsted Green.

Five years later came the case of the curate of Ruckinge near Maidstone being heard in the Archdeacons Court. The curate was playing at "cricketts" with some of his parishioners after divine service on a Sunday.

These stray references to cricket continue on through the seventeenth century. Plotting them on a map of the British Isles reveals that they are all confined to the south-east corner of England and form a rough crescent, from Chichester in the south-west up to Surrey and across to the south-west area of Kent. The crescent neatly encloses the Weald – that part between the North and South Downs, which in Tudor times was the Black Country of England. Some 80 iron and glass foundries flourished in the region, using the ample iron ore deposits and, for fuel, the charcoal which could be easily produced from the abundant supply of wood from the Ashdown and St Leonards forests.

It has been suggested by some historians that cricket as an organized game began among the shepherds on the Downs, the theory being that the shepherd's crook could be a bat and the wicket gate used for sheep pens could have been the stumps; in addition the pasture grazed by the sheep would have been an ideal surface on which to play. However, the first references to a cricket bat all note it to have been a small batten or staff, whereas a shepherd's crook was six or more feet in length. The sheep certainly grazed the pasture, but generally on the considerable slopes of the Downs, rather than on the flatter land which would be more useful for arable crops. The other argument against shepherds being the instigators of cricket is that looking after sheep is normally a rather solitary occupation.

It is far more likely that ironworkers and those involved in the trades connected with the iron industry were the ones playing cricket.

Whichever theory one accepts, cricket certainly became popular in the Weald, which was itself a rather enclosed community. The game therefore took many years to emerge from the south-east corner of England. In any case most other regions had their own games

CRICKET IN THE VICTORIAN ERA *An illustration from* Every Boy's Book *by Edmund Routledge (1868).*

involving balls being hit with sticks: Yorkshire had knurr and spell, Gloucestershire had stoolball, Scotland had golf, and Ireland had hurling.

In the second half of the seventeenth century cricket began to attract spectators and gamblers. In 1668 there comes a mention of men selling drink at a cricket match near Maidstone and later the accounts of two landed gentry show money being paid for cricketing purposes, especially by the Earl of Sussex who resided at Herstmonceux Castle in East Sussex, and by Sir John Pelham, who lived at Halland, north-east of Lewes.

In 1700 a series of matches was played on Clapham Common with the players each betting £10, and in 1705 there is a mention of cricket being played on Walworth Common. Cricket was about to

take London by storm. The first reference to a team styled "London" comes in a newspaper notice of 1707, when there were two "great matches" between London and Croydon, one in Croydon, the other in Holborn. The days were now clearly gone when the landed gentry and the people of the capital had no knowledge of cricket. A political pamphlet of 1712 attacking the Duke of Marlborough and Lord Townshend features the two playing cricket supposedly near Fern-hill in Windsor Forest for 20 guineas.

That match may be fanciful, but cricket was certainly established at Trinity College, Cambridge, before then – Thomas Blomer, a fellow of the college, wrote in 1710 that the undergraduates were eating their meals too fast, in order to go out and play cricket.

The first detailed description

of a cricket match was published in 1706 in London. The author was William Goldwin, who was educated at Eton and King's College, Cambridge, and had gone up to the university in 1700. The description was written in Latin but a translation shows that the game Goldwin described would be easily recognizable as the game played today, with stumps and bails, a level pitch, two umpires and batsmen being dismissed bowled or caught, and the scoring of runs, which were recorded by a scorer.

With cricket now a common game among the landed gentry, as well as among the general public (a diary kept by Thomas Marchant, of Hurstpierpoint in Sussex, makes frequent references to inter-village matches in the locality), and with considerable sums of money being wagered on games, there must have been an agreed set of laws. It is most

frustrating for historians that the earliest set extant date only from 1744, though it has been proved fairly conclusively that the 1744 version is a revision of an earlier code.

Several of the great landowners in the south-east were no longer content to go to matches and simply place their bets. They decided to form their own cricket teams and challenge each other. A letter of 1725 reveals that such challenges were taking place between the Duke of Richmond and his side from Goodwood, near Chichester, and Sir William Gage's side from Firle near Seaford. A third challenger was Edwin Stead of Kent. These challenges were usually played on the country estates of the patrons involved, but by 1730 a major enclosed ground in London was in use – the Artillery Ground, which still exists in City Road,

THE DUKE OF RICHMOND *one of cricket's early patrons.*

generated and the vast sums wagered, the laws of the game were redrafted. James Love was commissioned to write a heroic poem describing the match which was published a month after the game. Love, whose real name was Dance, was the son of the architect of the Mansion House in the City.

Over the next decade cricket matches were increasingly reported in the press, though not the detailed scores, only the results and team totals. The crowds became more unruly; an indication of the social standing of cricket in the 1740s is the position in the game of Robert Colchin. He was one of the best batsmen of the London Club and at the same time a major figure in the criminal underworld of the period. The point was reached where respectable people did not attend matches and eventually the Honourable Artillery Company, owners of the Artillery Ground,

stopped the playing of public matches there. At the public schools and at Oxford and Cambridge the authorities tended to discourage cricket – as late as 1796 the Eton headmaster flogged the Eton team for playing a match against his wishes.

In 1751, the dissolute Prince of Wales died, in some reports as a result of being hit in the chest by a cricket ball. The other cricket patrons of the period faded away, and what major matches there were tended to be played back on the country estates, rather than in London.

FROM HAMBLEDON TO MARYLEBONE

A combination of apparently unrelated events, however, rescued cricket from the mire and took the game to new heights. Richard Nyren, whose uncles had been part of an outstanding team raised by

Moorfields. The landlord of the public house on the corner of the ground had a wall built round it and in the 1740s is recorded as charging spectators to watch the cricket.

At the same time as spectators began to be charged, cricket's first professional players were emerging. The Duke of Richmond and other members of the upper class who raised teams were employing men who were good cricketers as grooms, bailiffs and the like on their estate. One of the first such was Thomas Waymark, who is mentioned several times in contemporary reports. He was employed by Richmond.

Aside from the teams raised by Richmond, Gage and Stead, the principal side of the 1730s was the London Club whose home venue was the Artillery Ground. A report of 1732 ends with the comment: "This is the thirteenth match the London gamesters have played this year and not lost one match."

The stakes for matches were now reported to be £100 – a vast sum at that time. Frederick Louis, Prince of Wales, the eldest son of George II, had not long come from Hanover to England when he discovered that

cricket was an ideal game for betting purposes. In 1733 he had picked a side and challenged Edwin Stead's Kent team for £30. In 1735 the stakes had risen to £1,000 and the Prince's opponent was the Earl of Middlesex, eldest son of the Duke of Dorset.

It need hardly be said that the major cricket matches in London soon began to attract every rogue and vagabond in the metropolis, as well as many from outside.

"THE GREATEST CRICKET MATCH EVER KNOWN"

It had been the habit of aspiring teams to challenge the London Club, but in 1744 Kent, raised by the Sackville family at Sevenoaks, challenged the rest of England. Played on the Artillery Ground, the game was described in the press as "the greatest Cricket Match ever known". The Prince of Wales, the Duke of Cumberland, the Duke of Richmond and many other notables attended the game. Kent won by one wicket and this is the first major match whose detailed score survives.

Because of the enormous interest

PRINCE FREDERICK ADOLPHUS *with a cricket bat (late seventeenth century).*

PRECURSOR TO LORD'S *Cricket played near White Conduit House, 1787.*

the Duke of Richmond and centred on the village of Slindon on the Goodwood Estate, became the landlord of an inn in the Hampshire village of Hambledon. The Reverend Charles Powlett, son of the Duke of Bolton and educated at Westminster and Trinity, Cambridge, was a curate of Itchen Abbas from 1763; his family home was near Basingstoke. Both men were passionately fond of cricket. The meeting of Nyren, Powlett and other interested parties resulted in the creation of the Hambledon Cricket Club some time in the mid-1760s. The club struggled for some years before it really took off around 1772. Through the decade which followed, the Hambledon Club built up a Hampshire side, capable of taking on and often beating the rest of England.

Richard Nyren captained the side, which was normally an all-professional eleven. Several players came from Hambledon itself but others came from places

a good few miles distant, such as Noah Mann from Northchapel and later William Beldham from Wrecclesham.

Many of the gentry whom Powlett persuaded to join the club also took part in the social life of London and met at the Star and Garter Tavern in Pall Mall, which had been the unofficial headquarters of cricket and horse-racing for many years. The Jockey Club had been founded there and the laws of cricket revised there. In the 1780s the members of the Star and Garter played cricket among themselves on White Conduit Fields in Islington. They decided that they would like a private ground, rather than using White Conduit Fields to which the public had access.

In 1786, two members of the Star and Garter, the Earl of Winchelsea and Colonel Lennox, the son of the Duke of Richmond, asked Thomas Lord, who was paid to help with the matches on White Conduit Fields, if he would find a suitable piece of land and set out a

private ground. Winchelsea and Lennox promised Lord their full support and Lord created what was to become known as Lord's Cricket Ground in Marylebone. The first matches were played there in 1787. The cricket club of the Star and Garter, which was also described as the White Conduit Club, soon became known as the Marylebone Cricket Club. The club itself can be traced back to the earliest known revision of the laws in 1744.

Owing to building development and the building of the Regent's Canal, Lord twice moved his ground and the present Lord's was established in 1814. The Marylebone Club attracted most of the wealthy supporters of cricket, particularly those educated at the major public schools and Oxford or Cambridge. The club continued to be the forum for the revision of the laws and was the most opulent cricket club in the British Isles. Its position as the world's premier

club has remained unchallenged since it was established.

CRICKET CONQUERS THE WORLD

Cricket as a popular game was spread from its south-east England birthplace throughout the British Isles by the landed gentry. In some places, such as Leicester, Nottingham and Sheffield, it was soon adopted by the locals. In others, Ireland being an extreme example, the game scarcely moved outside the landowners' parks.

During the Napoleonic Wars, soldiers in some regiments were encouraged to play cricket – Colonel Lennox, for instance, organized inter-militia matches in the 1790s and a game of cricket was played prior to the Battle of Waterloo.

As the British Empire grew, the army garrisons stationed in its various outposts took cricket with them. On the continent of Europe, British residents in Paris, Rome and other cities played the game, though the local inhabitants, whether part of the Empire or not, initially paid little attention to this strange British ritual. North America, with its large number of residents of British descent, was the only part of the world outside the British Isles where cricket became established in the eighteenth century.

The American War of Independence caused a hiccup in the game's development in what was to become the United States, but cricket recovered and the first-ever English touring team overseas went to Canada and the United States in 1859: this was an all-professional side and the trip was profitable. The first genuine international match – the United States versus Canada had taken place 15 years earlier, in 1844.

The American Civil War brought a temporary end to matches between the States and Canada, put a stop to possible visits by an

England team and found the embryonic game of baseball an easier game to play in wartime conditions. From the time the war ended, baseball grew in stature at the same speed as cricket languished. From the 1870s the only stronghold of cricket was in the Philadelphia area.

So cricket was to remain a minority sport in North America, but across the world in Australia the game grew as the number of emigrants from Britain increased. The development of Australia into its various colonies – Van Diemens Land (Tasmania), New South Wales, Victoria, South Australia, Queensland and Western Australia – led to cricketing rivalry between those colonies. The first inter-colonial game was between Tasmania and Victoria in 1850–51, then came the matches between Victoria and New South Wales, which were regarded as the great

contests of the season until overshadowed by Test cricket. With an England side unable to go to America in the early 1860s because of the Civil War and its aftermath, it was a fortunate coincidence that an entrepreneur decided to arrange for an England team to tour Australia. The leading England players refused to go, but an England "Second" Twelve went and were highly successful financially, even though no team in Australia was capable of opposing them evenhanded (in most matches 22 Australians played 11 of England).

The first people of non-British stock to take to cricket in an organized fashion were the Parsee community of Bombay. They began playing in the 1840s and by the 1880s were sending touring teams to England. From the Parsees, cricket spread to the other Indian communities and what developed was the great Bombay Tournament

between Europeans, Parsees, Hindus and Muslims. Until the Ranji Trophy (the Indian equivalent of the County Championship) was founded in the 1930s, the Bombay Tournament was the major cricket contest in India.

Development of cricket in both the West Indies and South Africa was initially through the military personnel stationed in those territories. In South America, especially the Argentine, the game was well established, but only among the English communities.

The first team to come to England on a cricket tour was in fact a side of Australian Aborigines in 1868. The team was not of first-class standard, but opposed local club sides in an over-ambitious programme of 47 two- and three-day games. The side was captained by the former Surrey county cricketer, Charles Lawrence. It was an experiment not repeated (at least until the 1990s).

FIRST TESTS *The Australian touring team of 1882.*

SWEET SUMMER SCENE *A cricket field at Bourneville, Birmingham, where recreational facilities were supplied by Cadbury's for their employees.*

The legalisation of over-arm bowling in 1864 is generally considered to be the starting point of 'modern' cricket. In the following years the immortal W.G. Grace began his career and created many of his records which succeeding generations aimed to equal or beat. By that date first-class cricket was being played in Australia, in New Zealand, where inter-provincial games had commenced in the 1860s, in the West Indies, where the first inter-colonial game was staged also in the 1860s, and of course in England, where the modern County Championship had begun with a match between Sussex and Kent in 1825. The first recognized first-class game in the United States was played in 1878 when Australia opposed Philadelphia. Some 10 years later, the match between England and South Africa at Port Elizabeth marks the start of South African first-class cricket,

whilst 1891–92 saw the first-class England tour to India and the first first-class match between Europeans and Parsees. Cricket

flourished in many of the British colonies and in particular in Fiji – the Fijian touring side to New Zealand was ranked first-class in

1894–95. But outside the Empire and isolated pockets such as Philadelphia, cricket remained a mystery!

PIONEERS OF CRICKET

**ROBERT COLCHIN
(1713–1750)**

The most famous professional of the 1740s, but it is believed that he was also a figure noted in the underworld, particularly for smuggling.

**JOHN MINSHULL
(1741–1793)**

Employed by the Duke of Dorset because of his batsmanship, he was the first player to score a century, in August 1769.

**RICHARD NYREN
(1734–1797)**

Landlord of the Bat and Ball Inn, Hambledon and captain of the famous side organized by the Hambledon Club in the 1760s and 1770s.

**DAVID HARRIS
(1755–1803)**

A fast under-arm bowler and the greatest bowler for the Hambledon Club. Much troubled by gout, he came to some matches on crutches, but still played.

**9TH EARL OF WINCHELSEA
(1752–1826)**

A notable patron who persuaded Thomas Lord to open his first ground. Lord Winchelsea was a talented player and staged many matches at Burley, his Rutland country seat.

**4TH DUKE OF RICHMOND
(1764–1819)**

His grandfather, the 2nd Duke had organized many matches in the 1720s and 1730s; Goodwood, the

family seat in Sussex, was a major centre of cricket. The 4th Duke continued the tradition and played at Lord's from its foundation.

**3RD DUKE OF DORSET
(1745–1799)**

Promoted many matches at Sevenoaks and as Ambassador to France was partially responsible for the English cricket tour to Paris in 1789 (aborted due to the Revolution).

**NOAH MANN
(1756–1789)**

He came from North Chapel in Sussex, but played for the Hambledon Club as a good all-rounder. He came to a sad end by going to sleep in front of a fire. His clothes caught alight and he died from burns.

CRICKET AROUND THE WORLD

Wherever English people settled, cricket went with them. English soldiers, merchants and missionaries played the game in most countries of the world. In Europe the locals ignored the strange rituals as did the Chinese and Japanese in the Far East, but in India, Pakistan, Ceylon (now Sri Lanka) and the West Indies things were different.

ENGLAND

The owners of the great estates in the south-east of England, when they became involved in cricket and staged matches against each other, named the sides they raised after the county in which they resided. At the same time, a town side opposing another, but from a different county, often entitled the match as one between two counties, rather than two towns, in order to bolster the standing of the match. The fashion of using county titles therefore was established long before such organizations as county clubs existed. With large sums wagered on these county matches, rules were established as regards the status of players qualified to play – *bona fide* resident or born inside the county boundaries was the usual agreed condition.

Following the famous Kent versus England match in 1744, county patrons' ultimate ambition for their team was to beat the rest of England. Surrey, Sussex, Kent and Hampshire all aspired to this great achievement; so much so that in the first two decades of the nineteenth century a county versus the rest was virtually the only major county contest – actual inter-county games were unfashionable.

In the early 1820s, however, James Ireland took over the old Brighton cricket ground, which had been laid out for the Prince of Wales (later George IV). He believed that money could be made staging matches between Sussex and Kent and, after much disappointment, he managed to set up home and away fixtures in 1825. With the Hambledon Club having folded in the 1790s and the famous cricketers who made up that club's Hampshire team all gone, and with Surrey lacking any central organization, Sussex and Kent were the only major cricketing counties which could field good-class teams. So Ireland's idea caught on and each season from

ORIGINALS *The Nottinghamshire Eleven of 1884.*

WILLIAM CLARKE *Founder of Trent Bridge and of the All England Eleven.*

1825, Sussex and Kent battled it out for the county championship.

In the 1830s the Nottingham team, which had beaten every side in the Midlands, joined the inter-county contest by challenging Sussex. In 1845, Surrey finally got its act together, formed a county club and established its home at Kennington Oval. Sussex had become a county club in 1839 and Nottingham's county club first emerged in 1841. Thus individual patrons raising and running county sides had given way to groups of subscribers putting up money to pay for players and their expenses for away games. The extensive space the newspapers of the 1830s and 1840s devoted to these inter-county games gives an indication of their importance.

In 1846, however, William Clarke, captain of Nottinghamshire, and founder of Trent Bridge, engaged the leading players of the day for a side which was to become known as the All England Eleven. At a stroke, he deprived the major counties of their "stars" and within a year or two had built up a full fixture list for his England team, playing what amounted to exhibition matches in whatever town would pay his expenses. The star players preferred Clarke's team to their county side simply because Clarke offered full-time employment through the summer, whereas the county teams only arranged a handful of games.

It took a dozen or so years for the craze of what were called wandering professional elevens (there were in time rivals to Clarke's outfit) to reach its peak. Then inter-county cricket not only re-emerged but increased rapidly. The 1860s saw the creation of clubs for Glamorgan, Gloucestershire, Worcestershire, Lancashire, Middlesex, Somerset and Yorkshire (of the present day first-class counties) as well as a goodly number of clubs among the lesser counties.

Not that all the seven listed suddenly began to challenge Kent, Nottinghamshire, Surrey and Sussex for the title of "champion county" – only Lancashire, Middlesex and Yorkshire rose to first-class rank immediately on the creation of a county organization. The romanticism surrounding Hampshire, fuelled by tales of the great Hambledon days, meant that various patrons and groups made attempts to raise Hampshire sides, but usually with dire results. Derbyshire was created as a county club in 1871, but struggled to produce a worthwhile side; in contrast, Cambridgeshire had a worthwhile team in the 1860s, but failed to create a satisfactory county club.

With all these sides, it became impractical to decide which county was the best on a challenge basis so the press began making up crude league tables.

COUNTY CRICKET

Since cricket at this time was the only popular team ball game with nationally, indeed internationally, recognized laws and in England was the major participatory game, both for playing and watching, the general public had an enormous interest in which county, in each season, was the best. In 1873, after some years of dispute, it was decided to lay down clearly the qualification rules for county cricketers; players had been taking advantage of the loose rule that they could play for county of residence or of birth and had in some cases played for both in the same season. This duality was stopped and a more careful record kept to see that players genuinely resided in a county.

In the same year, the MCC decided to stage a knockout county competition. Only one match was played, however, before the scheme collapsed. The two main reasons for its failure were, first that all matches were fixed to be played at Lord's and, second, that by the very nature of a knockout competition players would not know whether they were required on a given match day until each round had been played. Most professional players had signed agreements with local clubs which meant they could not be released willy-nilly to play for other teams, but only for set county and major matches on dates that were fixed.

The press continued to decide on the county champion and on how the league tables were presented each year, through the 1870s and into the 1880s. The situation was not very satisfactory, especially since there was no hard and fast rule as to which counties were included in the results as shown in a league table of top teams. Somerset, Hampshire and Derbyshire were the three sides which caused the press most problems.

In 1887, the editor of *Wisden's Cricketers' Almanack* decided to take a firm line. He cut out the three counties noted above and formulated a new "points" system. To his embarrassment, in 1889 his system resulted in a three-way tie at the head of a table which contained just eight counties: Gloucestershire, Kent, Lancashire, Yorkshire, Middlesex, Nottinghamshire, Surrey and Sussex. The counties themselves decided to act and for 1890 devised a new "points" system, though they kept to the eight-county league. Somerset were particularly upset at being excluded; and the following year simply forced their way into the league by arranging matches with the top counties.

The *Wisden* editor then came up with the idea of creating three leagues of eight teams each with promotion and relegation, but any hope of this sensible arrangement collapsed in 1895 when Derbyshire, Essex, Hampshire, Leicestershire and Warwickshire were all given a place in the "County Championship". All the other counties with teams that wanted to play competitive county cricket then joined together to form a separate Minor Counties' Cricket Association. The architect of this plan was Worcestershire's Secretary, P.H. Foley, and it began in 1895.

In effect, this pattern of county cricket – First Class County Championship and Minor Counties Championship – has remained unaltered ever since. No county has been demoted from first-class to minor, but Worcestershire (in 1899), Northamptonshire (six years later), Glamorgan (1921) and Durham (1992) have joined the top grade.

For the first two decades of intercounty games, which involved only Kent, Nottinghamshire and Sussex, Kent was the predominant shire. Their supporters had persuaded the greatest batsman of the day, Fuller Pilch, to move from East Anglia and play for them. In the 1820s, bowling style switched from under-arm to round-arm and Pilch was the first batsman to master thoroughly the new style. The county also possessed the best bowler in Alfred Mynn. Sussex's answer to these players was William Lillywhite, uncle of the first England Test captain. Lillywhite was 30 years old before he came into his own as slow medium round-arm bowler – and he was 60 when he played his final game for his county. Nottinghamshire had cunning under-arm bowler, William Clarke, and an elegant batsman in Joe Guy, but they were no match for Kent.

A combination of events in 1844 and 1845 led first to the conversion of a market garden into the Kennington Oval Cricket Ground and then to the formation of Surrey County Cricket Club. Within a few years, this new club had thoroughly shaken the three senior counties and the 1850s belonged to Surrey.

This Championship side was characterized by its all-round strength, rather than reliance on one or two stars. Tom Lockyer kept wicket, William Caffyn was the all-rounder and Julius Caesar of Godalming the principal batsman. Heathfield Stephenson, the captain of the first side to Australia, was another all-rounder, whilst George Griffiths was the tearaway fast bowler who hit sixes. In 1864 Surrey won six of their eight championship games, drawing the other two. No one seeing the side that year could dream that 23 years would elapse before Surrey regained the title.

Next it was the turn of Nottinghamshire to hold centre stage. Between 1865 and 1886, they were champions 14 times. In Alfred Shaw and Fred Morley they possessed the finest pair of bowlers in England; Billy Barnes and Wilfred Flowers were two all-rounders – the former was the first professional to achieve the "double" of 1,000 runs and 100 wickets in the same season. A succession of brilliant batsmen headed the run-getting. George Parr of Radcliffe-on-Trent succeeded Fuller Pilch as the best professional batsman in England, then Richard Daft, born in Nottingham, took over the crown, to be followed in his turn by Arthur Shrewsbury, who was to become the first man to reach 1,000 Test runs. Rather like the Surrey side of 1864, the Nottinghamshire team of 1886, having won the championship, faded away and, apart from the infamous triple tie of 1889, Nottinghamshire had to wait until 1907 for their next success.

THE THREE GRACES

In covering briefly the 20 years from 1865 onwards, one fact has been omitted and it is an Everest of an omission. A 16-year-old youth named William Gilbert Grace appeared in his first first-class match in 1865 – by the 1880s he was to vie with W.E. Gladstone as the best-known Englishman.

Born in a village near Bristol, he effectively belonged to no major county – Gloucestershire did not really exist in cricketing terms in 1865. His family remedied this shortcoming by single-handedly creating Gloucestershire County Cricket Club. Grace had two brothers, E.M. and G.F., both by any standards brilliant cricketers, but both played in the shadow of W.G. – as did everyone. Gloucestershire played their first first-class, intercounty game in 1870; in 1873 they were acclaimed as the joint champions with Nottinghamshire. The county of the Graces, as they were quickly christened, retained the title in 1874, lost it to Nottinghamshire in 1875, but regained it in 1876 and 1877. Too much depended on W.G. Grace and, though he continued to lead the county until deposed in

1899, Gloucestershire never again ended a season on top of the table. A peculiarity of the Gloucestershire side of the 1870s was that it contained only amateurs whereas Nottinghamshire generally fielded a side made up of all-professionals.

Throughout this period, Sussex and Kent, the oldest counties, went through some hard times; Yorkshire could field a good side, but their professionals were a wayward lot; Lancashire tied for the title with Nottinghamshire in 1879 and captured it in their own right in 1881, when most of Nottinghamshire's top professionals were on strike; Middlesex, through their London connections, had some fine amateurs qualified by residence or birth, but rarely managed to field a full-strength side; Derbyshire and Hampshire flirted on the fringes, without causing the top counties much trouble.

The late 1880s saw Surrey return to the fore. They were champions every year from 1887 to 1895 – except 1893. Walter Read and Read, unrelated, were Surrey's principal middle-order batsmen; Bobby Abel opened the innings, while George Lohmann, an outstanding medium-fast bowler, was partnered by Bill Lockwood in the attack. The County Championship – especially in the years when Australia did not tour England – drew enormous crowds for the top matches. It was at this time that the tradition of Lancashire playing Yorkshire and of Nottinghamshire meeting Surrey over the Whitsun and August Bank Holiday weekends was established.

THE SLEEPING GIANT AWAKENS

The decade of the 1890s saw the sleeping giant of cricket finally realize its potential. Yorkshire had found in Lord Hawke a leader who was capable of instilling some discipline into the professional ranks – one or two notable players were warned and then consigned to the scrapheap, but Yorkshire had ample reserves. Although, like all teams, the White Rose County had its less successful summers, for the next 70 years Yorkshire was the one side that was always feared.

Yorkshire's power base was founded on twin all-rounders: two complementary characters whose records, were the equal of anyone (except of course W.G.) who had participated in the game of cricket. George Hirst of Kirkheaton is the only man to score 2,000 runs and take 200 wickets in a single summer – when asked what he felt like, having reached this peak, he is reported as saying "tired". Wilfred Rhodes, Hirst's partner, and fellow left-arm bowler – and also from Kirkheaton – is the only man to take more than 4,000 first-class wickets. His batting was almost as impressive with 39,969 runs. He achieved the "double" 16 times to Hirst's 14. Not satisfied with two outstanding all-rounders, the county possessed a third in the amateur F.S. Jackson, but business commitments and his service in the Boer War meant that he was not always available for his county. Jackson captained England to the Ashes victory in 1905, but, with Lord Hawke in office, was never Yorkshire's official leader.

In the period up to 1914, despite Yorkshire's great superiority, the county did not take the title in the way Nottinghamshire and Surrey had earlier. Lancashire and Middlesex were allowed their turn and Nottinghamshire won in 1907. Even Warwickshire took a turn in 1911, but the strongest rival to Yorkshire in the years leading up to the First World War was Kent.

Lord Harris, one of the greatest figures in English cricket, had devoted himself to the revival of Kent cricket. Cricketers such as Blythe and Woolley made the county once more a stronghold of the game. A comment must be made on Warwickshire's single success, due almost entirely to their captain Frank Foster who topped both batting and bowling averages.

The 21 years between the wars might be described as a second War of the Roses; Yorkshire won 12 championships, Lancashire five, Middlesex two, Nottinghamshire and Derbyshire once each. Yorkshire boasted a team of stars, from opening batsmen Herbert Sutcliffe and Percy Holmes through to Hedley Verity and Bill Bowes. In the late 1930s came Len Hutton and

Ellis Robinson. Lancashire had Ernest Tyldesley as their batting stalwart, Dick Tyldesley as the principal slow bowler, as well as Eddie Paynter and Cyril Washbrook.

Middlesex's years were 1920 and 1921, with Patsy Hendren and Jack Hearne; Nottinghamshire, always a formidable batting side, won in 1929 when Harold Larwood and Bill Voce were at the top.

Derbyshire also owed their championship to the emergence of some sharp bowlers, Bill Copson and Alf Pope in particular. When cricket returned to normal after the Second World War, Yorkshire were again champions, but, after years of modest returns, Surrey came back with a vengeance. Led by the inspiring Stuart Surridge, the county had a perfect attack. In 1953, for example, the four Surrey bowlers, Alec Bedser, Peter Loader, Jim Laker and Tony Lock, were all in the top 10 in the English bowling averages. Laker (off spin) and Lock (left arm) were the slower bowlers, whilst Bedser and Loader opened. Surrey shared the title with Lancashire in 1950, then won it outright for seven successive years commencing 1952.

Yorkshire climbed back in 1959 and gained seven of the next ten titles. In those 20 or so post-war years, three of the former also-rans had their moments of glory: Glamorgan won in 1948 and 1969, Worcestershire in 1964 and 1965 and Hampshire in 1961.

LIMITED-OVERS CRICKET

With county cricket in a parlous state financially in the late 1950s and early 1960s, the time had come for change. A one-day limited-overs knockout competition– the Gillette Cup – began in 1963: in 1969 it was joined by a 40-overs-a-side Sunday League and a third – a 55 overs-a-side competition – started in 1972.

In 1968 the authorities broke with tradition by allowing counties to play overseas cricketers. The immediate effect of this was that the domination by the counties with large populations was broken. Yorkshire alone decided to stick with players born within the county boundary.

Essex and Middlesex came to the fore in the 1970s. The former, led by Keith Fletcher, possessed a fine attack, with John Lever and Neil Foster the principal seam bowlers and Ray East and David Acfield as spinners. The batting line-up included the captain and Graham Gooch and Ken McEwan, whilst Derek Pringle was the all-rounder. Middlesex were led by the most talented captain of the day, Mike Brearley. Their spin attack revolved around John Emburey and Phil Edmonds, the West Indian Wayne Daniel opened the bowling, and Mike Gatting, who succeeded Brearley as captain, was the leading run-getter. In a golden period in the late 1970s and 1980s, Middlesex won the County Championship seven times and gained seven one-day trophies. Essex won 11.

YORKSHIRE'S OPENERS *Herbert Sutcliffe and Percy Holmes scored over 100 runs for the first wicket no fewer than 69 times.*

With counties fielding overseas players and with the movement of players between counties on the increase, the spread of trophies was greater than in the past. Aside from Essex and Middlesex, seven counties – Hampshire, Kent, Lancashire, Nottinghamshire, Somerset, Warwickshire and Worcestershire – won at least five titles and, Durham apart, all the rest boasted at least one. Warwickshire, with the services of Brian Lara in 1994 and Allan Donald in 1995, won the championship both seasons, and in 1994 also gained the Sunday League and Benson & Hedges titles. This was the season in which Lara recorded the first first-class innings of more than 500 – 501 not out against Durham at Edgbaston.

A fundamental change took place in County cricket in the late 1990s. In 1999 the 40-over Sunday League was split into two nine-team divisions, with three up and three down. In 2000, the County Championship adopted the same format, all matches being played over four days. For the Sunday League the counties chose wacky nicknames and teams played two day-night fixtures in the league with batsmen being accompanied to the wicket by their own signature tunes, usually one of the latest chart-topping songs, wearing brightly-coloured clothing.

In 2001, Yorkshire recaptured the County Championship, which it had last won in 1968. In 2003 Sussex, which had competed in the County Championship since 1864, won the title for the first time. However, the decision to split the Championship into two sections did not have the desired effect of creating two "classes" of county, simply because promotion and relegation was based on three up, three down. In most seasons the margins between counties promoted or relegated and the others were very slight. In the five seasons 2001 to 2005, five different clubs headed Division One, a state of affairs that had happened just once in the previous century. The promotion system was changed from 2006, with two counties going up and down.

As far as the one-day competitions were concerned, the Benson & Hedges Cup was replaced after 2002 by a 20 overs a side competition – called Twenty20 – and run on similar lines to the B&H, except that the two semi-finals and the final were staged on the same day at the same venue. Each innings lasted about one hour and a complete game two and a half hours. Twenty20 proved very popular with the public. The unpopular "Sunday League" 45-over format will be abandoned in 2006 and revert to 40 overs a side. The C&G Trophy for 2006 will become a competition based on mini-leagues followed by finals between the top sides, rather than the straight knock-out formula which has reigned since its inception.

One rule, which has crept into the county circuit in recent years, is the "borrowing" of players from their registered county to another county. Thus for the first time since 1872, players can appear in competitive matches for more than one county in the same season. The use of "replacement" overseas stars when the main overseas player is unavailable has become increasingly employed.

SCOURGE OF BOWLING *Flintoff finally replicated his county form with the bat for England.*

TWENTY 20

2003 At Trent Bridge
Semi-final 1: Warwickshire beat Leicestershire by 7 wickets
Semi-final 2: Surrey beat Gloucestershire by 5 runs
Final: Surrey 119–1 (10.5 overs) beat Warwickshire 115 (18.5 overs) by 9 wickets

2004 At Edgbaston
Semi-final 1: Leicestershire beat Glamorgan by 21 runs
Semi-final 2: Surrey beat Lancashire by 1 run
Final: Leicestershire 169–3 (19.1 overs) beat Surrey 168–6 (20 overs) by 7 wickets

2005 At the Oval
Semi-final 1: Lancashire beat Surrey by 22 runs
Semi-final 2: Somerset beat Leicestershire by 4 runs
Final: Somerset 118–3 (14.1 overs) beat Lancashire 114–8 (16 overs) by 7 wickets

COUNTY CHAMPIONS SINCE 1864

Year	Champion	Year	Champion	Year	Champion	Year	Champion
1864	Surrey	1894	Surrey	1933	Yorkshire	1972	Warwickshire
1865	Nottinghamshire	1895	Surrey	1934	Lancashire	1973	Hampshire
1866	Middlesex	1896	Yorkshire	1935	Yorkshire	1974	Worcestershire
1867	Yorkshire	1897	Lancashire	1936	Derby	1975	Leicestershire
1868	Nottinghamshire	1898	Yorkshire	1937	Yorkshire	1976	Middlesex
1869	Nottinghamshire, Yorkshire	1899	Surrey	1938	Yorkshire	1977	Kent, Middlesex
1870	Yorkshire	1900	Yorkshire	1939	Yorkshire	1978	Kent
1871	Nottinghamshire	1901	Yorkshire			1979	Essex
1872	Nottinghamshire	1902	Yorkshire	1946	Yorkshire	1980	Middlesex
1873	Gloucestershire, Nottinghamshire	1903	Middlesex	1947	Middlesex	1981	Nottinghamshire
1874	Gloucestershire	1904	Lancashire	1948	Glamorgan	1982	Middlesex
1875	Nottinghamshire	1905	Yorkshire	1949	Middlesex, Yorkshire	1983	Essex
1876	Gloucestershire	1906	Kent	1950	Lancashire, Surrey	1984	Essex
1877	Gloucestershire	1907	Nottinghamshire	1951	Warwickshire	1985	Middlesex
1878	Undecided	1908	Yorkshire	1952	Surrey	1986	Essex
1879	Nottinghamshire, Lancashire	1909	Kent	1953	Surrey	1987	Nottinghamshire
1880	Nottinghamshire	1910	Kent	1954	Surrey	1988	Worcestershire
1881	Lancashire	1911	Warwickshire	1955	Surrey	1989	Worcestershire
1882	Nottinghamshire, Lancashire	1912	Yorkshire	1956	Surrey	1990	Middlesex
1883	Nottinghamshire	1913	Kent	1957	Surrey	1991	Essex
1884	Nottinghamshire	1914	Surrey	1958	Surrey	1992	Essex
1885	Nottinghamshire	1919	Yorkshire	1959	Yorkshire	1993	Middlesex
1886	Surrey	1920	Middlesex	1960	Yorkshire	1994	Warwickshire
1887	Surrey	1921	Middlesex	1961	Hampshire	1995	Warwickshire
1888	Surrey	1922	Yorkshire	1962	Yorkshire	1996	Leicestershire
1889	Surrey, Lancashire, Nottinghamshire	1923	Yorkshire	1963	Yorkshire	1997	Glamorgan
1890	Surrey	1924	Yorkshire	1964	Worcestershire	1998	Leicestershire
1891	Surrey	1925	Yorkshire	1965	Worcestershire	1999	Surrey
1892	Surrey	1926	Lancashire	1966	Yorkshire	2000	Surrey
1893	Yorkshire	1927	Lancashire	1967	Yorkshire	2001	Yorkshire
		1928	Lancashire	1968	Yorkshire	2002	Surrey
		1929	Nottinghamshire	1969	Glamorgan	2003	Sussex
		1930	Lancashire	1970	Kent	2004	Warwickshire
		1931	Yorkshire	1971	Surrey	2005	Nottinghamshire
		1932	Yorkshire				

GILLETTE/NATWEST/C&G TROPHY

1963 Sussex 168 (60.2 overs) beat Worcestershire 154 (63.2 overs) by 14 runs

1964 Sussex 131–2 (43 overs) beat Warwickshire 127 (48 overs) by 8 wkts

1965 Yorkshire 317–4 (60 overs) beat Surrey 142 (40.4 overs) by 175 runs

1966 Warwickshire 159–5 (56.4 overs) beat Worcestershire 155–8 (60 overs) by 5 wkts

1967 Kent 193 (59.4 overs) beat Somerset 161 (54.5 overs) by 32 runs

1968 Warwickshire 215–6 (57 overs) beat Sussex 214–7 (60 overs) by 4 wkts

1969 Yorkshire 219–8 (60 overs) beat Derbyshire 150 (54.4 overs) by 69 runs

1970 Lancashire 185–4 (55.1 overs) beat Sussex 184–9 (60 overs) by 6 wkts

1971 Lancashire 224–7 (60 overs) beat Kent 200 (56.2 overs) by 24 runs

1972 Lancashire 235–6 (56.4 overs) beat Warwickshire 234–9 (60 overs) by 4 wkts

1973 Gloucestershire 248–8 (60 overs) beat Sussex 208 (56.5 overs) by 40 runs

1974 Kent 122–6 (56.4 overs) beat Lancashire 118 (60 overs) by 4 wkts

1975 Lancashire 182–3 (57 overs) beat Middlesex 180–8 (60 overs) by 7 wkts

1976 Northamptonshire 199–6 (58.1 overs) beat Lancashire 195–7 (60 overs) by 4 wkts

1977 Middlesex 178–5 (55.4 overs) beat Glamorgan 177–9 (60 overs) by 5 wkts

1978 Sussex 211–5 (53.1 overs) beat Somerset 207–7 (60 overs) by 5 wkts

1979 Somerset 269–8 (60 overs) beat Northamptonshire 224 (56.3 overs) by 45 runs

1980 Middlesex 202–3 (53.5 overs) beat Surrey 201 (60 overs) by 7 wkts

1981 Derbyshire 235–6 (60 overs) beat Northamptonshire 235–9 (60 overs) by losing fewer wkts

1982 Surrey 159–1 (34.4 overs) beat Warwickshire 158 (57.2 overs) by 9 wkts

1983 Somerset 193–9 (50 overs) beat Kent 169 (47.1 overs) by 24 runs

1984 Middlesex 236–6 (60 overs) beat Kent 232–6 (60 overs) by 4 wkts

1985 Essex 280–2 (60 overs) beat Nottinghamshire 279–5 (60 overs) by 1 run

1986 Sussex 243–3 (58.2 overs) beat Lancashire 242–8 (60 overs) by 7 wkts

1987 Nottinghamshire 231–7 (49.3 overs) beat Northamptonshire 228–3 (50 overs) by 3 wkts

1988 Middlesex 162–7 (55.3 overs) beat Worcestershire 161–9 (60 overs) by 3 wkts

1989 Warwickshire 211–6 (59.4 overs) beat Middlesex 210–5 (60 overs) by 4 wkts

1990 Lancashire 173–3 (45.4 overs) beat Northamptonshire 171 (60 overs) by 7 wkts

1991 Hampshire 243–6 (59.4 overs) beat Surrey 240–5 (60 overs) by 4 wkts

1992 Northamptonshire 211–2 (49.4 overs) beat Leicestershire 208–7 (60 overs) by 8 wkts

1993 Warwickshire 322–5 (60 overs) beat Sussex 321–6 (60 overs) by 5 wkts

1994 Worcestershire 227–2 (49.1 overs) beat Warwickshire 223–9 (60 overs) by 8 wkts

1995 Warwickshire 203–6 (58.5 overs) beat Northamptonshire 200 (59.5 overs) by 4 wkts

1996 Lancashire 186 (60 overs) beat Essex 57 (27.2 overs) by 129 runs

1997 Essex 171–1 (26.3 overs) beat Warwickshire 170–8 (60 overs) by 9 wkts

1998 Lancashire 109–3 (30.2 overs) beat Derbyshire 108 (36.4 overs) by 7 wkts

1999 Gloucestershire 230–8 (50 overs) beat Somerset 180 (45.1 overs) by 50 runs

2000 Gloucestershire 122–3 (29.4 overs) beat Warwickshire 205–7 (50 overs) by 22 runs (D/L method)

2001 Somerset 271–5 (50 overs) beat Leicestershire 230 (45.4 overs) by 41 runs

2002 Yorkshire 260–4 (48 overs) beat Somerset 256–8 (50 overs) by 6 wkts

2003 Gloucestershire 150–3 (20.3 overs) beat Worcestershire 149 (46.3 overs) by 7 wickets

2004 Gloucestershire 237–2 (43.5 overs) beat Worcestershire 236–9 (50 overs) by 8 wickets

2005 Hampshire 290 (50 overs) beat Warwickshire 272 (49.2 overs) by 18 runs

Minor Counties Champions

Year	Champion	Year	Champion	Year	Champion	Year	Champion
1895	Norfolk–Durham–Worcestershire	1923	Buckinghamshire	1955	Surrey II	1981	Durham
1896	Worcestershire	1924	Berkshire	1956	Kent II	1982	Oxfordshire
1897	Worcestershire	1925	Buckinghamshire	1957	Yorkshire II	1983	Hertfordshire
1898	Worcestershire	1926	Durham	1958	Yorkshire II	1984	Durham
1899	Northamptonshire–Buckinghamshire	1927	Staffordshire	1959	Warwickshire II	1985	Cheshire
1900	Glamorgan–Durham–Northamptonshire	1928	Berkshire	1960	Lancashire II	1986	Cumberland
1901	Durham	1929	Oxfordshire	1961	Somerset II	1987	Buckinghamshire
1902	Wiltshire	1930	Durham	1962	Warwickshire II	1988	Cheshire
1903	Northamptonshire	1931	Leicestershire II	1963	Cambridgeshire	1989	Oxfordshire
1904	Northamptonshire	1932	Buckinghamshire	1964	Lancashire II	1990	Hertfordshire
1905	Norfolk	1933	Undecided	1965	Somerset II	1991	Staffordshire
1906	Staffordshire	1934	Lancashire II	1966	Lincolnshire	1992	Staffordshire
1907	Lancashire II	1935	Middlesex II	1967	Cheshire	1993	Staffordshire
1908	Staffordshire	1936	Hertfordshire	1968	Yorkshire II	1994	Devon
1909	Wiltshire	1937	Lancashire II	1969	Buckinghamshire	1995	Devon
1910	Norfolk	1938	Buckinghamshire	1970	Bedfordshire	1996	Devon
1911	Staffordshire	1939	Surrey II	1971	Yorkshire II	1997	Devon
1912	In abeyance	1946	Suffolk	1972	Bedfordshire	1998	Staffordshire
1913	Norfolk	1947	Yorkshire II	1973	Shropshire	1999	Cumberland
1914	Staffordshire	1948	Lancashire II	1974	Oxfordshire	2000	Dorset
1920	Staffordshire	1949	Lancashire II	1975	Hertfordshire	2001	Cheshire/Lincolnshire
1921	Staffordshire	1950	Surrey II	1976	Durham	2002	Herefordshire/Norfolk
1922	Buckinghamshire	1951	Kent II	1977	Suffolk	2003	Lincolnshire
		1952	Buckinghamshire	1978	Devon	2004	Bedfordshire/Devon
		1953	Berkshire	1979	Suffolk	2005	Cheshire/Suffolk
		1954	Surrey II	1980	Durham		

Benson & Hedges Cup

Year	Result
1972	Leicestershire 140–5 (46.5 overs) beat Yorkshire 136–9 (55 overs) 5 wkts
1973	Kent 225–7 (55 overs) beat Worcestershire 186 (51.4 overs) by 39 runs
1974	Surrey 170 (54.1 overs) beat Leicestershire 143 (54 overs) by 27 runs
1975	Leicestershire 150–5 (51.2 overs) beat Middlesex 146 (54.2 overs) by 5 wkts
1976	Kent 236–7 (55 overs) beat Worcestershire 193 (52.4 overs) by 43 runs
1977	Gloucestershire 237–6 (55 overs) beat Kent 173 (47.3 overs) by 64 runs
1978	Kent 151–4 (41.4 overs) beat Derbyshire 147 (54.5 overs) by 6 wkts
1979	Essex 290–6 (55 overs) beat Surrey 255 (51.4 overs) by 35 runs
1980	Northamptonshire 209 (54.5 overs) beat Essex 203–8 (55 overs) by 6 runs
1981	Somerset 197–3 (44.3 overs) beat Surrey 194–8 (55 overs) by 7 wkts
1982	Somerset 132–1 (33.1 overs) beat Nottinghamshire 130 (50.1 overs) by 9 wkts
1983	Middlesex 196–8 (55 overs) beat Essex 192 (54.1 overs) by 4 runs
1984	Lancashire 140–4 (42.4 overs) beat Warwickshire 139 (50.4 overs) by 6 wkts
1985	Leicestershire 215–5 (52 overs) beat Essex 213–8 (55 overs) by 5 wkts
1986	Middlesex 199–7 (55 overs) beat Kent 197–8 (55 overs) by 2 runs
1987	Yorkshire 244–6 (55 overs) beat Northamptonshire 244–7 by losing fewer wkts
1988	Hampshire 118–3 (31.5 overs) beat Derbyshire 117 (46.3 overs) by 7 wkts
1989	Nottinghamshire 244–7 (55 overs) beat Essex 243–7 (55 overs) by 3 wkts
1990	Lancashire 241–8 (55 overs) beat Worcestershire 172 (54 overs) by 69 runs
1991	Worcestershire 236–8 (55 overs) beat Lancashire 171 (47.2 overs) by 65 runs
1992	Hampshire 253–5 (55 overs) beat Kent 212 (52.3 overs) by 41 runs
1993	Derbyshire 252–6 (55 overs) beat Lancashire 246–7 (55 overs) by 6 runs
1994	Warwickshire 172–4 (44.2 overs) beat Worcestershire 170 (55 overs) by 6 wkts
1995	Lancashire 274–7 (55 overs) beat Kent 239 (52.1 overs) by 35 runs
1996	Lancashire 245–9 (50 overs) beat Northamptonshire 214 (48.3 overs) by 31 runs
1997	Surrey 215–2 (45 overs) beat Kent 212–9 (50 overs) by 8 wkts
1998	Essex 268–7 (50 overs) beat Leicestershire 76 (27.4 overs) by 192 runs
1999	Gloucestershire 291–9 (50 overs) beat Yorkshire 167 (40 overs) by 124 runs
2000	Glamorgan 225 (49.3 overs) beat Gloucestershire 226–3 (46.5 overs) by 7 wkts
2001	Surrey 244 (49.4 overs) beat Gloucestershire 197 (45.5 overs) by 47 runs
2002	Warwickshire 182-5 (36.2 overs) beat Essex 181–8 (50 overs) by 5 wkts

Sunday League Champions

Year	Champion	Year	Champion
1969	Lancashire	1988	Worcestershire
1970	Lancashire	1989	Lancashire
1971	Worcestershire	1990	Derbyshire
1972	Kent	1991	Nottinghamshire
1973	Kent	1992	Middlesex
1974	Leicestershire	1993	Glamorgan
1975	Hampshire	1994	Warwickshire
1976	Kent	1995	Kent
1977	Leicestershire	1996	Surrey
1978	Hampshire	1997	Warwickshire
1979	Somerset	1998	Lancashire
1980	Warwickshire	1999	Lancashire
1981	Essex	2000	Gloucestershire
1982	Sussex	2001	Kent
1983	Yorkshire	2002	Glamorgan
1984	Essex	2003	Essex
1985	Essex	2004	Glamorgan
1986	Hampshire	2005	Essex
1987	Worcestershire		

Second XI One Day Competition

Year	Champion
1986	Northamptonshire
1987	Derbyshire
1988	Yorkshire
1989	Middlesex
1990	Lancashire
1991	Nottinghamshire
1992	Surrey
1993	Leicestershire
1994	Yorkshire
1995	Leicestershire
1996	Leicestershire
1997	Lancashire
1998	Northamptonshire
1999	Middlesex
2000	Middlesex
2001	Hampshire
2002	Kent
2003	Hampshire
2004	Worcestershire
2005	Sussex

Second XI Champions

Year	Champion
1959	Gloucestershire
1960	Northamptonshire
1961	Kent
1962	Worcestershire
1963	Worcestershire
1964	Lancashire
1965	Glamorgan
1966	Surrey
1967	Hampshire
1968	Surrey
1969	Kent
1970	Kent
1971	Hampshire
1972	Nottinghamshire
1973	Essex
1974	Middlesex
1975	Surrey
1976	Kent
1977	Yorkshire
1978	Sussex
1979	Warwickshire
1980	Glamorgan
1981	Hampshire
1982	Worcestershire
1983	Leicestershire
1984	Yorkshire
1985	Nottinghamshire
1986	Lancashire
1987	Kent, Yorkshire
1988	Surrey
1989	Middlesex
1990	Sussex
1991	Yorkshire
1992	Surrey
1993	Middlesex
1994	Somerset
1995	Hampshire
1996	Warwickshire
1997	Lancashire
1998	Northamptonshire
1999	Middlesex
2000	Leicestershire
2001	Surrey
2002	Kent
2003	Yorkshire
2004	Somerset
2005	Kent

AUSTRALIA

The colonies of New South Wales and Victoria opposed each other in a first-class cricket match for the first time in 1855–56. Prior to that, the only major inter-colonial games had been between Tasmania and Victoria. In the period 1855–56 to 1871–72, Victoria generally got the better of their arch-enemy. The wickets were dreadful and in the first 10 years it was unusual for an innings total to exceed 100. In 1862–63, when New South Wales won the annual match after losing five in succession, an umpiring dispute caused the game to be cancelled for the next two seasons.

The first individual hundred in the series, and indeed the first first-class hundred ever scored in Australia, came in 1867–68, when Dick Wardill hit 110 for Victoria. Wardill, a Liverpudlian, captained Victoria and was one of the main promoters behind the English team, led by W.G. Grace, which came out to Australia in 1873–74. Wardill, however, did not play against Grace's side. In the winter of 1873, it was found he had embezzled his employers out of £7,000. He eluded the police, but committed suicide.

Whilst Wardill was the outstanding batsman of the era, Sam Cosstick was Victoria's greatest bowler – fast round-arm – and a slogging bat.

Of the two established English players who were tempted to stay in Australia, after touring with the English team, Charles Lawrence was employed by the Albert Club in Sydney, whilst William Caffyn was initially in Melbourne, but after one season switched to Sydney.

With Victoria apparently too good for New South Wales, it was decided in 1872–73 that Victoria should not only play a combined New South Wales, Tasmania and South Australia team, but that the latter should be allowed 13 men! The odds were too great, Victoria losing by five wickets.

Two months later Victoria opposed New South Wales in an XI-a-side game and, mainly thanks to Cosstick's 11 for 51, the former won.

From 1874–75 it was New South Wales' turn to dominate. Playing home and away each year, New South Wales won seven straight games – Charles Bannerman, who was to score the first Test hundred, was the batting star, whilst F.R. Spofforth (The Demon) developed into a unique bowler. He was quite lethal whatever the wicket. In the 1880s the two sides were evenly matched; frequently one victory in the first fixture was reversed in the second. Billy Murdoch scored the first triple hundred for New South Wales in 1881–82. Fast-medium bowler Charles Turner (The Terror) also belonged to New South Wales.

South Australia opposed Victoria in a first-class match for the first time in 1880–81 (the former had previously played Tasmania). The Adelaide side found an outstanding all-rounder, George Giffen. His figures were quite formidable: in one game against Victoria he hit 271 and took 16 wickets; other combinations were 237 and 12, 135 and 13, 166 and 14. He was considered Australia's answer to W.G. Grace.

THE SHEFFIELD SHIELD

Lord Sheffield, the leading patron of Sussex cricket, agreed to finance an English team to Australia for the 1891–92 season. Soon after his arrival in Australia, in November 1891, Lord Sheffield offered to pay for a trophy which could be competed for by the three main cricketing colonies. By the end of this tour, the cricketing authorities in Australia had set up the Australasian Cricket Council, one of whose tasks was to purchase a suitable trophy, with money which Lord Sheffield donated. The three colonies each played home and away matches with the other two in 1892–93. Matches were timeless and Victoria won all their four contests, thus being the first winners of the Sheffield Shield.

This three-way contest continued as such until 1925–26. Of the 30 seasons played (it was suspended from 1915–16 to 1918–19), New South Wales won 17 times, Victoria 10 and South Australia three.

The best sequence of wins came between 1901–02 and 1906–07 when New South Wales recorded six successive titles. Victor Trumper, the outstanding batsman of his generation, was New South Wales's great run-getter in this period. Albert Cotter, the fastest bowler of the day, also represented New South Wales.

A major change came for the 1926–27 season. Queensland were admitted to the Sheffield Shield and simultaneously timeless matches for the Shield were abandoned, with four-and-a-half day matches introduced. Queensland hadtaken part in first-class matches since 1892–93. This season was also unusual as South Australia claimed the title for the first time since 1912–13. South Australia relied on the brilliant leg breaks of Clarrie Grimmett.

Don Bradman arrived and dominated Australian domestic cricket, just as he did Test cricket. Initially he played for New South Wales, but the season he switched to South Australia, the latter immediately won the title again. Queensland remained the minnows, winning only 12 times in their first 83 matches up to the Second World War.

Western Australia took their first title in their first Shield season of 1947–48. However, they played only four matches, whilst the rest played seven. This system remained in place until 1956–57 – with the exception of 1954–55 when a bizarre arrangement was tried whereby Western Australia played only two games and the rest only four.

New South Wales had a run of nine consecutive Shield titles from 1953–54 to 1961–62. They had two great all-rounders in Richie Benaud and Alan Davidson, as well as the batting of Norman O'Neill. Ray

BRADMAN *The greatest of all batsmen. His Test batting average of 99.94 says it all.*

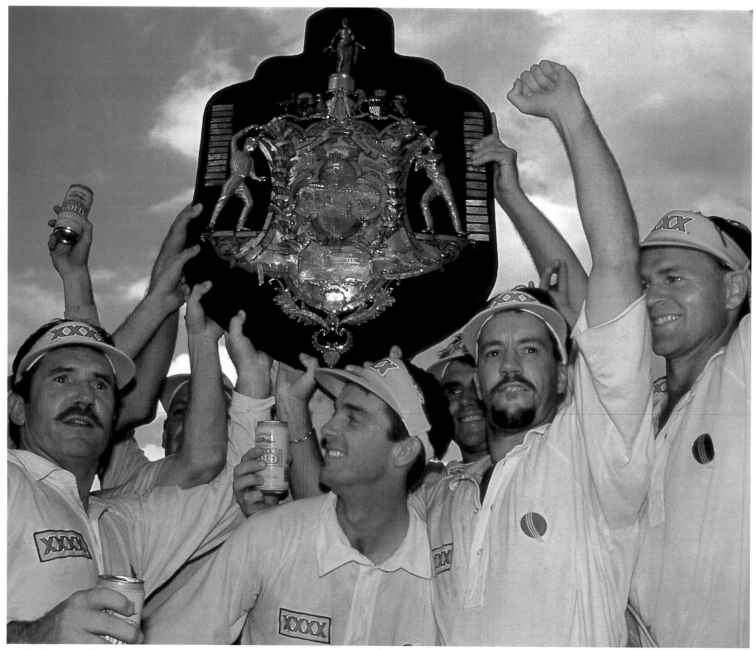

HISTORIC SHEFFIELD SHIELD *Australia's principal cricket trophy: Queensland's success in 1994–95.*

Lindwall, the fearsome fast bowler, switched from New South Wales to Queensland for the 1954–55 season.

In 1961–62, three West Indian Test players, Gary Sobers, Rohan Kanhai and Wesley Hall, were imported for the Sheffield Shield. Hall took 43 wickets for Queensland, Kanhai made 533 runs for Western Australia and Sobers topped both batting and bowling for South Australia. More importantly, the crowds flocked to see them – South Australia's gate receipts rose by two and a half times.

The 1970s saw Western Australia out in front – six titles in nine seasons to 1980–81. The period also saw

seasons when the Australian Packer players were banned from the Shield and the increase of international games meant that the top players missed many matches. Attendances at Shield games dropped to new lows.

Tasmania rose to Shield status for the 1977–78 season. In their first five seasons, they played one match against each opponent, while the rest played home and away. To avoid a percentage system, the points gained by Tasmania were multiplied by nine and divided by five.

A one-day knockout competition began in 1969–70. Tasmania participated from the start as did New

Zealand – in fact the Kiwis won the first title. An innings was limited to 40 eight-ball overs until 1978–79 and since then 50 six-ball overs. In 1978–79 Tasmania won the competition. In the same year, they won their first Shield match. Much of the team's success was due to the skills of Jack Simmons, the Lancashire all-rounder. Queensland finally won the Sheffield Shield in 1994–95.

It took until the autumn of 1999 for a sponsor to be be found for the Sheffield Shield. National Foods Ltd paid A\$22 million per annum for four years and the competition was renamed the Pura Milk Cup.

THE CRICKET ACADEMY

In 1987–88, the Australian Cricket Board appointed Jack Potter to head the Australian Cricket Institute of Sport's Youth Squad – 16 of Australia's most promising young players were brought together in Adelaide for special training, seminars and coaching. This was the start of the Australian Cricket Academy. The idea was based on the enormous success of East Germany's training programme of athletes for the Olympics.

Six years later, the Academy's "graduates" included Shane Warne, Michael Bevan, Michael Slater and

Glenn McGrath. The Academy led to schools of sporting excellence being set up in every state. They pick up potential players at a very young age, with the best transferring to the Academy at age 19. This system has meant that from the mid-1990s Australia became the world's top cricketing nation.

On the domestic front, the unremitting international schedule has meant that top players are rarely seen. The authorities tried day-night first-class matches, but these totally failed to attract spectators and have been generally abandoned. So poor were attendances that Melbourne Cricket Ground, the traditional home of cricket, deliberately staged football matches on the same dates as Victoria had arranged cricket matches – hitherto unheard of, but TV now controls everything.

A new team was introduced into the major one-day domestic competition – Australian Capital Territory – but they dropped out in 2000 after three seasons. Domestic first-class cricket is now almost totally ignored by the media – both broadcast and written. Pura Milk Cup crowds are pitiful – 166 people watched Victoria play Queensland in 2003–04.

Also in 2003–04, the Australian Cricket Board re-branded itself as "Cricket Australia".

SHEFFIELD SHIELD

SHEFFIELD SHIELD		**1922–23**	New South Wales	**1954–55**	New South Wales	**1980–81**	Western Australia
1892–93	Victoria	**1923–24**	Victoria	**1955–56**	New South Wales	**1981–82**	South Australia
1893–94	South Australia	**1924–25**	Victoria	**1956–57**	New South Wales	**1982–83**	New South Wales
1894–95	Victoria	**1925–26**	New South Wales	**1957–58**	New South Wales	**1983–84**	Western Australia
1895–96	New South Wales	**1926–27**	South Australia	**1958–59**	New South Wales	**1984–85**	New South Wales
1896–97	New South Wales	**1927–28**	Victoria	**1959–60**	New South Wales	**1986–87**	Western Australia
1897–98	Victoria	**1928–29**	New South Wales	**1960–61**	New South Wales	**1987–88**	Western Australia
1898–99	Victoria	**1929–30**	Victoria	**1961–62**	New South Wales	**1988–89**	Western Australia
1899–00	New South Wales	**1930–31**	Victoria	**1962–63**	Victoria	**1989–90**	New South Wales
1900–01	Victoria	**1931–32**	New South Wales	**1963–64**	South Australia	**1990–91**	Victoria
1901–02	New South Wales	**1932–33**	New South Wales	**1964–65**	New South Wales	**1991–92**	Western Australia
1902–03	New South Wales	**1933–34**	Victoria	**1965–66**	New South Wales	**1992–93**	New South Wales
1903–04	New South Wales	**1934–35**	Victoria	**1966–67**	Victoria	**1993–94**	New South Wales
1904–05	New South Wales	**1935–36**	South Australia	**1967–68**	Western Australia	**1994–95**	Queensland
1905–06	New South Wales	**1936–37**	Victoria	**1968–69**	South Australia	**1995–96**	South Australia
1906–07	New South Wales	**1937–38**	Victoria	**1969–70**	Victoria	**1996–97**	Queensland
1907–08	Victoria	**1938–39**	South Australia	**1970–71**	South Australia	**1997–98**	Western Australia
1908–09	New South Wales	**1939–40**	New South Wales	**1971–72**	Western Australia	**1998–99**	Western Australia
1909–10	South Australia	**1946–47**	Victoria	**1972–73**	Western Australia		
1910–11	New South Wales	**1947–48**	Western Australia	**1973–74**	Victoria	**PURA MILK CUP**	
1911–12	New South Wales	**1948–49**	New South Wales	**1974–75**	Western Australian	**1999–00**	Queensland
1912–13	South Australia	**1949–50**	New South Wales	**1975–76**	South Australia	**2000–01**	Queensland
1913–14	South Australia	**1950–51**	Victoria	**1976–77**	Western Australia	**2001–02**	Queensland
1914–15	Victoria	**1951–52**	New South Wales	**1977–78**	Western Australia	**2002–03**	New South Wales
1919–20	New South Wales	**1952–53**	South Australia	**1978–79**	Victoria	**2003–04**	Victoria
1921–22	Victoria	**1953–54**	New South Wales	**1979–80**	Victoria	**2004–05**	New South Wales

LIMITED-OVERS COMPETITIONS

V & G AUSTRALASIAN COLA-COLA COMPETITION

1969–70 New Zealand 140–4 (31.4 overs) beat Victoria 129 (34.6 overs) by 6 wkts

1972–73 Western Australia 170 (38.2 overs) beat Queensland 79 (23.5 overs) by 91 runs

AUSTRALASIAN COCA-COLA COMPETITION

1969–70 Victoria 192–2 (33.4 overs) beat South Australia 190 (38.7 overs) by 8 wkts

1972–73 New Zealand 170–9 (35 overs) beat Queensland 132 (31.3 overs) by 38 runs

GILLETTE CUP

1973–74 Western Australia 151–3 (26.6 overs) beat New Zealand 150 (36.3 overs) by 7 wkts

1974–75 New Zealand 77–2 (17 overs) beat Western Australia 76 (26.1 overs) by 8 wkts

1975–76 Queensland 236–7 (40 overs) beat Western Australia 232 (39 overs) by 4 runs

1976–77 Western Australia 165–9 (39.3 overs) beat Victoria 164 (37.3 overs) by 1 wkt

1977–78 Western Australia 185–3 (37.1 overs) beat Tasmania 184-9 (40 overs) by 7 wkts

1978–79 Tasmania 180–6 (40 overs) beat Western Australia 133 (50 overs) by 47 runs

MCDONALD'S CUP

1979–80 Victoria 199–6 (47.4 overs) beat New South Wales 198–8 (50 overs) 4 wkts

1980–81 Queensland 188–9 (48 overs) beat Western Australia 116 (32.5 overs) by 72 runs

1981–82 Queensland 224–8 (47 overs) beat New South Wales 197 (44.4 overs) by 27 runs

1982–83 Western Australia 198–6 (49.1 overs) beat New South Wales 195–6 (50 overs) by 4 wkts

1983–84 South Australia 256–6 (49 overs) beat Western Australia 248–9 (49 overs) by 8 runs

1984–85 New South Wales278–7 (50 overs) beat South Australia 190 (45.5 overs) by 88 runs

1985–86 Western Australia 167 (38 overs) beat Victoria 148 (36.5 overs) by 19 runs

1986–87 South Australia 325–6 (50 overs) beat Tasmania 239–9 (50 overs) by 86 runs

1987–88 New South Wales 219–7 (50 overs) beat South Australia 196–6 (50 overs) by 23 runs

FEDERATED AUTOMOBILE INSURANCE

1988–89 Queensland 253–4 (50 overs)beat Victoria 90 (32.4 overs) by 163 runs

1989–90 Western Australia 88–3 (19.1 overs) beat South Australia 87 (34.5 overs) by 7 wkts

1990–91 Western Australia 236–3 (44.5 overs) beat New South Wales 235–7 (50 overs) by 7 wkts

1991–92 New South Wales 199–9 (50 overs) beat Western Australia 130 (40.1 overs) by 69 runs

MERCANTILE MUTUAL CUP

1992–93 New South Wales 187–6 (49.4 overs) beat Victoria 186 (50 overs) by 4 wkts

1993–94 New South Wales 264–4 (50 overs) beat Western Australia 218–9 (49 overs) on faster scoring rate

1994–95 Victoria 170–6 (44.5 overs) beat South Australia 169 (46.4 overs) by 4 wkts

1995–96 Queensland 167–6 (44.5 overs) beat Western Australia 166 (49.1 overs) by 4 wkts

1996–97 Western Australia 149–2 (35 overs) beat Queensland 148 (40.1 overs) by 8 wkts

1997–98 Queensland 167–8 (47.5 overs) beat New South Wales 166 (49.3 overs) by 2 wkts

1998–99 Victoria 231 (50 overs) beat New South Wales 192 (45.3 overs) by 39 runs

1999–00 Western Australia 301–6 (50 overs) beat Queensland 256 (45.2 overs) by 45 runs

2000–01 New South Wales 273–4 (48.2 overs) beat Western Australia 272–7 (50 overs) by 6 wkts

2001–02 New South Wales 204 (50 overs) beat Queensland 185 (48.5 overs) by 19 runs

ING CUP

2002–03 New South Wales 208–3 (26.5 overs) beat Western Australia 207 (49.5 overs) by 7 wkts

2003–04 Western Australia 248–6 (49.4 overs) beat Queensland 244 (49.1 overs) by 4 wkts

2004–05 Tasmania 247–3 (47.1 overs) beat Queensland 246–7 (50 overs) by 7 wkts

SOUTH AFRICA

The first competition organized for major teams in South Africa was instituted in 1876. The silver inscription on the competition trophy – a cricket bat – reads: "Presented to the cricketers of the Colony of Good Hope by the municipality of Port Elizabeth". Named the Champion Bat Competition, the trophy was won twice by King William's Town, and once each by Kimberley, Port Elizabeth and Western Province. The final competition took place in 1890.

The Champion Bat Competition, which was granted first-class status only in 1890, was put in abeyance when the Currie Cup was established. Sir Donald Currie, the founder of the Castle Shipping Line, which carried passengers and goods between the United Kingdom and South Africa, donated a cup to be presented to the South African team which performed best against the 1888–89 England tourists.

Kimberley were awarded the Cup and from 1889–90 onwards the Currie Cup was competed for by the major sides in the country. In the first year, just one Currie Cup game took place, Transvaal challenging and beating Kimberley. The second season was a repeat of the first, except that Kimberley won the cup back. There was no competition in 1891–92 because of the tour of an England side – this was indeed to be the pattern for many years to come. If a first-class touring side visited South Africa, the Currie Cup was abandoned for the season.

Frank Hearne, the Kent all-rounder, emigrated to South Africa and was engaged as coach to Western Province from 1889. He also played for them, making a material difference to the strength of that side. They won the Currie Cup in 1892–93 and took the title in three out of the next four competitions.

The Boer War caused a gap from 1898–99 to 1901–02, then Transvaal won the title, all the matches being staged in Port Elizabeth.

It is amusing now to note the career of P.H. de Villiers. He had played for Western Province, but moved to Transvaal and fought on the Boer side. According to legend, he was wearing his cricketing gear when captured by the British, shipped out as a P.O.W. to Ceylon, where he organized what he called the Curry Cup, amongst fellow prisoners, then a P.O.W. team against Ceylon match, which the Governor of Ceylon attended.

The Edwardian era saw the emergence of some quite brilliant googly bowlers: Aubrey Faulkner of Transvaal; A.E.E. Vogler, who played for three different provinces; and Gordon White of Transvaal. A fourth notable spin bowler was Reggie Schwarz. When he toured England with the 1907 South Africans, he topped the first-class bowling table with 137 wickets at 11.79 each. Curiously, whilst at Cambridge University, Schwarz had not only failed to gain a blue, but he never played in a first-class game for the University. He played for Transvaal from 1902–03 to 1909–10.

The great batsman of this era was Dave Nourse, whose career began with Natal in 1896–97 and ended with Western Province in 1935–36. Long before his final game, he was known as the Grand Old Man of South African cricket.

Virtually all cricket in South Africa had been played on matting wickets, but this changed and by the time Wally Hammond's England side toured in 1938–39, all the principal grounds had turf wickets. The only matting wickets encountered by the tourists were in Rhodesia.

A major change in the Currie Cup Competition occurred in 1951–52 when the provincial sides were divided into two sections. Section A comprised Eastern Province, Natal, Transvaal and Western Province; Section B comprised Orange Free State, Rhodesia, Border, North-Eastern Transvaal and Griqualand West. The authorities reverted to a single division in 1960–61, but in 1962–63 went back to two divisions.

Natal were, by and large, the strongest team from the 1930s right through to the late 1960s and had three notable players in the 1950s and early 60s: Roy McLean, Jackie McGlew and Trevor Goddard.

Transvaal wrested the cup from Natal in 1968–69. They were to dominate the competition for the next 20 years during which, because of the political situation, South Africa was excluded from the Test arena.

In 1982–83, Transvaal played in all the competition's 22 matches and lost just one. The team was led by Clive Rice; the leading scorer was Jimmy Cook; the bowling was opened by Vincent van der Bijl; and

OLD ENOUGH *Graeme Smith was made captain of South Africa at the age of 22.*

Alan Kourie, slow left arm, was the principal wicket-taker.

The major domestic limited-overs competition began in 1969–70 on an unofficial basis – sponsored by Gillette – but in the second year it was recognized and ran on a knock-out basis until 1979–80, after which the semi-finals were played over two legs (home and away). From 1986–87, the teams were divided into two pools with the top two sides going into the semi-finals.

In 1981–82 a new competition, played under lights and sponsored by Benson & Hedges, was introduced. This, using coloured clothing and other novelties, took the public interest away from the original competition, so much so that 1992–93 saw the end of the daytime limited-overs competition.

CURRIE BECOMES CASTLE

The beginning of the 1990s saw the political situation in South Africa change. The two governing bodies of cricket in the country, the South African Cricket Union and the South African Cricket Board, joined to form the United Cricket Board of South Africa. One of the consequences of the amalgamation was a restructuring of the Currie Cup. The name was changed to the Castle Cup and two new regions were granted first-class status: Western Transvaal and Eastern Transvaal.

Eastern Province wrested the top place in domestic cricket from Rice's Transvaal during this period – in 1991–92 Eastern won the Castle Cup for the third time in four years. Another side to flourish was Orange Free State, managed by Eddie Barlow, whose stars were the West Indian Franklyn Stephenson and the fast bowler Allan Donald. Below the top level, further changes took place in that the lower division of the first-class scene was divided into two sections, the UCB Bowl and the President's Competition. The latter was for B sides or Second XIs. However, in 1992–93 first-class status was revoked for the B sides, but this lasted just one season. The efforts made by Barlow in the Free State paid off as the side won the Castle Cup for the first time in 1992–93, then the following year

TREVOR GODDARD AND JACKIE MCGLEW *Two of South Africa's greatest batsman through the 1950s and 1960s.*

performed the double by retaining the title and taking the Benson & Hedges Night Competition as well.

The Castle Cup was replaced by the Super Sports Series in 1996–97, and there were several name changes: Transvaal became Gauteng; Western Transvaal became North West and Northern Transvaal became Northerns.

Cricket in South Africa is proving ever more popular and its base is growing as the talents of the black and coloured cricketers are being discovered and utilized, notably in Soweto. In order to reflect the racial mix of the country, it was made compulsory for first class provincial sides to include at least one coloured player in any eleven, in 1999. Also in that year the Super Sports Series rules were altered. Instead of a single league, the teams were divided into two pools. The top four in each pool then went on to a Super Eight Final League.

The defeat of South Africa by Australia in 2000–01 and the apparent decline of cricket standards in provincial matches, prompted the United Cricket Board to appoint a firm of independent consultants to review cricket overall and make recommendations. The result was that six professional teams were created from the existing principal provincial sides, for example Gauteng and North West were reformed as the "Lions"; Free State became the "Eagles". In 2003–04, these new teams played in a new competition based on the English Twenty20 concept. It was enormously successful with 153,000 spectators watching the 17 matches.

In 2004–05, the same six teams competed in the first-class competition. The eleven old clubs were formed into an amateur league, whilst a third tier of clubs had a similar competition at a still lower level.

CASTLE CUP/SUPERSPORT SERIES

CASTLE CUP

Season	Winner
1889–90	Transvaal
1890–91	Kimberley
1892–93	Western Province
1893–94	Western Province
1894–95	Transvaal
1896–97	Western Province
1897–98	Western Province
1902–03	Transvaal
1903–04	Transvaal
1904–05	Transvaal
1906–07	Transvaal
1908–09	Western Province
1910–11	Natal
1912–13	Natal
1920–21	Western Province
1921–22	Natal, Transvaal, Western Province
1923–24	Transvaal
1925–26	Transvaal
1926–27	Transvaal
1929–30	Transvaal
1931–32	Western Province
1933–34	Natal
1934–35	Transvaal
1936–37	Natal
1937–38	Natal, Transvaal
1946–47	Natal
1947–48	Natal
1950–51	Transvaal
1951–52	Natal
1952–53	Western Province
1954–55	Natal
1955–56	Western Province
1958–59	Transvaal
1959–60	Natal
1960–61	Natal
1962–63	Natal
1963–64	Natal
1965–66	Natal, Transvaal
1966–67	Natal
1967–68	Natal
1968–69	Transvaal
1969–70	Transvaal, Western Province
1970–71	Transvaal
1971–72	Transvaal
1972–73	Transvaal
1973–74	Natal
1974–75	Western Province
1975–76	Natal
1976–77	Natal
1977–78	Western Province
1978–79	Transvaal
1979–80	Transvaal
1980–81	Natal
1981–82	Western Province
1982–83	Transvaal
1983–84	Transvaal
1984–85	Transvaal
1985–86	Western Province
1986–87	Transvaal
1987–88	Transvaal
1988–89	Eastern Province
1989–90	Eastern Province, Western Province
1990–91	Western Province
1991–92	Eastern Province
1992–93	Orange Free State
1993–94	Orange Free State
1994–95	Natal
1995–96	Western Province

SUPERSPORT SERIES

Season	Winner
1996–97	Natal
1997–98	Free State
1998–99	Western Province
1999–00	Gauteng
2000–01	Western Province
2001–02	Kwazulu-Natal
2002–03	Easterns
2003–04	Western Province
2004–05	Eagles, Dolphins

BENSON & HEDGES NIGHT SERIES

Season	Result
1981–82	Transvaal 265–7 (47.3 overs) beat Natal 263 (49.3 overs) by 3 wkts
1982–83	Transvaal 277–4 (42.0 overs) beat Western Province 275–9 (45 overs) by 6 wkts
1983–84	Natal 125–3 (29.2 overs) beat Eastern Province 124 (37.3 overs) by 7 wkts
1984–85	Transvaal 179–3 (36.2 overs) beat Northern Transvaal 176 (43.1 overs) by 7 wkts
1985–86	Western Province 265–4 (45 overs) beat Northern Transvaal 253–9 (45 overs) by 12 runs
1986–87	Western Province 205–6 (45 overs) beat Transvaal 164 (41.4 overs) by 41 runs
1987–88	Western Province 190–5 (44 overs) beat Transvaal 189 (44.3 overs) by 5 wkts
1988–89	Orange Free State 213 (45 overs) beat Western Province 152 (39.4 overs) by 61 runs
1989–90	Eastern Province 205–9 (45 overs) beat Natal 202 (44.5 overs) by 1 wkt
1990–91	Western Province 168–4 (39.3 overs) beat Natal 164–8 (45 overs) by 6 wkts
1991–92	Eastern Province 246–4 (44.1 overs) beat Western Province 244–2 (45 overs) by 6 wkts
1992–93	Transvaal 193–7 (45 overs) beat Natal 192–8 (45 overs) by 1 run
1993–94	Orange Free State 108–3 (28.1 overs) beat Natal 103 (36.2 overs) by 7 wkts
1994–95	Orange Free State 291–8 (50 overs) beat Eastern Province 177–8 (50 overs) by 113 runs
1995–96	Orange Free State 290–6 (45 overs) beat Transvaal 148 (37.4 overs) by 142 runs
1996–97	Natal beat Western Province winning two out of three finals
1997–98	Gauteng 193–7 (43.2 overs) beat Northerns 192 (40.5 overs) by 3 wkts
1998–99	Griqualand West 199–4 (40.2 overs) beat Border 198–6 (45 overs) by 6 wkts
1999–00	Boland 209–6 (45 overs) beat Eastern Province 173–8 (45 overs) by 36 runs
2000–01	Kwazulu-Natal 217–7 (44 overs) beat Northerns 214 (45 overs) by 3 wkts
2001–02	Kwazulu-Natal 223–6 (45 overs) beat Western Province 195–9 (45 overs) by 28 runs

STANDARD BANK CUP

Season	Result
2002–03	Western Province 129–1 (12.5 overs) beat Griqualand West 125 (38.2 overs) by 9 wkts
2003–04	Gauteng 146–3 (33.3 overs) beat Easterns 144 (43.3 overs) by 7 wkts
2004–05	Eagles 259–3 (43.4 overs) beat Titans 258–5 (45 overs) by 7 wkts

BATTING STAR *Herschelle Gibbs has scored more than 11,000 runs in Tests and one-day internationals for South Africa.*

UCB BOWL

Season	Winner	Season	Winner
1977–78	Northern Transvaal	1990–91	Border, Western Province B
1978–79	Northern Transvaal	1991–92	Eastern Transvaal
1979–80	Natal B	1992–93	Boland
1980–81	Western Province B	1993–94	Transvaal B, Western Province B
1981–82	Boland		
1982–83	Western Province B	1994–95	Natal B
1983–84	Western Province B	1995–96	Griqualand West
1984–85	Transvaal B	1996–97	Eastern Province B
1985–86	Boland	1997–98	North West
1986–87	Transvaal B	1998–99	North West
1987–88	Boland	1999–00	Western Province B
1988–89	Border	2000–01	Western Province B
1989–90	Border, Western Province B		

NEW ZEALAND

The first three-day game between two New Zealand provinces – Otago v Canterbury – at Dunedin in January 1864 is considered as the starting point of first–class cricket in the country. They met annually in the single New Zealand first-class game until 1873–74, when Auckland, Nelson and Wellington joined the sides designated first-class. Taranki acquired first-class status in 1882–83 and Hawkes Bay in 1883–84.

The provinces were presented with a trophy by Lord Plunket, the Governor-General, in 1906–07. The New Zealand Cricket Council awarded it to Canterbury on the grounds that the province had given the best performance against the MCC side which had just toured.

The trophy – a shield – was to be competed for on a challenge basis. Auckland in December 1907 were the first successful challengers and they managed to retain it for more than three years.

In 1921 the New Zealand Cricket Council decided to set up a league. Despite the fact that various New Zealand sides had imported professionals from England to improve the standard, it cannot be said that the quality prior to the First World War was high. There was no question of New Zealand warranting Test-match status and touring sides to the country were not up to Sheffield Shield rank.

The four major associations which comprised the initial Plunket league were Auckland, Canterbury, Otago and Wellington. Hawkes Bay was designated a minor association. The Hawke Cup was the trophy for the minor associations and continued to be run on a challenge basis.

After the Second World War, two more sides were promoted to first-class status and joined the Plunket Shield, Central Districts, in 1950–51, and Northern Districts, in 1956–57. In general, the sides were fairly evenly matched and, apart from a four-season period in the 1930s –

when Auckland won successive titles – no side has been champion for more than two consecutive summers. Notable Auckland players of that purple patch were batsmen Mervyn Wallace, Graham Vivian and Bill Carson and fast bowlerJack Cowie.

Directly after the Second World War, New Zealand produced a record-breaking batsman, Bert Sutcliffe. Initially, he played for Auckland, but then switched to Otago, for whom he hit two triple-centuries, the highest being 385 against Canterbury in 1952–53. This remains the Plunket Shield record.

After the appearance of Bert Sutcliffe, came the debut of John Reid, who played for Wellington from 1947–48 to 1964–65, apart from two seasons with Otago. The Hadlee family were the major force for Canterbury. Walter Hadlee's career commenced in the 1930s and continued until 1951–52. His three sons all represented the province and one, Richard Hadlee, was the greatest cricketer New Zealand has yet produced. Initially a tearaway fast bowler, he developed into not only the most accurate bowler of his generation, but also a very aggressive left-hand middle-order batsman. The brothers Martin and Jeff Crowe, first with Auckland until Martin moved to Central Districts, were major batsmen of the 1980s.

In 1975–76 Shell Oil took over sponsorship of the Plunket Shield. At first there was a Shell Cup for the league winners and a Shell Trophy for a knockout competition, but in the 1979–80 season the trophy was given to the league winners and the cup to the winners of a limited-overs competition which had commenced in 1971–72.

In 1997–98 "Conference Cricket" was introduced, with four teams, three from New Zealand and Bangladesh. The teams competed in both four-day and one-day matches. In 1998–99 the one-day matches were ditched and Pakistan A

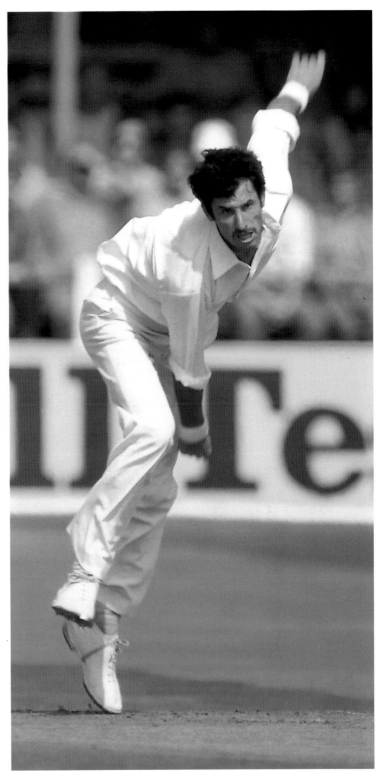

SIR RICHARD HADLEE *His 431 Test wickets created a new record.*

replaced Bangladesh. The whole plan was scrapped for 2000–01.

In 2002–03, the Cricket Players Association, formed in 2001, saw how much money the Board was earning through TV deals and demanded a 60 per cent pay rise for their 128 members. When this was rejected, the players went on strike.

The strike lasted six weeks. Stephen Fleming and Chris Cairns acted as negotiators on behalf of the players and eventually a four-year contract system was agreed together with a 15 per cent pay rise.

The first-class State Championship had a revised format in 2001–02, and yet another one for 2003–04.

SLOW LEFT-ARM *Daniel Vettori, New Zealand's top spinner from the 1990s.*

LIMITED-OVERS COMPETITIONS

NZ MOTOR CORPORATION TOURNAMENT

Season	Result
1971–72	Canterbury 129–3 (33.3 overs) beat Wellington 127 (36.5 overs) by 7 wkts
1972–73	Auckland 209–6 (40 overs) beat Otago 144 (34 overs) by 65 runs
1973–74	Wellington 212–9 (34 overs) beat Auckland 209–7 (35 overs) by 1 wkt
1974–75	Wellington 181–7 (35 overs) beat Northern Districts 165–8 (35 overs) by 16 runs
1975–76	Canterbury 233–6 (35 overs) beat Wellington 153–7 (35 overs) by 80 runs
1976–77	Canterbury 178–7 (34.1 overs) beat Northern Districts 176–7 (35 overs) by 3 wkts

GILLETTE CUP

Season	Result
1977–78	Canterbury 211–9 (30 overs) beat Northern Districts 154–9 (30 overs) by 57 runs
1978–79	Auckland 156 (34.6 overs) beat Canterbury 143–9 (35 overs) by 13 runs

NATIONAL KNOCKOUT TOURNAMENT

Season	Result
1979–89	Northern Districts 183–8 (50 overs) beat Otago 182–8 (50 overs) by 2 wkts

SHELL CUP KNOCKOUT TOURNAMENT

Season	Result
1980–81	Auckland 188–7 (49.1 overs) beat Canterbury 186 (49.3 overs) by 3 wkts
1981–82	Wellington 205–2 (47.5 overs) beat Canterbury 204–7 (50 overs) by 8 wkts
1982–83	Auckland 212–5 (49.1 overs) beat Northern Districts 210 (49.2 overs) by 5 wkts
1983–84	Auckland 130–5 (33.3 overs) beat Wellington 129–6 (35 overs) by 5 wkts
1984–85	Central Districts 156–2 (43.2 overs) beat Wellington 153 (48.2 overs) by 8 wkts
1985–86*	Canterbury
1986–87*	Auckland
1987–88*	Otago
1988–89*	Wellington
1989–90	Auckland 198–8 (50 overs) beat Central Districts 176–9 (50 overs) by 22 runs
1990–91	Wellington 214–8 (50 overs) beat Central Districts 140 (42.4 overs) by 74 runs
1991–92	Canterbury 252 (49.4 overs) beat Wellington 249 (49.4 overs) by 3 runs
1992–93	Canterbury 183–8 (50 overs) beat Otago 169–9 (50 overs) by 14 runs
1993–94	Canterbury 240–7 (50 overs) beat Central Districts 215 (49 overs) by 25 runs
1994–95	Northern Districts 256–8 (50 overs) beat Wellington 108(29.3 overs) by 148 runs
1995–96	Canterbury 329–5 (50 overs) beat Northern Districts 213 (44.4 overs) by 116 runs
1996–97	Canterbury 204–7 (50 overs) beat Wellington 81 (33.5 overs) by 123 runs
1997–98	Northern Districts 189–9 (50 overs) beat Canterbury 134 (33.1 overs) by 55 runs
1998–99	Canterbury 217–7 (50 overs) beat Wellington 168 (44 overs) by 49 runs
1999–00	Canterbury 225–3 (41.5 overs) beat Auckland 224–6 (50 overs) by 7 wkts
2000–01	Central District beat Canterbury winning two out of three finals.
2001–02	Wellington 200–9 (50 overs) beat Canterbury 147 (44.3 overs) by 53 runs
2002–03	Northern Districts 234–7 (50 overs) beat Auckland 217–7 (50 overs) by 17 runs
2003–04	Central Districts 354–5 (50 overs) beat Canterbury 255 (41.2 overs) by 99 runs
2004–05	Northern Districts 190–9 (50 overs) beat Central Districts 170 (48.2 overs) by 20 runs

*These teams were the winners when this competition was run on a league basis during these seasons.

PLUNKET / SHELL

PLUNKET SHIELD

Canterbury	to Dec 17, 1907
Auckland	Dec 17, 1907 to Feb 1, 1911
Canterbury	Feb 1, 1911 to Feb 12, 1912
Auckland	Feb 12, 1912 to Jan 31, 1913
Canterbury	Jan 31,1913 to Dec 27, 1918
Wellington	Dec 27, 1918 to Jan 24, 1919
Canterbury	Jan 24, 1919 to Jan 4, 1920
Auckland	Jan 4, 1920 to Jan 10, 1921
Wellington	from Jan 10, 1921

Season	Winner
1921–22	Auckland
1922–23	Canterbury
1923–24	Wellington
1924–25	Otago
1925–26	Wellington
1926–27	Auckland
1927–28	Wellington
1928–29	Auckland
1929–30	Wellington
1930–31	Canterbury
1931–32	Wellington
1932–33	Otago
1933–34	Auckland
1934–35	Canterbury
1935–36	Wellington
1936–37	Auckland
1937–38	Auckland
1938–39	Auckland
1939–40	Auckland
1940–45	No competition
1945–46	Canterbury
1946–47	Auckland
1947–48	Otago
1948–49	Canterbury
1949–50	Wellington
1950–51	Otago
1951–52	Canterbury
1952–53	Otago
1953–54	Central Districts
1954–55	Wellington
1955–56	Canterbury
1956–57	Wellington
1957–58	Otago
1958–59	Auckland
1959–60	Canterbury
1960–61	Wellington
1961–62	Wellington
1962–63	Northern Districts
1963–64	Auckland
1964–65	Canterbury
1965–66	Wellington
1966–67	Central Districts
1967–68	Central Districts
1968–69	Auckland
1969–70	Otago
1970–71	Central Districts
1971–72	Otago
1972–73	Wellington
1973–74	Wellington
1974–75	Otago

SHELL TROPHY

Season	Winner
1975–76	Canterbury (Cup), Canterbury (Trophy)
1976–77	Northern Districts (Cup), Otago (Trophy)
1977–78	Canterbury (Cup), Auckland (Trophy)
1978–79	Otago (Cup), Otago (Trophy)
1979–80	Northern Districts
1980–81	Auckland
1981–82	Wellington
1982–83	Wellington
1983–84	Canterbury
1984–85	Wellington
1985–86	Otago
1986–87	Central Districts
1987–88	Otago
1988–89	Auckland
1989–90	Wellington
1990–91	Auckland
1991–92	Central Districts, Northern Districts
1992–93	Northern Districts
1993–94	Canterbury
1994–95	Auckland
1995–96	Auckland
1996–97	Canterbury
1997–98	Canterbury
1998–99	Central Districts
1999–00	Northern Districts
2000–01	Wellington
2001–02	Auckland
2002–03	Auckland

STATE CHAMPIONSHIP

Season	Winner
2003–04	Wellington
2004–05	Auckland

PAKISTAN

The Dominion of Pakistan was created on July 18, 1947. It was formed from two separate parts of the former Indian Empire: in the West, there was Baluchistan, Sind, North West Frontier Province and West Punjab; Eastern Pakistan was made up of East Bengal and the Sylhot district of Assam. The three main cricketing centres in Pakistan were all in the west – at Lahore, Karachi and Peshawar. (In March 1971, East Pakistan became Bangladesh.)

The only first-class matches involving a Pakistan side staged in 1947–48 were Sind v Bombay, in Bombay, and Punjab University v Punjab Governor's XI. In 1948–49, the West Indian side touring India played two first-class matches in Pakistan and a few months later a Pakistan team toured Ceylon.

Pakistan was admitted as a member of the ICC in July 1952 and played its first Test, against India, in the 1952–53 season. The first domestic first-class competition in Pakistan was arranged for the following season. The competition was called the Qaid-i-Azam ("The Great Leader") Trophy, a reference to Mohammad Ali Jinnah, who founded the Pakistan State.

Seven teams competed in the first competition: Punjab, Karachi, Sind, North West Frontier Province, Bahawalpur, Services and Railways. Two other sides were entered, East Pakistan and Baluchistan, but both withdrew. They did, however, compete in the second season, 1954–55. It was soon clear that the sides were ill-matched and it was agreed that in 1956–57 Karachi and Punjab should enter three teams each. There have been numerous changes both in the teams taking part and in the way the competition has been run.

In 1960–61 the Board of Control instituted the President Ayub Trophy, donated by Field-Marshal Ayub Khan. In 1970–71, this was replaced by the BCCP Trophy, which lasted two seasons, to be replaced by the Patron's Trophy.

The Patron's Trophy was downgraded to non-first-class – with matches of two-day duration – in 1999–00, but reinstated as first class for 2000–01. In 2002–03 it was merged with the Qaid-i-Azam Trophy.

From the late 1950s, a number of other competitions were granted first-class status for a few seasons.

The principle limited-overs competition is for the Wills Cup. This began in 1980–81 as a 45-overs-a-side contest, the teams being divided into two leagues with the top two teams in each league meeting in a knockout semi-final round.

The Pakistan Board of Control has tinkered with the game's domestic structure almost annually over the last decade. In 2002–03 for example, the regional and departmental teams had competed alongside each other for the Q-e-A Trophy, then in 2003–04, they were once again split, whilst the Patron's Trophy was revived after having lapsed for one season. Teams' identities change quite frequently. Faisalabad absorbed Sargodha, Bahawalpur became Multan and Sialkot was a merger of Gujranwala and Sheikhupura.

In 2004–05, the first-class competition was regionally based, but extended to eleven teams, with Karachi and Lahore fielding two teams each. The Patron's Trophy was altered to include new teams – Defence Housing Authority (DHA), Karachi Port Trust (KPT) and Pakistan Telecom Company Limited (PTCL). Agricultural Development Bank of Pakistan changed its name to Zarai Taraquiati Bank Limited. The non-first-class Cornelius and Kardar Trophies, which were the second divisions of the Q-e-A and Patron's Trophies, were scrapped.

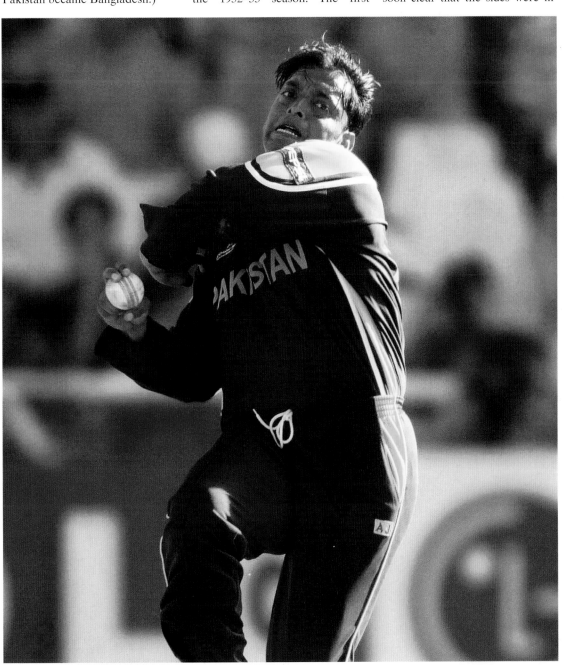

SHOAIB AKHTAR *Pakistan's fast-bowling sensation.*

QAID-I-AZAM TROPHY

1953–54	Bahawalpur	1982–83	United Bank
1954–55	Karachi	1983–84	National Bank
1956–57	Punjab	1984–85	United Bank
1957–58	Bahawalpur	1985–86	Karachi
1958–59	Karachi	1986–87	National Bank
1959–60	Karachi	1987–88	PIA
1961–62	Karachi Blues	1988–89	ADBP
1962–63	Karachi A	1989–90	PIA
1963–64	Karachi Blues	1990–91	Karachi Whites
1964–65	Karachi Blues	1991–92	Karachi Whites
1966–67	Karachi	1992–93	Karachi
1968–69	Lahore	1993–94	Lahore
1969–70	PIA	1994–95	Karachi Blues
1970–71	Karachi Blues	1995–96	Karachi Blues
1972–73	Railways	1996–97	Lahore City
1973–74	Railways	1997–98	Karachi Blues
1974–75	Punjab A	1998–99	Peshawar
1975–76	National Bank	1999–00	PIA
1976–77	United Bank	2000–01	Lahore Blues
1977–78	Habib Bank	2001–02	Karachi Whites
1978–79	National Bank	2002–03	PIA
1979–80	PIA	2003–04	Faisalabad
1980–81	United Bank	2004–05	Peshawar
1981–82	National Bank		

PATRON'S TROPHY

Year	Winner	Year	Winner
1970–71	PIA	1987–88	Habib Bank
1971–72	PIA	1988–89	Karachi
1972–73	Karachi Blues	1989–90	Karachi Whites
1973–74	Railways	1990–91	ADBP
1974–75	National Bank	1991–92	Habib Bank
1975–76	National Bank	1992–93	Habib Bank
1976–77	Habib Bank	1993–94	ADBP
1977–78	Habib Bank	1994–95	Allied Bank
1978–79	National Bank	1996–97	United Bank
1979–80	IDBP	1997–98	Habib Bank
1980–81	Rawalpindi	1998–99	Habib Bank
1981–82	Allied Bank	1999–00	Lahore City Blues
1982–83	PACO	2000–01	Customs
1983–84	Karachi Blues	2001–02	National Bank
1984–85	Karachi Whites	2002–03	No competition
1985–86	Karachi Whites	2003–04	ZT Bank Ltd
1986–87	National Bank	2003–04	Habib Bank, PIA

WILLS CUP/TISSOT CUP

Year	Result
1980–81	PIA 230 (45 overs) beat United Bank 225 (44.1 overs) by 5 runs
1981–82	PIA 132–3 (32.5 overs) beat Lahore 131 (42.3 overs) by 7 wkts
1982–83	PIA 206–9 (45 overs) beat Habib Bank 173 (43.2 overs) by 33 runs
1983–84	Habib Bank 182–3 (41 overs) beat PIA 181 (39.4 overs) by 7 wkts
1984–85	No competition
1985–86	PIA 257–3 (45 overs) beat United Bank 254–9 (45 overs) by 3 runs
1986–87	Habib Bank 155–7 (49.2 overs) beat United Bank 154 (48.1 overs) by 3 wkts
1987–88	PIA 212–8 (47.4 overs) beat United Bank 206–8 (49 overs) by 2 wkts
1988–89	United Bank 228–6 (45 overs) beat PIA 228 (45 overs) by losing fewer wkts
1989–90	Habib Bank 178–2 (42.4 overs) beat PIA 177 (46.3 overs) by 8 wkts
1990–91	Habib Bank 241–4 (45 overs) beat United Bank 185–9 (45 overs) by 6 wkts
1991–92	Habib Bank 254–5 (39 overs) beat PIA 234–4 (43 overs) by 5 wkts
1992–93	National Bank 272–5 (48 overs) beat Habib Bank 269–6 (50 overs) by 5 wkts
1993–94	Habib Bank 249–5 (50 overs) beat Rawalpindi 203–8 (50 overs) by 46 runs
1994–95	National Bank 215–2 (43.2 overs) beat PIA 211 (44.4 overs) by 8 wkts
1995–96	PIA 125–3 (30.5 overs) beat Rawalpindi 124 (42.4 overs) by 7 wkts
1996–97	Allied Bank 252–4 (42.1 overs) beat Nat. Bank 251–9 (50 overs) by 6 wkts
1997–98	Allied Bank 248 (48 overs) beat PIA 216 (48.3 overs) by 32 runs
1998–99	Allied Bank 260-6 (47.4) beat Pakistan Customs 259–9 (50 overs) by 4 wkts
1999–00	PIA 310–4 (50 overs) beat Redco 272–9 (50 overs) by 38 runs
2000–01	Karachi Whites 278–5 (50 overs) beat Sheikhupura 199 by 79 runs
2001–02	PIA 236–9 (50 overs) beat Habib Bank 230 (49.5 overs) by 6 runs
2002–03	PIA 273–7 (50 overs) beat WAPDA 218–9 (50 overs) by 55 runs
2003–04	Habib Bank 266–7 (50 overs) beat PIA 135 (39.1 overs) by 131 runs
2004–05	WAPDA 288–9 (50 overs) beat PIA 252 (49.2 overs) by 36 runs

WASIM AKRAM *Combined with Waqar Younis to provide Pakistan's opening attack.*

WEST INDIES

LEARIE CONSTANTINE *The star all-rounder for West Indies in the 1930s.*

The match between Barbados and Demerara played in Bridgetown on February 15 and 16 1865 is considered as the start of first-class cricket in the West Indies. In 1868–69, Trinidad played Demerara in two matches, both in Port of Spain, and are considered "first-class" from those matches. Matches between the three colonies continued intermittently for 20 years or more, but attempts to organize some sort of proper competition between the colonies came to nothing – despite the fact that in 1886 G.N. Wyatt of British Guiana had managed to pick a fairly representative West Indian side to tour the United States.

In September 1891, Trinidad agreed to play in a triangular intercolonial tournament in Bridgetown. Barbados won it, mainly thanks to brothers Clifford and Percy Goodman, the former a fast-medium bowler and the latter a batsman.

Jamaica was too far away to compete in this tournament and they had to wait for overseas touring sides before it could field a representative XI. Jamaica's first first-class game was against R.S. Lucas's English touring team in 1894–95.

Between 1911–12 and 1921–22 the Intercolonial Tournament was not staged. The next competition, in Georgetown, saw Barbados win by an innings in the final. In 1924–25, Jamaica opposed Barbados for the first time in Bridgetown, having played another island in first-class matches only once before, when Trinidad visited Kingston in 1905–06. All three games in 1924–25 ended as draws, the pitches being perfect for batting.

In the 1920s, Trinidad gradually overtook Barbados as the major force in the Caribbean. British Guiana were also building up their strength and in 1929–30 won the Intercolonial Trophy for the first time since 1895–96 – throughout the 1930s, the trophy was in the hands of either Guiana or Trinidad and the once all-powerful Barbados team was out in the cold.

Trinidad's outstanding cricketer from the First World War was Learie Constantine, an all-rounder who could change the course of any match. In the mid-1930s, however, he more or less emigrated to England. George Headley was the second great international West Indian star; his career batting record gave an average just a shade under 70. Unfortunately, he lived in Jamaica and thus took no part in the Intercolonial Trophy matches.

THE SHELL SHIELD

The 1938–39 season saw the end of the old trophy, and a proper competition did not re-emerge until 1965–66 when Shell Oil sponsored a trophy. At first the competition involved Barbados, British Guiana, Jamaica, Trinidad and Combined Islands (Leewards and Windwards). In the second season, the Leewards and Windwards played as separate sides, but from 1969 to 1981 the two groups united again. From 1981–82, the Leewards and Windwards have participated as individual competitors. In 1987–88, the Shell Shield was replaced by the Red Stripe Cup.

Barbados were the major force in the days of the Shell Shield, winning the trophy 12 times out of the 21 occasions on which it was held. In the 1960s, Barbados had Gary Sobers, the most talented cricketer of his time. Conrad Hunte and Seymour Nurse were the main batsmen and Charlie Griffith led the bowling attack. In the late 1970s, Barbados won five titles in a row, with a fast bowling attack of Wayne Daniel, Joel Garner and Vanburn Holder, and opening batsmen Gordon Greenidge and Desmond Haynes. The Leeward Islands found two quite outstanding cricketers, Viv Richards and Andy Roberts, and took the title in 1980–81.

The principal limited-overs competition began as the Gillette Cup in 1975–76.

Two countries in the West Indies have also had their own internal first-class competition. In British Guiana (Guyana since 1966), the Jones Cup – later the Guystac Trophy and Sookram Trophy – was originally contested by the three counties, Demerara, Berbice and Essequibo, from 1954 to 1991. And in Trinidad and Tobago, the Beaumont Cup, was competed for from 1926 to 1979–80.

In 1996–97 it was decided that the first-class teams should play each other home and away, thus doubling the number of games. This proved financially disastrous. The following season the competition reverted to five matches per side; Red Stripe transferred their sponsorship to the One Day Competition and the first-class competition was renamed the President's Cup. In 1998–99 a new sponsor was found and the first-class competition was for the Busta Cup.

Serious financial losses by the West Indies Cricket Board, plus the on-going controversy over the Test leadership led to much unrest among the first-class West Indian cricketers in the late 1990s. The doubling of Red Stripe Cup fixtures in 1996–97 had cost the Board dearly, added to this was the lack of a sponsor in 1997–98, when the Red Stripe Company switched its support to the one-day competition.

There was further embarrassment for the Board when it was discovered that seven of the players they had picked for the Under-19 World Cup squad were ineligible, being over age.

A disastrous tour of South Africa in 1998–99, which began with an infamous row at Heathrow Airport, did nothing to enhance West Indies' most famous cricketer, Brian Lara. Politicians and academics became involved in West Indies cricket in 1999–2000 in an effort to discover what was wrong with the game in the islands. The result was a severe criticism of the standard of the first-class competition. Pat Rousseau, the long serving Board President was succeeded by Wes Hall.

In Grenada, a cricket academy was opened, under the control of Rudi Webster, but financial problems reduced the options open to the Board. One idea that was implemented was the introduction of an overseas team into the domestic tournament. England 'A' took part in 2000–01 and Bangladesh 'A' in 2001–02. But this proved too expensive as was the plan to invite Bermuda and the USA to take part in the major one-day competition.

In 2002–03, the Board actually showed a surplus of $1 million, having lost $15 million in the previous three years. The spectre of rows between the Board and the players, plus the financial position continues to dog progress in the West Indies.

GILLETTE CUP

1975–76 Barbados 191 (49.3 overs) beat Trinidad 148 (39.5 overs) by 43 runs

1976–77 Barbados 97–2 (27 overs) beat Trinidad 95 (33.3 overs) by 8 wkts

GEDDES GRANT-HARRISON LINE TROPHY

1977–78 Jamaica and Leeward Islands shared the trophy as the final was abandoned

1978–79 Trinidad 214–9 (50 overs) beat Barbados 158 (47.1 overs) by 56 runs

1979–80 Guyana 327–7 (50 overs) beat Leeward Islands 224 (41.1 overs) by 103 runs

1980–81 Trinidad 128–6 (42 overs) beat Barbados 127 (49 overs) by 4 wkts

1981–82 Leeward Islands 95–5 (29.3 overs) beat Barbados 94 (37.5 overs) by 5 wkts

1982–83 Guyana 211–8 (41 overs) beat Jamaica 83 (25 overs) by 128 runs

1983–84 Jamaica 213–7 (41 overs) beat Leeward Islands 212–9 (42 overs) by 2 wkts

1984–85 Guyana 140–5 (41 overs) beat Jamaica 139 (46.1 overs) by 5 wkts

1985–86 Jamaica 173–4 (34.3 overs) beat Leeward Islands 169–8 (39 overs) by 6 wkts

1986–87 Jamaica 252–6 (46 overs) beat Barbados 249–3 (49 overs) by 4 wkts

1987–88 Barbados 219–9 (46 overs) beat Jamaica 218–8 (46 overs) by 1 wkt

GEDDES GRANT SHIELD

1988–89 Windward Islands 155–9 (49.3 overs) beat Guyana 154–9 (50 overs) by 1 wkt

1989–90 Trinidad 180–5 (44.2 overs) beat Barbados 178–9 (47 overs) by 5 wkts

1990–91 Jamaica 232–6 (49.5 overs) beat Leeward Islands 228–8 (50 overs) by 4 wkts

1991–92 Trinidad 167–2(37.3 overs) beat Barbados 163 (49.3 overs) by 8 wkts

1992–93 Guyana and Leeward Islands shared the shield as the final was abandoned

1993–94 Leeward Islands 289–6 (50 overs) beat Barbados 255 (46.1 overs) by 34 runs

SHELL-SANDALS TROPHY

1994–95 Leeward Islands188 (49 overs) beat Barbados 110 (31 overs) by 78 runs

1995–96 Trinidad and Guyana joint winners after rain prevented the final being completed

1996–97 Trinidad and Tobago 236–4 (50 overs) beat Guyana 227 (49.3 overs) by 9 runs

RED STRIPE BOWL

1997–98 Leeward Islands 245 (49.4 overs) beat Guyana 215–9 (50 overs) by 30 runs

1998–99 Guyana 226–7 (50 overs) beat Leeward Islands 174 (45.5 overs) by 52 runs

1999–00 Leeward Islands 228–7 (50 overs) lost to Jamaica 177–6 (38 overs) – D/L method

2000–01 Windward Islands 164 (42.5 overs) beat Leeward Islands 163–8 (50 overs) by 5 wkts

2001–02 Guyana 223–4 (46.5 overs) beat Barbados 221–5 (50 overs) by six wkts

2002–03 Barbados 241–8 (50 overs) beat Jamaica 208 (46.2 overs) by 33 runs

2003–04 Guyana 212–9 (50 overs) beat Barbados 156 (36 overs) by 27 runs (D/L method)

2004–05 Trinidad 161–6 (39.2 overs) beat Guyana 160 (43.4 overs) by 4 wkts

CHAMPION TEAMS

1891–92	Barbados
1893–94	Barbados
1895–96	Demerara
1897–98	Barbados
1890–00	Barbados
1901–02	Trinidad
1903–04	Trinidad
1905–06	Barbados
1907–08	Trinidad
1908–09	Barbados
1909–10	Trinidad
1910–11	Barbados
1911–12	Barbados
1921–22	No result
1922–23	Barbados
1923–24	Barbados
1924–25	Trinidad
1925–26	Barbados
1926–27	Barbados
1928–29	Trinidad
1929–30	British Guiana
1931–32	Trinidad
1933–34	Trinidad
1934–35	British Guiana
1935–36	British Guiana
1936–37	Trinidad
1937–38	British Guiana
1938–39	Trinidad

SHELL SHIELD

1965–66	Barbados
1966–67	Barbados
1967–68	No competition
1968–69	Jamaica
1969–70	Trinidad
1970–71	Trinidad
1971–72	Barbados
1972–73	Guyana
1973–74	Barbados
1974–75	Guyana
1975–76	Barbados, Trinidad
1976–77	Barbados
1977–78	Barbados
1978–79	Barbados
1979–80	Barbados
1980–81	Combined Islands
1981–82	Barbados
1982–83	Guyana
1983–84	Barbados
1984–85	Trinidad
1985–86	Barbados
1986–87	Guyana

RED STRIPE CUP

1987–88	Jamaica
1988–89	Jamaica
1989–90	Leeward Islands
1990–91	Barbados
1991–92	Jamaica
1992–93	Guyana
1993–94	Leeward Islands
1994–95	Barbados
1995–96	Leeward Islands
1996–97	Barbados

PRESIDENT'S CUP

1997–98	Leeward Islands/ Guyana

BUSTA CUP

1998–99	Barbados
1999–00	Jamaica
2000–01	Barbados
2001–02	Jamaica

CARIB BEER CUP

2002–03	Barbados
2003–04	Barbados
2004–05	Jamaica

DESMOND HAYNES *Prolific batsman for the West Indies, Barbados and Middlesex.*

INDIA

At first it appears odd that the first major cricket club in India should be established in Calcutta and through the nineteenth and much of the twentieth century be regarded as the premier club in India, when the most important competition in the sub-continent until the 1930s was centred 1,000 miles away in Bombay.

The origins of the Calcutta Cricket Club are obscure. What is known is that in 1792 the club was established at Eden Gardens and in 1804 Robert Vansittart, an Old Etonian, hit the first recorded century on the Eden Gardens ground. The Calcutta Club, however, was exclusively European and as such gave no encouragement to the Indians to learn or participate in cricket. It was aloof and remained so well into the twentieth century.

In contrast, the Parsees of Bombay took readily to cricket. Their first organized club was set up in 1848 and in 1877 the Parsees opposed the Europeans for the first time – the Indians lost. Undeterred by their defeat, the number of Parsees playing cricket multiplied as did their clubs and in 1886 they were able to finance a team to tour England. A programme of 28 matches was arranged against modest opposition – as the organizers pointed out, this was a tour on which to learn. Socially the matches were a great success and, at Queen Victoria's behest, the Parsees played at Windsor against Prince Christian Victor's Team. A second such tour took place in 1888. On this visit was M.E. Pavri, who was to become the greatest Parsee cricketer of his day. He played for Middlesex in 1895, while he was in England qualifying as a doctor.

First-class cricket in India began in 1892–93 when the Parsees opposed the Europeans of Bombay Presidency, in two matches arranged for three days each. This fixture then became the major annual contest in India. In that first season, an English team toured the sub-continent, playing four first-class games.

In 1905–06, the Hindus joined in the European-Parsee contest, which therefore became a triangular series.

In 1912–13, with the advent of a Muslim side, the contest became quadrangular, but it remained confined to Bombay and Poona. Similar communal tournaments were later arranged in Nagpur (Central Provinces Quadrangular), Lahore (Northern India Tournament) and Karachi (Sind Tournament). Apart from the Bombay Tournament, the status of the matches in these communal contests is very complicated and readers interested in the subject are advised to consult the *Guide to First Class Cricket Matches Played in India* published in 1986.

It was not until the MCC toured India in 1926–27 that any substantial moves were made to create an Indian Cricket Board of Control. A board was duly formed and encouraged the formation of cricket associations based on the various Indian provinces.

Apart from the Ranji Trophy and the various communal tournaments between the wars, the most notable competition was the Moin-ud-Dowlah Gold Cup. This was originally staged at Secunderabad in 1927–28. Run by the Nawab Behram-ud-Dowlah, it was strictly for invited teams and the various Indian rulers gathered together notable players in order to build a strong XI and win the trophy. The tournament lapsed when the founder died in 1938. It was revived in 1948–49 but ended in 1978–79.

No look at Indian first-class cricket would be complete without a mention of the Maharajkumar of Vizianagram. A major patron of Indian cricket between the wars he vied with the Maharajah of Patiala for having the last word on cricketing affairs. In 1930–31, the MCC cancelled their proposed tour of India owing to the civil unrest created by Gandhi's independence movement. Vizianagram chose a picked team of Indian players and engaged the leading England batsmen, Hobbs and Sutcliffe. He then tried to fulfil the fixtures left vacant by the MCC. A fixture list of 16 matches was arranged plus entry into the Nawab's Gold Cup.

VIJAY MERCHANT *India's premier batsman in the 1930s and 1940s.*

Indian independence in 1947 saw the end of the communal tournaments, though the Cricket Club of India staged a zonal tournament in Bombay for three seasons, the last being 1948–49.

THE RANJI TROPHY

In a meeting held in Simla in July 1934, the Board arranged a Cricket Championship of India which became known as the Ranji Trophy, when H.H. Sir Bhupindra Singh Mahinder Bahadur, Maharaja of Patiala, presented a trophy for the new competition in memory of K.S. Ranjitsinhji who had recently died. India is divided into five zones, North, South, East, West and Central, and each runs a league competition. The winners then went into a national semi-final and then a final to decide the ultimate winners.

The Ranji Trophy is India's equivalent of the County Championship in England. Zones disappeared in 2003 and a promotion–relegation system

RANJITSINHJI *The Indian Prince who played Test cricket for England.*

now exists between the Elite and Plate sections, each divided into two sections. For 2005–06 the teams were (with Ranji One Day Trophy zones):

Elite A: Karnataka (s), Bengal (E), Gujarat (w), Delhi (N), Mumbai (w), Railways (C), Maharashtra (w), Tamil Nadu (s)

Elite B: Services (N), Haryana (N), Andhra (s), Punjab (N), Baroda (w), Hyderabad (s), Uttar Pradesh (C)

Plate A: Saurashtra (w), Tripura (E), Orissa (E), Goa (s), Vidarbha (C), Himachal Pradesh (N)

Plate B: Assam (E), Jharkhand (E), Madhya Pradesh (C), Rajasthan (C), Jammu & Kashmir (N), Kerala (s)

Bombay (now Mumbai) has dominated throughout the 70-odd years of the competiton, winning 34 times; no other side has claimed the title more than six times. Over the past decade the standard of cricket in the lesser known outposts of Indian cricket has improved quite markedly. For example, in 2000–01, Baroda, Railways, Orissa and Punjab – teams that in the past were usually on the fringes of the competition – were the semi-finalists in the Ranji Trophy.

The outstanding feature of the Ranji Trophy has been the high scores achieved. More than 60 batsmen have averaged more than 100 and three have exceeded 200, with Rusi Modi in 1944 hitting 1,008 at an average of 201.60. He played for Bombay as did such noted batsmen as Sunil Gavaskar, Vijay Merchant, Ajit Wadekar and Polly Umrigar. Among the bowlers, the Haryana left-arm spinner Rajinder Goel took 640 Ranji Trophy wickets – 100 more than the second on the list – but never played Test cricket.

In 1961–62 the Board of Control established a new competition which was aimed to give a higher standard of cricket than the Ranji Trophy. It was named the "Zonal Tournament" for the Duleepsinhji Trophy – but was more usually known as the "Duleep Trophy". Duleepsinhji was a nephew of Ranjitsinhji and both played Test cricket for England.

The two major limited-overs competitions of the present day are the Deodhar Trophy and the Wills Trophy. The former, established in 1973–74, involves teams on the same basis as the Duleep Trophy. The Wills Trophy is competed for by the five zonal winners of the Ranji Trophy, plus two representative sides which draw their players from the Ranji Trophy teams not involved. This competition began in 1977–78.

In March 2000 a betting scandal unfolded and with such personalties as Kapil Dev, the national coach, and Azharuddin being the centre of accusations, the press almost ignored domestic cricket for the next year.

However, like all Test playing nations, India saw less and less international stars appearing in domestic first-class cricket especially when, in 2002–03, central contracts for twenty top players were introduced.

The Duleep Trophy also saw a major change with three 'Elite' elevens and two 'Plate' elevens competing. The limited-overs Deodhar Trophy saw another basic change. England 'A' was invited to take part, while each of the Indian sides co-opted an overseas fast bowler in order to improve batting standards against seamers.

An unusual scandal emerged in November 2003 when Abhijit Kale was suspended for allegedly offering bribes to selectors in exchange for selection on India's tour to Australia.

KAPIL DEV *Took 434 wickets for India in Test cricket.*

DULEEP TROPHY			
This competition is run between the five zones formerly used in the Ranji Trophy and an overseas guest team. Originally a knockout competition, it is now played on a two-group system with a final for the group winners.		1979–80	North Zone
		1980–81	West Zone
		1981–82	West Zone
		1982–83	North Zone
		1983–84	North Zone
		1984–85	South Zone
		1985–86	West Zone
1961–62	West Zone	1986–87	South Zone
1962–63	West Zone	1987–88	North Zone
1963–64	West Zone	1988–89	North Zone, West Zone
1964–65	West Zone	1989–90	South Zone
1965–66	South Zone	1990–91	North Zone
1966–67	South Zone	1991–92	North Zone
1967–68	South Zone	1992–93	North Zone
1968–69	West Zone	1993–94	North Zone
1969–70	West Zone	1994–95	North Zone
1970–71	South Zone	1995–96	South Zone
1971–72	Central Zone	1996–97	Central Zone, West Zone
1972–73	West Zone	1998–99	Central Zone
1973–74	North Zone	1999–00	North Zone
1974–75	South Zone	2000–01	North Zone
1975–76	South Zone	2001–02	West Zone
1976–77	West Zone	2002–03	Elite C
1977–78	West Zone	2003–04	North Zone
1978–79	North Zone	2004–05	Central Zone

RANJI TROPHY							
1934–35	Bombay	1952–53	Holkar	1970–71	Bombay	1988–89	Delhi
1935–36	Bombay	1953–54	Bombay	1971–72	Bombay	1989–90	Bengal
1936–37	Nawangar	1954–55	Madras	1972–73	Bombay	1990–91	Haryana
1937–38	Hyderabad	1955–56	Bombay	1973–74	Karnataka	1991–92	Delhi
1938–39	Bengal	1956–57	Bombay	1974–75	Bombay	1992–93	Punjab
1939–40	Maharashtra	1957–58	Baroda	1975–76	Bombay	1993–94	Bombay
1940–41	Maharashtra	1958–59	Bombay	1976–77	Bombay	1994–95	Bombay
1941–42	Bombay	1959–60	Bombay	1977–78	Karnataka	1995–96	Karnataka
1942–43	Baroda	1960–61	Bombay	1978–79	Delhi	1996–97	Karnataka
1943–44	Western India	1961–62	Bombay	1979–80	Delhi	1997–98	Karnataka
1944–45	Bombay	1962–63	Bombay	1980–81	Bombay	1998–99	Karnataka
1945–46	Holkar	1963–64	Bombay	1981–82	Delhi	1999–00	Mumbai (formerly Bombay)
1946–47	Baroda	1964–65	Bombay	1982–83	Karnataka	2000–01	Baroda
1947–48	Holkar	1965–66	Bombay	1983–84	Bombay	2001–02	Railways
1948–49	Bombay	1966–67	Bombay	1984–85	Bombay	2002–03	Mumbai
1949–50	Baroda	1967–68	Bombay	1985–86	Delhi	2003–04	Mumbai
1950–51	Holkar	1968–69	Bombay	1986–87	Hyderabad	2004–05	Railways
1951–52	Bombay	1969–70	Bombay	1987–88	Tamil Nadu		

This competition is played between the five zonal teams. Originally played on a knockout basis, it was changed to a league from 1993–94. The competition has been held in a single zone over two weeks with two matches played on each of five days. The overs limit was 60 until 1979–80 and thereafter has been 50.

DEODHAR TROPHY

1973–74 South Zone 185 (52.1 overs) beat West Zone 101 (38 overs) by 84 runs

1974–75 South Zone 263–5 (60 overs) beat West Zone 255–9 (60 overs) by 8 runs

1975–76 West Zone 185 (55.2 overs) beat South Zone 161 (49 overs) by 24 runs

1976–77 Central Zone 207–7 (56 overs) beat South Zone 206–9 (60 overs) by 3 wkts

1977–78 North Zone 177–0 (38.5 overs) beat West Zone 174 (53 overs) by 10 wkts

1978–79 South Zone 247 (59.4 overs) beat North Zone 218 (56.1 overs) by 29 runs

1979–80 West Zone 246–6 (48 overs) beat North Zone 245–9 (50 overs) by 4 wkts

1980–81 South Zone 275–5 (50 overs) beat West Zone 189–7 (50 overs) by 86 runs

1981–82 South Zone 260–5 (50 overs) beat Central Zone 147 (50 overs) by 113 runs

1982–83 West Zone 198–9 (46 overs) beat North Zone 185–9 (46 overs) by 13 runs

1983–84 West Zone 309 (48.4 overs) beat North Zone 266 (47.2 overs) by 43 runs

1984–85 West Zone 218–4 (37.5 overs) beat North Zone 214–8 (45 overs) by 6 wkts

1985–86 West Zone 227–9 (47 overs) beat North Zone 196 (44.5 overs) by 31 runs

1986–87 North Zone 207–1 (39.5 overs) beat West Zone

206–9 (48 overs) by 9 wkts

1987–88 North Zone 223–3 (45.2 overs) beat West Zone 221–7 (50 overs) by 7 wkts

1988–89 North Zone 243–6 (45 overs) beat South Zone 239–8 (46 overs) by 4 runs

1989–90 North Zone 319–6 (50 overs) beat South Zone 263–8 (50 overs) by 56 runs

1990–91 West Zone 304–3 (44 overs) beat East Zone 260 (41.4 overs) by 44 runs

1991–92 South Zone 158–7 (35 overs) beat Central Zone 122 (33.2 overs) by 36 runs

1992–93 East Zone 257–9 (50 overs) beat North Zone 254–4 (50 overs) by 1 wkt

1993–94 East Zone

1994–95 Central Zone

1995–96 North Zone

1996–97 East Zone

1997–98 North Zone

1998–99 Central Zone

1999–00 North Zone

2000–01 North Zone

2001–02 South Zone

2002–03 North Zone

2003–04 East Zone

2004–05 North Zone

This competition is played on a knockout basis between the five zonal winners of the previous seasons's Ranji Trophy plus two representative sides, who choose their players from the other Ranji Trophy teams. The overs limit is 50 per side, although in the first two seasons 60 overs per side were played. In 1993–94, Ranji Trophy one-day matches were introduced as qualification for the following season's Wills Trophy.

WILLS TROPHY

1977–78 Wills XI 214–3 (52.3 overs) beat President's XI 213–4 (60 overs) by 7 wkts

1978–79 Delhi 253–7 (60 overs) beat Bombay 253 (56.1 overs) by losing fewer wickets

1979–80 No competition

1980–81 Wills XI 218–7 (49.3 overs) beat President's XI 216–8 (50 overs) by 3 wkts

1981–82 Bombay 225–7 (50 overs) beat President's XI 210–8 (50 overs) by 15 runs

1982–83 Bombay 158 (47.1 overs) beat Delhi 99 (42.1 overs) by 59 runs

1983–84 President's XI 269–6 (42 overs) beat Karnataka 242–9 (42 overs) by 27 runs

1984–85 Wills XI 252–4 (46.1 overs) beat President's XI 249 (49.4) by 6 wkts

1985–86 Bombay 228–9 (46.2 overs) beat Delhi 226–5 (47overs) by 1 wkt

1986–87 Delhi 258–8 (50 overs) beat Maharashtra 159 (37.4 overs) by 99 runs

1987–88 President's XI 244–5 (47 overs) beat Karnataka 184 (45.5 overs) by 60 runs

1988–89 Delhi 205–2 (44.1 overs) beat Railways 200 (48.2 overs) by 8 wkts

1989–90 Wills XI 265–4 (47.3 overs) beat Delhi 261–9 (49 overs) by 6 wkts

1990–91 Bombay 257–3 (46.5 overs) beat Wills XI 254–9 (49 overs) by 7 wkts

1991–92 President's XI 234–8 (50 overs) beat Wills XI 206–8 (50 overs) by 28 runs

1992–93 President's XI 128 (43.2 overs) beat Delhi 128 (44.4 overs) on scoring rate

1993–94 No competition

1994–95 Bombay 265–1 (36.4 overs) beat Haryana 263–7 (50 overs) by 9 wkts

1995–96 Wills XI 299–5 beat Bengal 224–6 by 75 runs

1996–97 Bombay

1997–98 Mumbai (formerly Bombay)

1998–99 Bombay

1999–00 Bombay

2000–01 Board President's XI

2001–02 India 'A'

BCCI TROPHY

2002–03 Tamil Nadu

RANJI TROPHY ONE DAY

2003–04 Mumbai

2004–05 Tamil Nadu, Uttar Pradesh

RUNS AND RUNS *Rahul Dravid has scored nearly 50,000 runs in all cricket.*

SRI LANKA

The Europeans v Ceylonese match was contested from 1887 to 1933. In the early twentieth century it was the biggest match on the island. A representative Ceylon Cricket Association was formed in 1922 and from 1924 organized a club championship.

There were 15 first-class teams in 1924, but most "first-class" matches were scheduled for one day only. In 1937, the championship became the Daily News Trophy, but was renamed the P. Saravanamuttu Trophy in 1950. It only gained first-class designation from 1988–89, and it was known as the Lakspray Trophy. Ceylon's best-known cricketers of this era were Dr C.H. Gunasekara and F.C. de Saram.

So far as recognized first-class matches are concerned, it was confined to matches played by representative teams overseas or games against visiting touring sides. Until the 1970s, most England and Australia Test teams sailing between the two countries refuelled at Colombo and, when at all possible, a match was arranged between the tourists and a team from the island.

The first game against the tourists took place in October 1882, when England opposed 18 of Colombo.

Eight years later the Australians played in Colombo. Between these two visits England first toured India and commenced their matches in Colombo. They played two games, a three-day fixture against All-Ceylon and a two-day match against Colombo CC, both of which were won by an innings. In 1924, England were bowled out for 73 in Colombo.

Sri Lanka – Ceylon's name from 1972 – was raised to full membership of the ICC in 1981 and gained Test-match status.

In 1990–91, the Lakspray Trophy was renamed the Sara Trophy after the new sponsors. In addition to the Sara Trophy, an inter-Provincial tournament started to be ranked as first-class from 1989–90, the sides

competing for the Singer Trophy.

A list of current first-class domestic sides is difficult to compile because clubs compete in a non-first-class section before being entered into the first-class part of the Sara Trophy.

In June 1990 an Inter-Provincial competition, sponsored by Singer and based on the Duleep Trophy was launched. Four teams competed, Southern, Central, Western and North-Western. Two other innovations at this time were an Under-23 limited overs competition for the Brown's Trophy and the Delmege Trophy. The Sara Trophy had no fewer than 30 teams competing in 1990–91, with the top 12 clubs playing three-day first-class matches. The other 18, having been eliminated played for

WORLD CUP WINNERS *Arjuna Ratatunga and Asanka Gurusinha are seen with the 1997 trophy.*

Bloomfield, whilst the Under-23 Trophy was renamed the GTE Yellow Pages Trophy and won by Nondescripts.

Sri Lanka's great, unexpected, success, in the 1996 World Cup caused a cricket boom on the island, though the Inter-Provincial Trophy was cancelled due to international commitments. However, the Sara Trophy was revamped with the number of matches virtually doubled to 104. In 1996–97 the Trophy was divided into two equal leagues with a knockout final section. Colombo C.C. ended as winners. The following year they were suspended due to irregularities.

Internal rows in 1998–99 led to a court suspending the Cricket Board executive committee. The Sports Minister appointed an interim committee. This put major domestic matches in abeyance for a month. The Premier Trophy superseded the Sara Trophy, though in 1999–2000 a new format was introduced with a final "super-league".

The cricket board was again dissolved by the Sports Minister in 2000–01. The historic Gopalan Trophy was revived having been in abeyance since 1982–83. Yet more alterations were made to the Premier Trophy and another new Invitation Trophy was brought in. The President of the Board announced plans to revamp the game and create "Sri Lanka Cricket", based on the Australian model, but in January 2004 he was arrested for alleged passport offences.

In December 2004, the tsunami put a temporary stop to internal bickering and over the last few years the major talking point has been the bowling of Muralitharan, especially his "doosra".

DULEEP MENDIS *He was captain of Sri Lanka in his country's first Test match in England, at Lord's in 1984.*

the Delmege Trophy. Only the final was first-class. Another innovation was the Pure Beverages Under-19 Championship, for schools and colleges. The star in 1990–91 was Muttiah Muralitharan, who took a record 127 wickets for St Anthony's College.

In 1991–92 a new floodlit competition was launched – the R. Premadasa Challenge Trophy.

Fourteen clubs were entered into the 1992–93 Sara Trophy first-class section, but in the following summer, the number was reduced to eight. A

"Super Tournament" was also tried with six teams competing in four-day matches, but the idea was ditched after just one season.

The R. Premadasa Trophy was replaced by the Hatton National Bank Trophy in 1994–95, won by

SARA TROPHY		
	1988–89	Nondescripts, Sinhalese SC
	1889–90	Sinhalese SC
	1990–91	Sinhalese SC
	1991–92	Colts
	1992–93	Sinhalese SC
	1993–94	Nondescripts
	1994–95	Bloomfield, Sinhalese SC
	1995–96	Colombo
	1996–97	Bloomfield
	1997–98	Sinhalese
	PREMIER TROPHY	
	1998–99	Bloomfield
	1999–00	Colts
	2000–01	Nondescripts
	2001–02	Colts
	2002–03	Moors
	2003–04	Bloomfield
	2004–05	Colts

ZIMBABWE

It is believed that the first cricket match took place in Zimbabwe (formerly Rhodesia) as early as August 1890 near Fort Victoria. The first English cricket side to visit was Lord Hawke's Team of 1898–99.

J.D. Logan, a well-known South African cricket patron, asked Lord Hawke to purchase a cup which could be used as a trophy competed for by the principal clubs in Rhodesia. It was not, however, until 1903–04 that a suitable competition was organized, with Matabeleland as the first winners.

Before Zimbabwe's independence in 1981, Rhodesia had played as a first-class team in the South African Currie Cup, albeit sporadically until 1946–47 and regularly thereafter.

The country was granted Test-match status in July 1992 and for the 1993–94 season organized a programme of domestic first-class games for the Logan Cup. However, in 1995–96, the cricket Board reduced the number of first-class sides to two, Mashonaland and Matabeleland, and they played three matches to decide the title. In 1999–2000 the Logan Cup expanded to five teams and first-class cricket reached hitherto unexplored parts of Zimbabwe.

Zimbabwe's most successful players since gaining Test status include David Houghton, Eddo Brandes, brothers Andrew and Grant Flower, and Heath Streak – plus John Traicos, the only cricketer to play Tests for both South Africa and Zimbabwe.

In 1996–97, with Alistair Campbell as captain, Zimbabwe had the better of England in two drawn Tests; then Sri Lanka, the World Cup holders, were beaten in Sharjah. They swept a triangular series with Kenya and Bangladesh in October 1998, showing evidence of the gap between the countries.

But, just as Zimbabwe cricket seemed to be on the rise, two problems emerged. First, Government funding for development was reduced, then Test players began to distrust the way the governing body was running the game.

During 2000–01, players alleged that there was political interference with the selection of the national side and resented the idea of a quota system promoting black players into the squad. Black players of Test standard were gradually emerging – Hamilton Masakadza was the first black Zimbabwean player to hit a century in domestic first-class cricket and for his country.

Australia's cancellation of their tour to Zimbabwe in 2001–02 badly affected the Board's finances. The question of whether they should co-host the 2003 World Cup dominated the preceding summer. Things went further downhill when Andy Flower and bowler Henry Olonga wore black armbands to mark the death of democracy in the country. They went into exile, substantially weakening the national team. Several other players also quit. Then Test captain Heath Streak was sacked after he confronted the board with his team's grievances.

The ICC sent a delegation to Zimbabwe to see if racism was dominating the country's cricket, but failed to find any evidence. Sadly, with so many of the players leaving the country, the team representing Zimbabwe five years into the new century is now only – in terms of a decade earlier – a "third eleven".

HEATH STREAK *Zimbabwe's opening bowler in their first match against England.*

ANDY FLOWER *Zimbabwe batsman.*

BANGLADESH

After the partition of India, the country now known as Bangladesh formed the eastern section of Pakistan. Four first-class teams from East Pakistan took part in competitions. Bangladesh became an independent nation in 1973, by which time cricket there was in a poor state. However, the MCC were persuaded to visit the country in 1976–77. A second tour took place in 1980–81.

Bangladesh have taken part in six ICC Trophy tournaments, winning in 1997 and reaching the semi-finals in 1982 and 1990. In 1988–89, they held their first official one-day international tournament, hosting India, Pakistan and Sri Lanka, but were outplayed by their visitors.

In 1999 Bangladesh beat Pakistan in a World Cup match, but this landmark was dwarfed on June 26, 2000, when ICC granted Bangladesh Test Match status. The country played its first Test against India in November 2000 in Dhaka. In May and June 2000, they staged the Asian Cup.

A major domestic "National League" competition was established in 1999–2000 comprising six teams: Dhaka, Chittagong, Khulna, Rajshadi, Barisaal and Sylhet. In 2000–01 the league increased to eight teams. Chittagong were the unexpected winners of the first-year, but the Board did not grant the competition first-class status.

In 2001–02 the National League (sponsored by Ispahani Mirzapore Tea) was regarded as first class, and won by Dhaka. Khulma were champions in 2002–03, but Dhaka claimed the title in both 2003–04 and 2004–05.

In 2001–02, Bangladesh struggled to compete at Test level and by July 2002, 12 of their 13 Tests had been lost, rain causing a draw in the other one. The country also lost 20 consecutive one-day internationals. The annual changes in the head coach did not help the Test squad's chances. Trevor Chappell was the third coach in three years in 2002.

Another 13 Test defeats were suffered in 2002–03, plus 25 one-day losses. A number of critics suggested that Bangladesh should lose its Test status, especially after a very poor showing in the 2003 World Cup. The fact that the head of the Cricket Board was a government appointee came in for adverse comment.

When Dav Whatmore was given the coach's job, the team did seem to improve and a first Test victory was achieved, though at the expense of a depleted Zimbabwe. Bangladesh toured West Indies and certainly the squad looked a more robust outfit, even if they failed to win.

The Under-19 World Cup was held in Bangladesh in 2004, when nearly every match was played in front of a capacity crowd – this demonstrates the enthusiasm for cricket in the country and in time that enthusiasm must translate itself into a viable Test team.

NON-TEST-PLAYING NATIONS

ARGENTINA

The first cricket club was not established in the Argentine until 1831. The continuing influx of Britons led to more clubs and more cricket, and in 1868 an Argentine side went to Montevideo in Uruguay.

The major match of the Argentine season, North v South, was founded in 1891, the principal cricketers of the day being the Leach family, several of whom had played for Lancashire. The Argentine Cricket Association was formed in 1913, by which time the first first-class matches had been played: the three games between the 1911–12 MCC side and a representative Argentine XI.

Between the two World Wars three sides from England – MCC in 1926–27, Sir Julien Cahn's in 1929–30 and Sir Theodore Brinckman's in 1937–38 – toured the country playing first-class matches. Argentina also opposed both Brazil and Chile during the same period. In 1932, a South American side, comprising mainly Argentine players, toured the British Isles and played a number of first-class matches. After the Second World War, the MCC sent a side to Argentina in 1958–59, but the major games were not considered first-class.

As an associate member of ICC, Argentina have taken part in the ICC Trophy, but with little success.

Argentina took part in the first ever Americas' Cup in Toronto in 2000, but finished bottom. In domestic cricket the four leading clubs now each field a professional and this is improving standards.

The second Americas' Cup was staged in Argentina in 2002 and won by the United States of America; Argentina failed to win any of their four matches.

BERMUDA

Although a British garrison was stationed in Bermuda fron 1701 until the 1950s, the first records of a cricket come in 1844. The following year Bermuda Cricket Club was formed. With the colony's close proximity to the United States, it is hardly surprising that the first team to tour Bermuda came from the States – Philadephia Zingari opposed the Garrison in three matches in 1891. The early years of the twentieth century saw regular tours between Bermuda and Philadelphia. The principal Bermudan cricketers of the period were the brothers J.R. and G.C. Conyers. The former was a fine batsman, whilst the latter bowled slow right arm. The 1912 Australian tourists to England played a game against Bermuda on their way home and had difficulty in beating the home side.

In the inter-war period, the most important event was the 1933 tour by Sir Julien Cahn's English team. Five matches were played and a general holiday was proclaimed for the major fixture against Somerset CC

After the Second World War, various West Indian sides visited Bermuda. The first tour by Bermuda to England took place in 1960, at which time W.F. Hayward was the driving force behind the team. Further tours took place, both to England and to Canada.

The major domestic match in Bermuda is the Cup Match between the two clubs, Somerset and St Georges. Alma Hunt is considered the best cricketer Bermuda has produced and he came close to being selected for the West Indies. Bermuda joined the ICC in 1966 and competed in the first ICC Trophy in 1979. The West Indies are continuing to encourage cricket in Bermuda and the country was invited to take part in the Shell–Sandals Limited-Overs competition, which involves the first-class West Indian sides, in October 1996. Though they failed to win a match, Bermuda impressed the West Indies Board and it is hoped that Bermuda will at some date in the near future compete in the first-class Red Stripe competition.

Bermuda took part in the West Indies Red Stripe One Day Competition in 1998-99 but lost all their matches; they did not repeat the experiment the following season. The suggestion that Bermuda take part in the first-class West Indian competition was not followed through.

BURMA

Some kind of cricket was played in Burma in 1824 when British troops took Rangoon. Through the nineteenth century cricket was regularly played among the various regiments stationed in the country. King Thebaw seemed quite keen on the game in the 1870s, but refused to field and "was in the habit of using very injurious language to anyone who bowled him".

Burma opposed the MCC in a first-class match in 1926–27, at a time when Hubert Ashton, the Essex cricketer, was working for the Burmah Oil Company.

After the Japanese occupation during the Second World War, there was limited cricket among the British residents, but in recent years it has all but died out as little or no cricket has been played there.

CANADA

Although there are stray references to cricket in Canada in the eighteenth century, it was during the 1820s that the game really became established. Toronto Cricket Club was founded in 1827 by George A. Barber, a master at Upper Canada College, who also encouraged cricket there. In 1859, George Parr's England side, sponsored by the Montreal Club, toured Canada and United States. By 1864 a club was formed in Winnipeg and in the next decade cricket reached the West Coast. In 1844, came the first Canada v USA match, attended by 5,000 spectators and at which it is reported $100,000 changed hands among the betting fraternity.

The Marquis of Lansdowne, Governor-General in the 1880s, was a very keen cricketer and gave much encouragement to the sport, helping to sponsor the 1887 Canadian tour to England: there had been an earlier one in 1880, but this had collapsed when it was discovered that the Canadian captain was in fact a deserter from the British Army.

England teams made a number of visits to Canada through the late nineteenth century and the first half of the twentieth century, but Canadian cricket was relatively weak.

The most famous inter-war event in Canadian cricket was the 1932 tour by the Australians – the visitors included Bradman in their side.

Although Canada toured England in 1954 and played some first-class matches, the game was not making great strides in Canada itself, as many of the players were British exiles. In the 1960s, though, due to the influx of immigrants from the West Indies and the Indian subcontinent, the number of active cricketers increased.

In 1968, the Canadian Cricket Association was incorporated. The country entered the ICC Trophy in 1979 and has competed in all the subsequent contests. In 1996, a series of one-day internationals between India and Pakistan were staged at the Toronto Cricket Club – the first matches of such standing to be played in Canada. Two difficulties face cricketers in Canada today: one is that most grounds are also public parks and the second is that government funding has been substantially reduced. It is estimated that there are at present about 10,000 adult players.

The Canadian cricket authorities are striving for status as a top class One Day International country. The inaugural Americas' Cup was staged in Canada in 2000 but there have been problems in the staging of what had become the annual India v Pakistan One Day International in Toronto. Ten new turf squares have been recently laid and it is hoped that this will improve standards and encourage more cricket. 22 teams competed in the ICC Trophy in Canada in June and July 2001. Canada came third in the competition, qualifying them for the 2003 World Cup, where they won just one match. Canada lost to Scotland in the Inter-continental Cup final in 2004.

CHINA

In the nineteenth century the main centre of cricket in China was Shanghai. The annual match between Shanghai and Hong Kong commenced in 1866 and Shanghai sent a team to Japan in 1893.

In 1929 there was a Shanghai Cricket League comprising six teams. Another centre of cricket at this time was Wei-Hai-Wei, most of the players there being from the Royal Navy.

The development of the game in Peking was spasmodic – when Peking Civilians opposed British Legation Guard in 1931, it was noted that this was the first game in the city for several years. The Mission Boys' School in Chungking also had an established cricket ground in the 1930s.

So far as the Chinese themselves were concerned, very few attempted to play the game, though B. Oeitiongham, from China, came close to obtaining a place in the Eton XI in 1926 and appeared for Eton 2nd XI. Later, the post-war period saw cricket disappear from China, but in the 1990s the Beijing International Sixes Tournament was founded and in the third such tournament in 1996 an all-Chinese team competed for the first time. It is to be hoped that cricket will grow in popularity.

CORFU

The single ground for cricket is in fact the main square in Corfu Town, part of the playing area being the tarmac of the car parking area round the square.

The Ionian Islands were a British Protectorate from 1815 to 1863 and inter-regimental games were played by the troops stationed there. The Greeks continued to play cricket after the islands reverted to Greece and two Greek clubs were established, playing either against each other or against visiting British sides. Sir Percy Kahn kept cricket going there between the wars, but the Second World War saw the end of matches.

A revival took place following an appeal in the *Cricketer* magazine in 1952. Since that date the popularity of Corfu with British tourists has meant that cricket is played on a regular basis.

DENMARK

Cricket was introduced to Denmark in the 1860s by the British engineers involved in laying out the country's railway system. It was not until after the First World War that teams from England began to make fairly regular visits to Denmark and not until the 1950s that Denmark began to play the Netherlands in "Test" matches.

In the ICC Trophy in both 1979 and 1986, they came third, losing in 1979 to Sri Lanka in the semi-finals and to the Netherlands in 1986. In 1997, Denmark made it as far as the quarter-finals.

The European Championship was inaugurated in 1996 and the initial tournament was staged in Denmark. The home side finished in third place, beating the England side in a play-off.

Denmark initially performed well in the 2001 ICC Trophy, topping the Division One, Group B table, but then failed to make much of a mark in the Super League which followed. The lack of turf pitches in the country is holding back its progress towards first-class status.

OLE MORTENSEN *Danish bowler who had a successful career with Derbyshire.*

FIJI

The first cricket in Fiji took place in about 1874. The founding father of cricket's rapid development was the Attorney-General, J.S. Udal. The islanders took to the game, so much so that in 1894–95 a Fijian team toured New Zealand and played the major provinces. The team comprised six Europeans and six Fijians. These games were recognized as first-class. In 1908, one of the smallest islands in the Fijian group actually sent a touring team to Australia.

The major problem in the colony was the lack of touring sides visiting the islands for any but the briefest of stays. In the late 1930s, Philip Snow came to Fiji. He made every effort to promote the game and two further tours were organized to New Zealand, in 1947–48 and 1953–54.

Fiji was elected an associate member of the ICC in 1965; in the 1970s, various Indian teams toured. The country has taken part in the ICC Trophy competitions, but the game is battling for popularity against rugby and is certainly not as strong as it was in the 1940s.

FRANCE

Considering the proximity of France to the Kentish heartland of cricket, it is surprising that the game has never really established itself among the French. A visit by English cricketers to Paris was arranged for 1789, but it was hastily cancelled – just before the team was to cross the Channel – because the Revolution had started.

In the 1820s and onward, cricket was played extensively in the Pas de Calais among the Nottingham lace workers who had emigrated there, but few French names are found in the extant scores. In the 1860s, fashionable Paris toyed with cricket and again one or two English touring sides were organized – this time they actually arrived! However, most of the "French" players were English residents in the capital.

This enthusiasm for cricket among English residents continued through to the twentieth century. In 1930, there was a French Cricket Federation and two leagues, one in Paris and the other in the north. The Standard Athletic Club of Paris sent a team to England annually, but no French players were among the sides. The only time cricket was part of the Olympic Games was in 1900 when the Devon County Wanderers, representing England, came up against "France". The former won by 158 runs.

After the Second World War various British army sides played cricket in France and made up so-called French teams to oppose Belgium and the Netherlands.

In the last 10 years or so, the number of French-born cricketers has grown and in 1995 the MCC toured France, playing seven matches. The country takes part in the European Nations Cup. Nottinghamshire also sent a team to play France in 1995. An application to join the ICC as an associate member was made but was turned down. A fresh application was made in 1998 and the France Cricket-Federation Française de Baseball, Softball et Cricket became associate members of the ICC.

GERMANY

There are many reports of cricket matches in Germany in the nineteenth century. A club was formed in Berlin in 1858 and Hamburg played Frankfurt in 1863. A cricket festival in Hamburg in 1865 included a match billed as France v Germany, but virtually all the players were English. A book of cricket instructions was published in Stuttgart in 1893; although the written part is fairly accurate, the illustrations were clearly by someone with no cricket knowledge. The bowlers were wearing pads and gloves, the bats resemble Indian clubs and the wicket is the same width as its height!

The Berlin Cricket League was founded in 1898 and even continued in the First World War. In 1927, a correspondent from Berlin wrote to *The Cricketer* suggesting that a German side should tour England. The tour eventually took place in 1930 and the German team – which significantly comprised German born players – played four matches. In 1937, the Gentlemen of Worcestershire paid a visit to Germany.

With many British troops stationed in Germany after the Second World War, there were frequent tours to Germany by English club sides, but their matches were. almost without exception, against British regimental sides rather than German-born cricketers. The resumption of cricket by German players has been a fairly recent development but there are now around 50 clubs.

In 1992, the German team was undefeated in the European Cricketer Cup held in England and went on to play the MCC at Lord's for the first time. It has to be admitted that not one of the German XI who played at Lord's was German-born. Nevertheless, Germany's cricket association became an affiliated member of the ICC in 1991 and in the last few seasons German cricket has begun to make progress beyond the British expatriate community. New leagues are springing up and matches being played against other European nations.

Now an Associate member of the ICC, Germany performed well in the 2000 European Championship held in Scotland and in 2001 travelled to Canada to participate, for the first time, in the ICC Trophy. As debutantes they made an immediate impression, managing to win three matches out of the five matches that they played, overcoming Italy, West Africa and Gibraltar. However, defeats at the hands of eventual group winners and tournament runners-up Namibia and Nepal – the latter by only two runs – saw them narrowly miss out on a place in the final Super League.

GIBRALTAR

The first recorded match in the colony took place in 1822. Most of the cricket on the Rock has involved the military stationed there.

Gibraltar Cricket Club was founded in 1883. The Gibraltar Cricket Association was formed in 1960 and nine years later joined the ICC as an associate member.

The Cryptics visited Gibraltar in 1927 and the Yorkshire Gents toured in 1935. Teams from Gibraltar have made some trips to Portugal. The principal team is Gibraltar Cricket Club – a reduction of British Forces in recent years has meant that this club dominates the domestic scene.

Gibraltar had to withdraw from the 1979 ICC Competition, but have taken part, with not much success, in the five subsequent tournaments. In Canada in 2001, Gibraltar won two out of their five matches.

HONG KONG

Britain acquired Hong Kong as a result of the Opium Wars of the 1840s and cricket is reported to have been played there as early as 1840. The Hong Kong Cricket Club was formed in 1851 and its series of matches against Shanghai commenced in 1866. In 1882, the Hong Kong side under Captain J. Dunn was travelling homeward from Shanghai when their ship was sunk in a typhoon, with all lives lost. In all, 37 matches were played between the two sides, the final game taking place in 1948.

In 1890, Hong Kong began its series against Singapore, and the colony has also played matches in more recent times against Malaysia. The Hong Kong teams have been predominantly British with the Chinese taking little interest, but in recent years there has been a growing number of Chinese playing at junior level. The Hong Kong Sixes competition has brought world-class players to the colony and the competition has drawn the cricket world's attention to the territory for the first time.

Hong Kong took part in the ICC Trophy for the first time in 1982 and have played in the four subsequent competitions. In 1994 and 1997, they did well enough to reach the second round, but both times, were out-played by the top ICC Trophy sides and ended up in eighth place.

In 2001, even though Hong Kong were seeded sixth for the tournament, the side performed poorly, winning just a single game, and failed to qualify for the second round in the ICC Trophy played in Toronto, Canada.

As a result of this poor showing Hong Kong were not invited to play in the 2005 competition.

IRELAND

Although there is a reference to cricket supposedly being banned in Ireland by Cromwell's Commissioners in 1656, it is very probable that hurling rather than cricket was the subject. Hurling goes back to 1200 BC according to the standard works of reference; cricket in Ireland does not appear until AD 1792. The match in question, played in Phoenix Park, Dublin, was arranged by Colonel Lennox, later the Duke of Richmond, and involved the Dublin Garrison against "All-Ireland". The Phoenix Club in Dublin was founded in about 1830 and at about the same time cricket was introduced into Dublin University.

The original Irish Cricket Union was formed in 1884–85, though the present governing body did not come into being until 1923. The most important matches by representative Irish teams in the nineteenth century were against the MCC, I Zingari and Scotland, and the first recognized first-class games by Ireland came in May 1902 when an Irish side came to England. Prior to this, the Dublin University team had played four first-class matches in 1895.

The status of matches by Ireland up to 1947 is very complex and readers are advised to study the *Guide to First-Class Matches in the British*

IRISH EYES ARE SMILING *Ireland celebrate their victory over Middlesex in the 1997 Benson & Hedges Cup.*

Isles, published by the Association of Cricket Statisticians, if they wish to know the full details.

At present, only Ireland's match against Scotland is given first-class status. In 1980, Ireland was admitted into the English Gillette Cup competition and has been a regular competitor since, but the side has yet to win a game. They have also taken part in the Benson & Hedges Cup since 1991.

In 1994, Ireland competed in the ICC Trophy for the first time, winning four games out of seven. In 1997, they had a successful run and reached the quarter-finals. Having finished third in the Emerging Nations Tournament in Harare in 2000, Ireland had high hopes in the 2001 ICC Trophy. They qualified for the Super League, but then failed completely, ending bottom of the eight nation league.

Ireland were hosts for the 2005 ICC Trophy and went all the way to the final before losing to Scotland.

ISRAEL

Part of the Ottoman Empire until 1917, the country became a British Mandate in 1920. Within a few years cricket was being played on a regular basis by the British Forces and civil administration in what was then Palestine. In 1935, Lord Melchett took a team to Palestine and five matches were played.

Israel became an independent state in 1948. Its national side took part in the first ICC Trophy Tournament in 1979 and has continued to play in the subsequent competitions. Its results, however, have been disappointing – after the first three tournaments, Israel had won only one out of 19 matches. Israel took part in the European Championships in 1996, but failed to win a single game.

The structure of cricket in the country is being revamped, and proper coaching schemes and cricket at youth level are now operating. These should improve the standard of the game considerably, especially after the appointment of a National Coach.

The first all-weather practice facility was officially opened in 2000 by the ICC Chief Executive, David Richards, who paid a three day visit to the country. Unfortunately Israel did not compete in the ICC 2001 Competition.

ITALY

Although there had been occasional cricket matches in Italy from the late eighteenth century, cricket on an organized basis and involving Italians did not really take off until the 1980s.

Italy became an associate member of the ICC in 1995 and played in the ICC Trophy, for the first time in 1997, but with little success. At club level, however, more has been achieved. The Cesena Club won the European Club Championship in 1996, and brought the title to Italy for the second year running.

JAPAN

Probably the first game in Japan took place in 1863 when British residents in Yokohama opposed visitors from the Royal Navy. According to reports, due to unrest in the city, the players were armed!

The one regular fixture before and after the First World War was Yokohama v Kobe. It commenced in 1884 and in the 1930s was a three-day match. In 1919, a team from Shanghai visited Japan and played in both Kobe and Yokohama, but such visits seem to have been rare.

In more recent years, cricket has had a slightly higher profile and a cup competition has been established since 1993. Some native Japanese are taking up the game, which in the past was exclusively played by expatriates. A hopeful sign is the emergence of five University sides, but there is a scarcity of suitable grounds.

KENYA

The British East Africa Company secured what was to become Kenya Colony in 1888; the first cricket match of note took place in 1899 and in 1910 the annual fixture Officials v Settlers was established.

In 1933 the Asian community had developed their cricket to the extent that a match against Europeans was arranged. This fixture vied with Officials v Settlers as the major game of the season, and both continued after the Second World War. The first "international" took place in 1951 when Kenya met Tanganyika and in 1953 came the formation of the Kenya Cricket Association.

The MCC toured East Africa, including Kenya, in 1957–58 under the leadership of former England Test captain Freddie Brown. Basil D'Oliveira led a South African non-European side to Kenya in 1958.

In the first ICC Trophy contest of 1979, Kenya played as part of East Africa, but in 1982 they broke away, playing as a separate country. The standard of cricket has improved over the years and in the 1997 ICC Trophy, Kenya reached the final.

The most important series of matches played in Kenya took place in Nairobi in September and October 1996, when Kenya, South Africa, Pakistan and Sri Lanka met. The competition, sponsored by the Sameer Group, was won by South Africa. Kenya had taken part in the World Cup of 1996 and caused a major upset by beating the West Indies, but it proved to be their only victory in their five matches.

In August 2001, West Indies made the first full tour by a Test-playing nation to Kenya and they won all three one-day matches. The ICC ruled that from 1997–98 Kenya would be granted first-class status.

Kenya were the surprise team in the 2003 World Cup, winning four pool match and qualifying for the Super Six play-offs. They took part in West Indies first-class cricket in 2003–04 but did not win a match. They lost to Scotland in the semi-final of the 2004 Inter-continental Cup.

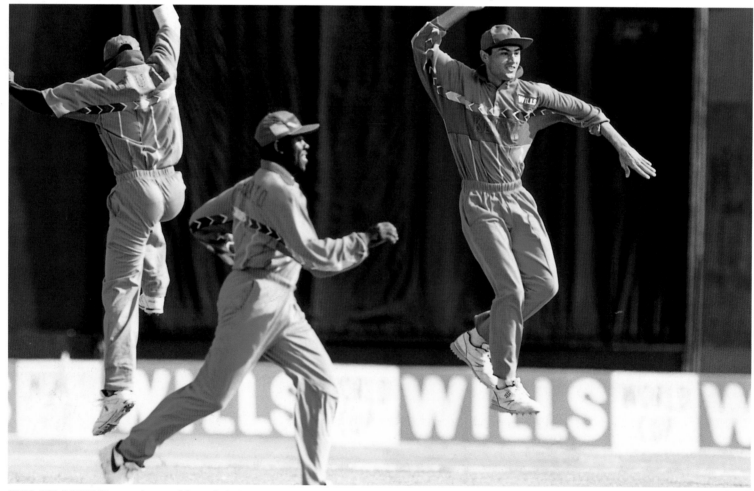

SONG AND DANCE *Kenyan players celebrate their victory over Australia at the 1996 World Cup.*

MALAYSIA

The present Malaysia Cricket Association was formed in 1963 and includes Sarawak and Sabah (formerly North Borneo). Cricket began there in the second half of the nineteenth century, when the Malay States came under the protection of the British Government.

The major match between the wars was Federated Malay States (i.e. Perak, Selangor and Negri Sembilan) against Straits Settlements (Singapore, Penang and Malacca). At this time, the Singapore Cricket Club acted as the unofficial controlling body.

In 1927, a strong Australian touring side was defeated in Kuala Lumpur and the All Malaya team of this period was probably about first-class standard, although their matches are not generally recognized as first-class.

In the first two ICC Trophy competitions, Malaysia failed to win a match, but in 1986 they gained three victories. The country only had moderate success in 1990 and 1994. The highly successful 1997 ICC competition was staged in Malaysia and, although the home side did not reach the final eight, cricket in the country as a whole is on the increase and the main domestic tournaments are flourishing.

Malaysia did not fare as well as expected in the 2001 ICC Trophy, failing to gain a place in the final Super League. They also took part in the Inter-continental Cup in 2004.

NAMIBIA

This sparsely populated country was a German colony from 1890 until 1915. From 1920 the League of Nations gave a mandate to South Africa to administer the country. Namibia became an independent nation in 1990. Namibia took part in the ICC Trophy competitions of 1994 and 1997, but with little success. From 1996 South Africa allowed Namibia to compete in the UCB Bowl. In April 1996, a South African Country Districts side visited Windhoek and played three one-day matches against local sides.

Namibia, who play regularly in South Africa, gained experience in the 2003 World Cup, but failed to win a match. Namibia also played in the Inter-continental Cup in 2004.

THE NETHERLANDS

Cricket in the Netherlands goes back to 1855, when some South African students at Utrecht University introduced the game, but it failed to take root and the first proper Dutch club was not formed until 1875.

In the 1880s, it is believed, there were some hundred or so clubs. In 1883, the Nederlandse Cricket-Bond was founded and in 1892 the first Dutch side visited Britain. Prior to the First World War, the best known Dutch cricketer was C.J. Posthuma, who appeared in some first-class matches in England.

Between the wars the major British club to visit the Netherlands, the Free Foresters, scarcely missed a single season without going across the North Sea. Despite the obvious difficulties, cricket continued to be played every season between 1940 and 1945, though owing to travel restrictions matches were played on a regional basis.

The Free Foresters resumed their annual tour in 1946. In 1964 the Australians, who went to the Netherlands briefly whilst on tour to England, were beaten in a one-day game. In the first two ICC Trophy contests, the Netherlands did not shine, but in 1986 they reached the final before being defeated by Zimbabwe. The 1990 final was a repeat of the 1986, with the same out. Four years later, the Netherlands finished in third place, beating Bermuda in the play-off. In the 1997 ICC Trophy, the Dutch team were unfortunate to come up against Bangladesh after having achieved a place in the last eight.

Due to their success in the 1994 ICC Trophy, the Netherlands qualified for the 1996 World Cup on the Indian sub-continent. However, they failed to win any of their five matches, their best performance being against England when they lost by 49 runs.

In 2000 the Dutch team won the European Championship and came second to Kenya in the Emerging Nations Tournament. In 2001 they were losing finalists in the ICC Trophy Competition.

Taking part in the 2003 World Cup, they won one match – against Namibia. The Netherlands took part in the Inter-continental Cup in 2004 and in the 2005 ICC Trophy, where they finished a disappointing fifth.

ZUIDERENT *Scored 54 against England the 1996 World Cup at Peshawar.*

NIGERIA

The British presence in Nigeria commenced with the annexation of Lagos island in 1861, but it was not until 1914 that the colony of Nigeria was established. The neighbouring Gold Coast had played for the first time in 1904. Matches between Gold Coast and Nigeria started in 1926 and continued through to recent times. In the mid-1930s, two Cricket Associations were formed, one for Europeans and one for Africans. The two organizations merged in 1956.

Nigeria is part of West Africa insofar as the ICC Trophy competition is concerned. West Africa first participated in 1982, when they failed to win a match. The side did not take part in the 1986 and 1990 tournaments, but returned in 1994 when, after again failing to win a match in the main competition, West Africa played in the Wooden Spoon Deluxe Group and won all three games. However, the 1997 tournament saw the side improving very little.

Nigeria won the 1988 triangular tournament against Ghana and Gambia in emphatic style, beating Gambia by 10 wickets and Ghana by an innings and 15 runs.

In the 2001 ICC Trophy, Nigeria remained part of the West African team, which failed to win a single match. In 2002 Nigeria – with around 1,000 players in a population of 150 million – were elected associate members of the ICC.

PAPUA NEW GUINEA

Until 1918, the country was divided into two halves, the northern half being a German colony, the southern a British colony. Cricket was taught at missionary stations in the British colony before the First World War, but the other half did not see cricket until about 1921, when it became a League of Nations Mandate.

In the 1930s, two mission stations, at Samarai and Kwato, played cricket against each other every Saturday – there was no time limit, but as soon as one match was complete the next commenced. In Port Moresby a competition was established in 1937 for sides in the capital.

A Board of Control was founded in 1972 and the country joined the ICC in 1973, two years before becoming independent. In the 1982 ICC Trophy, Papua finished third, beating Bangladesh in the play-off. The country reached the second round in 1990, but has not been so successful in the last three contests.

In July 2003 Papua New Guinea won the South Pacific Games.

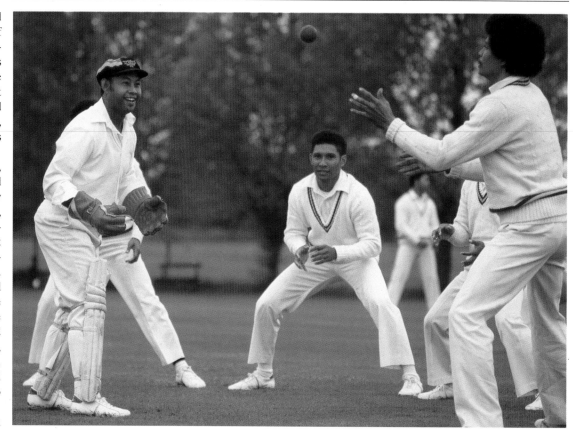

THE MATCH AT BANBURY *Papua New Guinea practise for their match against Argentina in the 1979 ICC Trophy.*

PORTUGAL

The British played some cricket in Portugal in the eighteenth century and there are references to informal games during the Peninsular Wars. A club was established in Oporto in 1855 and, when a second club came into being in Lisbon, an annual fixture began between the two sides, both being entirely composed of British residents. Cricket teams from England, notably the Cryptics, have made regular trips to Portugal since the 1920s.

In the nineteenth century, Tom Westray took a side out to Portugal once or twice. Pelham Warner gives an interesting account of his visit with Westray's side, when matches were played against Oporto and All-Portugal.

For many years Portugal and its cricketers remained aloof from competitive matches, but in 1995 it joined the European Nations Cup and, to the surprise of most rivals, took the title, but the majority of players are of English descent.

In the 1999 European Nations Cup, Portugal proved this was no flash in the pan by again reaching the final, but this time they finished as runners-up, losing to Greece.

SCOTLAND

There are odd references to cricket in Scotland in the eighteenth century, but the game did not become established in the country outside the military and landed gentry until the middle of the nineteenth century and the first match by a so-called Scotland team took place in 1865. The Scottish Cricket Union was formed in 1879, dissolved in 1883 and re-established in 1908. Much confusion was caused to cricket statisticians by the fact that Scotland apparently played two matches simultaneously in 1878, one against Yorkshire, the other against England. Closer inspection reveals, however, that Yorkshire played "Gents of Edinburgh".

The first first-class match involving Scotland took place in 1905, when the opponents were the Australian tourists. The West Indies were played in 1906 and South Africa in 1907.

The first recorded inter-county game was in 1851, East Lothian playing Stirling. The Scottish County Championship was established in 1902 and continued, with gaps for the two World Wars, until 1995. Aberdeen, Forfar, Perthshire and Stirlingshire played every year. Apart from those counties, others which at one time were champions were Clackmannan, Ayrshire and West Lothian.

In 1996, there was a drastic reorganization of major club cricket in Scotland. A new National Scottish League was created, of two divisions, with 10 clubs in each and with promotion and relegation. Division 1 comprises Aberdeenshire, Arbroath Utd, Carlton, Freuchie, Grange, Heriots FP, Prestwick, Strathmore, Watsonians and West Lothian. The authorities have, however, established a knockout competition for the old Scottish counties.

Scotland entered the English Benson & Hedges competition in 1980 and the NatWest Trophy in 1981. Their success was limited, with only two wins in the former and none in the latter. In 2003 – as the Scottish Saltires – they began a three-year spell in Division Two of the 45-over National (Sunday) League.

Scotland entered the ICC Trophy competition for the first time in 1997 and finished in third place.

Scotland gained a place in the 1999 World Cup, but failed to win a single match. In 2001, taking part in the ICC Trophy in Canada, Scotland won four out of five matches in the initial league stage, then qualified for the play-off for third place. They lost to Canada and therefore did not qualify for the 2003 World Cup. They were consigned to the tension of a play-off after a dramatic collapse against Namibia in their final Super League match when, needing ten runs to win off two overs with three wickets in hand, they lost.

Scotland beat Canada in the Intercontinental Cup Final in 2004 and continued their good form in the 2005 ICC Trophy in Ireland, where they defeated the hosts in the final.

SINGAPORE

Singapore was founded in 1819 and from 1826 formed part of the Straits Settlements. The first reported cricket took place in 1852 and Singapore was from then considered the centre of cricket in the Settlements.

In 1890–91, a triangular tournament was staged in Singapore between Hong Kong, Ceylon and the Settlements, the home side being victorious. Three years afterwards, a team was sent to Ceylon. Matches between the Federated Malay States and the Straits Settlements were played on a regular basis between the wars. In May 1927, a strong Australian side, including Bill Woodfull and Charles Macartney, played two games against Singapore, both of which the tourists won by an innings.

After the Japanese occupation, the Singapore Cricket Club was flourishing again in 1947; Hong Kong made several visits to both Singapore and Malaya. Singapore became an independent state in 1965 and its team has taken part in the ICC Trophy since 1979.

At present, there is a flourishing league with 19 teams split into two divisions. In April 1996, Singapore staged the Singer Tournament – limited-over matches between India, Pakistan and Sri Lanka.

SPAIN

Occasional cricket matches were played in Spain from the second half of the nineteenth century, but it cannot be said that any serious matches were staged until the British began to take up residence there after the Second World War. Spain joined the ICC in 1992 as an affiliated member and in 1995 played against both Italy and Portugal for the first time in matches arranged for two days. Barcelona and Javea are two of the main cricketing centres.

In June 1989, the first Spanish cricket tournament took place in the capital, Madrid, involving four teams: Madrid, Malaga, Balearic XI and Barcelona. The home team were the winners.

TANZANIA

Until the First World War Tanganyika was a German colony, whilst the second element of Tanzania was the British Protectorate of Zanzibar, ruled by the Sultan. There was some cricket in Zanzibar in the nineteenth century, but cricket in Tanganyika did not become established until the 1920s, and it was not until after the Second World War that, with the formation of the Twigas CC in 1951, international games commenced. The Twigas opposed the Kenya Kongonis and also toured England. The MCC visited Dar-es-Salaam for the first time in 1957–58 and the South African Non-European side also visited the country in the same season.

Tanzania came into being in 1964 and, in January 1974, under the captaincy of J.M. Brearley, the MCC toured the country. In the game against Tanzania at Dar-es-Salaam the home country had the better of a high-scoring draw, gaining a lead on first innings.

Tanzania participates in the ICC Trophy as part of East & Central Africa, a combination of countries which had been admitted to the ICC in 1966.

UGANDA

The first cricket in Uganda was played in Entebbe, which was the original government headquarters in 1893. The cricket ground there was considered the equal of any in central Africa. The country's first international game took place there in 1914 when Uganda met the British East African Protectorate (Kenya).

Between the two World Wars, the major domestic fixture was Armed Forces v Uganda Kobs, a two-day game staged to coincide with the King's birthday. The Uganda Kobs is an organization involved in all sports, not only cricket, and has been responsible for tours to England. There was also a triangular communal competition between European, Goan and Indian teams. Later it was expanded to include an African side.

When Idi Amin became head of state in 1971 and began his policy of expelling Asians, cricket was very seriously affected. Of the dozen or so clubs in existence prior to his taking over, only the African Club remained and even this struggled to exist. The game is slowly recovering, and it is estimated that there are now at least 200 adult cricketers playing.

In 1995, a team toured England, playing 12 matches. Uganda plays in the ICC Trophy as part of the East & Central Africa side. It had little success, however, in the 1997 competition. They also played in the Inter-continental Cup in 2004, but their grounds were not up to standard and their game was played in Kenya.

UNITED ARAB EMIRATES

On April 13, 1984, some four years after starting his project to build an international cricket stadium in Sharjah, Abdul Rehman Bukhatir saw his ambitions realized when the Asian Cup, involving India, Pakistan and Sri Lanka, was staged there. Some 15,000 spectators watched India beat Pakistan in the final

Since that momentous day, more one-day internationals have been played in Sharjah than at any other venue and in the 1995–96 season the total reached 100. Domestic cricket in the seven Emirates has flourished on the back of the international stadium and both leagues and knockout competitions are operating.

In 1994, the United Arab Emirates entered the ICC Trophy for the first time. They outplayed all their rivals, winning all nine matches, and beating Kenya in the final by two wickets. This success qualified the team for the 1996 World Cup. However, they failed to make much impression on the Test-playing opponents and the Emirates' only victory was at the expense of the Netherlands.

In the ICC Trophy of 2001, the Emirates failed to get into the Super League stage of the competition.

The Emirates lost to Canada in the semi-final of the Inter-continental Cup in 2004 and finished sixth in the 2005 ICC Trophy in Ireland.

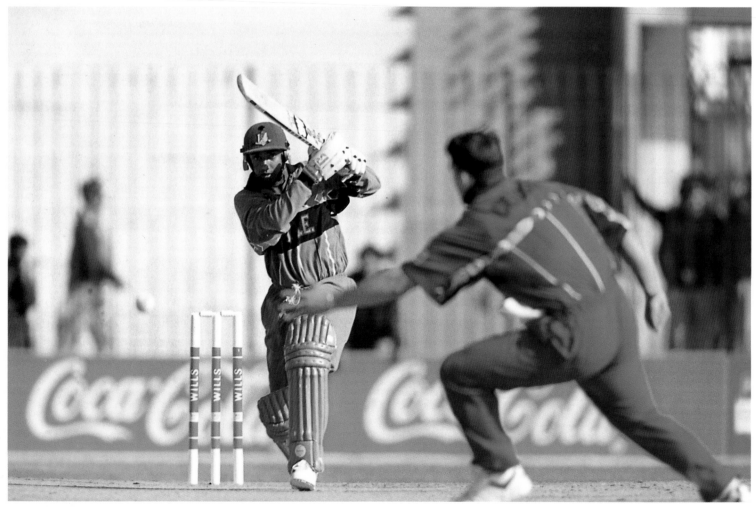

THE 1996 WORLD CUP *Mazhar Hussain hit the highest score, 33, for the United Arab Emirates against England in their 1996 World Cup match at Peshawar.*

UNITED STATES OF AMERICA

The first report of a match in New York was published in 1751. Between then and 1780, cricket flourished but the War of Independence seems to have brought cricket to a standstill. The game revived, though, and the creation of the St George's Club in 1839 had a great influence on cricket's popularity. The club sent a team to Toronto in 1840 and from this stemmed the first United States v Canada match of 1844.

By this time cricket was well-established in Philadelphia, and in the 1850s there were regular matches between various clubs from the two great cities. The first English touring side of 1859 played in both New York and Philadelphia.

The American Civil War had a disastrous effect on American cricket – not only were the international matches against Canada stopped for the duration, but financial problems prevented any English teams from touring. In addition, the war did much to encourage cricket's rival, baseball.

By the 1870s Philadelphia had become the cricketing centre of the States. When an international tournament was arranged in Halifax, Nova Scotia, in 1874, the United States were represented by the Philadelphians who duly won the tournament and the Halifax Cup. This cup was taken back to Philadelphia and used as the trophy for what was probably the first cricket league competition in the world. This "Halifax Cup Tournament" ran until 1926.

Although the Philadelphians toured England, playing county teams, from 1883 to 1908 and were granted first-class status for three of their five tours, first-class domestic cricket in the United States was a

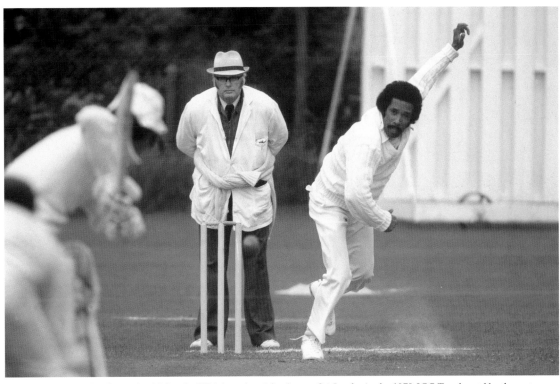

WALTER BOVELL *Took two for 29 for the USA in a six-wicket loss to Sri Lanka in the 1979 ICC Trophy at Northampton.*

very occasional affair: such contests as Gentlemen v Players, American-born v English Residents and Philadelphia v Rest of United States. No first-class competition was ever staged, the only other first-class games being between Philadelphia and the English or Australian tourists.

After the First World War cricket of any serious nature almost died out, though a league kept going in the Chicago area, and English residents in Hollywood, under the leadership of the film star and former England Test cricketer C. Aubrey Smith, played friendly games. The most outstanding American cricketer of the Edwardian era was the bowler J. Barton King; the best batsman was George Patterson.

The post-war revival of cricket was engineered by John Marder, who established the United States Cricket Association in 1961 and in 1968 organized a team to tour Britain, playing a series of 21 games.

They joined the ICC in 1965 and have been regular entrants in the ICC Trophy since it started in 1979.

But the rise of American cricket in the last 20 years has been largely due to players from the West Indies or the Indian sub-continent rather than any great development among American-born players. In 1996, a United States Cricket Federation was created as a rival to the 1961-vintage Cricket Association.

In October 2000, the United States beat Barbados in the Red Stripe, one-day cup competition. Earlier the same summer the United States toured England and gained victories both against MCC and Yorkshire 2nd XI. In the 2001 ICC Trophy, the side qualified for the Super League, but had disappointing results and therefore did not qualify for the World Cup in 2003. Off the field of play matters are fraught, with much bickering between officials. Uniformed security guards had to be hired at a general meeting of the country's Cricket Association, in order to maintain the peace.

The United States won the Americas' Cup in 2002.

The first first-class match in the USA since 1912 was staged at Fort Lauderdale, Florida, in May 2004, but the United States lost to Canada. And there was a disappointing tenth-place finish in the 2005 ICC Trophy.

VANUATU

Until 1980 this independent country was the Anglo-French condominium of the New Hebrides, situated between the Solomon Islands and Fiji.

At present, it is reported that there are some 400 active cricketers and 12 teams. South of Vanuatu are the Loyalty Islands of Mare, Lifou and Ouvea, and in the 1960s cricket was played there, having first come to the islands through the London Mission Society in the nineteenth century. It seems that little cricket is played in the Solomon Islands at the moment.

The man responsible for introducing of cricket to many South Pacific islands was an Oxford blue, the Rev. J.C. Patteson. He was appointed Bishop of Melanesia in 1861, but 10 years later was murdered by natives on Nukapu.

Strangely, Vanuatu, in the Southern Hemisphere, enjoys its main cricket season in the winter months.

TEST CRICKET

The first plans for international cricket were made in 1789, when the Duke of Dorset, a patron of Kent cricket and at the time the British Ambassador in Paris, arranged for a side captained by William Yalden, the Surrey wicket-keeper, to play matches in France. However, when the side reached Dover to board the ferry, they were met by the Duke coming the other way. He was fleeing from the French Revolution, and that was the end of that idea.

The world had to wait until 1844 before the first international cricket match took place, and this match nowadays sounds as unlikely as that abortive tour of France. It was a match between the United States and Canada, played in New York. In those days, North America was considered the strongest cricketing area outside England, and this was reflected in the calibre of the English side sent on the first cricketing tour. It went to Canada and the USA in 1859 under the captaincy of George Parr, captain of Nottinghamshire, and included the leading players of the day. The team won all five matches played (against 22 on the opposition side) and staged three exhibition matches.

Two years later, in 1861–62, a team toured Australia. Many of the 1859 tourists couldn't agree terms, but two went: H.H. Stephenson, the captain, and William Caffyn, both of Surrey, who had five Surrey colleagues with them. Again, most

EARLY TOUR *Stephenson and Caffyn.*

of the 12 matches were against 22 players, and two were lost. There were also two exhibitions, in one of which the World beat Surrey by six wickets.

There followed two more tours to Australia, during the second of which in 1873–74 W.G. Grace led the side, and two more to America,

one by an amateur team in which W.G. was merely the leading batsman, before the first important tour of Australia in 1876–77. The team for this tour was led by James Lillywhite (Jr) of Sussex, the nephew of Fred and cousin of James (Sr) and John, all of Sussex. They mostly played against sides of 15, 18 or 22 players but on this tour, for the first time, three matches were played which are considered now to be "first-class". The first was against New South Wales, who followed on but held on for a draw when an innings defeat was the likeliest outcome. The other two first-class games were against Australia and have come to be regarded as the first two Test matches.

Not that they were known as Test matches then, although the term "Test match" in relation to cricket had been used as early as the first English tour to Australia in 1861–62. This sentence regarding the tourists appeared in Hammersley's *Victorian Cricketer's*

Guide, published in Melbourne in 1862: "Of the thirteen matches played, five only can be termed 'test matches'; the three played at Melbourne and the two at Sydney". It wasn't until the 1880s that the term "Test match" to describe the England-Australia matches gradually became more widespread. Even then, which matches qualified for the description was disputed until the beginning of the twentieth century. It was then that the list in *Australian Cricket and Cricketers* by C.P. Moody, published in Melbourne in 1894, came to be regarded as the official list.

The series of matches which a Rest of the World team played in the 1970s, and the Australia v ICC World XI Super-Test of 2005, although officially designated Test matches, are not included in this section.

BRISBANE 2002 *Matthew Hayden smashes 197 off the England attack.*

ENGLAND v AUSTRALIA

The side captained by James Lillywhite in that first Test match at Melbourne on March 15, 16, 17 and 19, 1877 was not quite representative of England's best, as the leading batsmen Grace, Daft and Shrewsbury did not tour, but the bowling was up to scratch. England were also lacking their wicket-keeper, Ted Pooley of Surrey, who was under arrest in New Zealand. This came about because of a well-known betting ploy which Pooley had used to his advantage against the locals. He bet a spectator at one of the matches England played against 22 opponents that he could forecast the score of all 22 batsmen. The spectator gave him odds of 20–1 for each, which Pooley took at £1 to a shilling. He then wrote down 0 for each man, it being usual to have quite a few ducks in these games. In fact there were 11, so Pooley won £11 and lost 11s, i.e. he required £10.9s to settle. The spectator refused to pay, there was a fight causing damage to property, and Pooley was arrested. He was awaiting trial when the first-ever Test began. As the party consisted of only 12 players, opening batsman Selby was forced to keep wicket.

The first ball in the first of more than 1,400 Tests was bowled by Alfred Shaw of Nottinghamshire

ALFRED SHAW *First Test bowler.*

and received by Charles Bannerman of New South Wales. Five of the Australian team were born in the British Isles including the two who scored most runs, Bannerman and Tom Horan, and the two who got most wickets, Tom Kendall and W.E. Midwinter. Midwinter also played for England, and is the only player to have played for England in Australia and for Australia in England.

The star of the first Test was Charles Bannerman, who scored twice as many runs as any player on either side. Bannerman scored the first Test century, 165, before retiring hurt with a split finger. The English fielding was appalling, with half the team suffering from stomach upsets after the boat journey from New Zealand. Australia, 245 and 104, beat England, 196 and 108, by 45 runs. The Australian captain was D.W. Gregory.

UNBROKEN RECORDS

This first Test established three records of interest which still stand, and one will be impossible to break. This belongs to James Southerton, the England bowler from Petworth, Sussex who played most of his cricket for Surrey. Born on November 16, 1827, he was 49 at the time of the Test, and not surprisingly remains the "first-born" of all Test players. He also remains the oldest player to make his Test debut (although not the oldest Test player, a record held by Wilfred Rhodes). As it happens he was also the first Test player to die, in June 1880, three months before G.F. Grace. The other record is held by Charles Bannerman, whose first innings 165 was 67.3 per cent of his side's all-out total, the highest proportion still. It is strange to think that a record set in the first innings of the first Test still stands.

A second Test was arranged two weeks later for the benefit of the touring professionals, which led to cries of "fix" by gamblers who'd lost by betting on England in the first, and who claimed that England

deliberately lost to ensure a big return gate. If it were true it worked, for 15,000 saw England win by four wickets to square the rubber. An odd statistic of this match is that the five Yorkshiremen in the side (Andrew Greenwood, George Ullyett, Tom Emmett, Allen Hill and Tom Armitage) scored 329 of the 356 runs from the bat, or 92.5 per cent of the runs.

To emphasize the unrepresentative nature of early Tests, the next touring side was an amateur outfit led by Lord Harris, reinforced by two of the Yorkshire professionals named above. The match which became the only Test of the series was billed as Gentlemen of England (with Ullyett and Emmett) versus An Australian XI. The England team's one-Test collection included the improbable Test players The MacKinnon of MacKinnon and the Reverend Vernon Peter Fanshawe Archer Royle. Australia's new discovery, the "Demon Bowler" F.R. Spofforth, was far too good for them, taking 13 wickets including the first Test hat-trick, as Australia won by 10 wickets.

In 1880 an Australian team toured England under W.L. Murdoch (who later was to play one Test for England). No Tests had been arranged, because the English thought the Aussies incapable yet of facing the full might of England. However, Charles Alcock, secretary of Surrey (who years earlier had played in the first FA Cup Final and arranged the first soccer international match), arranged a Test at the Oval. The first Test match in England took place on September 6, 7 and 8. W.G. Grace played and scored 152, England forced the follow-on and won by five wickets. Spofforth couldn't play through injury, but there were three Graces in the England side, the brothers W.G., E.M. and G.F. G.F. Grace made a pair but took a brilliant catch. Sadly, he caught a chill and died at Basingstoke a fortnight later, the second Test player to die.

Australia really established their

BANNERMAN *Scored first Test century.*

credentials in the 1881–82 season, when they beat a strong English touring side 2–0 with two draws. In a match against Victoria, the state side needed only 94 in the fourth innings to win and the odds against England were 30–1. Most England players put £1 on themselves to win and, with Ted Peate getting six for 30, they dismissed Victoria for 75 and collected £30 winnings. But it then transpired that two England players, who had played noticeably badly, had been bribed with £100 to throw the match. They invited Midwinter to join them, but he reported the matter to the captain, Alfred Shaw. For his honesty, Midwinter was beaten up by the two conspirators.

HORNBY AND BARLOW

One of the big shocks in cricket came in 1882. There was one Test at the Oval, played on August 28 and 29. Unusually, both teams were at something like full strength, Murdoch captaining Australia and A.N. Hornby England (Hornby's Lancashire team-mate R.G. Barlow was also playing – the two are immortalized in Francis Thompson's

SHAW'S TEAM *Toured America, Australia and New Zealand in 1881–82.*

famous poem *At Lord's*, which contains the refrain "O my Hornby and my Barlow long ago").

Australia won the toss and batted, and were rushed out for 63. When England batted, Spofforth bowled W.G. Grace for 4, but England battled on to 101, a lead of 38. In Australia's second innings, Hugh Massie launched an attack on the England bowling and scored 55 in an opening stand of 66, but the batting collapsed again and Australia were all out for 122. England needed a mere 85 to win. Openers Hornby and Barlow were both bowled by Spofforth at 15, but Grace and Ullyett took the score past 50 and all seemed over. Yet both were out by 53, and Spofforth and his steady ally Henry Boyle gradually ate through the remaining England wickets until the last one fell at 77 – Australia won by seven runs. Spofforth took seven wickets in each innings. W.G. Grace described the Australian wicket-keeper J.M. Blackham as "perfection". Blackham was an outstanding keeper who played Test cricket for 18 years and was on the first eight tours to England.

English cricket followers could hardly believe this result – the masters, at full strength, had been beaten. The *Sporting Times* published its famous obituary notice, framed in a black border, which read: "In affectionate remembrance of English cricket which died at the Oval on 29th August 1882, deeply lamented by a large circle of sorrowing friends and acquaintances. R.I.P. N.B. – The body will be cremated, and the ashes taken to Australia."

THE ASHES

In the English winter after this defeat, the Honourable Ivo Bligh took a party to Australia at the invitation of the Melbourne Cricket Club. It consisted of eight amateurs and four professionals. Fast bowler Fred Morley was injured when the ship taking them to Australia collided with a sailing ship. Three matches were arranged against the Australian team which had won at the Oval, but these were still not recognized as part of a Test match series – indeed the matches were billed as "Mr Murdoch's XI against the Hon. Ivo F.W. Bligh's Team". The Honourable Ivo Bligh, before departure for Australia, said at a dinner that he would be bringing "the Ashes of English cricket" back to England.

Bligh appeared to have little chance when Australia won the first Test. The star of the second Test was Willie Bates of Yorkshire. He took seven wickets in each innings, including a hat-trick, England's first in Tests. He also scored 55 with the bat, becoming the first to score 50 and take 10 wickets in a Test. England won by an innings.

England won a well-fought decider at Sydney by 69 runs, with Dick Barlow the hero, taking seven for 40, off 34.2 overs, as Australia,

needing 153, were dismissed for 83.

At this juncture, according to legend, some Melbourne ladies burned a bail, placed the ashes in a small urn and presented them to Bligh as the "ashes of England cricket" which he had won back. The urn was labelled "The Ashes" and carried a short type-written poem. It was given to Bligh in an embroidered velvet bag, and urn and bag are now kept in the Memorial Gallery at Lord's.

However, after this a fourth Test was arranged for Sydney and finished in a four-wicket win for Australia despite A.G. Steel's 135 for England. Blackham made two 50s for Australia, the only wicket-keeper to achieve this in the first 50 years of Test cricket.

In 1884 England staged the first home Test series against Australia, as opposed to the single matches of 1880 and 1882. Although Australia had the better of two drawn matches, England won the only match to be decided, at Lord's, by an innings and five runs. A.G. Steel excelled again with 148 out of 379. In the final match at the Oval, the Australian captain, W.L. Murdoch, scored 211, the first double-century in Tests. That England saved the match was largely due to Surrey all-rounder Walter Read scoring 117 batting at number 10 and putting on 151 with William Scotton, the Nottinghamshire opener, who was ninth out for 90, scored in 340 minutes. The ninth-wicket stand remains the biggest for England against Australia.

END OF THE CENTURY

As the nineteenth century approached its end, big names and outstanding performances established the appeal of the Test match, in which England and Australia were now seen to compete on level terms. England won in 1884–85 by 3–2. There were more disputes over money (all tours were privately run) and Blackham's continuous spell of playing in all the first 17 Tests ended when the Australian team asked for 50 per cent of the takings from the second Test and were dropped wholesale. This tour, as were many around this

time, was organized by the trio of Arthur Shrewsbury and Alfred Shaw, of Nottinghamshire, and James Lillywhite, of the famous Sussex cricketing family, who was now an umpire. Shrewsbury, in the last Test, became the first Test captain to make a century.

In 1887–88 two rival teams went to Australia: that of Shrewsbury, Shaw and Lillywhite and G.F. Vernon's team captained by Lord Hawke. The two teams combined to play one Test at Sydney, with England winning after dismissing Australia for 42 and 82, George Lohmann and Bobby Peel taking 10 and nine wickets respectively.

The double tour was a financial disaster. This, plus the fact that in 1888–89 a third Test-playing country entered the lists with England taking a party to South Africa, meant the frequency of the meetings between England and Australia decreased. Australia exacted revenge for their dismal two-innings total of 124 at Sydney by dismissing England for 53 and 62 in the first Test of 1888. This caused W.G. Grace to assume the England captaincy for five years during which time England had the better of things.

The first Test of 1894–95 at Sydney was sensational. Australia made 586, with Syd Gregory scoring 201, the first Test double-century in Australia, George Giffen 161, and captain J.M. Blackham 74 at number 10, his ninth-wicket partnership with Gregory realizing 154, and remaining to this day a record for the series. England, out for 325, followed on and, thanks to 117 from opener Albert Ward and solid all-down-the-order contributions, made 437, setting Australia 177 to win. Bobby Peel (6 for 67) and Johnny Briggs then took advantage of a sticky sixth-day wicket to dismiss Australia for 166 and a 10-run victory. The aggregate runs scored, 1,514, was at the time a record for all first-class cricket. It was to be 87 years, when England again came from behind to beat Australia at Headingley in 1981, before the second instance of a side winning a Test after following on. England had to win the fifth Test to take the series 3–2.

DAWN OF THE GOLDEN AGE

The "Golden Age" of cricket was dawning, with great players and great deeds abounding. In the second Test of 1896, K.S. Ranjitsinhji of Sussex became the first Indian to play Test cricket and made a century (154 not out) on his debut, the second English batsman to do this after Grace. In the same match Australia's George Giffen, in his 30th Test, became the first player to complete 1,000 runs and 100 wickets in Tests. Bobby Peel ended his Test career with 6 for 23 in the final Test, having taken 102 Australian wickets – the following year Lord Hawke sacked him from Yorkshire for being drunk.

Under the captaincy of G.H.S. Trott, Australia had the ascendancy in the last two series of the nineteenth century, with the batting of Joe Darling and Clem Hill outstanding.

In the first Test of 1899 at Trent Bridge, which was drawn, W.G. Grace played his last Test, captaining England at the age of nearly 51. By coincidence, the player who was to break his record as the oldest Test player, Wilfred Rhodes, made his debut in the same match. Also making his debut (with a duck) was Victor Trumper, a batsman whom many Australians compared with the later Bradman. In the second Test, he made 135 not out to help win the only match of the series to be decided.

In 1901–02 A.C. MacLaren picked Syd Barnes, whose bowling had been mostly for Rishton and Burnley in the Lancashire League. The Yorkshire committee refused to allow the leading bowlers of the summer, Rhodes and George Hirst, to tour. Barnes took six wickets in the first Test, which England won by an innings and 124, and 13 wickets in the second Test, which Australia won (Monty Noble also took 13 wickets). Then Barnes injured his knee, and Australia won the series 4–1. With Trumper, Hill, Syd Gregory and Reggie Duff among the batsmen, and Hugh Trumble to bowl, Australia had one of its greatest sides.

When the party came to England in 1902, England too had one of its best sides, with MacLaren,

Ranjitsinhji, C.B. Fry, J.T. Tyldesley, F.S. Jackson and Gilbert Jessop among the batsmen and Rhodes, Hurst, Len Braund and W.H. Lockwood among the bowlers. Wicket-keeper A.F.A. Lilley was also outstanding.

In the first Test at Edgbaston, England made 376 for 9 declared (Tyldesley 138) and dismissed Australia for 36, still their lowest score in Tests (Rhodes 7 for 17). Australia were 46 for 2 in the follow-on when rain intervened. The Lord's Test was washed out with England 102 for 2 (Albert Hopkins had dismissed both Fry and Ranjitsinhji without a run on the board). Clem Hill made 119 in the only Test ever to be played at Sheffield (Bramall Lane) and Australia won by 143.

Australia won the series at Old Trafford. Trumper and Duff had 100 up in 57 minutes, and by lunch, at 173 for 1, Trumper had completed his century. But Jackson scored a century for England, Australia were shot out for 86 and England needed only 124 to win. At 92 for 3 and 107 for 5, it seemed a doddle. Alas, Fred Tate, father of the more famous Maurice, was making his Test debut. He had already expensively dropped Joe Darling, Australia's top scorer in the second innings, and now, coming in last with 8 to get, was bowled, giving Australia victory by three runs.

The last Test at the Oval, although "dead", was even closer, and one of the most exciting on record. Australia made 324 and 121, leaving England, with a first-innings 183, a target of 263, which looked hopeless when Jessop went in at 48 for 5. Jessop then played one of the most famous of all innings, 104 in 75 minutes (then the fastest, and still the second-fastest ever Test century), Hirst stuck for 58 not out and, when Rhodes came in as last man, 15 were still required, but they got them to record a famous one-wicket victory.

ENTER THE MCC

England regained the Ashes in 1903–04, when R.E. Foster, of the famous Worcestershire family of cricketers, made 287 on his debut in the first Test, which remained the highest Test score for 26 years. He

'GOLDEN AGE' GIANTS *Brilliant sportsmen C.B. Fry and Prince Ranjitsinhji.*

put on 130 for the last wicket with Rhodes (40 not out), the highest last-wicket stand for England in Tests. In the fifth Test Rhodes opened the innings. This was the first tour sponsored by the MCC rather than private sponsors. Such teams were always known as MCC until 1977–78 when the TCCB suggested that henceforth they should be called England.

The 1907–08 series was notable for the debut of C.G. Macartney of New South Wales in the first Test at Sydney, and the fact that Jack Hobbs of Surrey was only 12th man, even though the side was not the strongest. Australia, needing 274, were 124 for 6, but won by two wickets. Hobbs made his debut in the second Test at Melbourne and made 83 and 28, and England won by one wicket, thanks to a last-wicket stand of 39. A partnership which was then a record for Test cricket and remains Australia's highest for the eighth wicket turned the series Australia's way in the third, setting up a 4–1 win. Roger Hartigan of Queensland, batting at

number 8 in his Test debut, scored 116 at Adelaide, helping Clem Hill (160), who came in at 9, add 243 in the second innings.

England picked 25 players in the Test series of 1909, and lost 2–1. Australia's main debutant was Warren Bardsley, who in the fifth Test at the Oval made 136 and 130 to become the first to score centuries in each innings of a match.

The 1911–12 series in Australia was the last for Clem Hill, who led Australia, and Victor Trumper, who were the only batsmen at the time to have passed 3,000 Test runs. Trumper made 113 as Australia won the first Test, but England won the rest, with Jack Hobbs in the form that made him the best batsman of his day. He made 662 runs, average 82.75, including 178 at Melbourne out of 323 for the first wicket with Wildred Rhodes (179). This remains the highest opening stand for England against Australia, so Rhodes, the erstwhile number 11, still figures in the record Ashes stands for both England's first and last wickets.

TRIANGULAR TEST SERIES

There was a triangular Test series in England in 1912, the only one in Test history, in which Australia and South Africa were the visitors. England won it by beating Australia in a "timeless" Test in the 12th match, but rain spoiled the whole experiment, which wasn't repeated.

The First World War interrupted Test cricket, and Australia dominated on resumption in 1920–21. There were 14 centuries in the series, 10 for Australia, skipper Warwick Armstrong making three of them. Arthur Mailey of New South Wales took 9 for 121 in the fourth Test, the only time an Australian has taken nine wickets in an Ashes Test. Australia won the series 5–0.

Less than two months after the last Test they were beginning the first in England, and Australia continued their run by winning the first three Tests. The final two were drawn.

Before the next series, in 1924–25, Herbert Sutcliffe and Maurice Tate had made their Test debuts against South Africa. Sutcliffe was to form the best-known of all opening partnerships with Hobbs. Their first three opening stands against Australia were 157, 110 and 283. It was another series in which 14 centuries were scored, and half of them were scored by Hobbs (3) and Sutcliffe (4). Maurice Tate of Sussex took 38 wickets at 23.18 in the series. But Australia still managed to win the series 4–1. Newcomers Bill Ponsford of Victoria and Vic Richardson of South Australia both made centuries and Jack Ryder of Victoria made 201 not out.

England at last regained the Ashes in 1926. After four draws in a rain-affected season, England began their second innings at the Oval 22 in arrears. On a sticky wicket on the third day Hobbs (100) and Sutcliffe (161) opened with a legendary stand of 172. England won the match by 289 runs.

The majestic Walter Hammond of Gloucestershire, who made his Test debut against South Africa in the previous winter, was the star of the 1928–29 series, even though Don Bradman made his debut in the first Test. Patsy Hendren scored 169 and

Larwood took eight wickets in the match as England won the first Test by 675 runs. They won the second at Sydney by eight wickets as England scored 636, the highest Test innings so far, with Hammond getting 251. Hammond made 200 in the next Test and 119 not out and 177 in the fourth, establishing a third-wicket partnership of 262 with Douglas Jardine which remains England's highest for the wicket against Australia. He ended the series with what is still an Ashes record for England of 905 runs (average 113.12). Bradman made two hundreds and averaged 66.85 but, even in competition with Bradman and Hammond, the 19-year-old New South Wales batsman Archie Jackson, making his debut in the fourth Test, played one of the great innings of the series in his first knock, 164. Sadly ill-health cut short his career.

BRADMAN AND BODYLINE

The 1930 series was the last for Hobbs, and the one in which Don Bradman established his reputation as the greatest batsman the world has seen. England won the first Test, despite Bradman's 131 in the second innings. The series was levelled at Lord's with Bradman getting 254 in a brilliant innings, until 1990 the highest Test score made at Lord's. With skipper W.M. Woodfull getting 155, Australia totalled 729 for 6 declared, the highest ever made at Lord's. The third and fourth Tests were drawn, but Bradman established a new Test record with an innings of 334 at Headingley, including 309 on the first day, still a Test record. Despite 161 and 54 from Sutcliffe, Australia won the match by an innings and the series at the Oval, with Bradman getting 232 and W.H. Ponsford 110. Bradman's 974 runs in the series (average 139.14) is still a Test record.

In order to combat the new superbatsman, Douglas Jardine, the England captain for the 1932–33 tour to Australia, employed a tactic which he called leg-theory and which the Australians called bodyline. It produced the most bitter tour of all, with the Australian Board calling the English

unsporting, questions being raised in parliament and much diplomatic activity aimed at preventing a secession of Australia from the Empire. The method involved packing the leg-side with fielders and bowling short, with Harold Larwood being the main weapon.

The controversy itself is explained in another chapter, but the tactic worked. In Bradman's absence through illness, England won the first Test at Sydney overwhelmingly despite Stan McCabe's defiant 187 not out. Sutcliffe, Hammond and the Nawab of Pataudi each scored centuries. The Nawab followed Ranjitsinhji and his nephew Duleepsinhji in being the third Indian prince to play for England and the third to score a century on his debut against Australia. Australia won the second Test at Melbourne, when Bradman scored his only century of the series, but England

won the three remaining matches.

The bodyline argument came to its head in the third Test at Adelaide when Aussie captain Woodfull and wicket-keeper Bill Oldfield were both badly injured. Larwood did most to win the series with 33 wickets at 19.51, but such was the bitterness that he became a scapegoat and did not play for England again.

The 1934 series belonged to Bradman again, as Australia won 2–1. Australia won the first Test, which was notable for A.G. Chipperfield of New South Wales being the first man to be out for 99 on his debut. England won by an innings at Lord's when, on a sticky wicket, Yorkshire's Hedley Verity took 14 wickets for 80 on one day – the most taken in a day in an Ashes Test. Verity's 15 for 104 remains the third-best analysis in Ashes matches. Bradman made 304 in the drawn

RUN-GETTER SUPREME *Don Bradman (right) with Stan McCabe in 1934.*

fourth Test at Headingley and with Bill Ponsford (181) added 388 for the fourth wicket, then the highest stand in Ashes matches, and still the record for the fourth wicket. Australia won the series at the Oval, where Bradman (244) and Ponsford (266) did even better, adding 451 for the second wicket.

When England returned to Australia for the first series after the bodyline controversy, in 1936–37, Bill Voce, Larwood's main ally on bodyline, returned to the side, having been left out for the 1934 series. Voce proved the most successful bowler of the series with 17 wickets in the first two Tests, both won overwhelmingly by England. In the second, Voce took three wickets in four balls (O'Brien, Bradman and McCabe, all for ducks) to have Australia 1 for 3, after Hammond had made 251 not out for England. However, Bradman turned the tide in the third Test with clever captaincy. On a Melbourne sticky wicket, after England declared at 76 for 9, 124 behind, Bradman sent in his tailenders while the wicket eased. He came in at number 7 with the score 97 for 5. He scored 270, and shared a stand of 346 with Jack Fingleton (136). This remains the highest sixth-wicket partnership in Test cricket. A second-innings 212 at Adelaide after England led on first innings and 169 in the last Test at Melbourne were Bradman's further contributions as Australia came back from two down to win 3–2.

Opening bat Charlie Barnett of Gloucestershire got the 1938 series off to a good start by reaching 98 not out at lunch in the first Test at Trent Bridge, completing his century to the first ball afterwards. Len Hutton and Denis Compton each got a century in their first Ashes innings, and Lancashire left-hander Eddie Paynter topped them all with 216 not out. Stan McCabe made 232 in reply. He scored 72 of the 77 added for the last wicket with Fleetwood-Smith. Australia followed on, but centuries from W.A. Brown and Bradman saved the match. Hammond scored 240 and Brown 206 not out (carrying his bat) in a drawn second Test.

The third Test, at Old Trafford, was abandoned with no play at all.

LARWOOD *Controversial fast bowler.*

Australia finally forced a result in the fourth at Headingley, thanks to the bowling of Bill O'Reilly, who took five wickets in each innings. With the series undecided, the fifth Test at the Oval was played to a finish and records tumbled. Len Hutton scored 364 in 13 hours 17 minutes, then the highest score in Tests and still the highest in Ashes matches. L.O.B. Fleetwood-Smith conceded the most runs in a Test innings – 298 (he got one wicket). With Bradman and Fingleton absent hurt, England won by an innings and 579 runs, still the biggest margin of victory in a Test match.

After the war, the two batting giants of the 1930s, Hammond and Bradman, led the two sides in the 1946–47 series but, as after the First World War, England took a long time to regain form, and Australia won 3–0. In the first Test Bradman received a "not-out" decision to a strong appeal for a catch by Jack Ikin at second slip and went on to score 187, adding 276 with Lindsay Hassett (128) for the third wicket. Australia won by an innings and 322 runs. More records fell in the second Test at Sydney when Bradman and Sidney Barnes each scored 234 and made a fifth-wicket partnership of 405, a record for all first-class cricket. The drawn Adelaide Test was remarkable for the first of only two instances (1990–91 was the second) of two batsmen getting centuries in each innings of a Test – Denis Compton and Arthur Morris.

The Australian side which toured England in 1948 was possibly the strongest ever. It went through the season unbeaten, for the first time ever, and won the Tests 4–0. The first Test was most noticeable for Denis Compton's highest innings against Australia of 184. He played an even better innings in the drawn Test at Old Trafford: hit on the head at 4, he retired at 33 for 2, resumed stitched up at 119 for 5 and was not out 145 when the innings ended. Australia won at Headingley after N.W.D. Yardley's declaration at 365 for 8 set Australia 404 to win in 344 minutes on the last day. Arthur Morris (182) and Don Bradman (173 not out) put on 301 for the second wicket in 217 minutes and Australia won at 404 for 3.

Bradman made his last appearance in Tests at the Oval. England were dismissed for 52 (Ray Lindwall 6 for 20) with Hutton batting throughout the innings for 30. Bradman was cheered all the way to the wicket, given three cheers by the players, and then bowled second ball by Eric Hollies for 0 – a mere four runs would have given him a Test match career average of 100. Morris made 196 and Australia won by an innings.

HUTTON HITS BACK

Freddie Brown and Lindsay Hassett were the new captains for the tour of Australia in 1950–51, in which the Aussies won the first four Tests and England at last won the final match. The luck tended to go Australia's way, particularly in the first Test at Melbourne. Trevor Bailey and Alec Bedser did well to bowl Australia out for 228 on a good pitch. On an unplayable sticky pitch 20 wickets then fell on the third day. England declared at 68 for 7, Australia declared at 32 for 7, and England were reduced to 30 for 6. On the last morning Hutton, who was held back to number 8, scored 62 not out of the last 92 runs, but England were 70 short. There were remarkable innings at Adelaide: Morris 206 for Australia out of 371, Hutton 156 not out, carrying his bat out of 272. At Melbourne England won by eight

wickets. Hutton was easily the outstanding batsman, his average of 88.83 being more than twice that of anybody else on either side.

The Ashes returned to England in 1953, by virtue of an eight-wicket win at the Oval after four closely fought draws. Since the previous series, Len Hutton had become the first professional to be chosen to lead England on a permanent basis. Perhaps the best match was at Lord's, where Hutton played one of his best innings, 145, to give England a narrow first-innings lead. But at the close on the fourth day, England had been reduced to 20 for 3, needing 343. Willie Watson, in his first Ashes match, and not out overnight, then played a masterly defensive innings of 109 in 346 minutes and, with the help of Trevor Bailey (71 in 257 minutes), saved the day, England being 282 for 7 at the close.

By 1954–55 England had some fast bowlers in Frank Tyson and Brian Statham to challenge the dominance that Lindwall and Miller had established over England. In the first Test, however, Hutton put Australia in, and Morris (153) and Harvey (162) allowed them to declare at 601 for 8, and to win by an innings. But in the Tests in Sydney and Melbourne, Tyson bowled brilliantly in the fourth innings to win matches after Australia had led on first innings, and England recorded a 3–1 series victory.

England, now captained by Peter May, again came from behind in 1956 to win the series 2–1. The Surrey spinners, Jim Laker and Tony Lock, helped win the Headingley Test by an innings with 18 wickets between them, then at Old Trafford Laker produced the Test bowling performance of all time in another innings win, with 9 for 37 in the first innings and 10 for 53 in the second. His 19 wickets in the match is a record for all first-class cricket, let alone Tests, the next highest being 17. Laker's 46 wickets (at 9.60) in the series is also an England-Australia record.

BOWLED OVER BY BENAUD

Australia, led by Richie Benaud, regained the Ashes in 1958–59 emphatically, 4–0, but the tour was marred by bitterness over the bowling styles of the Australian bowlers Ian Meckiff, Keith Slater, Gordon Rorke and Jim Burke. Meckiff, Slater and Burke were eventually called for "throwing", while Rorke's drag helped get the Laws changed.

Australia's retention of the Ashes in 1961 was more satisfactory. After Australia had won at Lord's and England at Headingley, the series was won by Benaud's inspired bowling at Old Trafford. England were set 256 to win, after Alan Davidson (77 not out) and Graham McKenzie (32) had added 98 for Australia's last wicket. At 150 for 1, with Ted Dexter a dazzling 76 in 84 minutes, England were coasting, but Benaud had Dexter caught behind, May bowled round his legs for a duck, and England subsided to a 54-run defeat, with Benaud completing a spell of 5 for 12 in 25 minutes.

In a series mostly dominated by batsmen the 1962–63 series was drawn 1–1. It was the last series for the Australian stalwarts Neil Harvey and Alan Davidson.

Australia won the only match to be decided in 1964. At Headingley, Peter Burge of Queensland scored 160, the last 122 coming out of 211 as he nursed Australia from 178 for 7 to 389, a lead of 121. At Old Trafford Australia's 656 for 8 declared (new captain Bobby Simpson 311, Bill Lawrey 106) was replied to with 611 (Ken Barrington 256, skipper Ted Dexter 174). The main interest at the Oval was Fred Trueman becoming the first bowler to claim 300 wickets in Tests.

M.J.K. Smith was England's new captain in 1965–66 as the sides drew 1–1. Doug Walters of New South Wales made his Test debut at Brisbane with 155. England won at Sydney when Bob Barber made 185 out of 303 in less than five hours on the first day. Australia won at Adelaide with Simpson (225) and Lawry (119) opening with a stand of 244. Ken Barrington played his last match at Adelaide by scoring 60 and 102, thus completing 10 consecutive innings there of over 50. In the fifth Test at Melbourne, Bob Cowper

BENAUD *Successful Aussie skipper.*

made 307 for Australia.

There was another 1–1 in 1968. Australia won the first Test with a good all-round performance, but rain saved them in the second after they were out for 78. England squared the series at the Oval with five minutes left. With Australia needing 352 to win and being 86 for 5 at lunch, a freak storm flooded the ground. Spectators helped in mopping up and play started at 4.45. England grabbed the last five wickets for 15 runs, mainly through Derek Underwood (7 for 50).

Six Tests were arranged for 1970–71, when the English tourists were led by Ray Illingworth. The third Test, due to be played at Melbourne, was abandoned without a ball bowled, and was rearranged. Greg Chappell made his debut at Perth and made 108 in a draw. England won at Sydney by 299 runs with John Snow of Sussex taking 7 for 20 as Australia were out for 116. At the rearranged Melbourne Test, England were set to score 271 in four hours to win but, with two batsmen injured, did not attempt the task, Boycott and John Edrich batting out time at 161 for no wicket. Dennis Lillee made his Test debut at Adelaide and took five wickets in his first innings. England won again at Sydney in the last Test, when Lawry was dropped and Ian Chappell became captain. In

Australia's first innings a bouncer from Snow hit Terry Jenner on the head and he was taken to hospital. When Snow went to field on the boundary a drunk grabbed his shirt, and beer cans were thrown. Illingworth led the players off the field. Australia led by 80 after the resumption but, set 223 to win, were bowled out for 160. England took the series 2–0.

The 1972 series was closely fought. After England won the first Test by 89 runs, Bob Massie made an astonishing debut at Lord's, taking eight wickets in each innings (8 for 84 and 8 for 53), and Australia levelled the series. England won the fourth Test at Headingley when freak weather conditions caused the outbreak of a fungus on the wicket, and Underwood took 10 wickets in the match. An eighth-wicket stand of 104 between Illingworth and Snow to put England ahead was crucial. However, Australia drew the series by winning the last Test at the Oval by five wickets. Ian Chappell (118) and Greg Chappell (113) provided the first instance of brothers each scoring centuries in the same innings of a Test.

"LILIAN THOMSON"

Australia won decisively in 1974–75 by 4–1, thanks mainly to "Lilian Thomson", otherwise Jeff Thomson and Dennis Lillee, the opening fast bowlers. They took 57 wickets between them in the

first five Tests, England winning the last when Thomson was unfit and Lillee bowled only six overs.

The first World Cup competition, held in England in 1975, meant only a four-match rubber that year. A win in the first Test at Edgbaston was enough to give Australia the series. At Headingley the match was abandoned as vandals, protesting against the conviction of a man they claimed was innocent, wrecked the pitch with oil and knives.

A one-off Centenary Test was played in March 1977 at Melbourne and coincidentally was won by Australia by the same margin as the first-ever Test – 45 runs. The heroes were Dennis Lillee, with 11 wickets, and Derek Randall, who in his first England-Australia Test scored 174 as England reached 417, the highest fourth-innings score between the countries.

THE PACKER SERIES

The Centenary Test was used to finalize plans for Kerry Packer's World Series Cricket in which Packer bought up Test players for his own series of matches. The 1977 Ashes series was therefore deprived of the England captain, a ringleader in the project. Mike Brearley took over; England won 3–0. In the third Test, Ian Botham made his debut, taking five first-innings wickets. Geoff Boycott also returned to Test cricket after a 30-match disagreement with the selectors. At Headingley he scored 191, becoming the first player to complete his hundredth hundred in a Test match.

By the time England toured Australia in 1978–79, the whole group of Packer players had been named and were not considered for the Tests. England easily won the series by 5–1. Allan Border made his debut in the third Test at Melbourne, but the discovery of the tour was fast bowler Rodney Hogg, who topped the averages and took 41 wickets, a record for an Ashes series in Australia.

England also toured the following season, when WSC had been disbanded. Australia won all three matches in a series dominated by bowlers.

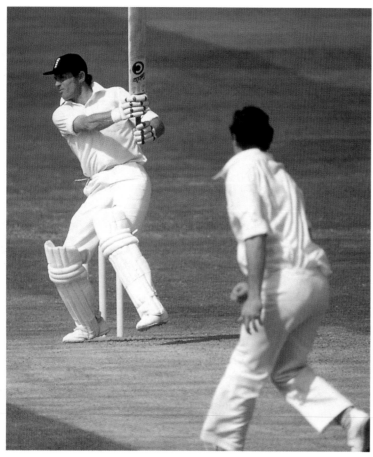

BOYCOTT *Batting at Headingley, 1977, where he scored his hundredth hundred.*

A second Centenary Test was played at Lord's in 1980, on the anniversary of the first Test played in England (though that was at the Oval). It was completely spoiled by rain and drawn.

The 1981 series was one of the most remarkable of all. Australia (with Kim Hughes as captain and Terry Alderman making his debut by taking nine wickets) won a low-scoring first Test by four wickets. At Lord's, where the match was drawn, England captain Ian Botham made a pair and was received back into the pavilion in complete silence. His 12 matches as captain had produced four draws and eight defeats. He was replaced at Headingley by Brearley, but remained in the team.

BOTHAM BOUNCES BACK

The third Test at Headingley saw a change in the fortunes of both England and Botham that came straight out of schoolboy fiction. Australia made 401 (Botham 6 for 49) and dismissed England for 174 (Botham 50). England followed on,

and when Botham arrived at the wicket were 105 for 5. Soon they were 135 for 7 – still 92 behind. Botham then proceeded to add 117 with Graham Dilley (56), 67 with Chris Old (29) and 37 with Bob Willis (2). He finished 149 not out. Botham's century came in 87 balls, 62 of the last 64 runs coming in boundaries. He scored 106 in the final session of the fourth day. It looked a magnificent but probably futile gesture, as Australia still needed a mere 130 runs to win. But Botham quickly got a wicket in Australia's second innings and so inspired Bob Willis that Willis grabbed eight wickets for 43 and at 111 all out Australia had been beaten by 18 runs. It was only the second time in 905 Tests that a team had won after following on.

Botham played a quiet role at Edgbaston until Australia, needing 151 to win, reached 105 for 4. He then took five wickets for one run in 28 balls and England had won by 29 runs. At Old Trafford he began his second innings at 104 for 5 and scored 118, reaching his century in

86 balls. England totalled 404, won by 103 and retained the Ashes. The sixth Test was drawn. Amid all this, Terry Alderman took 42 wickets, still the most in an Ashes series by an Australian.

Australia got back the Ashes 2–1 in 1982–83. England were weakened by the absence of players who had gone on a "rebel" tour to South Africa and been given a three-year ban. In a drawn match at Perth, some hooligans invaded the pitch and, in making a rugby tackle on one of them, Alderman dislocated his shoulder and took no further part in the series. Kepler Wessels, the first South African to play for Australia, scored 162 in the second Test to help Australia win by seven wickets. Australia won the third Test and England the fourth. This was very close, all four innings being between 284 and 294. Australia required 292, and were 218 when last man Jeff Thomson joined Allan Border. In a partnership of over two hours they refused 29 singles in order to manipulate the strike, but Thomson was out at 288 for 21, leaving Border 62 not out. The last wicket belonged to Botham who completed 1,000 runs and 100 wickets against Australia.

Allan Border and David Gower were the new captains for the 1985 series which, by winning the last two Tests by an innings, England took 3–1. England won the first Test, in which Tim Robinson made 175, and Australia the second, with Border getting 196. The next two Tests were draws. Rain at Edgbaston kept Australia, at 335 for 8 at the end of the second day, apparently safe from defeat, but England were inspired on the third day, grabbing the last two wickets and scoring 355 for 1 at the close. Gower (215) and Robinson (148) added 315 for the second wicket and England declared at 595 for 5. A controversial dismissal of Wayne Phillips on the last day sealed Australia's fate. He slashed, Allan Lamb jumped to avoid injury, the ball struck his foot in mid-air and was caught by Gower. He was given out by the square leg umpire. England won as clearly at the Oval, with Gooch getting 196 and Gower

157. With 732 runs (average 81.33) Gower was the most successful batsman, but Gatting with 527 (average 87.83) topped the averages. Allan Border also made more than 500 runs. Ellison, with 17 wickets at 10.88, topped the bowling but Botham had most wickets: 31.

England kept the Ashes in 1986–87 under the captaincy of Mike Gatting. They won the first and fourth Tests comfortably and Australia's victory in the last was academic. Chris Broad made centuries in three successive Tests and topped the batting averages at 69.57, but his 487 runs was topped by Australia's Dean Jones, who scored 511.

BROAD STUMPS UP

Australia celebrated the Bicentenary of British colonization in 1988 with a one-off Test match at Sydney. Chris Broad, out for 133, his fourth century in six Tests in Australia, smashed a stump out of the ground and was fined £500 by his manager. England forced Australia to follow on, but 184 not out by David Boon saved the game.

An under-rated Australian party in 1989 soon changed their opponents' estimation of them. At Headingley they made 601 for 7 declared to win by 210 runs. Australia then made it 2–0, winning by six wickets at Lord's. The next Test was spoiled by rain, but Steve Waugh, by scoring 43, took his total runs for the series to 393 before being out, a record in Ashes matches. A fourth Test win by nine wickets, Australia's 100th victory over England in 267 contests, sealed the Ashes for Australia. At Trent Bridge, Mark Taylor and Geoff Marsh batted throughout the first day, scoring 301 runs. Next day they took their stand to 329, beating the Hobbs and Rhodes stand of 323 in 1911–12. Australia won by an innings and 180. The sixth Test was drawn. For the first time in an Ashes series, three batsmen from one side topped 500 runs: Taylor, Dean Jones and Steve Waugh. Waugh topped the averages at 126.50, but Taylor's aggregate of 839 remains the third-highest in a Test series. By taking 41 wickets at 17.37, Terry Alderman became the first bowler to achieve the feat of taking 40 or more wickets in a Test series twice.

Graham Gooch was England captain in 1990–91. In a low-scoring game at Brisbane, which lasted only three days, England got a first-innings lead of 42 but set Australia only 157 to win – which Taylor and Marsh scored without loss. The story was repeated at Melbourne: an England first-innings lead of 46, a target of 197, an eight-wicket win for Australia. Bruce Reid took 13 wickets. The next two Tests were drawn, the most notable occurrence being the debut of Mark Waugh at Adelaide, making him and Steve the first twins to play Test cricket. Mark Waugh began his Test career with 138. Australia wrapped up the series 3–0 at Perth.

Allan Border captained Australia for the last time in Ashes matches on the tour of 1993. Shane Warne made an explosive entry into Ashes Tests by bowling Mike Gatting with a fizzing leg break on his first ball – the fifth bowler to take a wicket with his first ball in Ashes matches. Warne took eight wickets in the match and Australia won by 179 runs. Gooch, the England captain, was out "handled the ball" in the second innings for 133, having punched it away as it bounced up after a defensive shot.

At Lord's Australia declared at 632 for 4 and won by an innings and 62. Afer a draw at Trent Bridge, Australia repeated the old slaughter at Headingley, declaring at 653 for 4 (Border 200 not out, Steve Waugh 157 not out in an unbroken fifth-wicket stand of 332). Australia won by an innings and 148 runs, and Graham Gooch resigned the England captaincy. Mike Atherton took over for the last two Tests. Australia won by eight wickets at Edgbaston, but England at last managed a win at the Oval by 161 runs, their first against Australia in 19 Tests.

TAYLOR'S MEN DOMINATE

Mike Atherton took his first side to Australia in 1994–95, when Mark Taylor had assumed the Australian captaincy. Warne got the first hat-trick in Ashes Tests for 91 years as

Australia went two up. England had much the best of a drawn third Test and won the fourth Test comfortably by 106 runs. Looking to level the series in the last Test at Perth, they collapsed badly in the fourth innings to 27 for 6, were all out for 123 and lost by 329 runs.

Mark Taylor's side to England in 1997 won a six-Test series 3–2. At Edgbaston Australia were shot out for 118, and with Nasser Hussain (207) and Graham Thorpe (138) adding 288 for the fourth wicket, England declared and won by nine wickets. Rain had the last word at Lord's but Australia levelled the series at Old Trafford, winning by 268 runs. Steve Waugh made a century in each innings, the first to do so in Ashes Tests for 50 years, and Alec Stewart took eight catches (six in one innings), a record for an English keeper in Ashes Tests. Australia took the next two Tests comfortably, by an innings at Headingley and by 264 at Trent Bridge. With the Ashes lost, England won a low-scoring final Test at the Oval by 19 runs, dismissing Australia for 104 in the fourth innings. Phil Tufnell (eleven) and Caddick (eight) took all but one of the Australia wickets.

In 1998–99 Alec Stewart captained the England tourists to Australia. The first Test at Brisbane was drawn, with England hanging on, but Australia won the second Test at Perth in three days. Victory at Adelaide saw Australia retain the Ashes with two Tests remaining. England won an exciting fourth Test at Melbourne by 12 runs. In the final Test Darren Gough fought back and registered the only England hat-trick in Ashes Tests in the 20th century, and the match developed into an enthralling contest. England were dismissed for 220, and put out Australia for 184. Michael Slater played a remarkable innings of 123, thus making 66.8 per cent of the runs, the highest proportion since Charles Bannerman's 67.3 per cent in the very first Test match of all. Australia won eventually by 98 runs.

Steve Waugh captained Australia on the tour to England in 2001. At Edgbaston, Australia's numbers four, five and six each got a century:

STEVE WAUGH *At Lord's in 1989 during his run of 393 runs before being out.*

Steve Waugh 105, Damien Martyn 105 and Adam Gilchrist 152. Australia made 576, England could muster only 164 and lost by an innings. At Lord's where Australia won by eight wickets, Mark Waugh established a world record with his 158th Test catch. Australia retained the Ashes (thus holding them for the seventh successive series) at Trent Bridge, achieving a target of 158 for the loss of three wickets. Adam Gilchrist captained Australia at Headingley, Steve Waugh being injured, and set England 315 to win in 110 overs, of which 17.3 were immediately lost. On the last day, a magnificent innings of 173 not out by Mark Butcher steered England to a six-wicket victory. Steve Waugh returned for the final Test at the Oval and Australia won by an innings. Steve and Mark Waugh became the second brothers, after Ian and Greg Chappell, to each score a century in an Ashes Test.

England avoided a whitewash in their 2002–03 tour of Australia by winning the final Test. The scene was set at Brisbane, where crowds were the biggest for 70 years. Nasser Hussain put Steve Waugh's Aussies in and saw the score reach 339 before the second wicket fell. Australia won by 384 after bowling out England for a paltry 79 in the fourth innings.

The margin was an innings and 51 at Adelaide, where there were again

record crowds. Michael Vaughan scored 177 of England's 342 but Ricky Ponting got a second series ton. Another innings victory at Perth was followed by a five-wicket win at Melbourne, where Justin Langer scored 250 and Vaughan got a second hundred. At last England managed a victory at Sydney, by 225 runs, helped by 183 from Vaughan.

Vaughan's 633 runs (av. 63.30) was the outstanding batting performance of the tour, while three Aussies topped 400: Matthew Hayden (496, av. 62), Justin Langer (423, av. 52.87) and Ricky Ponting (417, av. 52.12). Jason Gillespie took 20 wickets at 24.60, as did Andy Caddick at 34.50, while Glenn McGrath had 19 wickets at 20.

FLINTOFF'S FEATS

The 2005 series in England was eagerly anticipated, as being between the world's strongest teams, with Australia the long-time champions. Nobody was disappointed, as the series developed into one of the best ever with four great last days. The first Test at Lord's was the exception, although it had its excitements as Australia won the toss, batted, and were dismissed for 190. But England made only 155, with McGrath, the Man of the Match, collecting his 500th Test wicket in a masterly display, taking 9 for 82 in the match. Australia eventually won by a full 139 runs.

McGrath was injured warming up for the second Test at Edgbaston, despite which Aussie skipper Ponting put England in. They raced to 407 in fewer than 89 overs on the first day, enough to earn a first innings lead of 99. Warne's six for 46 struck back in the second knock, and only a swash-buckling 73 from Flintoff, including his last-wicket stand of 51 with Simon Jones, got the score to 182. In his two innings Flintoff scored 68 and 73 from 148 balls and hit nine sixes, easily a record for Ashes Tests. Australia were set 282 runs to win, but lost seven wickets for 137. England claimed the extra half-hour on the fourth evening but could dismiss only Clarke just before the end, at 185. Although there were only two tail-enders to get out on the last morning, a large crowd came to watch. Warne and Lee took the score to 220, then last pair Lee and Kasprowicz edged towards victory, adding 59 as the tension became unbearable before Kasprowicz was caught behind off Harmison, with Australia two short of England's total. It was the narrowest winning margin in Ashes Tests. Flintoff took seven wickets altogether and was an outstanding Man of the Match.

McGrath returned at Old Trafford, but was ineffective in the first innings, where Vaughan, having won the toss and batted, made 166, the first century of the series. England made 444, during which Warne became the first man to take 600 Test wickets. He also scored 90 of Australia's reply of 302. Andrew Strauss scored 106 in England's second knock, but rain on the third day which cost 76 overs crucially delayed a declaration. At 280 for 6, England set Australia 413 to win. Man of the Match Ponting resisted for 275 minutes and 156 runs, but was out with four overs left. The last wicket pair of McGrath and Lee held out and Australia ended on 371 for nine.

With the series still level, England won the toss at Headingley, and the match was evenly poised at 241 for 5 on the second morning when Geraint Jones joined Flintoff. In the next 39 overs they added 177, Flintoff going on to 102 and Jones to 85. England made 477 and rushed Australia out for 218, Simon Jones getting 5 for 44. The follow-on was enforced. However, Jones bowled only four overs in the second innings before departing the series with an injured ankle. The substitute fielder, Gary Pratt, made a controversial contribution, sparking an outburst of temper from Ponting, by brilliantly running out the Aussie skipper for 48, making the score 155 for 3. The Aussies dug in and ground their way to a total of 387, leaving England only 129 to get to win. Yet Warne nearly had the final word, getting three quick wickets to reduce England from 32 without loss to 57 for 4. An almost identical situation was remembered from 1981 when Australia were set 130 to win after enforcing the follow-on, and were reduced to 58 for 4. They famously went on to lose but in 2005 Flintoff and Kevin Pietersen steadied the innings with a stand of 46. There was more excitement to come. At 116 for 7 it was still not settled, especially with Simon Jones injured, but Giles and Hoggard got the 13 needed to win.

England, needing to draw at the Oval to regain the Ashes, won the toss and began well, with Strauss going on to make 129, but with Warne grabbing four quick wickets, it needed Flintoff to join him and add 143 for the fifth wicket. He scored 72, the tail wagged, and England reached 373. With Langer (105) and Hayden (138) producing an opening stand of 185, and Ponting helping Hayden to get the score to 264 for one, England's total hardly seemed enough. Then Flintoff stepped in again, getting Ponting and Hayden, and when Hoggard helped him polish off the tail, the last five wickets falling for 11, England surprisingly had a lead of six. Flintoff finished with 5 for 78, bowling unchanged for almost three hours. It was still not over, and with Warne and McGrath striking regularly on the last day to get England at 126 for 5, the odds swung towards an Australia victory. Even at 199 for 7 the game wasn't safe, but Giles (59) joined Pietersen (158) and sometime during their

KEVIN PIETERSEN *His 158 at the Oval ensured the Ashes returned to England.*

stand of 109 the Ashes were won. England eventually totalled 335, with Warne getting 12 wickets in the match, and the Aussie openers went off for bad light after four deliveries. Pietersen's remarkable innings, which included seven sixes, made him Man of the Match.

There were two giants, one on each side, and they were made joint Players of the Series: Andrew Flintoff and Shane Warne. Flintoff made 402 runs (av. 40.20) at the fastest rate of anybody in the series, and was top England wicket-taker with 24 wickets at 27.29. Warne, who near the end of his career could also call himself an all-rounder, took 40 wickets (second best in a five-Test Ashes series to Laker) at 19.92, and scored 249 runs (av. 27.66).

TEST RESULTS

ENGLAND v AUSTRALIA

	Matches	Eng	Aus	Draw	Series	Eng	Aus	Draw
In Australia	160	54	80	26	37	12	20	5
In England	151	43	46	62	35	16	15	4
Totals	311	97	126	88	72	28	35	9

ENGLAND v SOUTH AFRICA

The third country to play Test matches was South Africa. The first touring party from England came in 1889 led by Major R. Gardner Watson. After playing sides of 15, 18 and 22 players, they played two matches against 11 South Africans. These two matches have become recognized as the first two Tests in South African cricket. England were overwhelmingly superior and remained so for some years. England won the matches, at Port Elizabeth and Cape Town, by eight wickets and an innings and 202 runs.

A strong touring side played one Test in South Africa in 1891–92 and won by an innings and 189. It included Australian Test players J.J. Ferris and W.L. Murdoch, who made their debuts for England. Similarly Frank Hearne of Kent, who had played twice for England against South Africa in 1888–89, made his debut for South Africa, having settled there. His brothers, Alec and George Gibbons, were in the England side, the second occasion on which three brothers had appeared in the same Test. Harry Wood, the Surrey wicket-keeper, scored 134 not out, the first instance of a wicket-keeper making a Test century.

Lord Hawke, the power behind Yorkshire for many years, took sides to South Africa in 1895–96 and 1898–99 which won all their Tests. In the second innings of the first Test in 1895–86, South Africa were dismissed for a record low score of 30. In the second tour, when England introduced nine new Test players, South Africa actually took a first-innings lead of 106 at Johannesburg but lost by 32 after Pelham Warner carried his bat for 132 not out, the first player to carry his bat on his Test debut. James Sinclair of Transvaal was run out for 86 in this match, South Africa's first 50, and in the second scored his country's first century. He also took 6 for 26 in England's first-innings 92, almost single-handedly giving South Africa a lead of 85, but South Africa were out for 35 in their second knock.

It was not till 1905–06 that the next party went to South Africa, led by Pelham Warner. In the first Test, at Johannesburg, South Africa were 93 behind on first innings and set 284 to win. They got to 239 for 9, when captain Percy Sherwell joined A.W. "Dave" Nourse, and the two put on a winning 48. They then won the second Test by nine wickets and the third by 243 runs. C.M.H. Hathorn and G.C. White made centuries, and in South Africa's first innings, 385, every player made double figures. England won the fourth Test, but South Africa took the last.

FIRST OVERSEAS TESTS

South Africa played their first Tests overseas in 1907, when the team that had beaten England in the winter played three Tests in England. The weather interrupted all three, the only result coming in a low-scoring match at Headingley, where England won by 53 runs.

Jack Hobbs went to South Africa in 1909–10 and topped the batting averages with 67.37, but South Africa won an exciting series 3–2. While Colin Blythe topped the bowling averages, it was Bert Vogler and Aubrey Faulkner who won the series, with 36 and 29 wickets respectively. In this series, England played George Simpson-Hayward of Worcestershire, the last of the great under-arm bowlers.

South Africa played in the rain-sodden triangular series in England in 1912, but lost all three games to England – largely because of Sydney Barnes, who took 34 wickets.

Barnes was also their tormenter in 1913–14. England sent their strongest tourists so far, with Hobbs, Wilfred Rhodes, C.P. Mead and Frank Woolley also in the party. England won 4–0. Barnes set a record for all Tests, which still stands, by taking 49 wickets in the series, and he played in only the first four Tests. His best haul was 9 for 103 in the second innings of the second Test at Johannesburg. He took 17 for 159 in this Test, a record which has been passed only once since, by Jim Laker in 1956.

It was not until after the First World War that another side went to South Africa, and Taylor made 176 in the first Test of 1922–23 to give South Africa a win. England won the second Test by one wicket, and then won the rubber in the final Test at Durban, when C.A.G. "Jack" Russell of Essex made 140 and 111, the second player and first Englishman to make a century in each innings of a Test.

The South African tourists in 1924 faced Hobbs and Herbert Sutcliffe, who made his Test debut in the first Test at Edgbaston. They put on 136 in their first opening stand, the first of their 15 Test century stands, but it was England's bowlers who caused the sensations. Maurice Tate, another debutant, took a wicket with his first ball in Tests and finished with 4 for 12, but partner A.E.R. Gilligan, the captain, had 6 for 7. Eleven extras helped South Africa to 30, equalling their record lowest score. It remains the second-lowest score in all Tests. Hobbs (211) and Sutcliffe (122) opened with a stand of 268 in the second Test at Lord's. England at 531 for 2 declared, lost only two wickets in winning by an innings, a Test record. By winning at Old Trafford, England won the series 3–0.

Walter Hammond made his Test debut in South Africa in 1927–28, an exciting series in which England won the first two matches, the third was drawn and South Africa won the last two. England won the only two Tests to be decided in 1929. It was a series in which English batsmen made 10 centuries, four to Herbert Sutcliffe.

The 1930s were better for South Africa. They won 1–0 in 1930–31 by winning the first Test by 28 runs and drawing the rest. The fourth Test was the last played in South Africa on matting wickets. In 1935, under Herbie Wade, they won their first Test in England and with it the series. In the Lord's Test Bruce Mitchell made 164 and X.C. Balaskas took nine wickets. South Africa drew the other games.

"TIMELESS TEST"

The 1938–39 series in South Africa featured the famous "timeless Test"

SHARP BOWLER *Bert Vogler.*

at Durban. England had taken a 1–0 lead in a batsman-dominated series, so the last Test, as it could decide the rubber, was played to a finish.

South Africa made 530, with P.G.V. van der Bijl and Dudley Nourse scoring centuries, and England 316. Then, with Melville getting 103, South Africa made 481, setting England 696 to win. Paul Gibb (120) and Bill Edrich (219) put on 280 for the second wicket, Hammond (140) and Edrich 89 for the third, and Hammond and Paynter (75) 164 for the fourth. Finally, at tea on the 10th day, with England still 42 short at 654 for 5, rain caused the match to be abandoned, as England had to leave on a two-day rail journey to catch their ship at Cape Town. It is the longest first-class match, and the 1,981 runs scored was a record, since beaten twice in India.

COMPTON RUNS AND RUNS

In the first series after the war, there was a run-feast for Compton, Edrich, Nourse, Melville and Mitchell. It was Compton's record-breaking season,

LEN HUTTON *Hits high to leg against South Africa at the Oval in 1947.*

decided at the Oval when England won by 92 runs. Peter May, the captain and top run-scorer in the series, made 89 not out in England's second innings.

In 1956–57 South Africa tied the rubber by winning the last two Tests after England had won the first two with the third a draw. South Africa collapsed in their second innings in the first two Tests, being out for 72 each time. In the second, at Cape Town, Russell Endean prevented a ball rebounding on to his stumps with his hand, and became the first player to be given out "handled the ball" in Tests. In the drawn match, Tayfield delivered a record 137 balls without conceding a run in the first innings, and took 8 for 69 in the second. In the fourth Test, which South Africa won by 17 runs, he took 9 for 113 in the second innings, a record for South Africa, and 13 wickets in the match. Tayfield was easily the best bowler of the series with 37 wickets, the most by a South African in a Test series. England won easily in 1960, where the most noteworthy incidents concerned Geoff Griffin at Lord's, in his second Test. After becoming the first South African to get a Test hat-trick, he was no-balled 11 times for throwing. It was the end of his Test career.

APARTHEID AND AFTER

England won the series 1–0 in 1964–65 by winning the first Test by an innings and then securing four draws. In a three-match series in 1965, however, South Africa won 1–0 by taking the second Test at Trent Bridge, thanks to 125 from Graeme Pollock and five wickets in each innings from brother Peter. Series planned for South Africa in 1968–69 and England in 1970 were cancelled because of apartheid and the D'Oliveira affair, which is dealt with elsewhere in this book. Unfortunately for South Africa, they were building at that time their strongest-ever side.

Cricket relations resumed in 1994 when South Africa toured England and played a three-match series. Kepler Wessels captained South Africa, having previously played for Australia. After making a century on his debut for Australia against

England in 1982–83, he made another on his debut for South Africa at Lord's. South Africa won convincingly by 356 runs. Following a high-scoring draw at Headingley, South Africa appeared in command at the Oval until England's last man, Devon Malcolm, was hit on the helmet by a bouncer on the morning of the third day. Vowing vengeance, he then took 9 for 57 in four hours to skittle South Africa for 172, leaving England to get 205 for 2 and an eight-wicket win. Malcolm's analysis was the sixth-best in Tests in all time.

England returned to South Africa in 1996–97 after 32 years. After a rain-spoiled first Test, England saved the second, at Johannesburg, when captain Mike Atherton (185 not out) and wicket-keeper Jack Russell (29 not out) batted for more than four-and-a-half hours. Atherton's innings lasted 643 minutes. Russell took 11 catches in the match, a record number of dismissals for all Test cricket. After two more draws, South Africa won the last Test and the series at Cape Town by 10 wickets.

South Africa visited England in 1998 captained by Hansie Cronje. After a rain-spoilt first Test, South Africa had 15 to knock off for a 10-wicket win at Lord's. They were unlucky not to win the third Test at Old Trafford. Gary Kirsten made 210 (at 650 minutes it was South Africa's longest Test innings) and Jacques Kallis 132 in an innings of 552 for five declared. England followed on and on the last day Robert Croft batted for three hours (37 not out) to save the match. The scores finished level with England ending on 369 for nine. England levelled the series at Trent Bridge. Cronje's 126 helped South Africa to 374, a lead of 38. But good bowling by Angus Fraser, who took five wickets in each innings (10 for 122 in all), restricted South Africa's second knock to 208, and England's target to 247. With Atherton (98 not out) the anchor, the match was won for the loss of only two wickets. It was all to play for at the Oval. South Africa got a first innings lead of 22 and after England made 240, their target was 219 to win. They were all out for 195, with Darren Gough taking six for 42, so England won the series 2–1. Atherton (493), Stewart (465) and Cronje (401) made most

when he scored more runs and centuries than anybody before or since. Compton made 753 in the Tests, at an average of 94.12, but Edrich had a higher average, 110.40, with 552 runs. Edrich proved his worth by topping the bowling averages, too, with 16 wickets at 23.12. Melville (189 and 104 not out) made a century in each innings in the first Test, and Mitchell (120 and 189 not out) did it in the fifth. Compton (208) and Edrich (189) added 370 for the third wicket at Lord's. Melville's 117 at Lord's was his fourth century in successive Test innings, dating back to before the war, all against England. South Africa drew the first and last Tests, but England won 3–0.

England continued to have the better of the exchanges. They won 2–0 in 1948–49. On the first day of Test cricket at Ellis Park, Johannesburg, Hutton (158) and Cyril Washbrook (195) put on 359 for the first wicket, then a record for

all Tests. England won 3–1 in 1951, when captain Dudley Nourse made 208 at Trent Bridge, batting in great pain from a fractured thumb. Eric Rowan made 236 at Headingley, which helped him top the batting averages. Peter May made a century here on his Test debut. Alec Bedser's 30 wickets really decided the series. The most remarkable incident occurred at the Oval, when Len Hutton, having played a ball from Athol Rowan into the air, played it again as it was about to land on the stumps. However, Russell Endean was moving to catch it, and Hutton became the only batsman in Test cricket to be given out "obstructing the field". In 1955 all five Tests produced a result, the first time this had happened in England. England won the first two Tests and South Africa the third and fourth. Alec Bedser's Test career ended at Old Trafford with a then world-record 236 wickets. An exciting series was

BEDSER *Last wicket v South Africa.*

The match ended on his dismissal at 572 for seven. South Africa took a winning 2–0 lead in the series at Cape Town, recording their biggest win against England – an innings and 37 runs. England won the final Test at Pretoria in unique circumstances. South Africa made 155 for six on a damp first day, then three days were washed out. On the last day Hansie Cronje declared by arrangement with Nasser Hussain at 248 for eight. England declared at nought for nought, and South Africa forfeited their second innings, in effect setting England a target to win of 249 in a possible 76 overs. It was a generous declaration, and England got there at 251 for eight. In the series Klusener, Kirsten, Cullinan, Hussain and Stewart did best with the bat, Donald and Pollock with the ball.

An exciting series in England in 2003 ended 2–2. The first Test was drawn, at the end of which Hussain resigned as England captain, to be replaced by Michael Vaughan. South Africa's new captain, 22-year-old Graeme Smith, was the star of the series, beginning with innings of 277, 85 and 259. In all he made 713 runs, average 79.33. Marcus Trescothick, with 219 and 69 not out at the Oval, did most to help England level the series. Gary Kirsten, Herschelle Gibbs, Andrew Flintoff and Mark Butcher joined Trescothick and Smith with over 400 runs in the series. Smith's 277 was the highest by a South African captain and by a South African in a Test in England, his stand of 338 with Gibbs (179) on the first day at Edgbaston was the biggest opening partnership against England.

STRAUSS WALTZ

Vaughan captained England to South Africa in 2004–05. In the first Test at Port Elizabeth, South Africa lost captain Graeme Smith without a run on the board, but totalled 337. England got a lead of 88 and then bowled out South Africa for 229 and won by seven wickets, thanks to Andrew Strauss, who added 94 not out to a first-innings 126. It was England's eighth successive Test win, a national record. Rain prevented this being improved in the second Test at Durban. Although South Africa, with Kallis scoring 162, led by 193 on first innings, England made 570 for 7 declared, with Trescothick, Strauss and Thorpe getting hundreds, and South Africa were 290 for 8 when the rain came. England's 13-match unbeaten run then ended at Cape Town. Another Kallis century and an England first-innings collapse meant a 196-run South African wicn.

England's 411 for 8 declared (Strauss 147) at Johannesburg was surpassed by South Africa's 419 (Gibbs 161). Trescothick (180) then helped England to 332 for 9 declared and Matthew Hoggard's 7 for 61 removed South Africa for 247 and a 77-run win for England. This was enough to win the series 2–1 as the fifth Test at Centurion was drawn. Strauss was Player of the Series with 656 runs at 77.88, while Kallis scored 625, average 60.44. Flintoff, Hoggard, Pollock and Makhaya Ntini all claimed more than 20 wickets.

TEST RESULTS

ENGLAND v SOUTH AFRICA

	Matches	Eng	SA	Draw	Series	Eng	SA	Draw
In South Africa	73	28	17	28	17	10	5	2
In England	52	26	9	22	13	9	2	2
Totals	130	54	26	50	30	19	7	4

runs, and Allan Donald (33 wickets at 19.79) and Fraser (24 at 20.50) were the most successful bowlers.

Nassar Hussain led England to South Africa in 1999–2000. The first Test at Johannesburg started sensationally on a damp pitch in poor light, England being reduced to two runs for four wickets, three to Allan Donald. They never recovered, and South Africa won by nine wickets. At Port Elizabeth Lance Klusener came in at number seven and smashed 174 as South Africa made 450. England replied with 360 (Atherton 108), so. South Africa's 224 for four set a target of 315. They batted out time at 153 for six. Bad light stopped play very early on Durban's first three days. England declared at the end of the second on 366 for nine (Hussain 146 not out), and shot out South Africa for 156 (Andy Caddick 7–46). Gary Kirsten then batted for over 14-and-a-half hours, the second longest in Test history, to reach 275.

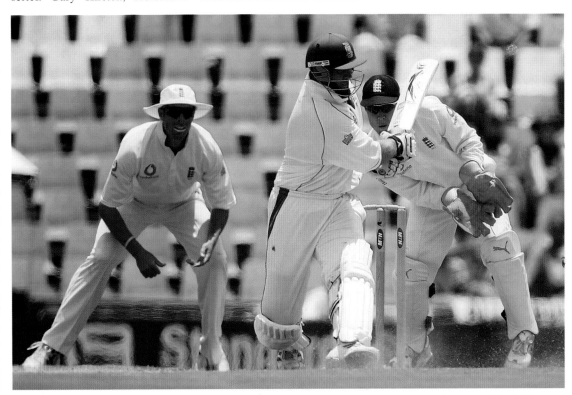

MORE RUNS *Jacques Kallis was South Africa's leading run-maker in the home 2004–05 series defeat against England.*

AUSTRALIA v SOUTH AFRICA

In 1902 the Australian party which won the Ashes in England played three Tests in South Africa on their way home. In the first they managed to save the game after following on, but they won the last two, despite Test South Africa's J.H. Sinclair scoring 100 in 80 minutes in the last Test, the fourth-fastest in Tests and still the fastest for South Africa.

The South Africans visited Australia in 1910–11 and lost 4–1. Although Trumper topped the batting averages, Aubrey Faulkner scored most runs – 732, a South African record for a series. South Africa failed to beat Australia in a Test after this until 1952–53, 25 Tests later. At Johannesburg in 1921–22, Jack Gregory scored a century in 70 minutes for Australia, still the fastest in Tests. In the two series in the 1930s, Australia won nine Tests and one was drawn. Bradman dominated the batting in Australia in 1931–32, making 806 runs and averaging 201.50. At Adelaide he made 299 not out, running out the number 11 batsman when going for a quick single at the end of an over.

It was 4–0 again for the Australians after the war when matches resumed in South Africa in 1949–50.

South Africa sent a young side under Jack Cheetham to Australia in 1952–53 with low expectations. After Robert Harvey had made his fifth century in successive matches to help win the first Test, South Africa won their second match ever against Australia at Melbourne, thanks largely to 162 not out from Endean and 13 for 165 by Tayfield, still the best analysis by a South African in Tests. South Africa then drew the series in the last Test at Melbourne. Australia, with Harvey making 205, totalled 520. South Africa made 435 and needed 295 in the fourth innings, and won by six wickets. Harvey made 834 runs in the series to average 92.66, the fourth-highest aggregate ever. Tayfield took 30 wickets.

Australia won 3–0 in South Africa in 1957–58, under Ian Craig, who in the fifth Test in 1952–53 had become Australia's youngest Test player at 17 years 239 days (a record he still holds), and now became the youngest Test captain of all (since superseded) in 1957–58 when he took a side to South Africa. Australia easily won 3–0. South Africa then narrowly failed to win the series in Australia in 1963–64, under Trevor Goddard. Australia won the first Test. Pollock made 122 at Sydney and, while still not 20 years old, 175 at Adelaide. He and Eddie Barlow (201) added 341 for South Africa's third wicket, a record for any wicket for South Africa and for the Australia-South Africa series. This levelled the series and the last Test was drawn.

CHRISTMAS PRESENT

There were to be no more close shaves. In 1966–67 in South Africa the home team won 3–1 for their first series win over Australia. Nobody would have guessed this outcome on the second day of the series, Christmas Eve, when Australia passed South Africa's total of 199 with only one wicket down. But South Africa made 620 in the second innings (Lindsay 182) and won by 233 runs, their first victory over Australia at home. Lindsay's six catches in Australia's first innings was at the time a Test record. After Australia won the second Test. South Africa won the third and the fifth for their historic win.

Even this performance was nothing to 1969–70 when South Africa won all four of the Tests played. Barry Richards made his debut in the first Test, and scored 140 in the second at Durban, where Graeme Pollock made 274, the highest score for South Africa in Tests. South Africa's 622 for 9 declared remains their highest. South Africa won by an innings and 129, and won the last two Tests by over 300 runs. Lindsay conceded no byes in any Test. Pollock and Richards topped the batting, It was Richards' only Test series before

South Africa were ejected from the Test arena. His average for Tests is therefore 72.57. Pollock ended his Test career with 2,256 runs.

The contests between the countries were revived in 1993–94 and three matches played in each country, the results being 1–1 with one draw each time. Australia came from behind in both series. In the last, Allan Border made his final Test appearance with a record number of appearances (156) and runs (11,174).

Australia won the next series in 1996-97 by 2–1 in South Africa. An innings and 96 runs separated the sides in the first Test. The second Test was much closer, with Australia winning by two wickets with Shaun Pollock unable to bowl after only six overs at the start of the match, when he bagged both openers for only six runs. As small consolation South Africa took the last Test by two wickets. Steve Waugh was the outstanding player of the series with 313 runs, average 78.25.

The teams met again in Australia in 1997–98, when Australia won 1–0. The first Test was drawn. Australia decisively won the second, and South Africa had the better of the draw in the third. Mark Taylor carried his bat in Australia's first innings for 169 not out from a total of 350. The series top scorers on each side made 279, Mark Waugh (average 69.75) and Gary Kirsten (55.80). Shane Warne took 20 wickets at 20.85.

The series in Australia in 2001-02 was billed as a world championship. Australia won by a knock-out, taking all three Tests by big margins: 246 runs, 9 wickets and 10 wickets. Matthew Hayden made a century in each match, aggregate

GREAT BATSMAN *Graeme Pollock.*

430 (av. 107.5). His first four innings took his Test aggregate for the year (2001) to 1,391, bettered only by Viv Richards in 1976 and Sunny Gavaskar in 1979.

A disappointed South Africa promised revenge at home some two months later, but Australia made 652 for 7 declared at Johannesburg and won by an innings and 360. South Africa fought back from 92 for 6 at Cape Town to lose eventually by only four wickets and beat Australia by five wickets in the final Test at Durban. Australia's Adam Gilchrist made 473 runs (av. 157.6) and claimed 15 victims behind the stumps. His 204 not out in the first Test was the fastest Test double century (212 balls) – but only for a little over two weeks.

		AUSTRALIA v SOUTH AFRICA							
		Matches	Aus	SA	Draw	Series	Aus	SA	Draw
T E S T R E S U L T S	In South Africa	39	20	10	9	10	7	2	1
	In Australia	29	17	5	7	7	4	0	3
	In England	3	2	0	1	1	1	0	0
	Totals	71	39	15	17	18	12	2	4

ENGLAND v WEST INDIES

An all-amateur English side toured the West Indies in 1894–95, and tours were made regularly after this from 1910. The first West Indian party toured England in 1900. It was during the fourth tour to England in 1928 that three Tests were played in the 41-match programme. England won all three by an innings. In 1929–30, however, the series was shared 1–1 with two draws. The England team was not the best, as England were also touring New Zealand. George Gunn, aged 50, was recalled after a record gap of 17 years, 316 days. The West Indians' J.E.D. Sealy, still their youngest Test player at 17 years, 122 days, had not been born when Gunn had played his previous Test. Clifford Roach made the West Indies' first Test century in the first Test, and George Headley, aged 20, on his debut, made 176 in the second innings. After England won the second Test (Patsy Hendren 205 not out), the West

Indies achieved their first Test victory in the third with Roach getting 209 and Headley a century in each innings. The fourth Test, at Kingston, Jamaica, was drawn.

In 1933 in England, West Indies fast bowlers Learie Constantine and Manny Martindale bowled bodyline at Old Trafford, but Jardine scored a century. England won 2–0.

There was an extraordinary match at Bridgetown in the first Test of 1934–35. The West Indies made 102 on a sticky wicket which grew more spiteful. R.E.S. Wyatt, the England captain, declared at 81 for 7. The West Indian captain, George Grant, reversed his batting order hoping the pitch might improve. But when Headley was dismissed for a duck at 51 for 6, he declared, giving England a day and a bit to get 73 to win! They were 29 for 4 and 48 for 6, but won by four wickets. Nevertheless the West Indies won the second and fourth Tests to win 2–1. Headley, who scored 270 in the latter Test, averaged 97.00.

In the last Test series before the war in 1939, England won at Lord's and drew the other two Tests. Headley scored a century in each innings at Lord's. After two draws, on resumption in 1947–48, the West Indies won the last two Tests.

GEORGE HEADLEY *The first outstanding West Indian batsman.*

CALYPSO CLASSIC

West Indian cricket really came of age in 1950, under the captaincy of John Goddard, and based on the batting of Frank Worrell, Everton Weekes and Clyde Walcott and two debutant slow bowlers, Alf Valentine and Sonny Ramadhin. Valentine must have wondered what it was all about as he took the first eight wickets to fall in his first Test at Old Trafford. He had taken only two wickets in first-class cricket before coming to England. Nevertheless, England won. It all turned round at Lord's in the second Test when Ramadhin took 11 wickets to add to Valentine's seven and the West Indies won by 322. Walcott got 168 not out, but the West Indian steel bands were telling everybody that it was "at Lord's where they done it … with those little pals of mine, Ramadhin and Valentine". The West Indies slaughtered England both at Trent Bridge and the Oval, and won the series 3–1.

Strangely, the West Indies did not win another series against England for 13 years. In 1953–54 the MCC

GREAT CAPTAIN *Frank Worrell.*

sent a strong team led by Len Hutton to the West Indies, but the West Indies won the first two Tests. England won at Georgetown, and there was a high-scoring draw at Trinidad. England squared the series by winning in Jamaica, on Gary Sobers' debut.

English batsmen finally found a way to play Ramadhin in the first Test of 1957 at Edgbaston. After being shot out for 186 (Ramadhin 7 for 49), and trailing by 288, they had reached 113 for 3. Peter May (285) and Colin Cowdrey (154) then added 411, still a record for the fourth wicket in all Test cricket. England won the series 3–0, with Peter Loader getting a hat-trick at Headingley.

England also won 1–0 in 1959–60, by virtue of winning the second Test in Trinidad.

WISDEN TROPHY

The Wisden Trophy was a new prize on offer in 1963. The West Indies won it 3–1.

Sobers was the captain defending the Trophy in 1966, and he did much to make sure the West Indies kept it 3–1 by scoring 722 runs, average 103.14, and taking 20 wickets and 10 catches.. At Lord's. he added 274 with his cousin David Holford for the sixth-wicket.

England, under Cowdrey, won the series 1–0 in 1967–68, thanks to a generous declaration by Sobers in the fourth Test which enabled them to win with three minutes to spare. In the last Test, England, chasing 308 to win, scraped a draw at 206 for 9. Sobers was again the best batsman, averaging 90.83, and John Snow took 27 wickets in four Tests. In 1969, England easily won a three-match series 2–0, but lost the Wisden Trophy in 1973 when the West Indies won 2–0. In this series, there was a bomb alert at Lord's which cost 89 minutes but allowed many of the public to tread the sacred turf.

A five-Test series in 1973–74 saw the West Indies win the first and England the last. Outstanding individual performances came in the second Test from Dennis Amiss, who saved the game with 262 not out in a total of 432 for 9, in the third from Lawrence Rowe, who made 302, and in the fifth from Tony Greig, who took 13 wickets in England's win. On the second day of the first Test, Greig ran out Kallicharran as the batsman was leaving the ground at close of play. Umpire Sang Hue had give him out, but an off-the-field conference between administrators, umpire and captains led to his reinstatement.

The West Indies, under Clive Lloyd, were beginning their long mastery of all countries in 1976, when they won the series 3–0. Vivian Richards scored 232 in his first innings against England. Gordon Greenidge made a century in each innings at Old Trafford and Richards made 291 at the Oval, bringing his total of runs in the calendar year to 1,710, still the world's record. Dennis Amiss's 203 was unable to affect the result. Richards made 829 runs in the series at an average of 118.42.

Richards topped the averages in 1980 and 1980–81 as well. The West Indies beat England, led by Ian Botham for the first time, 1–0 in 1980, by virtue of winning the first Test. Rain cut short the other games. The West Indies won 2–0 in 1980–81. England's manager, Ken Barrington, died of a heart attack during the third Test. It was a sad tour all round.

BLACKWASHED

In 1984 and 1985–86 the West Indies won all 10 Tests in what were called "blackwashes". All the margins were big. In both series it was the West Indian fast bowlers Malcolm Marshall and Joel Garner who did most damage to England. In 1984, in the second Test at Lord's, England got a first-innings lead, and David Gower was able to declare on the last morning and set the West Indies 342 to win. Greenidge made 214 not out and the West Indies won by nine wickets. Greenidge made another double-century at Old Trafford. In the 1985–86 series, 94 of the 98 England wickets to fall were taken by fast bowlers. Viv Richards made 110 not out in the fifth Test, his century coming in 56 balls, still the fastest hundred in terms of balls received in Test cricket.

England's run of defeats ended in the first rain-interrupted Test of 1988, but normal service was soon resumed and the West Indies won the next four in a rainy summer, in which only three centuries were made. For one reason or another, England had four captains in this series: Mike Gatting, John Emburey (two), Chris Cowdrey and Graham Gooch. Marshall, with 35 wickets, was the star.

England under Gooch unluckily lost 2–1 in 1989–90. England won the first Test by nine wickets, the second was washed out with no play at all, and in the third, chasing only 150, they were forced to come off at 120 for 5 because of bad light after Gooch's hand had been broken, amid suggestions of a West Indies' "go-slow" until it was too dark to continue. The West Indies levelled at Barbados, with Curtley Ambrose getting 8 for 45 in the second innings, and won the series at Antigua, where Greenidge and Haynes set a first-wicket partnership record for the West Indies with 298.

The 1991 series was drawn 2–2. England won at Headingley, where Graeme Hick made his long-awaited debut. But it was Graham Gooch, who carried his bat in the second innings for 154 out of England's 253, who was the hero. Rain spoiled an even Test at Lord's and the West Indies took a 2–1 lead by winning at Trent Bridge and Edgbaston. England tied the rubber at the Oval after the West Indies followed on.

The 1993–94 series, when Mike Atherton and Richie Richardson were captains, was the series of Brian Lara. The West Indies won the first three Tests, coming from behind in the third at Trinidad, bowling England out for 46 in the second innings, their lowest total against the West Indies and only one more than their lowest ever. Ambrose took 6 for 24. England then won in Barbados with Alec Stewart making a century in each innings. However, everything became secondary to Brian Lara's performance in the last Test in Antigua, where he scored 375 runs, the highest-ever Test innings. It took 766 minutes, and he faced 538 balls and hit 45 boundaries. His aggregate for the series was 798, average 99.75.

In 1995 Dominic Cork made an impressive debut for England at Lord's, with 7 for 43 in the second innings to get England level after the West Indies won at Headingley, but the West Indies went ahead again on a dangerous pitch at Edgbaston, exploited by the fast bowlers. A hat-trick by Cork helped level it again at Old Trafford, and the fifth and sixth Tests were drawn, with the West Indies making 692 for 8 declared at the Oval, their highest total against England.

England, led by Mike Atherton, visited West Indies in 1997–98. The first Test was one of the most extraordinary in Test history, lasting only 62 balls. A new pitch proved very fast and uneven. The English batsmen were constantly hit, and physio Wayne Morton was called on six times for injuries. England made 17 for three, when the umpires decided the pitch was unfit and the match abandoned as a draw, a unique occasion in Test cricket. The second Test was won by West Indies recovering from a first-innings deficit to win by three wickets, and the situation was reversed in the third Test, when England did the same. West Indies

TONY GREIG *In 1973–74, took wickets and involved in a controversial run-out attempt.*

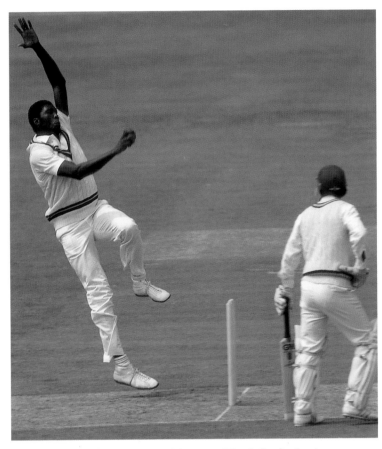

'BIG BIRD' *Joel Garner, the tall and dangerous West Indies fast bowler.*

decisively won the fourth and sixth Tests with the fifth drawn, to register a 3-1 series win.

Alex Stewart, 452 runs, average 45.20, Brian Lara, 417, average 52.12 and Graham Thorpe, 339, average 42.37 were the only batsmen to score over 300 runs. Curtly Ambrose, with 30 wickets at 14.26 was the most successful bowler.

Jimmy Adams captained West Indies in England in 2000, and began with an emphatic innings and 93 victory at Edgbaston. England made 179 and 125, West Indies 397. It was the 1500th Test match. England levelled the series in a remarkable turn-round at Lord's. West Indies made 267 for nine on the first day, then for the first time in Test history, part of all four innings took place on the second day. West Indies' last wicket

fell, England were dismissed for 134, West Indies for 54, their lowest total against England, thanks mainly to Andy Caddick's five for 16, and England were nought for nought overnight. Despite six wickets from Courtney Walsh, on the third day England reached 191 for eight to win. After a drawn third Test, England took the series lead at Headingley, winning by an innings, with Caddick (five for 14) and Darren Gough (four for 30) shooting out West Indies for 61 in their second innings. England's 158-run victory at Lord's clinched a 3–1 series win. Bowlers took the series honours, Walsh, who became the first bowler to pass 450 Test wickets, took 34 at 12.82.

A superb series followed in 2003–04. With Brian Lara and Michael Vaughan captains, England

impressively won the first three Tests. At Kingston, Steve Harmison destroyed the West Indies, with seven for 12 in a second innings of 47 all out, their lowest in Tests. Harmison and Simon Jones were the heroes of a seven-wicket win in Trinidad, with Jones and father Jeff becoming the only England father-and-son to get five wickets in an innings. At Bridgetown, Matthew Hoggard took a hat-trick and Andrew Flintoff seven wickets in all as England won by eight wickets. Graham Thorpe scored 119 not out in England's first innings of 226, with extras (20) being the next-highest scorer. But the performance of the series came in the fourth and final Test in Antigua, Lara regaining the world record Test score with 400 not out in a West Indies total of 751 for five declared, the highest total made against England. He and Ridley Jacobs (107 not out) added a West Indian sixth-wicket record of 282. England followed on, but easily saved the match.

WHITEWASH

Twenty years after the first "black-wash", England whitewashed the West Indies in 2004. It started at Lord's with a century in each innings by captain Michael Vaughan, another from Andrew Strauss and a double century from Robert Key. Shivnarine Chanderpaul made 128 and 97 in a losing cause. At Edgbaston, Marcus Trescothick scored a century in each innings, Andrew Flintoff made 167 and Ashley Giles had his second nine-wicket haul. Ramnaresh Sarwan made 139 for the West Indies. At Old Trafford West Indies had a first-innings lead of 65, but were skittled for 165 in the second innings. England completed the whitewash at the Oval, after forcing West Indies to follow on. Flintoff and Chanderpaul were joint Players of the Series, Flintoff heading England's batting and bowling averages with 387 (average 64.50) and 14 wickets at 21.21. Giles took

22 wickets. Chanderpaul scored 437 runs (av 72.83), and Chris Gayle 400 in a losing cause.

HARMISON *Bowled up a storm at Kingston in 2004.*

ENGLAND v WEST INDIES								
	Matches	Eng	WI	Draw	Series	Eng	WI	Draw
In England	74	25	29	20	17	7	8	2
In West Indies	60	13	23	24	13	3	4	6
Totals	134	38	52	44	30	10	12	8

TEST RESULTS

ENGLAND v NEW ZEALAND

New Zealand entered the Test fold in 1929–30 when England toured. The first Test was at Christchurch, and England won by eight wickets. C.S. Dempster proved the best New Zealand batsman, scoring his country's first century (136) at Wellington, and incidentally putting on 276 with John Mills (117) for the first wicket.

For the first 40 years or so of their meetings, England had much the better of the matches between the countries. In the second of the two-match 1932–33 series, Walter Hammond made 336 not out, the highest Test score at the time. Since he was only once out, his average of 563.00 for the series remains, unsurprisingly, a record for all Tests.

In 1949 at Lord's Martin Donnelly scored 206, the first double-century by a New Zealander against England. In 1954–55 at Auckland, New Zealand were dismissed for 26, the lowest score by any country in Tests. New Zealand were nevertheless given their only five-Test tour to date in 1958, managing only one draw, in a rain-ruined match at the Oval. In 1965 John Edrich scored 310 not out for England at Headingley. In another defeat for New Zealand in 1969, Glenn Turner carried his bat at Lord's for 43 not out in a total of 131. Dick Motz, at the Oval, became the first New Zealander to take 100 Test wickets.

Although New Zealand lost 2–0 in a three-match series in 1973, there was evidence that better things were coming. Set 479 to win at Trent Bridge, they passed 400 with only five out, but were all out for 440. At Lord's New Zealand made 551 for 9 declared. Captain Bev Congdon made 176 and 175 in these innings.

The 1974–75 series was overshadowed by the accident to New Zealand debutant Ewen Chatfield, whose heart stopped after a hair-line fracture of the skull caused by a ball from Peter Lever. Fortunately MCC physio Bernard Thomas resuscitated him and he made a full recovery.

ARISE, SIR RICHARD

England toured New Zealand after a tour of Pakistan in 1977–78. New Zealand won at Wellington, where Richard Hadlee took 6 for 26 (10 in the match) to dismiss England for 64 in the second innings. It was New Zealand's first win over England in their 48th Test. The series was drawn.

England made a clean sweep, 3–0, in 1978, but in 1983 New Zealand won their first Test in England, by five wickets at Headingley, although lost the series 3–1. The 1983–84 series saw New Zealand's big breakthrough. Dismissing England for 82 and 93 at Christchurch, they won by an innings and 132. Richard Hadlee was the star, taking eight wickets and top-scoring with 99 in 81 balls. Two draws gave New Zealand their first series win against England.

On their next trip to England in 1986, New Zealand repeated the formula, winning the middle one of three Tests for another 1–0 win.

A dull series in 1987–88 did not produce a win. England won the final Test to win 1–0 in 1990. A 2–0 series win in 1991–92 was notable for an unusual ending to the first Test. With New Zealand's last pair together, 4 needed to avoid an innings defeat, and three overs remaining, captain Martin Crowe decided a boundary would save the game, as England would not have time to bat. Trying to hit a 4, he miscued and was caught at cover.

Thanks to an innings win at Trent Bridge, England won the 1994 series 1–0, and then won the 1996–97 series 2–0, after New Zealand had saved the first Test at Auckland with a last-wicket stand of 166 minutes between Nathan Astle (102 not out) and Danny Morrison (14 not out).

New Zealand, under Stephen Fleming, visited England in 1999 and won a four-match series by 2–1.

In 2001–02 a remarkable first Test at Christchurch saw England, with Graham Thorpe scoring 200 not out and Andrew Flintoff 137 in a 281 sixth wicket stand set New Zealand 550 to win. Amazingly, they threat-

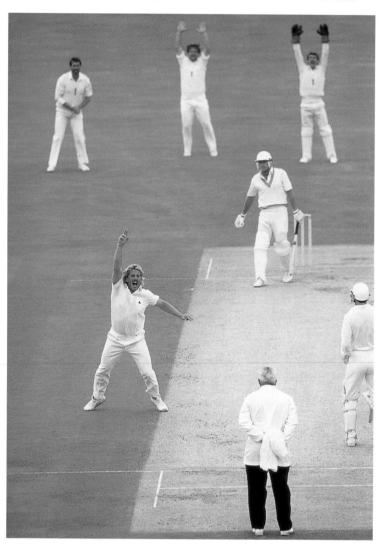

IAN BOTHAM'S *356th Test wicket; Jeff Crowe lbw breaks the record, Oval 1986.*

ened to do it, getting 451, the second-highest fourth-innings total in Tests. Astle cracked 222 from 168 balls, his 200 coming from 153 balls. New Zealand squared the series with a 78-run victory at Auckland.

At Lord's in 2004, Andrew Strauss made his England debut and scored 112 and 83 run out. The run-out came courtesy of Hussain when England were chasing 282 to win on the last afternoon. At 143 for 3 the match remained even, but Hussain made 103 not out and England won by seven wickets. At Headingley, England's victory was more clear-cut, by nine wickets, with Marcus Trescothick and Geraint Jones century-makers. A four-wicket win at Trent Bridge, led by Thorpe's hundred, completed a whitewash, though Stephen Fleming and Scott Styris made centuries for New Zealand.

		TEST RESULTS								
ENGLAND v NEW ZEALAND										
		Matches	Eng	NZ	Draw	Series	Eng	NZ	Draw
In New Zealand		41	16	3	22	16	9	1	6
In England		47	25	4	18	14	11	2	1
Totals		88	41	7	40	30	20	3	7

AUSTRALIA v WEST INDIES

The West Indies played their first Tests against Australia when touring in 1930–31. They lost the first four Tests, but won the last. The same 4–1 result was recorded in the West Indies' next tour in 1951–52, but the matches were more closely fought.

Ian Johnson led the first Australian Test tour to the West Indies in 1954–55 and won 3–0 in a series remarkable for heavy scoring, 21 centuries being scored. Clyde Walcott's series aggregate of 827, with five centuries, is sixth in the all-time list. Neil Harvey, however, topped the averages at 108.33.

FRANK WORRELL TROPHY

The series in Australia in 1960–61 is one of the great series, and led to the presentation of the Frank Worrell Trophy, named after the West Indian captain, to the winners. It got off to a superb start at Brisbane with the first of only two tied Tests. Australia required 233 to win and recovered from 92 for 6 to require 6 with three wickets left when the last over began, bowled by Wes Hall. A leg-bye was followed by Benaud caught behind for 52. A bye to the keeper came from the fourth ball and a single from the fifth. Grant was run out going for a third and winning run off the sixth – 232 for 9, level. On the seventh ball another winning run was tried but Solomon threw down the wicket from sideways on for another run out and the match was tied. Alan Davidson became the first player to complete 100 runs and 10 wickets in a Test. Australia won the second Test, the West Indies the third, and the fourth was drawn. Australia won the deciding Test by two wickets.

Australia beat an ageing West Indian touring side 3–1 in 1968–69 with Doug Walters making four centuries in four matches, including 242 and 103 in the fifth Test at Sydney. He averaged 116.50. Two wins kept Australia on top in the West Indies in 1972–73.

After the West Indies, with a new resurgent team led by Clive Lloyd, had won the first World Cup, the series in Australia in 1975–76 was billed as the "world championship". After Australia won the first Test and the West Indies the second, the West Indies disappointed, and Australia won the last four Tests.

World Series Cricket meant the teams in the West Indies in 1977–78 weren't representative. However, the West Indies' 3–1 win gave them the Frank Worrell Trophy which they were to hold for 17 years. Back with full-strength sides in Australia in 1979–80, the West Indies confirmed their new superiority. Their fast-bowling battery of Andy Roberts, Michael Holding, Joel Garner and Colin Croft were the masters. While the 1981–82 series was drawn 1–1, the West Indies won 3–0 at home in 1983–84 in a series remarkable for the fact that they did not lose a second-innings wicket all series.

The West Indies won a very bad-tempered series in 1984–85. Australian captain Kim Hughes resigned in tears after the second Test, and Allan Border took over. Australia's draw in the fourth Test ended a run of 11 successive wins by West Indies. Australia then won the fifth Test at Sydney.

Under Viv Richards, the West Indies won 3–1 in Australia in 1988–89. The West Indies won the first three Tests to ensure retention of the Frank Worrell Trophy. Courtney Walsh surprised himself with a hat-trick in the first Test, spread over both innings – the last wicket in the first and the third and fourth to fall in the second innings. In a brave 13-wicket performance at Perth, Merv Hughes bettered this with a unique Test hat-trick with wickets in three separate overs. In the West Indies' first innings he took the ninth wicket with the last ball of one over and the tenth with the first ball of the next. He completed the hat-trick with his first ball of the West Indies' second innings. In the third Test at Melbourne, Malcolm Marshall took his 300th Test wicket. Australia won the fourth Test and drew the last, with Dean Jones getting 216.

The West Indies maintained their superiority 2–1 in 1990–91, but it was another bad-tempered series, remarkable for the dismissal of Dean Jones in the second Test at Georgetown. Thinking he was bowled (not hearing a no-ball call), he was returning to the pavilion when Carl Hooper, who fielded the ball, pulled a stump from the ground. Jones was given run out, which eventually turned out to be an umpiring mistake.

The same 2–1 score for the West

GREG CHAPPELL *Had a superb series in 1975–76, averaging 117 and leading Australia to a 5–1 series victory.*

Indies was repeated in 1992–93 in Australia, but they had to win the last two Tests. Brian Lara announced his arrival in the top flight with an innings of 277 in the drawn third Test.

The West Indies won the fourth Test by one run. Australia were set 186 to win, and seemed out of it at 74 for 7, but the last-wicket pair put on 40 and just failed to clinch the series. Having escaped, the West Indies won the last Test in three days by an innings. Curtley Ambrose, with 19 wickets in the two Test wins and 33 in all, was the man of the series.

Australia, under Mark Taylor, at last beat the West Indies in 1994–95, West Indies' first series defeat in 15 years and the first on their own soil for 22 years. In fact, they had won 20 and drawn 9 of their 29 previous series. After three Tests, in which Australia won the first, rain the second and the West Indies the third, the final decisive Test was fought at Kingston, Jamaica. Australia won decisively by an innings and 53 runs, with outstanding contributions from the Waugh twins, Steve (200) and Mark (126), who put on 271 together, more than half of Australia's total and more than either of the West Indies' innings.

The West Indies went to Australia in 1996–97 to try to reassert their mastery but lost the first two Tests by 123 and 124 runs. They came back to win the third Test by six wickets, but Australia clinched the Frank Worrell Trophy in the fourth by an emphatic margin of an innings and 83 runs. An easy 10-wicket win for the West Indies in the final Test only narrowed the defeat to 3–2. Wicket-keeper Ian Healey topped the series' batting averages for Australia with 356 runs at 59.33 while Glenn McGrath topped the bowling with 26 wickets at 17.42. Rick Ponting achieved the curious bowling figures for the series of one wicket for no runs, having come on to complete an over when Steve Waugh was injured. So Australia emphasized that, for the time being, they were the world's leading power.

A series in West Indies in 1998–99 was drawn 2–2. A big win by 312 runs was registered by Australia in the first Test when West Indies were shot out for 51 in their second innings (Glenn McGrath 5 for 28, Jason Gillespie 4 for 18). But the West Indies fought back from this disaster in the second Test to win by ten wickets, after Brian Lara scored 231. West Indies won a very exciting third Test at Bridgetown. With Steve Waugh getting 199, Australia led on first innings by 161, but were dismissed for 146 in their second knock. Needing 308, West Indies were 105 for five, and 248 for eight, but Lara was playing a magnificent innings, and with the last man in he reached 153 not out and squeezed a one-wicket win. Australia came back in the fourth and final Test to win by 176 runs, tie the series 2–2 and retain the Frank Worrell Trophy. Lara topped the series batting with 546 runs, average 91.00. Steve Waugh, with 409, average 58.42 was best for the Aussies. McGrath, with 30 wickets at 16.93 was best bowler and Courtney Walsh, 26 at 20.88, was West Indies' best.

When West Indies went to Australia in 2000–01, Australia were established as the strongest side in the world, while West Indies were in the dumps. By winning the first two Tests by an innings, Australia established a record by winning twelve Tests in succession (beating West Indies' record). Australia went on to complete a 5–0 whitewash in the series. It was a team performance, with five different players collecting Man of the Match nominations: Glenn McGrath, Mark Waugh, Colin Miller, Steve Waugh and Michael Slater, respectively.

Australia, under the captaincy of Steve Waugh, won a four-Test series 3–1 in the West Indies in 2002–03. The West Indies won the final Test with a fourth-innings total of 418 for seven, but Australia's bowling were in control with Stuart McGill (20 wickets), Jason Gillespie and Brett Lee (17 each) the best. Jermaine Lawson took 14 wickets for West Indies. Ricky Ponting (523 runs, ave 130.75) and Brian Lara (533 runs, ave 66.62) were the leading batsmen.

TOP TEST BOWLER *Malcolm Marshall, the West Indies' fast bowler, in 1990–91.*

TEST RESULTS	AUSTRALIA v WEST INDIES							
		Matches	Aus	WI	Draw	Series	Aus	WI	Draw
	In Australia	57	30	18	9*	12	7	4	1
	In West Indies	42	15	14	13	9	4	4	1
	Totals	99	45	32	22*	21	11	8	2
	* includes one tie								

SOUTH AFRICA v NEW ZEALAND

The first Test series not to involve either England or Australia began in 1931–32 when the South African tourists played two Tests in New Zealand, winning both easily. Twenty-one years later South Africa won a repeat two-match tour 1–0.

In 1953–54 New Zealand toured South Africa for a five-match series. Although South Africa won 4–0, the series is remembered for the magnificent innings of 80 not out by Bert Sutcliffe in Johannesburg in a match which spanned Christmas. On Christmas Day, the New Zealand party was devastated as news came through of a train smash at home which killed 151 people, including the fiancée of tourist Bob Blair, who was playing. New Zealand had to go in to bat. The pitch was very fiery and South African fast bowler Neil Adcock, in his second Test, bowled Chapple and Poore off their chests and sent Sutcliffe and Miller to hospital. Sutcliffe, going in at 9 for 2, was immediately hit on the head (no helmets then) and sank to the turf. After five minutes, he was helped from the field and rushed to hospital, where he fainted under treatment. However, at 81 for 6, with New Zealand still needing 41 to avoid the follow-on, he returned to the wicket, face pale and head swathed in bandage, to a great welcome from the crowd. Inspired, Sutcliffe pulled his third ball for six, and when Adcock was brought on, cut him for four. He went on to play an innings of controlled, graceful violence. He was 55 not out when New Zealand reached 154 for 9, having had his bandages readjusted after they had been disturbed by his onslaught. And then the crowd stood in silence as 22-year-old Blair, who had been left in the hotel, came out to bat, to be met by Sutcliffe. They added 33 for the last wicket in 10 minutes, during which time Sutcliffe hit Tayfield for three sixes in an over and took a single to keep the strike, only to see Blair himself hit a six. It was Blair's only scoring stroke – he was soon stumped and walked off with Sutcliffe's arm around him.

In 1961–62 New Zealand won their first Tests overseas and drew the series 2–2. In 1963–64 in New Zealand, with anti-apartheid demonstrators in evidence, all three Tests were drawn, though South Africa might have won them all.

The countries resumed their matches with a three-match series in South Africa in 1994–95. New Zealand won the first Test but South Africa took the last two to become the first side to come from behind this century to win a three-Test series. South Africa were then guests at Auckland for New Zealand's centenary match and spoiled the party by overturning a first-innings deficit to win by 93 runs.

South Africa won a three-match series in New Zealand by 1–0 in 1998-99. In the first Test they made 621 for five declared (Daryll Cullinan 275 not out, a South African record, Gary Kirsten 128) but failed to dismiss New Zealand twice, partly because Geoff Allott set his own world record in batting for 101 minutes for 0. He was batting at number eleven. The second Test was drawn, mostly through rain, but Herschelle Gibbs managed to bat 659 minutes for 211 not out. South Africa won the third Test by eight wickets with Gibbs getting 120 and Cullinan 152. In the series Cullinan scored 427 for once out, Gibbs 365, average 121.66.

In 2000–01, South Africa won a three-match series 2–0, taking the first two matche, by five wickets and seven wickets, respectively. The third Test was a rain-affected draw. Young South African fast bowler Makhaya Ntini was Man of the Series.

A closely fought three-match series was drawn 1–1 in New Zealand in 2003–04. New Zealand's victory in the second Test was their first at home against South Africa. Scott Styris made 170 and Chris Cairns 158 in that match, while Gary Kirten's 78 in his final Test helped South Africa level the series.

TEST RESULTS	SOUTH AFRICA v NEW ZEALAND							
	Matches	SA	NZ	Draw	Series	SA	NZ	Draw
In New Zealand	14	6	1	7	6	4	0	2
In South Africa	16	10	3	3	8	6	0	2
Totals	30	16	4	10	14	10	0	4

ENGLAND v INDIA

Indian cricket has a long tradition, and an English side toured India in 1888, but outstanding Indian players such as Ranjitsinhji, Duleepsinhji and the Nawab of Pataudi played their Test cricket for England until 1932, when India's inaugural Test took place at Lord's. England beat a side led by C.K. Nayudu by 158 runs. In 1933–34 England toured India, who played their first three home Tests. England won 2–0. "Lala" Amarnath made his country's first Test century. However, on the 1936 tour of England, Amarnath, India's best player, was sent home before the first Test after dissension in the Indian camp. England won 2–0.

England were too strong in the first series after the Second World War and won the only match decided. India won their first Test in 1951–52, however. It was at Madras, the last of five, and it allowed India to tie the rubber 1–1.

The four-match series in 1952, which England won 3–0, was notable for the debut of Fred Trueman at Headingley. India were 0 for 4 in their second innings, Trueman having taken three wickets in eight balls. Things were even worse for India in 1959 when England recorded the first 5–0 success in any rubber in England. But it all changed when England sent a not-quite-representative side to India in 1961–62. After three draws, India won the last two Tests for their first series win over England. The Nawab of Pataudi Jr made his debut in this series, and captained India in their next two against England, but without registering a win in eight Tests.

Under Ajit Wadekar, however, India won the next two series. In 1971, John Snow knocked over Sunny Gavaskar as they collided when the opener was going for a quick single, and Snow was disciplined by being dropped for the second Test. After two draws, India came from behind to win the third and last Test at the Oval, when Chandrasekhar's 6 for 38 shot England out in the second innings for 101. It was England's first defeat in 27 Tests. In 1972–73, in a five-match series, India recovered from losing the first Test to win 2–1. Chandrasekhar took 35 wickets. England won all three Tests in 1974, the last for the loss of only two wickets. David Lloyd made 214 not out in his first Test series.

Captain Tony Greig led England to a 3–1 win in India in 1976–77, their first there for 43 years, contributing immensely himself with an innings of 103 at Calcutta, batting for 414 minutes, including the whole of one day. England won again, 1–0, in 1974, but the series will be remembered for Gavaskar's magnificent innings at the Oval, when India were set 438 to win. He batted for 490 minutes and made 221, by which time India were 389 for 4. They finished just short at 429 for 8.

England beat India by 10 wickets in India's Golden Jubilee Test at Bombay in 1979 (celebrating the formation of the Board of Control for Cricket). Two outstanding English performances came from Ian Botham (the first to score a century

GREAT ALL-ROUNDER *India's one-time leading Test wicket-taker, Kapil Dev.*

SUNNY DAY *Gavaskar during his double century at the Oval in 1973.*

and take 10 wickets in a match – in fact 114 and 13 for 106) and Bob Taylor (the first wicket-keeper to make 10 dismissals in a Test).

There were six Tests in India in 1981–82. India won the first; there then followed five long draws. Captain Gavaskar made 172 in the second Test, and was on the field for all but four balls of the five days. In Madras, Gundappa Viswanath, Gavaskar's brother-in-law, made 222. In 1982 England won the first Test and drew the remaining two.

TRAGIC TOUR

The series in 1984–85 was marked by tragedy. The Indian Prime Minister, Mrs Indira Gandhi, was assassinated and the British Deputy High Commissioner to Western India was murdered, having entertained the tourists the day before. England won the series 2–1, despite losing the first Test when 18-year-old spinner Laxman Sivaramakrishnan took six wickets in each innings, and despite Mohammad Azharuddin becoming the first Test cricketer to make centuries in each of his first three Tests. He averaged 109.75 in his first series. At Madras, Mike Gatting and Graeme Fowler each made double centuries in England's 652 for 7 declared.

India, led by Kapil Dev, had their revenge in 1986 in England, winning 2–0 with one drawn. Dilip Vengsarkar set a record by becoming the first overseas player to make three Test centuries at Lord's.

England's 1–0 win in three Tests in 1990 was notable for the match at Lord's when Graham Gooch made 333 and 123, the first being the highest innings in England-India Tests and his total of 456 being the highest aggregate in a Test. He is the only batsman in first-class cricket to score 300 and 100 in the same match. England's total of 653 for 4 declared is the highest in England-India Tests. For India, Azharuddin made a century in 87 balls; Kapil Dev, partnering the number 11, hit a Test-record four successive sixes in an over, the last saving the follow-on; and the 17-year-old Sachin Tendulkar took a breathtaking catch in the deep. At Old Trafford, Tendulkar, at 17 years 122 days, became the second-youngest Test century-maker, and at the Oval, India made their highest score against England: 606 for 9 declared. Gooch's aggregate of 752 runs (average 125.33) is a record for a three-match series. Azharuddin did his best for India with 426 runs.

India's revenge in 1992–93 was complete, as they won all three matches, two by an innings and the other by eight wickets. Newcomer Vinod Kambli made 224 in his third Test match. Both he and his former school-fellow Tendulkar averaged 100 for the series. In 1996 in England, the home side won a well-fought series 1–0. Saurav Ganguly became only the third batsman in history to score a century in his first two Test innings. He averaged 105.00 for the series.

Ganguly was captain when England toured in 2001–02. India's spinners Anil Kumble and Harbhajan Singh dominated the Tests. India won the first by ten wickets, while the other two were drawn. A few months later in England the home side won the opening Test at Lord's by 170 runs. India held on for a high-scoring draw at Trent Bridge, and then won by an innings at Headingley when Rahul Dravid (148), Sachin Tendulkar (193) and Ganguly (128) all made centuries. Both teams topped 500 in another draw at the Oval. Michael Vaughan (616 runs, average 102.6) and Dravid (602, average 100.3) both achieved century averages.

ENGLAND v INDIA								
	Matches	Eng	India	Draw	Series	Eng	India	Draw
In England	41	22	3	16	13	11	2	0
In India	43	10	11	22	10	4	4	2
Totals	84	32	14	38	13	15	6	2

AUSTRALIA v NEW ZEALAND

ALLAN BORDER *At Christchurch on his way to a record career Test aggregate.*

country. Australia won 2–0 at home and drew 1–1 away, when New Zealand recorded the first victory over their neighbours at Christchurch, with Glenn Turner (101 and 110 not out) becoming the first New Zealander to get a 100 in each innings of a Test. At Wellington, both Chappell brothers performed the feat for Australia: Ian 145 and 121 and Greg 247 not out and 133. Australia won the series in 1976–77 and 1980–81 before New Zealand again won a match to tie the series in 1981–82.

In 1985–86, New Zealand went to Australia and won the series 2–1, thanks largely to the brilliant bowling of Richard Hadlee, who took 33 wickets at 12.50. New Zealand proved it was no fluke by beating Australia 1–0 in the same season in New Zealand.

Australia won 1–0 in Australia in 1987–88 but only after their last pair held out for four overs to draw the last Test. In 1989–90, there was one Test in each country, New Zealand recording the only win at Wellington.

In New Zealand in 1992–93, Allan Border passed Sunil Gavaskar's Test aggregate of 10,122 runs. New Zealand won the third Test to square the series. In 1993–94,

Australia won 2–0 at home. At Brisbane, Allan Border played his 150th Test and held his 150th catch.

A three-match series in 1997–98 in Australia was won 2–0 by the hosts, Australia winning the first Test by 186 runs, and the second by an innings and 70. The third was drawn when New Zealand's last pair held out to thwart the Aussies.

In 1999–2000 New Zealand were hosts. Australia won the series 3–0, thus extending their winning sequence in Tests to ten. In the third, wicket keeper Adam Gilchrist took five catches in each innings, beating Gil Langley's Australian record of nine in a Test.

New Zealand visited Australia in 2001–2002 and gave the all-conquering Aussies a fright in a series of three draws. At 274 for 6 New Zealand fell 10 runs short of victory in the first Test and, in the second, Australia were hanging on with three wickets left at stumps.

Australia won both Tests by large margins in Australia in 2004–05, the highlights being Justin Langer's 215 in Adelaide, and Glenn McGrath's 61 batting at number 11 in Brisbane. Later in the season, in New Zealand, they won 2–0 with one draw. With two centuries, Adam Gilchrist was Player of the Series.

Surprisingly, Australia and New Zealand did not meet each other in Test cricket until a match played at Wellington on March 29 and 30 1946 was retrospectively granted Test status. New Zealand were dismissed

for 42 and 54 and Australia won by an innings and 103.

Although each country toured the other in the 1960s, Tests were not resumed until 1973–74 in Australia with a three-Test tour in each

TEST RESULTS	AUSTRALIA v NEW ZEALAND							
	Matches	Aus	NZ	Draw	Series	Aus	NZ	Draw
In New Zealand	22	10	5	7	9	4	2	3
In Australia	24	12	2	10	9	6	1	2
Totals	46	22	7	17	18	10	3	5

AUSTRALIA v INDIA

India's first Test series against Australia was played in 1947–48 and Australia won 4–0. They also won a shortened tour of India in 1956–57, and on their first full tour, in 1959–60, won 2–1. India's win by 119 runs in the second Test at Kanpur was due to Jasu Patel, who took 14 for 124.

In 1964–65 India drew a home series 1–1, a crowd of 42,000 watching

them scrape home on the last day at Bombay. Australia kept up their superiority through the rest of the 1960s and 1970s, winning 10 Tests and losing three, but in 1977–78 they scraped by in a home series by 3–2.

In 1979–80, in India, India won their first series against Australia 2–0, led by Kapil Dev's 28 wickets. The three-match series in the 1980s

ended tied at 1–1. Australia completely outplayed India in Australia in 1991–92, winning 4–0. Allan Border won his 126th cap in the first Test, passing Sunil Gavaskar's previous record of 125.

In 1996–97 Australia, in India for a one-day tournament, played a one-off Test at Delhi, which India won by seven wickets.

India won a three-match series at home in 1997–98 by 2–1, but Australia replied with a 3–0 whitewash at home in 1999–2000.

The three-match series in India in 2000–01 was one of the greatest. Australia won by ten wickets in the first Test. In the second, they made 445 (Harbhajan Singh's seven wickets for 123 included India's first Test hat-trick) and then bowled out India for 171. Following-on, and at 232 for four, Rahul Dravid (180) joined VVS Laxman (281) and the pair put on 376 to help India declare at 657 for seven, setting Australia 384 to win. Six for 73 by Harbhajan got them out for 212 and a win for India by 171. It was the third time in Test history that a team won after following on, and the victory ended Australia's sequence of 16 consecutive victories. The third Test lived up to the second, and provided a tense finish. India needed 155 to win. Laxman's 66 got them home with two wickets to spare. Harbhajan, the Man of the Series, scored the winning run. In the series, he took 32 of the 50 Australia wickets to fall, for 545 runs, average 17.03. Matthew Hayden of Australia

was the best batsman with 549 runs, average 109.20 (on the losing side!), while match-winner Laxman had 503 runs, average 83.88.

A magnificent four-match series in Australia in 2003–04 was drawn 1–1. Despite Ricky Ponting's 242, India came from behind for a four-wicket win at Adelaide, with Dravid making 233 and Laxman 138. Australia's nine-wicket win came at Melbourne, despite 195 from Virender Sehwag, with Ponting making 257 and Hayden 136. At Sydney, India made 705 for seven (Sachin Tendulkar 241 not out), but in captain Steve Waugh's last Test, Australia held on for the draw, Waugh getting 80 in his last innings. Ponting scored 706 runs (average 100.85), Dravid 633 (av. 123.80). Amid the batting heroics,

VVS LAXMAN *In action at Sydney during the fourth Test against Australia in 2004.*

AUSTRALIA v INDIA

	Matches	Aus	Ind	Draw	Series	Aus	Ind	Draw
In Australia	32	20	4	8	8	5	0	3
In India	36	12	11	13*	10	4	4	2
Totals	68	32	15	21*	18	9	4	5

* Includes one tie

Anil Kumble's 24 wickets at 29.58 was outstanding.

A four-Test return in India in 2004–05 was won decisively by Australia. Led by Adam Gilchrist, it was Australia's first series win in India for 35 years. The highlights

included Michael Clarke's century on his debut in the first Test, Anil Kumble's 13 wickets in the drawn second Test, Damien Martyn's run of 104, 114 and 97 in successive innings, and Clarke's 6 for 9 in the fourth Test, which India won.

WEST INDIES v INDIA

Tests between the West Indies and India started with J.D.C. Goddard's team visiting India for a five-Test series in 1948–49. Everton Weekes, having made a century in his last Test innings against England, scored centuries in his first four in India, including two in the third Test. Weekes was then run out for 90 when attempting a sixth successive century. The West Indies won the only match decided, the fourth Test. In the last, India, chasing 361 to win, were 355 for 8 at the close. Weekes made 779 runs, average 111.28.

The West Indies maintained their supremacy in four series in the 1950s and 1960s, winning 11 matches to none. In India in 1958–59, there were complaints about the use of bouncers by the West Indians Wes Hall and Roy Gilchrist and Gilchrist was sent home for bowling beamers. In

1961–62, the West Indies achieved a 5–0 whitewash. At Bridgetown the Indian captain, N.J. Contractor, suffered a fractured skull when hit by a ball from C.C. Griffith, which ended his Test career.

India's first victory against the West Indies in 1970–71 was enough to win the series. India at Port-of-Spain, the Test in which Sunil Gavaskar made his Test debut. He scored 65 and 67 not out. Dilip Sardesai made 112 as India won by seven wickets. Jack Noriega, whose four Tests all came in this series, took 9 for 95, the best analysis recorded by a West Indian. In the fifth Test (his fourth), Gavaskar became only the second batsman (after K.D. Walters) to score a century and a double-century in the same Test. He scored 774 runs in the series, average 154.80. Ajit Wadekar was the successful skipper.

With Clive Lloyd as captain, the

West Indies won excitingly in 1974–75 in India by 3–2. Gordon Greenidge (with 93 run out and 107) and Viv Richards (4 and 3) made their debuts in the first Test. The West Indies won the final deciding Test, by 201 runs, Lloyd making 242 not out, and topping the batting, while Andy Roberts' 32 wickets was then a series record for the West Indies.

The 1975–76 series in the West Indies was a sour affair. After the West Indies won the first Test, India levelled in the third with a magnificent win. They were set 403 to win in the fourth innings and, with Gavaskar getting 102 and Viswanath 112, won by six wickets. Their score of 406 for 4 was the highest fourth-innings total made to win a Test match. The West Indies won the fourth and final Test with what the Indians regarded as intimidatory bowling on a variable

pitch. In protest, Bedi declared India's first innings total at 306 for 6, with two players injured. India were all out 97 in the second innings with five players absent hurt, although at first it was assumed Bedi had declared with five wickets down to reinforce his protests about the dangerous bowling. The West Indies needed only 13 to win.

India took their revenge in 1978–79 with their first series win over the West Indies in India. Alvin Kallicharran and Gavaskar were captains. It was a high-scoring, six-Test series, with the only result coming in the fourth Test in Madras. India won by three wickets in a match which became a bouncer war. Gavaskar led the series batting with 732 runs, average 91.50, while Karsan Ghavri took 27 wickets.

In 1982–83, the West Indies won a Test remarkably by taking four

Indian wickets and scoring 173 for 6 in the final session of play, with four balls of their allotted 26 overs left. In 1983–84 at Ahmedabad, Gavaskar scored the runs that took his Test aggregate past the previous record of 8,114 runs set by the great Geoffrey Boycott.

In the tied series in India in 1987–88 there was a remarkable Test debut by Narendra Hirwani, a little-known bespectacled leg-spinner from Gorakhpur who took 8 for 61 and 8 for 75 in India's victory at Madras. His 16 for 136 are the best match figures by a debutant in a Test match.

In 1994–95, the West Indies tied the series in the last Test to maintain their 15-year unbeaten record. Jimmy Adams, who made 174 and 78, both times not out in the 243-run victory, finished the series with 520 runs and an average of 173.33.

With the batting geniuses Brian Lara and Sachin Tendulkar captaining the sides, the West Indies won the series of 1996–97 by virtue of a single win at Bridgetown. On an increasingly difficult wicket they were bowled out for 140 in the third innings but dismissed India, who needed only 120 runs in the fourth, for just 81.

In the first Test in the West Indies in 2001–02, home captain Carl Hooper made 233 and 144 not out, but India drew then won the second Test by 37 runs. West Indies took two of the last three Tests, however, to win 2–1. Hooper (579 runs at an average of 82.71) and Shivnarine Chanderpaul (562 runs, average 140.50) were the stars.

In India in 2002–03 India won 2–0 with one drawn. This time the outstanding player was a bowler, Harbhajan Singh, with 20 wickets at 16.75 each.

161 NOT OUT *Clive Lloyd on his way to 161 at Calcutta in 1983–84, when he led West Indies to a 3–0 series win.*

TEST RESULTS

WEST INDIES v INDIA

	Matches	WI	Ind	Draw	Series	WI	Ind	Draw
In India	40	14	7	19	9	5	2	2
In West Indies	38	16	3	19	8	7	1	0
Totals	78	30	10	38	17	12	3	2

WEST INDIES v NEW ZEALAND

J.D.C. Goddard's strong West Indian side played two Tests in New Zealand in 1951–52 and won 1–0.

New Zealand won a match in the West Indies' next visit in 1955–56, but lost the series 3–1. The third series in New Zealand, 1968–69, was drawn. Seymour Nurse played innings for the West Indies of 168 and 258, averaging 111.60 for the series. All five Tests were drawn in New Zealand's first tour to the West Indies in 1971–72, but in 1979–80 back in New Zealand they won the three-Test series 1–0. The West Indians behaved badly after New Zealand's one-wicket win (from a leg-bye) in the first Test, and only Desmond Haynes attended the presentation. In the second Test, the West Indies refused to take the field after tea on the third day as a protest against an umpire, but did so eventually and saved the match.

The West Indies got their revenge 2–0 in the Caribbean in 1984–85 amid a flurry of bouncers from Marshall and Garner. After a draw in 1986–87, the West Indies won two two-Test series in the 1990s 1–0, before New Zealand reversed the trend with a 2–0 home victory in 1999–2000. Chris Cairns was outstanding and Mathew Sinclair, making his Test debut, scored 214.

New Zealand at last won a two-match series in the West Indies in 2002-03. Captain Stephen Fleming made 130 as the Kiwis won by 204 runs in Bridgetown, while the second test was drawn.

TEST RESULTS

WEST INDIES v NEW ZEALAND

	Matches	WI	NZ	Draw	Series	WI	NZ	Draw
In New Zealand	19	7	6	6	7	3	2	2
In West Indies	13	3	1	9	4	2	1	2
Totals	32	10	7	15	11	5	3	4

INDIA v PAKISTAN

The bitter rivalry between India and Pakistan began in 1952–53, when India were the hosts for Pakistan's first Test series. India won the first match, Pakistan the second in a match where Nazar Mohammad of Pakistan carried his bat for 124 not out in a score of 331 and became the first player to be on the field for an entire Test match. India took the series 2–1. A run of 13 consecutive draws followed. The 1954–55 series in Pakistan was the first five-Test series not to produce a result and in India, in 1960–61, there were again five draws.

Tests resumed in 1978–79, when Pakistan won 2–0. India reversed the result in India the following season by winning 2–0. In 1982–83, it was Pakistan's turn. They won 3–0, captain Imran Khan's 40 wickets remaining the best series haul for any Pakistani in Tests. At Hyderabad, Mudassar Nazar (231) and Javed Miandad (280 not out) put on 451 for the third wicket, equalling the then highest stand in Test cricket. And at Lahore, Mudassar became the second Pakistani to carry his bat in a Test innings, the first having been his father, Nazar Mohammad.

The only series of four succeeding ones to produce a result was in 1986–87 in India when, after four dull draws, Pakistan won an exciting final Test by 16 runs having set India 221.

A series in 1989–90 in Pakistan produced four draws. The teams did not meet again for nine years when, in 1998–99, a two-match series in India resulted in a win for each side. Bowlers dictated, with Saqlain Mushtaq taking five wickets in all four innings, 20 for 403, average 20.15. India's Anil Kumble did even better by taking all ten (for 74 runs) in Pakistan's second innings in Delhi, only the second time a bowler had taken all ten in a Test. Later in 1998–99, they met again in Calcutta in the first match of the Asian Test Championship, which also involved Sri Lanka. Pakistan won by 46 runs.

Because of political troubles, it was 2003–04 before the sides met again. India won for the first time in Pakistan when, at Multan, Virender Sehwag (309) became India's first triple centurion. India scored 675 for five declared and won by an innings and 52 runs. A solid all-round performance in the second Test saw Pakistan draw level with a nine-wicket win, but India took the decider when Rahul Dravid made 270 out of a total of 600 at Rawalpindi and India won by an innings and 132 runs.

The return three-Test series in India was drawn 1–1. The third was notable for the barracking of India's captain Sourav Ganguly, who scored 1 and 2, and only 48 in the series. He was made the scapegoat for India's home loss to Australia a few months before, in particular for having withdrawn from the decisive match with a hip injury 30 minutes before the start, having previously complained about the greenness of the wicket.

LEADING THE WAY *Inzaman-ul-Haq made 184 against India at Bangalore in 2005.*

TEST RESULTS

INDIA v PAKISTAN

	Matches	Ind	Pak	Draw	Series	Ind	Pak	Draw
In India	30	6	5	19	7	2	1	4
In Pakistan	23	2	6	15	6	1	2	3
Totals	53	8	11	34	13	3	3	7

ENGLAND v PAKISTAN

Pakistan toured England in 1954 to play four Tests. England won the second Test, at Trent Bridge, by an innings, and in the draws at Lord's and Old Trafford dismissed Pakistan for 87 and 90 respectively. So it was a big shock when Pakistan tied the series at the Oval with a 24-run win.

Pakistan did not win another match for nine series, five of which England won.

Pakistan eventually won their second match against England at Lord's in 1982, when Mohsin Khan scored the first Test double-century there for 33 years, and Pakistan won by 10 wickets. England, however, won the series 2–1. But at home in 1983–84, Pakistan won their first series against England 1–0, by virtue of winning the first Test at Karachi. When set to score 65 in the fourth innings, they lost seven wickets getting them.

Pakistan then won the next four series. An innings win at Headingley was enough in 1987 when, in the Oval Test, Pakistan scored 708, their highest total in Tests.

The 1987–88 tour of Pakistan was notable for the argument in Faisalabad between England captain Mike Gatting and umpire Shakoor Rana, who refused to continue without an apology from Gatting. A whole day's play was lost until Gatting apologized under instruction from the TCCB. The only result went to Pakistan by an innings in the first Test, Abdul Qadir getting 9 for 56 in the first innings, the best Test analysis by a Pakistani.

Pakistan won 2–1 in 1992. At Lord's, needing 138, they were 95 for 8, but got home when fast bowlers Wasim Akram (45 not out) and Waqar Younis (20 not out) added 46 to win. There were reprimands for bad behaviour for Pakistani players at Old Trafford, as well as 205 from Aamir Sohail. England won at Headingley, but Pakistan took the series with a 10-wicket win at the Oval. The wickets of the fast bowlers

Wasim (21) and Waqar (22) made the vital difference.

In 1996, Pakistan won a three-match series 2–0, with five of their batsmen averaging over 60: Moin Khan (best with 79.00), Ijaz Ahmed, Salim Malik, Inzaman-ul-Haq and Saaed Anwar, while leg-spinner Mushtaq Ahmed took the most wickets.

In Pakistan in 2000–01, the first two Tests were draws, and the final Test seemed to be heading for a similar outcome when Pakistan began the last day on 71 for three, 88 ahead. But they allowed them-selves to be dismissed for 158, leaving England to get 176 in a minimum 44 overs to win the series. Encroaching darkness seemed Pakistan's best hope and their first seven overs to tea took 41 minutes, and in the interval captain Moin Khan was summoned by the match referee, Ranjan Madugalie, and reminded of the spirit of the game. The over rate in the evening continued to be slow, the darkness crept in so that the fielding side were appealing against it, but England continued to accumulate the runs and the umpires refused to end the game. Finally, in almost impossible light, Graham Thorpe and Graeme Hick guided England to a six-wicket win. It was the first time Pakistan had lost at Karachi – a record stretching over 34 matches since 1955.

Pakistan played a two-match series in England in 2001 and drew 1–1. England won by an innings and nine runs at Lord's, Gough and Caddick getting eight wickets apiece, and Pakistan won by 108 runs at Old Trafford.

TEST RESULTS

ENGLAND v PAKISTAN

	Matches	Eng	Pak	Draw	Series	Eng	Pak	Draw
In England	39	14	8	17	11	5	3	3
In Pakistan	21	2	2	17	7	2	2	3
Totals	60	16	10	34	18	7	5	6

NEW ZEALAND v PAKISTAN

New Zealand first toured Pakistan in 1955–56. Pakistan won the first two of a three-Test series.

New Zealand's first series win came in 1969–70 in Pakistan when they won by five wickets in Lahore. It was New Zealand's first series win against any opposition, 40 years after their first Test. In Karachi, Pakistan fielded the third instance of three brothers playing in one Test when Hanif, Mushtaq and Sadiq Mohammad all played. New Zealand's second series win was by 2–0 in New Zealand in 1984–85, revenge for a 2–0 defeat in Pakistan earlier in the season.

Richard Hadlee made his Test debut against Pakistan in 1972–73 but Pakistan won the only Test decided by an innings. In a drawn Test at Auckland, New Zealand's Brian Hastings and Richard Collinge added 151 for the last wicket, still the highest last-wicket stand in Tests.

Pakistan's batsmen were on top in the 1970s and 1980s, with Mushtaq Mohammed and Asif Iqbal making 350 together in 1972–73 and Javed Miandad getting a century in each innings in 1984-85.

In 1996–97, a two-match series in Pakistan ended 1–1, with Pakistan's debutant Mohammad Zahid taking 11 for 130 in the second Test at Rawalpindi, the best by a Pakistani on Test debut.

In New Zealand in 2000–01 Pakistan won the first Test and New Zealand levelled the series by winning the third Test The highlight was an over from Younis Khan which Craig McMillan hit for a Test record 26 runs: 4, 4, 4, 4, 6, 4. .

A scheduled two-match series in Pakistan in 2002–2003 was called off after the first Test when a bomb exploded outside the New Zealanders' hotel, killing 14. Pakistan had won the Test by an innings and 324 runs with Inzamam ul-Haq scoring 329.

In a two-match series in New Zealand in 2003–04, Pakistan won 1–0. At Wellington, they trailed by 170, but Shoaib Akhtar (six for 30) dismissed New Zealand for 103 and Pakistan made 277 for three to win.

TEST RESULTS

NEW ZEALAND v PAKISTAN

	Matches	NZ	Pak	Draw	Series	NZ	Pak	Draw
In Pakistan	21	2	13	6	8	1	6	1
In New Zealand	24	4	8	12	10	1	7	2
Totals	45	6	21	18	18	2	13	3

NEW ZEALAND v INDIA

Less than a week after completing their first Test series in Pakistan in 1955–56, New Zealand began their first series against India. India won two of the five-Test home series, both by an innings, and they also had the better of the three drawn games.

India won the two series in the 1960s, 1–0 at home in 1964–65 and 3–1 away in 1967–68 – their first Test win away from home – thanks to excellent spin bowling. Graham Dowling made 239 at Christchurch. New Zealand were deprived of their first series win over India in 1969–70 when rain ruined the deciding Test.

They had to wait until 1980–81 for their first series success, winning the only match decided by 62 runs at Wellington. Each side won at home in series in the late 1980s. A one-off Test in Hamilton in 1993–94 was drawn, and India retained their superiority with a 1–0 win in 1995–96, a victory at Bangalore being enough.

The first Test in New Zealand in 1998–99 was abandoned at Dunedin without a ball being bowled. New Zealand won the second, and the series when the third was drawn, despite Rahul Dravid compiling a century in each innings.

India won the middle one of three Tests in India in 1999–2000. Sachin Tendulkar was the outstanding batsman with 435 runs, average 108.75, and Anil Kumble was the best bowler with 20 wickets at 18.20.

India's batsmen failed miserably in New Zealand in 2002–03 as in four innings the side failed to reach 200. Daryl Tuffey (13 wickets at 8.69), Shane Bond (12 at 16.33) and Jacob Oram (11 at 11.09) ensured a 2–0 win.

Batsmen came out on top when both Tests were drawn in India in 2003–04. Nine players made hundreds, four in New Zealand's 630 for six declared in the second Test. In the first, Rahul Dravid made 222 for India.

TEST RESULTS

NEW ZEALAND v INDIA

	Matches	NZ	Ind	Draw	Series	NZ	Ind	Draw
In India	26	2	10	14	8	0	6	2
In New Zealand	18	7	4	7	7	4	2	1
Totals	44	9	14	21	15	4	8	3

AUSTRALIA v PAKISTAN

The first Test between the two countries came in 1956. The first day at Karachi, on a matting wicket, produced 95 runs, still the lowest for a full day's play in Tests: Australia 80, Pakistan 15 for 2. Pakistan eventually won by nine wickets.

Australia gained revenge 2–0 during a second visit in 1959–60. Single Tests in each country were played in 1964–65, both drawn.

Pakistan made their first three-match tour in 1972–73, and Australia won 3–0. Mushtaq Mohammad led Pakistan on tours in 1976–77 and 1978–79 and both tours ended 1–1. In the first, Imran Khan's hauls of six wickets in each innings at Sydney sealed Pakistan's first victory in Australia.

Pakistan's first rubber victory followed in 1979–80 in Pakistan. A seven-wicket win in Karachi was followed by two draws. At Lahore, Allan Border scored 150 and 153, the first player to reach 150 in each innings of a Test. Under Imran Khan, Pakistan won 3–0 in 1982–83, all easy wins. Leg-breaker Abdul Qadir's 22 wickets in the series were crucial.

The first five-Test series between the countries was won 2–0 by Australia at home in 1983–84. At the end of the series, three great Australians announced their retirements: Greg Chappell, Dennis Lillee and Rodney Marsh.

Pakistan won 1–0 in Pakistan in 1988–89, thanks partly to captain Javed Miandad's batting, but the Australians objected officially to the umpiring at Karachi. Australia won 1–0 in 1989–90, Pakistan 1–0 in 1994–95 and Australia 2–1 in 1995–96, all in their own countries. This last series began in a bitter atmosphere after Australian players had made allegations of attempted bribery by at least one Pakistan player to lose in Pakistan the previous season. However, the bad feeling passed and the series proved to be well-fought.

Australia won a high-scoring series in Pakistan in 1998–99 1–0, with two drawn. The Aussie captain, Mark Taylor, batted the first two days at Peshawar to make 334 not out from a total of 599 for four, thus equalling Donald Bradman's record Test score for Australia. Unselfishly he declared overnight, without attempting to better the record. Australia scored a 3–0 whitewash in Australia in 1999–2000, with an outstanding team performance.

The sides played a three match series in Sri Lanka and Sharjah in 2002–03. The temperature at Colombo touched 48°C in the first Test, which Australia narrowly won, but they won both of the Sharjah Tests by an innings, Pakistan scoring 59 and 53 in the first. Shane Warne was the dominant player, taking 27 wickets at 12.66.

In Australia in 2004–05, the Australians won all three Tests easily. Damien Martyn and Ricky Ponting both averaged over 100, and Glenn McGrath topped the bowling with 18 wickets at 14.44 each. Adam Gilchrist played his 65th consecutive Test since his debut, an Australian record.

TEST RESULTS

AUSTRALIA v PAKISTAN

	Matches	Aus	Pak	Draw	Series	Aus	Pak	Draw
In Pakistan	20	3	7	10	8	2	5	1
In Australia	29	18	4	7	10	7	0	3
In Sharjah	3	3	0	0	1	1	0	0
Totals	52	24	11	17	19	10	5	4

WEST INDIES v PAKISTAN

In 1957–58, A.H. Kardar took a Pakistan team on a five-match tour of the West Indies. It proved to be record–breaking. In the first Test at Bridgetown, Nasim-ul-Ghani of Pakistan became the youngest Test player till then at 16 years 248 days and, when Pakistan followed on 473 behind, Hanif Mohammad scored 337, the second-highest Test score till then, in 16 hours 10 minutes, then the longest innings in first-class cricket.

In the third Test at Kingston, Gary Sobers, aged 21, scored 365 not out, the highest score in Tests until 1993–94. With Hunte (260), he put on 446 for the second wicket. The West Indies made 790 for 3 declared. In the fourth Test, Sobers made a century in each innings. Pakistan won the last Test, the West Indies taking the series 3–1.

The following season, Pakistan won 2–1 in Pakistan, captain Fazal Mahmood getting 21 wickets in the three Tests. There was a gap of 15 years before the countries met again.

In 1974–75 at Karachi both sides made their highest scores in Pakistan. Pakistan made 406 for 8 declared, and West Indies replied with 493.

The final Test of 1976–77 in the West Indies was reached with the sides 1–1, West Indies winning the decider. In 1980–1981 in the Tests in Pakistan, West Indies won the only match decided.

There was a particularly fine performance by Abdul Qadir at Faisalabad in 1986–87 when he took 6 for 16 in helping rout the West Indies for 53. At Bridgetown in 1987–88, Pakistan had a great opportunity to win their first series in the West Indies when in the last Test the West Indies, set 266 to win, and so draw the series, were 207 for 8. Jeffrey Dujon (29) and Winston Benjamin (40) provided the runs. In this match, a spectator struck by Abdul Qadir after abusing him was paid not to press charges.

There was more trouble on Pakistan's next tour of the West Indies in 1992–93. Four Pakistan players were arrested on a beach in Grenada for "constructive possession" of marijuana. The Pakistanis, who protested their innocence, threatened to call off the tour, which was locally billed as for the "world championship". The charges were dropped, but the first Test was delayed by one day. The West Indies' eventual 2–0 win was the biggest since the first series in 1957–58. Richie Richardson was the winning captain.

However at home in 1997–98 Pakistan whitewashed West Indies 3–0, beating them by an innings twice and ten wickets. Inzamam-ul-Haq and Aamir Sohail each averaged over a hundred. By contrast, the 1999–2000 series in West Indies could not have been closer, with the West Indies winning the third Test by one wicket after two draws. Captain Jimmy Adams and Courtney Walsh added 19 for the last wicket.

The first-ever Test series at Sharjah was played in 2001–02, between Pakistan and West Indies. Pakistan won both of the Tests easily with good performances from all their players.

A poorly attended two-match series in the West Indies in 2004–05 was drawn 1–1. Brian Lara was Player of the Series with 331 runs (average 82.75).

TEST RESULTS

WEST INDIES v PAKISTAN

	Matches	WI	Pak	Draw	Series	WI	Pak	Draw
In West Indies	21	10	4	7	6	4	0	2
In Pakistan	18	4	7	7	6	1	2	3
In Sharjah	2	0	2	0	1	0	1	0
Totals	41	14	13	14	13	5	3	5

ENGLAND v SRI LANKA

Sri Lanka was the eighth country to achieve Test status when in 1981–82 England played a Test in Colombo after touring India. England won by seven wickets. Sri Lanka had the better of a draw at Lord's in 1984, when Sidath Wettimuny batted for 636 minutes, the longest Test innings at Lord's, to score 190, the highest score by a foreign batsman playing his first Test in England.

Until 2000–01 the teams had played only single Tests. England won in 1988 and 1991, but in 1992–93

Sri Lanka registered their first victory at Colombo, by five wickets.

Sri Lanka won their first Test in England at the Oval in 1998. England won the first series between the countries, 2–1 in Sri Lanka in 2000–01 – despite Marvan Atapattu's 201 not out in the first Test – and 2–0 in England in 2002.

But Sri Lanka deservedly won 1–0 at home in 2003–04, winning the third Test by an innings. Spinner Muttiah Muralitharan starred with 26 wickets, average 12.30.

FIRST TEST CAPTAIN *Bandula Warnapura at Colombo, February 1982.*

TEST RESULTS	ENGLAND v SRI LANKA								
		Matches	Eng	SL	Draw	Series	Eng	SL	Draw
	In Sri Lanka	8	3	3	2	2	1	1	0
	In England	7	4	1	2	1	1	0	0
	Totals	15	7	4	4	3	2	1	0

PAKISTAN v SRI LANKA

Sri Lanka visited Pakistan for a three-Test series in 1981–82 and Pakistan won 2–0. In 1985–86, the result was repeated in Pakistan, but in the series which followed in Sri Lanka, Sri Lanka won at Colombo and drew the series. Pakistan won the series in 1991–92 and 1993–94, when the third Test was cancelled owing to civil disturbances in Sri Lanka.

In 1995–96, however, Sri Lanka won the series in Pakistan 2–1. After losing the first Test by an innings, Sri Lanka won the second by 42 runs and then took the third by 144 runs.

A two-Test series in Sri Lanka ended in two draws, with Sri Lanka's Aravinda de Silva the star,

with 432 runs, average 216.00 and two not out centuries in one match. The teams then met twice in the Asian Test Championship in 1998–99. Their league match was drawn, with Wajahatullah Wasti getting a century in each innings for Pakistan in Lahore. The two teams then met in the final in Bangladesh. Pakistan won by an innings.

Sri Lanka won a series 2–1 in Pakistan in 1999–2000, winning the first Test by two wickets; Arjuna Ranatunga returned with a broken thumb when Sri Lanka needed 43 with eight wickets downto squeeze out the win. In a return in Sri Lanka Pakistan reversed the result 2–0, winning the first two Tests. In the

second, four Pakistan batsmen scored centuries in the same innings, and their bowler Abdul Razzaq became at 20 the youngest player to get a Test hat-trick. Rain wrecked the third Test, but Atapattu (207 not out) and Jayasuriya (188) put 335 runs for Sri Lanka's first wicket.

The teams met in the final of the Asian Test Championship in Lahore

in 2001–2002, Sri Lanka winning by eight wickets. The highlight was 230 from keeper Kumar Sangakkara.

A well-fought two-match series in Pakistan in 2004–05 was drawn 1–1. Sanath Jayasuriya was Player of the Series, his 424 runs averaging 106.00. Danish Kaneria's ten wickets was instrumental in the second Test, which Pakistan won by six wickets.

TEST RESULTS	PAKISTAN v SRI LANKA								
		Matches	Pak	SL	Draw	Series	Pak	SL	Draw
	In Pakistan	19	8	6	5	6	3	2	1
	In Sri Lanka	10	5	1	4	4	2	0	2
	In Bangladesh	1	1	0	0	-	-	-	-
	Totals	30	14	7	9	10	5	2	3

INDIA v SRI LANKA

Sri Lanka played a Test in Madras in 1982–83 which ended evenly poised with India needing 40 to win with three wickets left. In their first three-Test series, in Sri Lanka in 1985–86, Sri Lanka won 1–0, winning the

second Test at Colombo, their first Test win in their 14th Test.

In India in 1986–87 the Indian batting saw them to a 2–0 victory.

At Chandigarh in 1990–91, India's 21-year-old slow left-arm

Venkatapathy Raju took 6 for 12 in the first innings and ended the match with the astonishing analysis of 53.5-38-37-8.

After winning in Sri Lanka 1–0 in 1993–94, India won all three Tests

in India later in the season by an innings.

Two Tests in Sri Lanka in 1997–98 were drawn, the first being remarkable for Sri Lanka beating the 39-year-old record for the highest Test score by making 952 for six declared. Sashan Jayasuriya (340) and Roshan Mahanama (225) established a new record Test partnership of 576. A series in India the same season ended in three draws, as did a match in 1998-99 in Sri Lanka in the Asian Test Championship.

Sri Lanka won 2–1 in a home series in 2001–02. the star performer was Muttiah Muralitharan, who captured 23 wickets at 19.30, including eight for 87 in the first innings of the decisive first Test.

TEST RESULTS

INDIA v SRI LANKA

	Matches	Ind	SL	Draw	Series	Ind	SL	Draw
In India	11	6	0	5	5	3	0	2
In Sri Lanka	12	2	3	7	4	1	2	1
Totals	23	8	3	12	9	4	2	3

NEW ZEALAND v SRI LANKA

Sri Lanka visited New Zealand and Australia in 1982–83 with a weak side and lost both Tests comfortably.

New Zealand won 2–0 in Sri Lanka in 1983–84. In 1986–87 in Sri Lanka, only one drawn Test was played, the other two being cancelled after a bomb killed 150 near the tourists' hotel. There was another series without a result in 1990–91, but there were records in the first Test at Wellington. Sri Lanka made their then highest score, 497 for 9 declared, with Aravinda de Silva getting 267. Facing a deficit of 323, New Zealand then made 671 for 4, with Martin Crowe scoring 299. Crowe and Andrew Jones (186) put on 467 for the third wicket.

Sri Lanka won 1–0 in 1992–93 at home, but again there was a bomb before the Tests started, and six New Zealanders voted to return home. The first Test was drawn, but Sri Lanka won the second of a two-match series. The win was repeated in New Zealand in 1994–95. At least New Zealand had the consolation of wicket-keeper Adam Parore setting a new Test record of not conceding a bye while 2,323 runs were scored. New Zealand comfortably won a home series 2–0 in 1996–97.

Sri Lanka came back from losing the first Test to beat New Zealand 2–1 in Sri Lanka 1997–98.

Both matches were drawn in Sri Lanka in 2002–03. New Zealand captain Stephen Fleming made 274 and 69, both not out, in the first Test at Colombo. A heavy scoring two-match series in New Zealand in 2004–05 was won 1–0 by the home side. Lou Vincent's 224 in New Zealand's victory in Wellington was the highlight.

TEST RESULTS

NEW ZEALAND v SRI LANKA

	Matches	NZ	SL	Draw	Series	NZ	SL	Draw
In New Zealand	11	5	1	5	5	3	1	1
In Sri Lanka	11	3	3	5	5	1	2	2
Totals	22	8	4	10	8	4	3	3

AUSTRALIA v SRI LANKA

Australia won one Test in Kandy in 1982–83, and another in Australia in 1987–88, both by an innings. Since then, in two- or three-match series until 1999–2000, Sri Lanka did no better than draw, although in 1992–93 only a brilliant catch by Allan Border saved the Australians in Colombo, when Sri Lanka lost their last eight wickets for 37 runs to lose by 16.

Sri Lanka's win by four wickets in Kandy in 1999–2000 was their first defeat of Australia, and their first series win. In Sri Lanka in 2003–04, both Shane Warne and Muttiah Muralitharan were approaching 500 Test wickets. Warne won the race, reaching 500 in the first Test, Murali in the second. Australia batted first and trailed on first innings each time, but recovered to win all three times. Warne took 26 wickets, Murali 31.

In 2004–05, Australia won a two-Test series 1–0 at home. The most notable performance was Matthew Hayden's century in each innings in the drawn match. Murali – who didn't tour – and Warne ended the series with 527 wickets each.

TEST RESULTS

AUSTRALIA v SRI LANKA

	Matches	Aus	SL	Draw	Series	Aus	SL	Draw
In Sri Lanka	10	5	1	4	4	3	1	0
In Australia	8	6	0	2	4	4	0	0
Totals	18	11	1	6	8	7	1	0

SOUTH AFRICA v WEST INDIES

South Africa's re-admittance to Test cricket after the apartheid ban which lasted 22 years was marked by the first meeting between them and the West Indies in a one-off Test at Bridgetown, Barbados, in the 1991–92 season. Andrew Hudson immediately became the first South African to make a century on Test debut but the West Indies won.

West Indies toured South Africa in 1998–99 and were whitewashed 5–0. It was a good all-round performance, with Jacques Kallis (485 runs) the best batsman and Shaun Pollock (29 wickets at 16.65) and Allan Donald (23 at 17.17) the leading bowlers. South Africa won again, 2–1 in a five-match series, in the West Indies in 2000-01. Daryll Cullinan and captain Shaun Pollock were match-winners, while Courtney Walsh became the first bowler in Test history to reach 500 wickets.

TEST RESULTS

SOUTH AFRICA v WEST INDIES

	Matches	WI	SA	Draw	Series	WI	SA	Draw
In West Indies	10	2	4	4	2	0	2	0
In South Africa	9	0	8	1	2	0	2	0
Totals	19	2	12	5	4	0	4	0

South Africa easily won a four-match series 3–0 at home in 2003–04. Kallis again batted superbly, scoring 712 runs at an average of 178.00, while Herschelle Gibbs averaged 116.60. The stars in the bowling department were Makhaya Ntini, with 29 wickets at 21.37, and Andre Nel, 22 at 23.18.

In a four-match series dominated by batsmen in West Indies in 2004–05 South Africa won 2–0. In the fourth Test Chris Gayle scored 317, while four players on each side scored centuries. In the first Test, both Wavell Hinds and Shivnarine Chanderpaul hit double centuries. The middle two Tests were won by South Africa through better bowling, again mostly from Ntini and Nel.

INDIA v ZIMBABWE

Zimbabwe became the ninth Test-playing country in 1992–93 when they drew with India in Harare. Their captain, David Houghton, scored 121, became the first player to make a century in his country's inaugural Test since Charles Bannerman in the very first Test of all 116 years earlier. In Delhi later the same season India won easily. Zimbabwe beat India for the first time in Zimbabwe in 1998–99 winning by 61 runs. The first series of two Tests, between the countries took place in India in 2000–01, with India winning 1–0, despite Andy Flower scoring 540 runs in four innings, twice out. Rahul Dravid made 432 in three innings for once out and Sachin Tendulkar 362 in three innings, twice out. A return in Zimbabwe in June 2001 was drawn 1–1. India won 2–0 at home in 2001–02, with spinners Anil Kumble (16 wickets at 18.12) and Harbajan Singh (12 at 19.66) in control.

India won a two-match series in Zimbabwe in 2005–06, only needing to bat a second time in the second Test and then for only 14 balls.

TEST RESULTS	INDIA v ZIMBABWE							
	Matches	Ind	Zim	Draw	Series	Ind	Zim	Draw
In Zimbabwe	6	3	2	1	2	1	0	1
In India	5	4	0	1	2	2	0	0
Totals	11	7	2	2	4	3	0	1

NEW ZEALAND v ZIMBABWE

Ten days after their first-ever Test against India, Zimbabwe played New Zealand at Bulawayo, but rain prevented a result, which meant that Zimbabwe became the only Test country to avoid defeat in each of their first two Tests. In the second of a two-Test series, New Zealand won convincingly. Two Tests in New Zealand in 1995–96 were drawn, the first through rain, the second because batsmen were on top. Both Tests of a series in Zimbabwe in 1997–98 were drawn, with Grant Flower making a century in each innings in the first, and with New Zealand needing 11 with two wickets left at the end of the second. New Zealand won both Tests of a series at home later in the season. It was tighter, but still 2–0 for New Zealand in Zimbabwe in 2000–01, but Zimbabwe drew a one-off Test in New Zealand later that season. New Zealand easily won both matches of a series in Zimbabwe in 2005–06.

TEST RESULTS	NEW ZEALAND v ZIMBABWE							
	Matches	NZ	Zim	Draw	Series	NZ	Zim	Draw
In Zimbabwe	8	5	0	3	4	3	0	1
In New Zealand	5	2	0	3	2	1	0	1
Totals	13	7	0	6	6	4	0	2

SOUTH AFRICA v INDIA

South Africa entertained India in 1992–93 in their first home series since being banned from Test cricket. South Africa's Jimmy Cook immediately made history as the first debutant to be out first ball of a Test. The South African captain Kepler Wessels scored 118 and became the first player to score Test centuries for two different countries, having made four centuries for Australia. When India batted, Sachin Tendulkar became the first player to be given out (run out) by the third umpire watching the television slow-motion replay, this being the first series of "trial by television". South Africa won their first Test and series (with three draws) since their re-admission. Solid batting all through and 20 wickets from fast bowler Allan Donald made the difference between the sides.

A series in India in 1996–97 resulted in a 2–1 win for India. Gary Kirsten made a century in each innings for South Africa in Calcutta, but Mohammed Azharuddin was the series' best batsman. A return series in South Africa, however, ended 2–0 in favour of South Africa. The fast bowling of Allan Donald and Shaun Pollock and the all-round play of Brian McMillan, were decisive.

South Africa comfortably won both Tests of a two-match series in India in 1999–2000. South Africa, thanks largely to Pollock and Herchelle Gibbs, won 2–0 in 2001–02, a third Test, which South Africa also won, being declared unofficial after India refused to accept a one-match ban on Virender Sehwag for intimidatory appealing.

India deservedly won a two-match series 1–0 in India in 2004–05, the breakthrough on good batting wickets being made by Harbhajan Singh with seven for 87 in the second innings at Kolkata, where Anil Kumble equalled Kapil Dev's 434 Test wickets for India.

TEST RESULTS	SOUTH AFRICA v INDIA							
	Matches	SA	Ind	Draw	Series	SA	Ind	Draw
In South Africa	9	4	0	5	3	3	0	0
In India	7	3	3	1	3	1	2	0
Totals	16	7	3	6	6	4	2	0

SOUTH AFRICA v SRI LANKA

In 1993–94, South Africa played a three-match series in Sri Lanka, winning 1–0. They also won both matches of a home two-Test series in 1997–98, Daryll Cullinan getting two centuries. A three-match series in Sri Lanka in 1999–2000 was drawn, Sri Lanka winning the first Test by an innings. South Africa won 2–0 at home in both 2000–01 and 2002–03, with Shaun Pollock and Jacques Kallis men of the Series. Sri Lanka won a home series in 2004–05 1–0 with a double century in each match from Mahela Jayawardene (237) and Kumar Sangakkara (232).

TEST RESULTS

SOUTH AFRICA v SRI LANKA

	Matches	SA	SL	Draw	Series	SA	SL	Draw
In Sri Lanka	8	2	2	4	3	1	1	1
In South Africa	7	6	0	1	3	3	0	0
Totals	15	8	2	5	6	4	1	1

PAKISTAN v ZIMBABWE

Zimbabwe lost their first series in Pakistan 2–0 in 1993–94 but, next season, in Zimbabwe recorded their first Test win, by an innings and 64. Grant Flower scored 201 not out for Zimbabwe, adding 269 for the fourth wicket with his brother Andy (156). Pakistan won the series 2–1. In 1996–97 and 1997–98 Pakistan won 1–0. In former, Wasim Akram made 257 not out for Pakistan, the highest score by a number 8. His stand of 313 with Saqlain Mushtaq (79) was a Test record. In a rain-affected 1998–99 series, Zimbabwe won 1–0, but lost 2–0 in Zimbabwe in 2002–03.

TEST RESULTS

PAKISTAN v ZIMBABWE

	Matches	Pak	Zim	Draw	Series	Pak	Zim	Draw
In Pakistan	7	3	1	3	3	2	1	0
In Zimbabwe	7	5	1	1	3	3	0	0
Totals	14	8	2	4	6	5	1	0

WEST INDIES V SRI LANKA

TEST RESULTS

WEST INDIES v SRI LANKA

	Matches	WI	SL	Draw	Series	WI	SL	Draw
In Sri Lanka	6	0	5	1	3	0	2	1
In West Indies	4	2	0	2	2	2	0	0
Totals	10	2	5	3	5	2	2	1

Rain spoiled the first Test at Moratuwa in 1993–94. Hosts West Indies won 1–0 in 1996–97. A 3–0 home Sri Lanka win in 2001–02 hid some remarkable statistics. Muttiah Muralitharan took 21 wickets in the first two Tests, while Chaminda Vaas took 14 in the third. Brian Lara scored 688 runs, Hashan Tillekeratne 403 in reply. The West Indies won 1–0 at home in 2002–03. Muralitharan, back from injury, took 17 wickets and Vaas 13 to help Sri Lanka win a two-match series 2–0 at home in 2005–06.

SOUTH AFRICA v PAKISTAN

Pakistan visited Johannesburg for a single Test in 1994–95, which South Africa won by 324 runs.

A series of three Tests in Pakistan in 1997–98 was won by South Africa 1–0 after two rain-affected draws. A return that season in South Africa was drawn 1–1. The highlight was 108 by Pat Symcox batting at number ten in the drawn Test.

South Africa easily won two home Tests in 2002–03. Outstanding was an opening stand of 368 at Cape Town between Hershelle Gibbs (228) and Graeme Smith (151). Pakistan then won 1–0 at home in 2003–04.

TEST RESULTS

SOUTH AFRICA v PAKISTAN

	Matches	SA	Pak	Draw	Series	SA	Pak	Draw
In South Africa	6	4	1	1	2	1	0	1
In Pakistan	5	1	1	3	2	1	1	0
Totals	11	5	2	4	4	2	1	1

SRI LANKA v ZIMBABWE

TEST RESULTS

SRI LANKA v ZIMBABWE

	Matches	SL	ZIM	Draw	Series	SL	ZIM	Draw
In Zimbabwe	8	3	0	5	3	2	0	1
In Sri Lanka	7	7	0	0	3	3	0	0
Totals	15	10	0	5	6	5	0	1

Test cricket's then youngest nations met in Zimbabwe in 1994–95, and drew three times. David Houghton's 266 remains Zimbabwe's highest Test innings. Sri Lanka won both home series 2–0 in 1996–97 and 1997–98 and won a three-Test series 1–0 in Zimbabwe in 1999–2000, though Andy Flower topped the batting with 388 for Zimbabwe. Sri Lanka won 3–0 at home in 2001–02 and in 2003–04 destroyed a dispute-ridden Zimbabwe with two innings defeats, Marvin Atapattu getting 249 and Kumar Sangakkara 270 in an innings of 713 for 3 in Bulawayo.

SOUTH AFRICA v ZIMBABWE

South Africa won a single Test match against Zimbabwe in Harare in 1995–96 season. Allan Donald, took 8 for 71, his best in Tests. They also won both matches played in 1999–2000, one in each country, by an innings in each case. South Africa won 1–0 in Zimbabwe in 2001–02. In the defeat Zimbabwe's Andy Flower scored 142 and 199 not out, more than half his side's total runs.

Jacques Kallis starred with bat and ball, as South Africa enjoyed two innings victories at home in 2004–05. Zimbabwe were dismissed for their lowest-ever 54 in Cape Town.

TEST RESULTS

SOUTH AFRICA v ZIMBABWE	Matches	SA	Zim	Draw	Series	SA	Zim	Draw
In Zimbabwe	4	3	0	1	1	1	0	0
In South Africa	3	3	0	1	1	1	0	0
Totals	7	6	0	1	2	2	0	0

ENGLAND v ZIMBABWE

England played a two-match Test series in Zimbabwe in 1996–97. In the first Test at Bulawayo, England gained a first-innings lead of 30 and, when Zimbabwe were dismissed for 234 in their second knock, needed 205 to win in a minimum 37 overs. A second-wicket partnership of 137 between Nick Knight and Alec Stewart took the score to 154, but England failed to press home the advantage and finished on 204 for 6, managing only a draw with the scores level, the first such instance in Test cricket. The second Test was spoiled by rain and ended in a draw.

Zimbabwe toured England in 2000 and 2003, losing three of the four Tests by an innings, with rain spoiling the other (in 2000).

TEST RESULTS

ENGLAND v ZIMBABWE	Matches	Eng	Zim	Draw	Series	Eng	Zim	Draw
In Zimbabwe	2	0	0	2	1	0	0	1
In England	4	3	0	1	2	2	0	0
Totals	6	3	0	3	3	2	0	1

ENGLAND CAPTAIN *Mike Atherton cuts hard behind point.*

AUSTRALIA v ZIMBABWE

Australia visited Zimbabwe in 1999–2000 and played a single Test, winning by ten wickets. Zimbabwe made 194 and 232 (Murray Goodwin was top-scorer for the hosts with 91), while Steve Waugh made the only century of the match, 151 not out, in Australia's 422 all out.

In 2003–04 Australia won both Tests. Matthew Hayden dominated, making a record Test score (since surpassed) of 380 at Perth. At Sydney he made 20 and 101 not out, to average 250.50 for the series.

TEST RESULTS

AUSTRALIA v ZIMBABWE	Matches	Aus	Zim	Draw	Series	Aus	Zim	Draw
In Zimbabwe	1	1	0	0	0	0	0	0
In Australia	2	2	0	0	1	1	0	0
Totals	3	3	0	0	1	1	0	0

WEST INDIES v ZIMBABWE

Zimbabwe toured West Indies in 1999–2000. In the first Test, they dismissed West Indies for 187 then 147 after making 236 in their first innings (Andy Flower 113 not out) Zimbabwe needed only 99 to win but were out for 63. West Indies were captained by Jimmy Adams for the first time. They won the second Test by ten wickets, a match notable for Courtney Walsh passing Kapil Dev's world record of 434 Test wickets in front of his home crowd at Sabina Park. West Indies won 1–0 in Zimbabwe in July 2000 and by the same margin in 2003–04, when the West Indies' last pair batted for 71 minutes to save the first Test.

TEST RESULTS

WEST INDIES v ZIMBABWE	Matches	WI	Zim	Draw	Series	WI	Zim	Draw
In West Indies	2	2	0	0	1	1	0	0
In Zimbabwe	4	2	0	2	2	2	0	0
Totals	6	4	0	2	3	3	0	0

INDIA v BANGLADESH

INDIA v BANGLADESH

	Matches	Ind	Ban	Draw	Series	Ind	Ban	Draw
In Bangladesh	3	3	0	0	1	1	0	0
Totals	3	3	0	0	1	1	0	0

On 10 November 2000 Bangladesh became the tenth Test playing country when the met India in a one-off match in Dhaka, a Test India won by 10 wickets. India toured Bangladesh in 2004–05 and won both Tests by an innings. Sachin Tendulkar scored 248 not out in the first Test and Bangladesh's Mohammad Ashraful 158 not out in the second. India's Irfan Pathan was Player of the Series with 18 wickets, while Anil Kumble passed Kapil Dev's 434 Test wickets for India.

ZIMBABWE v BANGLADESH

ZIMBABWE v BANGLADESH

	Matches	Zim	Ban	Draw	Series	Zim	Ban	Draw
In Zimbabwe	4	3	0	1	2	2	0	0
In Bangladesh	4	1	1	2	2	1	1	0
Totals	8	4	1	3	4	3	1	0

The two newest Test nations met in Zimbabwe in 2000–01. Zimbabwe won 2–0. Bangladesh's Javed Omar (85 not out) became the second man to carry his bat on his Test debut. Andy Flower equalled the record of Everton Weekes in scoring seven Test fifties in a row.

Zimbabwe won two rain-spoiled series 1–0 away in 2001–02 and at home in 2003–04.

Bangladesh won their first Test at the 35th attempt and first series 1–0 against Zimbabwe at home in 2004–05. Enamul Haque jnr, with 18 wickets, was Player of the Series.

PAKISTAN v BANGLADESH

Pakistan played Bangladesh in the Asian Test Championship in August 2000 in Multan and lost only three wickets in winning by an innings and 264 runs. Pakistan's next two Tests were in January, also against Bangladesh – but on tour – and were both won by an innings.

Three Tests in Pakistan in 2003–04 were all won by the home team. In the first Test, Yasir Hamed made a century in each innings for Pakistan. After two easy victories, Pakistan won by one-wicket in the final Test at Multan, with local hero Inzamam-ul-Haq scoring 138 not out.

PAKISTAN v BANGLADESH

	Matches	Pak	Ban	Draw	Series	Pak	Ban	Draw
In Pakistan	4	4	0	0	1	1	0	0
In Bangladesh	2	2	0	0	1	1	0	0
Totals	6	6	0	0	2	1	0	0

SRI LANKA v BANGLADESH

SRI LANKA V BANGLADESH

	Matches	SL	Ban	Draw	Series	SL	Ban	Draw
In Sri Lanka	5	5	0	0	2	2	0	0
Totals	5	5	0	0	2	2	0	0

Sri Lanka beat Bangladesh by an innings and 137 runs in the Asian Test Championship in September 2001 in Colombo. A series in Sri Lanka in July 2002 was won 2–0 by Sri Lanka, despite Sri Lanka making eight changes for the second Test.

Pinnaduwage De Silva and Sanath Jayasuriya put on 234 runs for the fifth wicket in the first Test, De Silva making 206. Michael Vandort, opening in the second Test, top scored with 140. Sri Lanka won a two-Test series both by an innings in 2005–06.

NEW ZEALAND v BANGLADESH

Bangladesh went to New Zealand for a two-match series in 2001–02 and lost both Tests by an innings. Mark Richardson and Craig McMillan put on 190 for the fifth wicket in the first Test, 15 runs short of Bangladesh's entire total. In the second Test the visitors were skittled out for 132 and 135. New Zealand visited Bangladesh in 2004–05 and again won both Tests by an innings. Player of the Series Daniel Vettori took 20 wickets. Stephen Fleming scored a double century in the second Test and James Franklin performed the hat-trick in the first.

NEW ZEALAND V BANGLADESH

	Matches	NZ	Ban	Draw	Series	NZ	Ban	Draw
In New Zealand	2	2	0	0	1	1	0	0
In Bangladesh	2	2	0	0	1	1	0	0
Totals	4	4	0	0	2	2	0	0

SOUTH AFRICA v BANGLADESH

South Africa first played a two-Test series at home to Bangladesh in 2002, which they won 2–0, with Gary Kirsten scoring a century in each match. They were far too strong for Test cricket's newest country, and won both matches by an innings.

In 2003 South Africa repeated the feat in Bangladesh. In the first Test, Jacques Rudolph made 222 not out on debut for South Africa – in a 429-run third-wicket partnership with Boeta Dippenaar (177) – and added 71 in the second Test to average 293.

TEST RESULTS

SOUTH AFRICA V BANGLADESH

	Matches	SA	Ban	Draw	Series	SA	Ban	Draw
In South Africa	2	2	0	0	1	1	0	0
In Bangladesh	2	2	0	0	1	1	0	0
Totals	4	4	0	0	2	2	0	0

WEST INDIES v BANGLADESH

Bangladesh hosted the West Indies in a two-match series in 2002-03. Although losing the first Test by an innings and 310 runs, they had the satisfaction of making the West Indies bat again for 111 in the second, and took three second-innings wickets. Jermaine Lawson of the West Indies took six wickets for three runs in the second innings.

In the West Indies in 2003–04, Bangladesh led on first innings and drew the first Test, but they lost the second, and the series by an innings, with Ramnaresh Sarwan scoring 261 not out.

TEST RESULTS

WEST INDIES V BANGLADESH

	Matches	WI	Ban	Draw	Series	WI	Ban	Draw
In Bangladesh	2	2	0	0	1	1	0	0
In West Indies	2	1	0	1	1	1	0	0
Totals	4	3	0	1	2	2	0	0

AUSTRALIA v BANGLADESH

Currently the most powerful side in the world, Australia took on the latest Test nation, Bangladesh, in a two-match series in Australia in June/July 2003, and predictably won both matches by an innings. Australian skipper Steve Waugh became the captain with the most wins (38) and the first to score 150 against each of the other nine Test countries and Darren Lehmann (two) and Martin Love also made centuries. The matches were played in Darwin and Cairns.

TEST RESULTS

AUSTRALIA V BANGLADESH

	Matches	Aus	Ban	Draw	Series	Aus	Ban	Draw
In Australia	2	2	0	0	1	1	0	0
Totals	2	2	0	0	1	1	0	0

ENGLAND v BANGLADESH

England were the last of the Test-playing countries to take on Bangladesh. They played a two-match series in Bangladesh in 2003–04, and won both matches, but needed to bat twice in each. England's total of 295 in the first Test was the lowest Test score by a touring side in Bangladesh.

England lost only three wickets per match in beating Bangladesh twice by an innings in a home series in early summer 2005. Marcus Trescothick scored 194 and 151, and Michael Vaughan and Ian Bell scored hundreds.

TEST RESULTS

ENGLAND V BANGLADESH

	Matches	Eng	Ban	Draw	Series	Eng	Ban	Draw
In Bangladesh	2	2	0	0	1	1	0	0
In England	2	2	0	0	1	1	0	0
Totals	4	4	0	0	2	2	0	0

TEST RESULTS

TOTAL TEST RESULTS 1876–77 TO 2005

	Played	Won	Lost	Draw	Tied	Wins/losses ratio
Australia	670	304	178	186	2	1.708
England	839	293	241	305	0	1.216
Pakistan	312	96	82	134	0	1.171
West Indies	423	149	130	143	1	1.146
South Africa	303	99	106	98	0	0.934

	Played	Won	Lost	Draw	Tied	Wins/losses ratio
Sri Lanka	153	41	58	54	0	0.707
India	387	84	127	175	1	0.661
New Zealand	324	59	128	137	0	0.461
Zimbabwe	83	8	49	26	0	0.163
Bangladesh	40	1	35	4	0	0.029

THE CRICKET WORLD CUP

For many years the pinnacle of the soccer world has been the World Cup. Although cricket's rules and regulations pre-date soccer's by over one hundred years, it was not until 1975 that the cricket authorities managed to organize a similar event. Even then, instead of being Test cricket it was confined to one-day matches. The World Cup, held every four years, has proved a popular success and nothing was more appropriate than that the 1996 World Cup should be won by Sri Lanka, until then considered by many to be inferior to the senior Test playing sides.

The first attempt in England to organize an international competition which involved more than one other country was staged in 1912. England invited Australia and South Africa to come and play a Triangular Tournament of Test Matches. Unfortunately, to quote a contemporary source "we had one of the most appalling summers ever known, even in England." It rained and rained. The cricket press forecast that it was an idea which would probably not be repeated for a generation. And so it proved.

In 1975 for the first World Cup, the *Wisden Almanack* commenced its report with "The First World Cup cricket tournament proved an outstanding success. Blessed by perfect weather, ideal conditions prevailed." Unlike the 1912 Triangular tournament, the authorities did not have to wait a generation to repeat the experiment.

HAPPY DAYS *The Australian squad celebrate their 125-run win over India in the World Cup final, 2003.*

WORLD CUP 1975

Venue: England

FIRST BLOOD TO WEST INDIES

The first World Cup was staged in England in June 1975. The trophy at stake was the Prudential Cup, Prudential having sponsored the competition to the tune of £100,000. There were eight countries competing: the six current Test-playing nations plus East Africa and Sri Lanka. It was noted with regret that South Africa were omitted. The teams were divided into two groups of four and the top two in each group would then meet in a knockout semi-final round. Each match would consist of 60 overs per side – the number used in the English Gillette Cup competition.

The first four matches commenced on June 7 at Lord's, Headingley, Old Trafford and Edgbaston. The most popular game was Australia v Pakistan at Headingley, where the ground sold out. Australia, batting first, reached 278 for 7, with Ross Edwards making a hard-hit 80. Pakistan lost Sadiq, Zaheer and Mushtaq cheaply and the game seemed all over, but Majid Khan was joined by Asif Iqbal and the score rose to 181 for 4 off 41 overs. Dennis Lillee returned to demolish the tail and bring Australia an easy win.

At Lord's, England completely outplayed India, after Dennis Amiss hit 137 – India's style was utterly cramped as they could only score 132 for 3 off their 60 overs, England winning by 202 runs. The minnows, Sri Lanka and East Africa, fell to the West Indies and New Zealand, Glenn Turner making 171 not out for the latter.

The second batch of games saw England beat New Zealand, Keith Fletcher making 131; Australia beat Sri Lanka, though only by 52 runs, a margin which would have been less if Jeff Thomson had not forced Wettimuny and Mendis to retire hurt when both were well established. India walked over East Africa – winning by 10 wickets with 30.1 overs to spare. The most exciting game was at Edgbaston,

where an incredible tenth-wicket stand of 64 by Deryck Murray and Andy Roberts produced a one-wicket victory for the West Indies over Pakistan. Sarfraz Nawaz had blown away the top West Indian batsmen.

The third batch of games saw England outplay East Africa, while Pakistan, put in to bat, dealt convincingly with Sri Lanka. The most exciting game was West Indies v Australia at the Oval. Clive Lloyd put Australia in and the fast attack led by Andy Roberts kept the Australia total below 200. For Australia everything depended on Lillee and Thomson, but the former was out of sorts and a brilliant batting display by Alvin Kallicharran, who hit 35 off 10 deliveries from Lillee, saw the West Indies win with 14 overs to spare.

In the other game, an unbeaten century by Glenn Turner saw New Zealand home against India at Old Trafford.

The first semi-final produced bitter criticism of the Headingley pitch, which was green and damp. Australia put England in and none of the home batsmen could master the conditions. England were bowled out for 93, with Gary Gilmour, the left-arm seamer, returning figures of six for 16. Australia's batsmen found the pitch difficult but Gilmour hit an unbeaten 28 and his team won by four wickets.

In the second semi-final, the winner of the toss, Clive Lloyd, also

EASY VICTORY *for Alvin Kallicharran and the West Indies over Australia.*

put the opposition in. New Zealand fared better on the Oval pitch than England had done at Headingley, but they could only make a modest 158 and Kallicharran again starred as the outstanding Caribbean batsman.

The final was staged at Lord's between Australia and the West Indies before a capacity crowd of 26,000. The West Indies were put in and lost their first three wickets for 50. Clive Lloyd joined Rohan Kanhai in a partnership which changed the game. Lloyd was on his best form, as was demonstrated when he hooked Lillee for six. With the latter batsmen all making useful contributions, the West Indian total reached

a very respectable 291 for eight.

Australia were not daunted by the target set. Ian Chappell batted very competently for 62, opener Alan Turner made 40, but some brilliant fielding allied to a casual approach to running meant that no fewer than four Australians were run out, including most importantly both Greg and Ian Chappell. Despite these errors, Australia lost only by the narrow margin of 17 runs, the game not ending until nearly quarter to nine. Prince Philip presented the trophy to Clive Lloyd amid great cheers from the large contingent of West Indian supporters in the crowd. Clive Lloyd was also given the Man-of-the-Match award.

RESULTS	FINAL QUALIFYING TABLE				
	GROUP A				
		P	**W**	**L**	**Pts**
	England	3	3	0	12
	New Zealand	3	2	1	8
	India	3	1	2	4
	East Africa	3	0	3	0
	GROUP B				
		P	**W**	**L**	**Pts**
	West Indies	3	3	0	12
	Australia	2	2	1	8
	Pakistan	3	1	2	4
	Sri Lanka	3	0	3	0

SEMI-FINALS *England* 93 (36.2 overs); *Australia* 94–6 (28.4 overs)
Australia won by four wickets
Man of the Match: G.J. Gilmour

New Zealand 158 (52.2 overs); *West Indies* 159–5 (40.1 overs)
West Indies won by five wickets
Man of the Match: A.I. Kallicharran

FINAL *West Indies* 291–8 (60 overs); *Australia* 274 (58.4 overs)
West Indies won by 17 runs
Man of the Match: C.H. Lloyd

WORLD CUP 1979

Venue: England

ENGLISH WEATHER CAN'T KEEP THE CARIBS DOWN

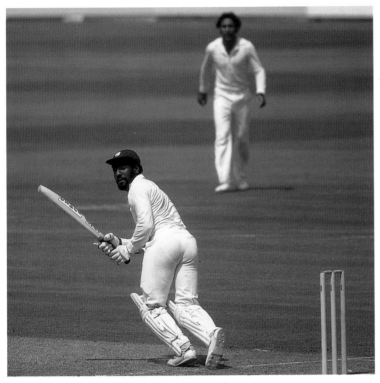

138 NOT OUT *for Viv Richards in the 1979 Final.*

In 1975, the World Cup had been played in a flaming English June; four years later June was not quite so kind, though only one match was totally washed out. However the Prudential Assurance Company upped their sponsorship to £250,000 and, because of increased prices, the receipts for matches were nearly double those of 1975 though the spectator numbers dropped by 28,000. The format was the same as for the first World Cup and there was only one team change, Canada replacing East Africa. Each side was allowed 60 overs, but the umpires were now instructed to deal more harshly with wides and bumpers.

The first batch of matches took place on June 9 at Edgbaston, Lord's, Headingley and Trent Bridge, the match of the round being that at headquarters between England and Australia. All tickets were sold prior to the day, and Mike Brearley, viewing a dull grey morning, put the opposition in. Runs came very slowly – only 14 off the first 10 overs – and by the time the first wicket fell the scoreboard read 56 off 21 overs. Brearley amazed everyone by putting Geoff Boycott on to bowl, but his tactic proved correct as Boycott removed both Andrew Hilditch and Kim Hughes. This was followed by a rash of run outs – four in all – and England were set just 160 to win. Graham Gooch made 53, Brearley 44 and England won by six wickets.

In the three other games, the West Indies crushed India. 75 from Viswanath enabled the Indians to make 190 all out before Gordon Greenidge and Desmond Haynes opened for the West Indies with a stand of 138. The former went on to a century and, in partnership with Viv Richards, brought a nine-wicket victory. The Pakistan v Canada match saw a very similar result, Pakistan cruising home by eight wickets, with Sadiq making a top score of 57 not out.

The same scenario occurred at Trent Bridge, where New Zealand won by nine wickets against Sri Lanka, Glenn Turner being the star batsman with 83 not out.

The weather affected the second batch of matches – all three days of the West Indies v Sri Lanka game saw the players sitting in the Leeds pavilion. At Old Trafford, the first day of England v Canada was washed out. The match began an hour late on day two in very poor conditions. Canada were bowled out for 45, Chris Old taking four for 8. It took England 13.5 overs to knock off the runs.

At Trent Bridge play was possible on the first day of Australia v Pakistan. Australia were without Rodney Hogg and Pakistan scored freely to reach 286 for seven on a rain-interrupted day. On the second day, the Australian batting never looked like scoring the runs required and Pakistan sailed home. New Zealand's batsmen found no difficulty in scoring the 183 required off India's attack – Bruce Edgar hit 84 and with John Wright added 100 before the first wicket fell.

In the third batch of games, Sri Lanka took centre stage, being the first non-Test-playing country to win a game in the World Cup. Playing India at Old Trafford, they were without their captain, Anura Tennekoon, but still hit 238 for five, with three players making fifties. The Indian innings did not begin until the second day. India seemed confident whilst Sunil Gavaskar and A.D. Gaekwad put on 60 for the first wicket, but the leg breaks of Somachandra de Silva caused the middle order problems and Sri Lanka dismissed their opponents for 191.

Brilliant sunshine greeted the semi-finals. There was a very exciting game at Old Trafford. New Zealand put England in and, though both Mike Brearley and Graham Gooch made fifties, Richard Hadlee caused all the early batsmen problems. Derek Randall came in at number 7 to make the tail wag and push the total over 200. With John Wright batting well, New Zealand kept in touch with the target and required 14 from the final over – they couldn't manage it, England winning by nine runs. In the other semi, the West Indies scored a rapid 293 for six, Gordon Greenidge being the top run-getter with 73.

For Pakistan, Majid Khan and Zaheer added 166 for the second wicket in 36 overs, before Colin Croft took three wickets in 12 balls and seized the initiative.

A full house at Lord's saw an outstanding batting display by Viv Richards, 138 not out and, though Mike Brearley and Geoff Boycott opened England's reply with a stand of 129, the scoring rate was too low. Viv Richards was Man of the Match as the West Indies won by 92 runs.

RESULTS

FINAL QUALIFYING TABLES

GROUP A

	P	W	L		Pts
England	3	3	0		12
Pakistan	3	1	2		8
Australia	3	1	2		4
Canada	3	0	3		0

GROUP B

	P	W	L	NR	Pts
West Indies	3	2	0	1	10
New Zealand	3	2	1	0	8
Sri Lanka	3	1	1	1	6
India	3	0	3	0	0

SEMI-FINALS *England* 221–8 (60 overs);
New Zealand 212–9 (60 overs)
England won by nine runs
Man of the Match: G.A. Gooch

West Indies 293–6 (60 overs);
Pakistan 250 (56.2 overs)
West Indies won by 43 runs
Man of the Match: C.G. Greenidge

FINAL *West Indies* 286–9 (60 overs);
England 194 (51 overs)
West Indies won by 92 runs
Man of the Match: I.V.A. Richards

WORLD CUP 1983

Venue: England

UNDERDOGS INDIA BEAT THE ODDS

The third World Cup, again sponsored by Prudential, saw the company put £500,000 into the kitty. The total attendance rose to 232,081, but the number of matches was substantially increased, each team in the group playing six games instead of three. Again the competition was staged in England, with one team change from the previous tournament: Zimbabwe replaced Canada. The weather was much kinder than in 1979, though England suffered a very wet May.

The sensation of the first batch of matches came at Trent Bridge where Zimbabwe beat Australia by 13 runs. The Zimbabwean captain Duncan Fletcher rescued his side from a poor start with an innings of 69 and the total was 239–6. Fletcher then took four for 42 as Australia struggled against some accurate bowling and good fielding.

India also caused an upset by beating the West Indies at Old Trafford. For once, the Caribbean batting was not up to the mark, Andy Roberts and last man Joel Garner being their highest scorers as India won by 34 runs.

In the second batch of games the West Indies recovered their poise with a 101-run win over Australia, Winston Davis returning figures of seven for 51. England always looked like beating Sri Lanka, David Gower scoring 130, and for New Zealand Richard Hadlee bowled brilliantly as Pakistan crashed to three down before a run was on the board. New Zealand won by 52 runs.

Australia won at last in the third batch of games, trouncing India by 162 runs; Trevor Chappell made 110 and Ken MacLeay took six for 39. Zimbabwe were brushed aside by the West Indies at Worcester, Gordon Greenidge making 105 not out.

Round four saw a nail-biting finish at Edgbaston, where New Zealand beat England with one

delivery unbowled and two wickets in hand. David Gower was again in splendid form for the home country, making 92 not out, but few of his compatriots could master Richard Hadlee. John Bracewell hit the penultimate ball for four to seal England's fate.

Australia managed to put Zimbabwe in their place when they played the return fixture at Southampton, whilst all England's batsmen – Fowler, Tavare, Gower and Lamb – flourished at the expense of Pakistan. On the same day, however, at Derby, Sri Lanka gained their single victory of the tournament, beating New Zealand by three wickets; Ashantha de Mel took five for 32 as the Kiwis were dismissed for 181, then Roy Dias hit 64 not out to bring Sri Lanka victory by three wickets. Zimbabwe nearly pulled off a sensation against India at Tunbridge Wells: India were five down for 17 and seven for 78, but Kapil Dev, coming in at number 6 hit 175 and, with Kirmani, added 126 for the 9th wicket. Even so, Zimbabwe batted well in reply, losing by just 31 runs. India went on to beat Australia by 118 runs at Chelmsford, Madan Lal taking four for 20 as Australia collapsed in the final innings, being 129 all out. This gave India a place in the semi-finals, against all the bookmakers' odds.

In the first semi-final, India met England at Old Trafford. To everyone's surprise, the England batting failed to score with any authority against a modest Indian attack and India had no trouble in reaching their target of 214, Yashpal Sharma hitting 61. In the other semi-final, Pakistan had the more difficult task of scoring from the formidable West Indian attack. Mohsin Khan made 70, but no one stayed with him and the West Indies were left needing 185. Viv Richards was in top form, making 80 not out as the Caribs won with 11.2 overs and eight wickets in hand.

The underdogs India therefore came to Lord's to meet Clive Lloyd's West Indians. Lloyd duly won the toss and naturally put India in. Facing Roberts, Garner, Marshall and Holding, the Indian batsmen were dismissed for 183, only Srikkanth managing to top 30.

For the crowd it seemed as if the West Indies merely had an afternoon's stroll in order to win the £20,000 prize. Gordon Greenidge, that most prolific of one-day batsmen, was out for a single – a minor disappointment. Desmond Haynes and Viv Richards took the total to 50 in an easy manner, then Madan Lal, bowling medium-pace seamers, struck. He dismissed Haynes, Richards and Gomes. Clive Lloyd fell to Binny and the score was suddenly 66 for five, then 76 for six. Malcolm Marshall came to partner wicket-keeper Dujon. Three figures were on the board. Gradually the two seemed to be turning the game the West Indies' way, but Mohinder Amarnath dismissed both and India won by 43 runs.

ALL ROUND CRICKET *from Mohinder Amarnath helped India to the final at Lord's.*

FINAL QUALIFYING TABLES			
GROUP A			
	P	W	L	Pts
England	6	5	1	20
Pakistan	6	3	3	12
New Zealand	6	3	3	12
Sri Lanka	6	1	5	4
GROUP B			
	P	W	L	Pts
West Indies	6	5	1	20
India	6	4	2	16
Australia	6	2	4	8
Zimbabwe	6	1	5	4

SEMI-FINALS *England* 213 (60 overs); *India* 217–4 (54.4 overs) *India won by six wickets* Man of the Match: M. Amarnath

Pakistan 184–8 (60 overs); *West Indies* 188–2 (48.4 overs) *West Indies won by eight wickets* Man of the Match: I.V.A. Richards

FINAL *India* 183 (54.4 overs); *West Indies* 140 (52 overs) *India won by 43 runs* Man of the Match: M. Amarnath

WORLD CUP 1987

Venue: India and Pakistan

AUSSIES BATTLE THROUGH

BORDER AND GATTING *the captains greet each other at the 1987 Final.*

The fourth World Cup, sponsored by Reliance, was staged in India and Pakistan. The same eight sides as played in 1983 were assembled and, as in the third cup, each team played six matches to settle positions in two group tables. The number of overs per side was reduced from 60 to 50. The Group A matches were played in India and Group B in Pakistan. Each country staged a semi-final, with the final held in Calcutta.

The competition got off to an exciting start in Madras. Geoff Marsh hit 110 as Australia began the game by making 270–7. India made a confident reply, Gavaskar, Srikkanth and Sidhu all in good form, so that the total rose to 207 for two. Craig McDermott, however, removed India's middle order and Australia won off the penultimate ball by one run. The next day in Hyderabad saw a match of almost equal excitement, when New Zealand beat Zimbabwe by three runs. The Kiwis made 242. Zimbabwe seemed a one-man band as David Houghton batted totally unsupported and the score

slumped to 104 for seven. Then Butchart arrived at number 9, the total doubled before the next wicket went down and New Zealand only won by dint of two run-outs, when Zimbabwe required six from the final over.

Heavy rain at Indore meant that the first Australia v New Zealand game was put off to the second day, and reduced to 30 overs per side. Through David Boon and Dean Jones, Australia made 199 for four. New Zealand made good progress and were 133 for two. They needed seven from the final over, but lost three wickets and made only three runs.

For the rest of the matches in Group A, the advantage remained with Australia and India, who both won five of six matches. In the final four games, India beat Zimbabwe by seven wickets and New Zealand by nine wickets, Sunil Gavaskar hitting a marvellous unbeaten 103 in the second game. Australia beat New Zealand by 17 runs, with Geoff Marsh scoring 126 not out, and Zimbabwe by 70 runs, Boon making 93.

Over in Pakistan, the host country had a tight match against Sri Lanka, winning by 15 runs only, in spite of 103 by Javed Miandad. A well-fought battle in Gujranwala, gave England a two-wicket win over the West Indies, Allan Lamb scoring 67, but England then came unstuck against Abdul Qadir whose spin brought Pakistan victory by 18 runs at Rawalpindi.

Pakistan went on to victory by one wicket over the West Indies.

Pakistan also beat England, but by a much larger margin, when Qadir again proved the best bowler. On the same day in Karachi, Viv Richards broke the World Cup record with an innings of 181 off 125 balls; Desmond Haynes also hit a century in the same game as Sri Lanka conceded 360 runs and lost by 191 runs. In the return fixture, Sri Lanka did much better but, needing 37 off the final four overs, Sri Lanka couldn't score off Patterson and Benjamin, so the West Indies won by 25. England, though, did manage to beat the West Indies in Jaipur and thus qualify for the semi-finals. Graham Gooch made 92.

In the first semi in Lahore, Australia batted well to make 267

for eight – for once Qadir failed to take a wicket. Javed Miandad and Imran Khan added 112 for the fourth Pakistani wicket after the first three batsmen fell cheaply, but Craig McDermott bowled accurately, taking five for 44 as the later home batsmen contributed little.

India put England in in Bombay. Gooch mastered the slow pitch and scored 115, giving England a total of 254. India looked on target so long as Azharuddin was attacking but, once Eddie Hemmings had him leg before, the English bowler took command. About 70,000 spectators came to watch the final in Calcutta. Australia decided to bat first. David Boon and Geoff Marsh took full advantage of some erratic opening overs by De Freitas and Small and this, in the end, proved the vital concession of the match. Allan Border and Mike Veletta kept Australia's runs flowing, so that England required 254. Gooch and Bill Athey took the England score to 66 for one; Mike Gatting and Allan Lamb made useful contributions, but England were gradually slipping behind the run rate. They needed 46 runs off the last five overs, but it was only narrowed to 17 off the final McDermott over, a task beyond Foster and Small. Australia, therefore, took the fourth World Cup by seven runs.

The main difference between this cup on the Indian subcontinent and those held in England was that the spin bowlers had much more opportunity – Hemmings and Emburey, for example, bowled 20 overs in the final – which was bound to add to the interest and break the dreadful monotony of pace.

RESULTS

FINAL QUALIFYING TABLES				
GROUP A				
	P	W	L	Pts
India	6	5	1	20
Australia	6	5	1	20
New Zealand	6	2	4	8
Zimbabwe	6	0	6	0
GROUP B				
	P	W	L	Pts
Pakistan	6	5	1	20
England	6	4	2	16
West Indies	6	3	3	12
Sri Lanka	6	0	6	0

SEMI-FINALS *Australia* 267–8 (50 overs);
Pakistan 249 (49 overs)
Australia won by 18 runs
Man of the Match: C.J. McDermott

England 254–6 (50 overs);
India 219 (45.3 overs)
England won by 35 runs
Man of the Match: G.A. Gooch

FINAL *Australia* 253–5; *England* 246–8
(50 overs)
Australia won by seven runs
Man of the Match: D.C. Boon

WORLD CUP 1992
Venue: Australia and New Zealand

IMRAN HAS THE LAST LAUGH

FINAL BAT *Imran Khan in the Final.*

There was a sensible format for the fifth World Cup in Australia and New Zealand in 1992. With South Africa recently returned to the fold of international cricket and Zimbabwe joining the Test match countries for the first time, there were nine entrants who played each other on a league basis, the top four qualifying for the semi-finals and final. So every country played at least eight matches. However, in the event, neither finalist could claim to have got there without luck or controversy – Pakistan by virtue of a point awarded for a "no-result" in a match they would almost certainly have lost, and England with the help of a "wet weather" rule which guaranteed them a semi-final win when the match was still in the balance.

The tournament was sold with the maximum amount of aggressive hype by Australian television, but the home country's expected easy ride to the knockout stages received a jolt in the first match,

when joint hosts New Zealand beat them by 37 runs. The New Zealand captain Martin Crowe made 100 not out in a total of 248 for six, and then, despite 100 from David Boon, Australia were bowled out for 211.

It was the start of a spectacular run by the New Zealanders who won their first seven matches and lost only to Pakistan in their last, by which time they had long qualified for the semi-finals. Martin Crowe, with 456 runs, was the highest scorer of the tournament, his average of 114 being 45 higher than the next best.

Australia also lost their second match, comprehensively beaten by nine wickets by South Africa, who made 171 for one wicket in reply to 170 for nine. Kepler Wessels, the South African captain, who had played Tests for Australia, made 81 not out. "This is the greatest moment in South African cricket," said Ali Bacher.

Apart from New Zealand, the only other team to march impressively on and clinch an early place in the semi-finals were England. A thrilling opening match with India was won by nine runs, and after six matches they had won five and drawn unluckily with Pakistan. After bowling Pakistan out for 74 (Pringle three for eight) England were 24 for one when persistent rain ended it. England finally lost to New Zealand and Zimbabwe when it didn't matter, giving Zimbabwe their only points.

South Africa became the third team to book a semi-final place by beating India in their last match, but the fourth semi-final place rested on the matches on the last day of the league section. The West Indies could have it by beating Australia, Australia could have it by beating the West Indies, but only if Pakistan lost, and Pakistan, who had started disastrously, could have it by beating New Zealand, provided Australia beat the West Indies. This last was what happened, thanks to Wasim

Akram taking four for 32 and an innings of 119 not out by opener Ramiz Raja.

As it happened, Pakistan had to play New Zealand again in the semi-final in Auckland. New Zealand made an excellent 262 for seven, with Martin Crowe run out for 91, but Pakistan achieved the runs thanks to a patient 57 not out by Javed Miandad, who anchored the innings, and a spectacular knock by Man-of-the-Match Inzamam-Ul-Haq, who came in at 140 for four and scored 60 in 37 balls.

In the other semi-final, South Africa put England in and bowled only 45 overs in their allotted time, from which England made 252 for six. With 10.10 p.m. fixed for the end of the day-night match, South Africa had reached 231 for six with 13 balls remaining when a downpour stopped play. When the players returned, the umpires decreed there was time for only seven balls but, as under the rules the lowest-scoring over of England's innings was discarded, the target was not reduced. However, before play could begin, there was another stoppage, reducing the time allowed

to only one ball. This time the target was reduced by one run to 21, and that was that.

Pakistan started slowly in the final, but scraped 249 for six. England batted disappointingly and were all out in the last over for 227, with Wasim Akram, who not only took three wickets but scored a vital 33 in 18 balls at the end of the Pakistan innings, becoming Man of the Match.

Martin Crowe was "Champion Player" of the tournament, winning cash and a Nissan motor car. Javed Miandad and South Africa's Peter Kirsten were the other batsmen to top 400 runs, while David Boon of Australia and Ramiz Raja each made two centuries. Wasim Akram took most wickets, 18, at the best average, 18.78, while Chris Harris (New Zealand), Ian Botham (England) and Mushtaq Ahmed (Pakistan) all captured 16 wickets.

The Pakistan skipper Imran Khan accepted the biggest prize, however, and couldn't help beaming at the way fortune had smiled for his team at half-way – after winning only one of their first five matches, they won all five thereafter.

RESULTS

FINAL QUALIFYING TABLES GROUP A						
	P	W	L	NR	Pts	NRR
New Zealand	8	7	1	0	14	0.59
England	8	5	2	1	11	0.47
South Africa	8	5	3	0	10	0.14
Pakistan	8	4	3	1	9	0.16
Australia	8	4	4	0	8	0.2
West Indies	8	4	4	0	8	0.07
India	8	2	5	1	5	0.14
Sri Lanka	8	2	5	1	5	-0.68
Zimbabwe	8	1	7	0	2	-1.14

NRR = Net Run Rate, calculated by subtracting runs per over conceded from runs per over scored, to be used in the event of a tie on points.

SEMI-FINALS *New Zealand* 262–7 (50 overs) (M.D. Crowe 91)
Pakistan 264–6 (49 overs) (Inzamam-Ul-Haq 60, Javed Miandad 57 not out)
Pakistan won by four wickets
Man of the Match: Inzamam-Ul-Haq

England 252–6 (45 overs) (Hick 83)
South Africa (revised target 252 in 43 overs)
232–6 (43 overs)
England won by 19 runs
Man of the Match: G.A. Hick

FINAL *Pakistan* 249–6 (50 overs) (Imran Khan 72, Javed Miandad 58, Pringle 3–22) *England* 227 (49.2 overs)
(Fairbrother 62, Wasim Akram 3–49, Mushtaq Ahmed 3–41)
Pakistan won by 22 runs
Man of the Match: Wasim Akram

WORLD CUP 1996

Venue: India, Pakistan and Sri Lanka

SRI LANKA CONQUER THE WORLD

There were 12 participants in the 1996 World Cup – the nine from 1992 (Zimbabwe was now a Test-playing country) plus Kenya, the Netherlands and the United Arab Emirates. The teams were split into two groups of six, each team to play the five others in their group, the top four in each group to play in the quarter-finals of the knockout stage. The whole tournament lasted 33 days in which 35 matches were played. The schedule consisted of 37 matches, but both Australia and the West Indies forfeited their matches against Sri Lanka, refusing to travel there after a terrorist bomb had killed 80 people in Colombo.

Sri Lanka, who were given the points for a win, were therefore more or less guaranteed a quarter-final place, but they nevertheless earned it by beating their other three opponents, Zimbabwe, India (in Delhi) and Kenya, against whom they made a world record for a one-day international of 398 for five.

The group produced one of cricket's biggest shocks when Kenya defeated the West Indies. With only one professional in the side, Kenya made 166 and dismissed the West Indies for 93. The result caused a crisis meeting of the West Indian Board, and Richie Richardson was lucky to retain the captaincy. However, 93 not out in the West Indies' final match, helping them beat Australia and qualify for the quarter-finals, proved his character.

In Group B, South Africa were impressive in winning all five matches, but there were no real surprises.

In the first quarter-final, Sri Lanka confirmed their form with an exciting victory over England. Sri Lanka were responsible in this tournament for a tactical innovation in limited-overs cricket by launching a batting assault from the first ball, the philosophy being to score fast while the fielding restrictions are in force, rather than build a foundation for a late assault. Coming together at 12, Jayasuriya and Gurusinha added 100 in 65 balls. Jayasuriya made 82 in 44 balls, including 22 in one over from De Freitas.

The sub-continent would have liked to see India play Pakistan in the final, but the two met at Bangalore in the quarters. With Pakistan's skipper, Wasim Akram unfit, India won by 39 runs, after Pakistan had forfeited an over of their innings for a slow bowling rate.

The new favourites, South Africa, were beaten by 19 runs by a rejuvenated West Indies, for whom Brian Lara made 111, while Australia beat New Zealand, despite a final New Zealand total of 286 for nine, of which Chris Harris made 130 and Lee Germon 89. Mark Waugh's 110 helped Australia to a comfortable win in the end by six wickets. Thus all four sides from Group A qualified for the semi-finals. Both of these were extraordinary matches, one in cricketing terms, the other because of crowd disturbances.

At Calcutta, India put in Sri Lanka. Both openers were out in the first over, caught at third man. In fact, the first three batsmen contributed two runs, but Aravinda de Silva continued attacking, reaching 53 in 32 balls, and Sri Lanka recovered to 251 for eight. India reached 98 for one, but Sanath Jayasuriya then dismissed both Tendulkar (65) and Manjrekar (25) and India collapsed in disarray. At 120 for eight after 34.1 overs, the 110,000 crowd began throwing bottles on the pitch, and referee Clive Lloyd took the teams off for a 20-minute cooling-off period. However, when the players returned, the bottle-throwing resumed, and Lloyd awarded the match to Sri Lanka by default.

In the other semi-final, Australia began disastrously, and were 15 for

ARAVINDA DE SILVA *in the final.*

four before Stuart Law (72) and Michael Bevan (69) squeezed the total to 207 for eight. At 165 for two, with Chanderpaul (80) and Richie Richardson established, the West Indies needed 43 in seven overs to win, but Shane Warne (4–36) inspired a panic. The last eight wickets went for 37 in 50 balls, leaving Richardson stranded on 49 not out and the West Indies five runs short of Australia.

Australia started well in the final, had 82 up in the first 15 overs and reached 137 before the second wicket fell, but Sri Lanka's bowlers then bowled very well and kept the final total down to a manageable 241 for seven. When Sri Lanka batted, a brilliant innings of 107 by Aravinda de Silva took his country to a convincing victory with runs and wickets in hand. Among the individual performances, Sachin Tendulkar made most runs, 523, while Australia's Mark Waugh and Aravinda de Silva of Sri Lanka also topped 400. Arjuna Ranatunga, the winning captain, averaged 120 by virtue of four not-outs.

RESULTS

FINAL QUALIFYING TABLES

GROUP A

	P	W	L	Pts
Sri Lanka	5	5	0	10
Australia	5	3	2	6
India	5	3	2	6
West Indies	5	2	3	4
Zimbabwe	5	1	4	2
Kenya	5	1	4	2

GROUP B

	P	W	L	Pts
South Africa	5	5	0	10
Pakistan	5	4	1	8
New Zealand	5	3	2	6
England	5	2	3	4
United Arab Emirates	5	1	4	2
The Netherlands	5	0	5	0

QUARTER-FINALS *England* 235–8; *Sri Lanka* 236–5 (40.4 overs)
India 287–8; *Pakistan* 248–9
West Indies 264–8; *South Africa* 245
New Zealand 286–9; *Australia* 289–4 (47.5 overs)

SEMI-FINALS *Sri Lanka* 251–8; *India* 120–8 (34.1 overs)
(Play ended because of crowd encroachment – match awarded to Sri Lanka)
Man of the Match: P. A. de Silva
Australia 207–8; *West Indies* 202
Australia won by five runs
Man of the Match: S. K. Warne

FINAL *Australia* 241–7 (Taylor 75, de Silva 3–42);
Sri Lanka 245–3 (46.2 overs) (Gurusinha 65, de Silva 107 notout)
Sri Lanka won by seven wickets
Man of the Match: P. A. de Silva

WORLD CUP 1999

Venue: England, Wales, Scotland, Ireland, the Netherlands

RUN OUT MIX-UP HELPS THE AUSSIES

ALLAN DONALD *run out in the semi-final with the scores level.*

Twelve teams competed in 1999, Scotland and Bangladesh replacing the Netherlands and the United Arab Emirates from 1996. From two initial groups of six, the top three went forward to the second stage, called the Super Six. Each team played three matches against the three teams from the opposite group, so that all six teams had then played each other once. The top four in the league table produced by these results provided the semi-finalists.

While most matches were played in England, two (involving Scotland) took place in Edinburgh, and one each in Cardiff, Dublin and Amstelveen in Holland.

In the opening match at Lord's, England beat the holders, Sri Lanka, who went on to lose twice more in Group A and were eliminated at the earliest stage. South Africa, India and Zimbabwe led the group, with England (on net run rate) and Kenya also being eliminated. The surprise team was Zimbabwe who, after beating Kenya, beat India by three runs. India, chasing 253, lost their last three wickets to Henry Olonga in one over. In their last match Zimbabwe beat South Africa by 48 runs. Neil Johnson opened both batting and bowling for Zimbabwe, scoring 76 and taking three for 27.

India's batsmen provided the record-breaking in this group. Against Kenya, Sachin Tendulkar (140) and Rahul Dravid (104) put on 237 unbroken for the third wicket against Kenya, a record World Cup partnership which lasted only until India's next match, when Dravid again (145) and Saurav Ganguly (183) added 318 for the second wicket against Sri Lanka.

In Group B Australia, after beating Scotland, lost their next two matches. New Zealand beat them by five wickets, with Roger Twose getting 80 not out, after Geoff Allott had four Aussie wickets for 37. Then in a thrilling game at Headingley, Pakistan beat Australia by 10 runs. The Aussies, set 276, needed 13 in the last over, but skipper Wasim Akram grabbed the last two wickets. Pakistan, Australia and New Zealand progressed. Bangladesh, who also beat Scotland, provided the shock of the tournament by beating Pakistan by 62 runs. A sell-out 7,000 crowd at Northampton went ballistic.

In the Super Six, Australia won all their three matches, but Zimbabwe caused momentary anxiety at Lord's. Chasing 304, they stood at 153 for one after 28 overs, but couldn't maintain the pace, and ended at 259 for six. Neil Johnson cored 132 not out from 144 balls.

Pakistan were beaten by India and South Africa. South Africa were set 221 to win, and were 58 for five. But Lance Klusener, the batsman who most excited the World Cup audiences, cracked 46 off 41 balls to win it by three wickets with an over to spare.

New Zealand made 241 for seven in the first semi-final at a sold-out Old Trafford. Shoaib Akhtar was the main destroyer. Pakistan began with a World Cup record opening stand of 194 between Saeed Anwar (113 not out) and Wajahatullah Wasti (94) and a 12-minute pitch invasion was all that delayed Pakistan thereafter.

At Edgbaston, another sell-out, Australia made 213 (Shaun Pollock 5-36). With six down for 175 Klusener (31 not out) came in. He faced the last over from Fleming with nine wanted and the last pair together. He hit two fours,

and off the fourth ball charged down the pitch for the winning run after a push past the bowler. He made his ground, but Allan Donald, his partner, was slow to respond, the ball was rolled back from bowler to keeper and Donald was run out halfway down the pitch. A great match was tied, but Australia went to the final on a better net run rate in the Super Six.

At Lord's, 30,000 saw a disappointing final. Pakistan failed to perform and were out for 132 (Warne 4-33). Australia knocked off the runs in the 21st over for an eight-wicket win.

Dravid was top batsman of the tournament with 461 runs, followed by Steve Waugh, Saurav Ganguly, Mark Waugh, Saeed Anwar and Neil Johnson (all 367 plus). Geoff Allott and Shane Warne (20) had most wickets, followed by Glenn McGrath, Lance Klusener and Saqlain Mushtaq.

RESULTS

FINAL QUALIFYING TABLES						
GROUP A						
	P	W	L	NR	PTS	NRR
South Africa	5	4	1	0	8	0.85
India	5	3	2	0	6	1.28
Zimbabwe	5	3	2	0	6	0.01
England	5	3	2	0	6	-0.33
Sri Lanka	5	2	3	0	4	-0.80
Kenya	5	0	5	0	0	-1.19
GROUP B						
	P	W	L	NR	PTS	NRR
Pakistan	5	4	1	0	8	0.50
Australia	5	3	2	0	6	0.73
New Zealand	5	3	2	0	6	0.57
West Indies	5	3	2	0	6	0.49
Bangladesh	5	2	3	0	4	-0.52
Scotland	5	0	5	0	0	-1.92
SUPER SIX						
	P	W	L	NR	PTS	NRR
Pakistan	5	3	2	0	6	0.65
Australia	5	3	2	0	6	0.36
South Africa	5	3	2	0	6	0.17
New Zealand	5	2	2	1	5	-0.52
Zimbabwe	5	2	2	1	5	-0.79
India	5	1	4	0	2	-0.15

SEMI-FINALS

New Zealand 241-7
Pakistan 242-1
Man of the Match: Shoaib Akhtar

Australia 213
South Africa 213
Man of the Match: Shane Warne
(Australia go through on net run rate in Super Six)

FINAL

Pakistan 132
Australia 133-2
Man of the Match: Shane Warne

CHAMPIONS *The Australian team celebrate with the World Cup trophy.*

WORLD CUP 2003

Venue: South Africa, Zimbabwe, Kenya

UNBEATEN AUSTRALIA NEVER THREATENED

RICKY PONTING *blasts a six to help the Aussies on the way to victory.*

The format for the 2003 World Cup played on the African continent was the same as that for the 1999 renewal, except that 14 teams competed instead of 12. Scotland was the only country missing from the 1999 competitors, with the Netherlands, Namibia and Canada coming in. All Zimbabwe's six Pool matches were scheduled for Harare or Bulawayo, while two of Kenya's were to be played in Nairobi. All other games took place at 12 venues in South Africa. Nine of the 54 matches were timed for 2.30 starts, with floodlit finishes, which, as the tournament progressed, seemed to give the side batting first a slight advantage.

Prolonged controversy surrounded the ICC decision to play matches in Zimbabwe, there being strong political objections from many sides because of the oppressive Zimbabwe regime. In the end, after bitter debates in the countries due to play there, only England refused, a decision largely taken by the players themselves in opposition to the England and Wales Cricket Board. New Zealand meanwhile declined to play in Nairobi on safety grounds.

England therefore forfeited their match to Zimbabwe and New Zealand likewise to Kenya. The decisions proved crucial to England's chance of reaching the Super Six stage, but New Zealand overcame the loss of points by beating the West Indies and South Africa in a dramatic match in which captain Stephen Fleming was inspirational.

There was sensation even before the matches began. Shane Warne, who announced before leaving for the World Cup that it would be his farewell to one-day internationals, was sent home from South Africa before a ball was bowled having been tested positive for taking a banned substance, in this instance some diuretics, allegedly on the advice of his mother. He was banned by the Australian Cricket Board for a year.

The matches themselves started with a shock, when the main hosts, South Africa, anxious to make up for their disappointing semi-final exit in 1999, lost the opening match to the West Indies by three runs. A scintillating 116 by Brian Lara turned the match. South Africa were then beaten by New Zealand, when rain reduced the Kiwis' target and they galloped to a nine-wicket win. Despite this, South Africa might have saved themselves by beating Sri Lanka in their last match, but miscalculated the Duckwith-Lewis figures and tied a match they could have won. Sri Lanka, New Zealand and Kenya (who beat Sri Lanka and took the points from the cancelled game with New Zealand) qualified from Pool B.

In Pool A, the Zimbabwe players Andy Flower and Henry Olonga issued a statement before their opening match 'mourning the death of democracy in our beloved Zimbabwe' and wore black armbands during the game. Olonga was dropped from subsequent matches, but a players' revolt saved Flower when the selectors

later wished to drop him, too. Having lost to India and Australia, who were to head Pool A, England's last hope of the Super Six disappeared when Zimbabwe received two points for a 'no result' against Pakistan, and took third place.

The Super Six provided no real shocks, but Kenya's place as third in the table, and thus in the semi-finals, would have been a major surprise before the event. Their forteited match against New Zealand meant they carried forward ten points to the Super Six, and defeating Zimbabwe was enough to get them through.

In the semis, Australia's batting was saved at 144 for 5 by Andrew Symonds, and Sri Lanka never got going. When rain sent the result to

Duckworth-Lewis, Australia were in the driving seat. Kenya's dream predictably came to an end with defeat by India.

Australia won the final, in style, making a big score and dismissing Tendulkar for 4. From then on, there was no doubting the winner.

The best batsman in the series was Sachin Tendulkar, with 673 runs (av. 61.18). Saurav Ganguly scored 465 (av. 58.12), Ricky Pointing 411 (av. 51.37), Adam Gilchrist 408 (av. 40.80) and Marvan Atapattu 368 (av. 61.33). Best bowlers were Chaminda Vaas (20 wickets at 14.85), Glenn McGrath (19 at 18.68), Andy Bichel (18 at 10.66, the best all-rounder of the tournament) and Shoaib Akhtar (17 at 17.05, and who reached 100 mph).

RESULTS

FINAL QUALIFYING TABLES
POOL A

	P	W	L	T	NR	PTS	SS BONUS*
Australia	6	6	0	0	0	24	4
India	6	5	1	0	0	20	4
Zimbabwe	6	3	2	0	1	14	3.5
England	6	3	3	0	0	12	-
Pakistan	6	2	3	0	1	10	-
Holland	6	1	5	0	0	4	-
Namibia	6	0	6	0	0	0	-

POOL B

	P	W	L	T	NR	PTS	SS BONUS*
Sri Lanka	6	4	1	1	0	18	3.5
Kenya	6	4	2	0	0	16	2
New Zealand	6	4	2	0	0	16	4
West Indies	6	3	2	0	1	14	-
South Africa	6	3	2	1	0	14	-
Canada	6	1	5	0	0	4	-
Bangladesh	6	0	5	0	1	2	-

*Qualifiers carried forward 1 bonus point to the Super Six for a win against a non-qualifier (0.5 point for a tie or no result).

SUPER SIX

	P	W	L	T	NR	PTS*
Australia	5	5	0	0	0	24
India	5	4	1	0	0	20
Kenya	5	3	2	0	0	14
Sri Lanka	5	2	3	0	0	11.5
New Zealand	5	1	4	0	0	8
Zimbabwe	5	0	5	0	0	3.5

*Including bonus points carried forward

SEMI-FINALS   *Australia* 212-7 (50 overs)
Sri Lanka 123-7 (38.1 overs)
Man of the Match: Andrew Symonds

India 240-7 (50 overs)
Kenya 179 (46.2 overs)
Man of the Match: Saurav Ganguly

FINAL   *Australia* 359-2 (50 overs)
India 234 (39.2 overs)
Man of the Match: Ricky Pointing

LEGENDS OF CRICKET

Becoming a legend in cricket is not a question of outstripping everyone else in statistics. Character, style, approach and temperament make mere figures secondary. In any case conditions change so much from era to era and from country to country that comparisons of figures tell only half the story. A player becomes a legend when he dominates an era, or shapes the course of cricket, or so transcends the game that he appeals to a wider audience. In short, he is a player who leaves a mark on the game and on the lives of those who follow it. All eleven in this section – including four players knighted for their services to cricket – comfortably satisfy the criteria. They represent cricket and sportsmanship at their best.

Another dozen players at least could easily have been included. Slow bowlers Rhodes, Grimmett, O'Reilly or Laker would clearly not be out of place, nor wicket-keepers Knott and Marsh. Many will wonder about the omission of Hutton, Compton, Trueman, George Headley, Worrell, Weekes, Barry and Viv Richards, Hanif, Kapil Dev, Doug Walters, Border and other famous players going back to the turn of the century, such as the immortal batsman, Victor Trumper. Short biographies of all of these and many more are included in the 'The Great Cricketers'.

The eleven players featured here represent well over 100 years of cricket history, from the 1870s and W.G. Grace to the present day and Brian Lara and Shane Warne. They include at least one player from six of the seven long-established Test countries and four men who have been knighted for their services to the game: Hobbs, Bradman, Sobers and Hadlee.

Five are all-rounders: Grace, Sobers, Botham, Hadlee and Imran Khan – the last three in the exclusive club (Kapil Dev the only other member) of players with 3,000 runs and 300 wickets in Tests. Four are batsmen: Hobbs,

'The Master' of England; Tendulkar, 'The Little Master' of India; Bradman of Australia, the greatest run-maker in history; and Lara, today's West Indian record-breaker. Two Australian bowlers complete the line-up: Dennis 'The Menace' Lillee and Shane Warne – the man who has done so much to encourage the new breed of spin bowler that has so dominated cricket in recent times..

LEAVING A MARK *Brian Lara will forever be a legend to the young fans who in 1994 witnessed – and celebrated – his world-record innings of 501 not out for Warwickshire against Durham.*

BOTHAM

Ian Botham was the typical schoolboy hero who could turn a match round in a couple of hours of extravagant strokeplay or bowling. He was a player who could make things happen.

BOTHAM *bowling in his last Test series, v Pakistan 1992.*

BEEFY TO THE RESCUE

Ian Terance Botham should really have been a Yorkshireman, like his father, but he was born prematurely in Cheshire, which at the time meant he was not qualified for Yorkshire. Their loss was Somerset's gain. Making his debut for the county in 1974, the 18-year-old Botham soon showed the swashbuckling characteristics which were to make him famous. In a Benson & Hedges Cup match at Taunton, a fast short ball from West Indian fast bowler Andy Roberts struck the helmetless Botham on the face, half felling him. The blow cost him four teeth but, with the last man in, Botham, in great pain, won the match with a boundary: 45 not out, and the 6,500 crowd had had the privilege of seeing the first significant signs of an outstanding batting career.

It wasn't long before Botham was England's best all-rounder – an aggressive batsman, fine swing bowler and brilliant and charismatic fielder. He made his Test debut against the Australians at Trent Bridge in 1977, and soon had his first wicket – Aussie skipper Greg Chappell. He claimed five wickets in the Australian first innings, and repeated the feat in the following Test match, England winning both.

In the winter, he scored his first Test century, against New Zealand (and also took eight wickets in the match). By the following summer, when he hit two centuries against Pakistan and achieved his best-ever bowling performance, 8–34, the 22-year-old was the hottest property in cricket.

Over a quarter of Botham's first-class matches were Tests, well over

and 100 Test wickets in his 21st Test, two fewer than the previous quickest (Mankad), and in 1979–80, in India's Golden Jubilee Test in Bombay, he became the first player to score a century and take 10 wickets in the same Test (114 and 13 for 106).

Botham became captain of England in 1980, but this proved to be the only area in which he failed. His form suffered and, after the second Test against Australia in 1981, he resigned the captaincy. This followed a chilling demonstration at Lord's when, after being bowled first ball in the second innings – to complete a pair – his return to the pavilion was marked by a frosty silence.

In answer, at Headingley in the next match, Botham produced one

BOTHAM AT BAT *for Queensland in 1987–88.*

> ## "Ian Botham had the mourners dancing in the aisles at Headingley last night with the greatest comeback since Lazarus."
>
> *PAT GIBSON, reporting on the 1981 England v Australia Test*

a quarter of his total runs were made in Tests, and practically a third of his total wickets were taken in Tests. The Test match arena became his natural habitat. In 1979, he passed 1,000 Test runs

of the greatest and most amazing all-round performances ever. Having taken six for 95 and scored 50 in the first innings, he went out to bat with England, following on, 105 for 5 in the second innings. Later, at 135 for 7 England still required 92 to avoid an innings defeat, with bookmakers quoting a victory at 500–1. In a heroic display of hitting, Botham smashed 149 not out and, with Bob Willis inspired to his best-ever bowling, helped dismiss Australia for 111 and give England an 18-run victory. He was only the second (after J.M. Gregory in 1920–21) to score a century and take five wickets in an innings in an Ashes Test.

And that was not all – at Edgbaston in the next Test, Botham claimed five wickets for one run to finish off the Aussies and give England a 29-run win, and then a magnificent, controlled 118 at Old Trafford gave England a third consecutive win. In his 12 matches as England captain, he had failed to register a win – in the

next three matches, he performed wonders to inspire three victories.

If his subsequent career did not produce comparable fireworks, the figures were outstanding nevertheless. He became the third (after Benaud and Sobers) to 2,000 Test runs and 200 Test wickets, and the youngest of them all at just over 26. Then in 1984 he became the first-ever Test player to reach 3,000 runs and 300 wickets.

In 1986, Botham became the leading wicket-taker in Test history when he passed Dennis Lillee's total of 355 (although with the current proliferation of Tests his own final tally of 383 wickets has been well surpassed).

Throughout his career, Botham made his own rules and was the centre of much controversy. There have been court appearances over drugs (a fine) and assault (dismissed), disparaging remarks about touring Pakistan (apologized for), dissent in a Test (reprimand), a well-publicized row with Somerset (he went to Worcestershire and helped win championships in 1988 and 1989), a row over ball-tampering with Imran Khan, accusations of being too domineering and getting too fat, and countless tabloid stories of reckless behaviour.

In retirement, there have been well-publicised walks for charity, and much successful television work, such as a team captaincy in the BBC quiz *A Question of Sport*, and latterly extensive commentating. He is still a true all-rounder.

CAREER FACT FILE

Born:	November 24, 1955, Oldfield, Heswell, Cheshire
Teams:	Somerset (1974–86), Worcestershire (1987–91), Durham (1992–93), Queensland (1987–88)
Tours:	Pakistan 1977–78; New Zealand 1977–78, 1983–84, 1991–92; Australia 1978–79, 1979–80, 1982–83, 1986–87; India 1979–80, 1981–82; Australia and New Zealand (World Cup) 1991–92; Worcestershire to Zimbabwe 1990–91.
First-class career:	(1974–93, 402 matches)
Batting:	runs 19,399; average 33.97; highest score 228; centuries 38
Bowling:	wickets 1,172; runs 31,902; average 27.22; best 8–34
Catches:	354
Tests:	(1977–92, 102 matches)
Batting:	runs 5,200; average 33.54; highest score 208; centuries 14
Bowling:	wickets 383; runs 10,878; average 28.40; best 8–34
Catches:	120

BRADMAN

Bradman dominated batting as no player before or since. His figures remain about 50 per cent better than those of anybody else in cricket history.

BRADMAN *going out to bat in his testimonial match, Melbourne, 1948. He scored 123.*

RELENTLESSLY FLOWS THE DON

HIP HIP HOORAY *Bradman (left) receiving three cheers from the England players before his last innings in Tests, Oval, 1948.*

There can be no other choice than Sir Donald George Bradman as the best batsman the world has ever seen. Arguments have been advanced for other players, usually on the grounds of Bradman having good firm Australian wickets to bat on, but it is clutching at straws because Bradman's record on his four tours of England is phenomenal: he scored 9,837 runs, averaging 96.44. Because of the increase nowadays in the number of matches, especially Test matches, many have surpassed him in aggregates, but his career average stands on its own 24 above the next player's, and his Test average is nearly 40 above anybody else's. A measure of his stature is that his worth as a Test run-getter practically equalled that of Allan Border and Viv Richards added together!

Bradman spent his boyhood in Bowral, 80 miles from Sydney, and developed his hand and eye coordination by hitting golf balls against a wall with a stump. In his first Sheffield Shield match aged 19 he scored 118, and throughout his career he continued to score a century for every three innings he played. And not only single centuries – 37 times he went past 200, six times past 300, both still records. His highest score is 452 not out. And he scored his runs quickly, only 12 times in his career batting for longer than six hours. His runs came all round the wicket, from a great variety of shots, with the pull shot, in which he took a ball sometimes from around or outside off-stump and smashed it through midwicket, being particularly associated with him.

He came to England in 1930 with a huge reputation, and scored 236 in the first match at Worcester (he repeated the double-century on his next two visits). In the Headingley Test, he came in at number 3 and was 309 not out at close, eventually going on to 334, an Ashes record at the time (he repeated the triple-century on his next Test at Headingley). Many consider his innings in the Lord's Test his finest. Coming to the wicket in mid-afternoon, he was not out 155 at the close, and went on to 254. He himself picked this innings as his greatest because "every ball went where I wanted it to go". Never, at Test level, had an innings been so dominating. In that series, Bradman scored 974 runs, still a record for a single series, and averaged 139.14.

Bradman's dominance was such that "bodyline" was used to counter him in 1932–33, and it worked, as his average was "only" 56.57 – still the best on either side. He was dominant again in 1934 and was captain on his tour of England in 1938. The Second World War took six years out of Bradman's career and his health

> ## "Every ball's the first ball whether I've just come to the wicket or reached 200. And I never consider the possibility that anybody will get me out."
>
> *Don Bradman, on his batting*

wasn't perfect when cricket resumed. Nevertheless, he carried on at only slightly below his peak and led an Australian side to England in 1948 that remained unbeaten and is generally considered the best side to tour England. When he went out to bat in his last Test at the Oval, he needed only four runs to make sure of a Test average of 100, but he was bowled for a duck, some said because he still had a tear in his eye from his reception. If so, it would have been untypical of Bradman, who had the self-sufficiency of a genius.

Apart from his batting, Bradman was a brilliant fielder at cover-point and a very shrewd and thoughtful captain. He was knighted in 1949 and on his retirement became an influential figure in Australian cricket as an administrator. He was awarded Australia's highest honour, the companion of the Order of Australia, in 1981.

CAREER FACT FILE	
Born:	August 27, 1908, Cootamundra, New South Wales, Australia
Died:	February 25, 2001, Adelaide, South Australia
Teams:	New South Wales (1927–28 to 1933–34), South Australia (1935–36 to 1948–49)
Tours:	England 1930, 1934, 1938, 1948
First-class career:	(1927–28 to 1948–49, 234 matches)
Batting:	runs 28,067; average 95.14; highest score 452 not out; centuries 117
Bowling:	wickets 36; runs 1,367; average 37.97; best 3–35
Catches:	131 (plus 1 stumped)
Tests:	(1928–29 to 1948, 52 matches)
Batting:	runs 6,996; average 99.94; highest score 334; centuries 29
Bowling:	wickets 2; runs 72; average 36.00; best 1–8
Catches:	32

GRACE

"W.G." was the most famous cricketer of all, a law unto himself, who with his brothers made Gloucestershire a first-class county.

W.G. GRACE *on an 1896 calendar.*

THE DOCTOR

GRACE AND FRIENDS *W.G., captain of the Gentlemen v Players at Lord's, 1894.*

William Gilbert Grace was not only the most famous cricketer of all time, but in his day the best-known Englishman. With his big beard and burly frame, he was instantly recognizable. He came from a cricketing family, the second-youngest of five brothers, and was coached as a boy in the back garden by an uncle, with his mother giving strong support. His brothers E.M., G.F., and Henry all played first-class cricket for Gloucestershire, the first two also for England (all three played together in one Test).

match to win a 440-yard hurdles championship at Crystal Palace.

He dominated the Gentlemen (i.e. amateurs) v Players match, which was to remain one of the showpieces of the season for 156 years. The Gentlemen had won only seven times in 35 years before Grace played for them, but the Players would win only seven times in 50 years afterwards. He began playing for Gloucestershire in 1868 and, when Gloucestershire became first-class in 1870, he captained them till 1898, when there was a dis-

> ## "No one has by prowess and personality alike so long and so indisputably dominated the field."
>
> *Cricket historian H.S. ALTHAM*

His son, W.G. Jr, played for Gloucestershire, and another, C.B., for London County. Two nephews also played first-class cricket, one for Gloucestershire.

Grace scored 32 against an All-England XI when 15, and made his first-class debut aged 16 for Gentlemen of South. When he was 18, he scored 224 not out for England against Surrey at the Oval. An athlete in his younger days, he slipped off during the

pute. Grace then moved to London County in 1900 and captained them for four years, during which time they were regarded as first-class, too.

When 23, Grace had one of his best seasons, establishing a record aggregate of runs, 2,739, and the highest average, 78.25. His average was more than double the second highest, the 37.66 of Notts batsman Richard Daft. In this season, 1871, Grace also became

the first to score 10 centuries in a season. He was the first to perform the double of 1,000 runs and 100 wickets in 1874 – although some record books claim he did it in 1873. The fact is that, such was Grace's charisma, a certain amount of fiddling with scores took place that year to give him the honour – the Society of Cricket Statisticians and Historians have now corrected Grace's figures. This fiddling reflected Grace's stature in the game, which has led to stories of his grandeur, such as the famous placard for a match: "Entrance 6d; if W.G. Grace plays, one shilling" and the occasion when, given out early, he refused to go, telling the umpire that the crowd had come to see him bat, not the umpire giving him out. Of course, some of the extra entrance money mentioned above would have gone to Grace, who although a "Gentleman" was far from being an amateur.

As a batsman, Grace was a master, seeing the ball early and sound in judgement of length. He scored all round the wicket. Although he scored 344 for the MCC against Kent in 1876, his career batting average of just under 40 would not be remarkable today. But one has to consider the genuinely fast bowling he faced and mastered on pitches which by today's standards would be regarded as extremely danger-

ous. Grace was the first player to score 20,000 runs, and the first to each target up to 50,000. He was the first to score 100 centuries.

As a bowler, his style has been described as "high, home and easy", delivering slows with the round-arm action of his day, but no doubt using all the cunning and competitiveness that made him stand out. He established yet another first – the first player to take 2,000 wickets.

At his peak he was called "the champion". He had already reached his peak before Test match cricket began. He toured North America in 1872 and took a team to Australia in 1873–74, but there were no first-class matches on the itinerary. Although he played his first Test in 1880, and captained England from 1888 to 1899, including the tour to Australia in 1891–92, he played only 22 Tests. He hit the first England Test hundred in his first innings in Tests, 152 at the Oval, the first Test played in England. Although his powers began to wane in the 1890s, he had a magnificent season in 1895, when he became the first batsman to score 1,000 runs in May – in 22 days, in fact. That season he completed his hundredth hundred. No wonder a "shilling testimonial" for him realised £9,000. In his later years, he became a bowls enthusiast and helped form the English Bowling Association in 1903.

CAREER FACT FILE

Born:	August 18, 1848, Downend, Bristol
Died:	October 23, 1915, Mottingham, Kent
Teams:	Gloucestershire (1870–99); Kent (1877 – 1 match as "given man"); London County (1900–04)
Tours:	North America 1872 (not first-class); Australia 1873–74 (not first-class), 1891–92
First-class career:	(1865–1908, 869 matches)
Batting:	runs 54,211; average 39.45; highest score 344; centuries 124
Bowling:	wickets 2,809; runs 50,980; average 18.14; best 10–49
Catches:	875 (plus 5 stumped)
Tests:	(1880–99, 22 matches)
Batting:	runs 1,098; average 32.29; highest score 170; centuries 2
Bowling:	wickets 9; runs 236; average 26.22; best 2–12
Catches:	39

HADLEE

With mental as much as physical assets, Hadlee became his country's greatest cricketer and the first bowler in the world to take 400 Test wickets.

HADLEE *batting for Notts in 1986.*

SIR RICHARD THE LIONHEART

Born: July 3, 1951, St Albans, Christchurch, New Zealand
Teams: Canterbury 1971–72 to 1988–89, Nottinghamshire 1978–87, Tasmania 1979–80
Tours: Australia 1972–73, 1973–74, 1980–81, 1982–83 (not first-class), 1984–85 (not first-class), 1985–86, 1987–88; England 1973, 1975 (World Cup), 1978, 1979 (World Cup), 1983, 1986, 1990; India 1976–77, 1988–89; Pakistan 1976–77; Sri Lanka 1983–84, 1986–87; West Indies 1984–85; Sharjah 1986–87 (not first-class)
First-class career: (1971–72 to 1990, 342 matches)
Batting: runs 12,052; average 31.71; highest score 210 not out; centuries 14
Bowling: wickets 1,490; runs 26,998; average 18.11; best 9–52
Catches: 198
Tests: (1972–73 to 1990, 86 matches)
Batting: runs 3,124; average 27.16; highest score 151 not out; centuries 2
Bowling: wickets 431; runs 9,611; average 22.29; best 9–52
Catches: 39

on form, and in England in 1984 he performed the double of 1,000 runs and 100 wickets, a very rare event since the introduction of one-day cricket. He also hit his highest score, 210 not out against Middlesex.

Because of the strains of the English season, he modified his run-up to a shorter one, more economical on energy, and reaped great rewards. In Australia in 1985–86, he achieved his best analysis, 9 for 52, and his 33 wickets in the three-match series gave New Zealand their first series victory over Australia.

Hadlee said farewell to Nottinghamshire in 1987 by helping them to win the championship again. His Test wicket-taking continued: in 1988–89 he passed Ian Botham's world record by capturing his 374th wicket in India; he passed 400 in 1989–90 on his home ground of Christchurch and finished in 1990 with 431. It had taken only 86 Tests, a remarkable strike rate of five wickets per match. In nine of those Tests he had taken 10 wickets; 36 times he took five wickets in an innings. He was awarded an MBE in 1980 and a knighthood in 1990 on his final tour to England.

In retirement, he took on the running of a plant nursery in Christchurch with his wife, and travelling the world, being frequently seen at Trent Bridge.

> **"A world-class fast bowler whose aggressive left-handed batting entitles him to all-rounder status."**
>
> *Five Cricketers of the Year, Wisden 1982*

If *Wisden* had made Richard Hadlee one of their Cricketers of the Year in 1990, rather than 1982, the quote on this page might have read slightly differently: the world-class fast bowler had established a class of his own by being the first ever to take 400 Test wickets.

Richard John Hadlee comes from a cricketing family. His father, W.A., captained New Zealand, and of his four cricketing brothers D.R. played for New Zealand, and B.G. for Canterbury. His wife, Karen, played for New Zealand Women.

Tall and wiry rather than muscular, he began playing for Canterbury in 1971–72 and a year later made his Test debut against Pakistan. He really came to the fore in 1975–76 against India when, in the third Test, he took 4 for 35 and 7 for 23 to help win the match by an innings and square the series. These were the best match figures produced by a New Zealander at the time. In 1977–78 at Wellington, he was instrumental in New Zealand beating England for the first time, in the 48th match between them. He took 10 wickets, his 6 for 26 in the

second innings skittling England for 64 when they were chasing 137. In 1979–80, he scored his first Test hundred, and his 11 wickets in the first Test against the West Indies set up the one-wicket win which gave New Zealand their first Test rubber at home after 50 years trying.

Hadlee then began an astonishing revival in the fortunes of Nottinghamshire, for whom he signed in 1978. In 1981, he took 100 wickets, the only bowler to do so, and Nottinghamshire won the championship for the first time for 62 years. From 1980 to 1987 at Nottinghamshire, he achieved complete domination over county batsmen, finishing top of the bowling averages five times and second twice.

Meanwhile he revived New Zealand, and had a hand in everything they achieved in the 1980s and beyond. New Zealand's win at Headingley in 1983 caused such euphoria that back home the demands on Hadlee led him to suffer a kind of mental breakdown. But a quick course in motivation by a psychologist soon had him back

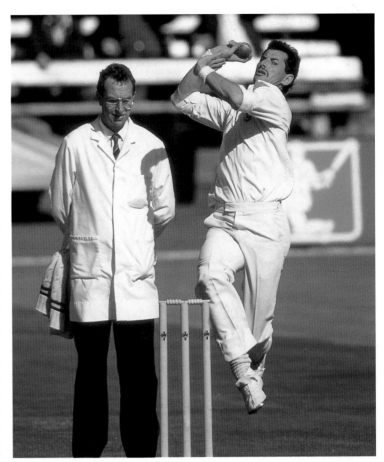

WICKET RECORD *Hadlee helped to win the Championship in 1987.*

HOBBS

Hobbs was more than the finest batsman of his generation; he was an attractive stroke-maker and gallant opponent who cared little for statistics.

JACK HOBBS *going out to bat.*

THE MASTER

There are those who still regard John Berry Hobbs as the greatest batsman of all, although his figures were eclipsed by Bradman. They base their view on his style, grace and mastery in all conditions, including the sticky wickets which do not occur in cricket in these days of covering whenever it rains. Hobbs himself would not have been the least concerned about his place in the pantheon. To quote Robertson-Glasgow, who bowled to him when he broke Grace's record of centuries, "he had the gift of smiling quietly at failure and triumph alike". Not that he failed often. He scored more runs and more centuries than any cricketer in history.

Hobbs joined Surrey in 1905 after playing four seasons for Cambridge, following in the footsteps of Tom Hayward, who was to be his opening partner and mentor till the First World War. W.G. Grace was captain of the Gentlemen of England in the first match Hobbs played for Surrey, in which he scored 88. Hobbs was soon into his stride. In 1907, he and Hayward shared four opening stands of over a hundred in one week and in 1909 put on 352 against Warwickshire. In 1907–08, Hobbs went to Australia and averaged 43.14 in his four Tests: in four more tours there he never averaged fewer than 50 in the Tests. In

1911–12, he enjoyed an outstanding tour, scoring 662 Test runs, average 82.75, and sharing with Wilfred Rhodes an opening stand of 323 at Melbourne, which remained an Ashes record opening stand for 77 years.

The war took seven years from Hobbs' career in what would have been his prime. Afterwards he had a new partner for Surrey, Andy Sandham, with whom he shared 63 opening stands of 100 or more, including a Surrey record of 428 against Oxford University in 1926. But the opening partner with whom Hobbs is most closely associated is Yorkshire's Herbert Sutcliffe, who began his Test career in 1924. Seven times they put on 200-plus together, and passed 100 on 26 occasions, 15 in Tests. In

AFTER THE ASHES *Jack Hobbs batting in 1926, the year he helped England regain the Ashes after 14 years.*

Australia in 1924–25, they had consecutive stands in Tests of 157, 110 and 283. Their most famous partnership occurred at the Oval in

1926, when they were required to open the second innings on a difficult rain-affected pitch and put on 172 (Hobbs 100), establishing a base for England to regain the

Ashes after 14 years. A similar stand of 105 (Hobbs 49) in 1928–29 on one of the most spiteful of Melbourne stickies paved the way for a three-wicket win and a 3–0 winning lead in the series.

On the domestic front, Hobbs caused tremendous excitement in 1925 as he closed in on Grace's record of centuries (then held to be 126). He was in tremendous form, and each time he didn't quite make a century it was said he'd "failed again". On August 15 he went to Taunton to play against Somerset and equalled the record in the first innings and passed it in the second. That season he scored 16 centuries, a record until surpassed by Denis Compton in 1947, and 3,042 runs, average 70.32. In 1926, when he averaged 77.60, he made his highest score, 316 not out for Surrey against

Middlesex at Lord's, the highest score made at Lord's until Graham Gooch beat it 64 years later.

Hobbs had overlapped Grace in his first match for Surrey, and in his last Test series in 1930, when he was 47, he overlapped Bradman, then on his first triumphant tour of England. So Hobbs passed on the mantle of the world's leading batsman, having been the first to score 5,000 runs in Test cricket.

In his first-class career, Hobbs was involved in no fewer than 166 opening stands of 100 or more. His total of runs, 61,760, remains a record more than 60 years after his retirement, as does his total of centuries, 199. These two records appear slightly different, 61,237 and 197, in *Wisden*, which has preferred to stick with tradition rather than correct them in the light of research by the Association of Cricket Statisticians and Historians. It is of little concern. It was the manner of the runs not the number that counted. It is said that Hobbs could have had many more had he not often surrendered his wicket on scoring a century.

Hobbs was an outstanding fielder at cover, and a pretty reasonable swing bowler, who opened the bowling in three Tests in South Africa. He was knighted in 1953, and every year on his birthday, until his death in 1963, "the master" was feted at a special dinner organized by admirers, of whom John Arlott was delighted to be at the fore.

> ## "He was the most perfectly equipped by art and temperament for any style of innings on any sort of wicket against any quality of opposition."
>
> *R.C. ROBERTSON-GLASGOW, cricketer and writer*

CAREER FACT FILE

Born:	December 16, 1882, Cambridge
Died:	December 21, 1963, Hove, Sussex
Teams:	Surrey (1905–34)
Tours:	Australia 1907–08, 1911–12, 1920–21, 1924–25, 1928–29; South Africa 1909–10, 1913–14; India and Ceylon (Vizianagram's XI) 1930–31
First-class career:	(1905–34, 834 matches)
Batting:	runs 61,760; average 50.70; highest score 316 not out; centuries 199
Bowling:	wickets 108; runs 2,704; average 25.04; best 7–56
Catches:	342
Tests:	(1907–08 to 1931, 61 matches)
Batting:	runs 5,410; average 56.94; highest score 211; centuries 15
Bowling:	wickets 1; runs 165; average 165.00; best 1–19
Catches:	17

IMRAN

One of the game's greatest all-rounders, Imran moulded the differing factions of Pakistani cricket into a major world power.

IMRAN KHAN *his greatest triumph: holding the World Cup aloft in 1992.*

CAPTAIN MARVEL

Imran Khan Niazi had a strange cricket career. A fierce critic of the structure of the first-class game in Pakistan, he did not play domestic cricket in his own country after 1980–81. Although he played county cricket in England from 1971 to 1988, his appearances were limited, as they were in his season in Australia, when he played five times for New South Wales. At the end of his career he was playing international cricket only.

He has a remarkable cricketing pedigree. Eight first cousins played first-class cricket, two of them, Majid Khan and Javed Burki, captaining Pakistan, as he himself was to do. Two uncles, Baqa Jilani and Jahangir Khan, played for India. While still at school, he made his first-class debut, aged 16½, for Lahore as a medium-fast bowler and opening bat. The chairman of selectors was his uncle, the captain

his cousin. He was picked for the tour of England in 1971, making his Test debut at Edgbaston, aged 18½. He failed to take a wicket, but had already agreed to play for Worcestershire while studying at Worcester Royal Grammar School. He went to Oxford University and won blues in 1973–75. In 1974, after coming down from Oxford, he played in three Tests for the Pakistani touring side, with slightly disappointing returns (he took just five wickets). After leaving Oxford he played for Pakistan International Airways for six years, after which he left Pakistani domestic cricket. At the same time he played in England, moving from Worcestershire to Sussex in 1977.

He was given a third chance to establish himself in the Pakistan Test side in 1976–77 and seized it. With a yard or two of pace added, he was a genuine and thoughtful fast

ANOTHER WORLD CUP *Imran bowling against Australia in the World Cup 1975.*

bowler. In three series that season, against New Zealand, Australia and the West Indies, he took 57 wickets. Twelve in the third Test at Sydney against Australia helped Pakistan win in Australia for the first time.

By 1981–82 he had become his country's leading wicket-taker, overtaking Fazal Mahmood, but internal strife in Pakistan's cricket politics led to eight players, including Imran, being omitted from the first two Tests against Sri Lanka. Restored in the third Test, Imran

He was not fully fit until 1985–86, the following season taking 18 wickets at only 11.05 each against the West Indies. In 1987, he led Pakistan to their first series victory in England, topping the series bowling with 21 wickets at 21.67, and scoring an imperious 118 at the Oval. In the West Indies the following winter, he took 23 wickets at 18.31, but Pakistan narrowly lost the final Test when they could have made themselves cricket's unofficial world champions. However, Imran

Born: November 25, 1952, Lahore, Pakistan
Teams: Lahore (1969–70 to 1970–71), Worcestershire (1971–76), Oxford University (1973–75), Dawood Club (1975–76), PIA (1975–76 to 1980–81), Sussex (1977–88), New South Wales (1984–85)
Tours: England 1971, 1974, 1975 (World Cup), 1979 (World Cup), 1982, 1983 (World Cup), 1987; Sri Lanka 1975–76, 1985–86; Australia 1976–77, 1978–79, 1981–82, 1983–84, 1984–85 (not first-class), 1986–87 (not first-class), 1988–89, 1989–90, 1991–92; West Indies 1976–77, 1987–88; New Zealand 1978–79, 1988–89; India 1979–80, 1986–87, 1989–90 (not first-class); Sharjah (not first-class) 1984–85, 1985–86, 1988–89, 1989–90, 1990–91, 1991–92; Australia and New Zealand 1991–92 (World Cup); Rest of World to England 1987, 1988
First-class career: (1969–70 to 1991–92, 382 matches)
Batting: runs 17,771; average 36.79; highest score 170; centuries 30
Bowling: wickets 1,287; runs 28,726; average 22.32; best 8–34
Catches: 117
Tests: (1971 to 1991–92, 88 matches)
Batting: runs 3,807; average 37.69; highest score 136; centuries 6
Bowling: wickets 362; runs 8,258; average 22.81; best 8–58
Catches: 28

"The sense of responsibility (of being captain) turned a fine cavalier into a great cricketer."

Five Cricketers of the Year, Wisden 1983

achieved his best Test bowling, 8 for 58, at Lahore (and 6 for 58 in the second innings).

After the turmoil, Imran was chosen as captain for the tour of England in 1982. Captaincy inspired him and, although the three-match series was lost 2–1, he took 21 wickets and scored 212 runs. Back in Pakistan, his side won all three Tests against Australia and then beat India 3–0 in a six-Test series. He took 53 wickets in the two series at an average of 13.75.

A shin injury kept him out of cricket for a season, but in Australia in 1983–84 he played in the last two Tests as captain and batsman only – a tribute to his genuine all-round qualities. He averaged 56.66.

achieved this in another way when he led Pakistan to win the World Cup in Australia in 1991–92, beating England in the final. He retired from cricket after this.

An inspirational and skilful captain, he remains one of the handful of all-rounders (including Ian Botham, Richard Hadlee, Kapil Dev and Shaun Pollock) who have scored 3,000 runs and taken 300 wickets in Tests.

After raising funds for a cancer hospital following his mother's death in 1985, he became a prominent figure in politics while at the same time, by marrying (then separating from) a society heiress, retaining the fascination that he is held in by the popular press.

LARA

The record-breaker
who leapt into
immortality with 876
runs which broke two
of the most treasured
records in cricket.

LARA on his way to 132 against
Australia, Perth, 1996–97.

THE SEVENTH SON

ON THE WAY *Lara on his way to a century v England, Trent Bridge, 1995.*

To break one of cricket's greatest records would ensure a batsman a place in the record books forever, and a position in any gallery of greats. To break another, seemingly even more impregnable, only seven weeks later, sounds like something out of fiction. Yet Brian Charles Lara did it, and his place among the all-time greats was already secure at the age of 25.

Lara, the seventh son of 11 children, was born in the village of Cantaro in Santa Cruz, four miles out-side Port of Spain. Aged seven, he was taken to the Harvard Club by an older sister for cricket coaching. Former West Indies opening bat Joey Carew took him in hand and at 14 he was scoring centuries at Fatima College. He toured India with a schools team and later led the West Indies Youth team to the Youth World Cup in Australia, and took a B side to Zimbabwe. He made his Trinidad debut in 1987–88 and showed his class with 92 against Barbados fast bowlers, Garner and Marshall.

Lara was devastated when his father Bunty died in 1988, just as he was chosen for the West Indies squad for the third Test against India at his local Queen's Park Oval. Unfortunately he was made 12th man and did not play.

His Test debut came in the final Test at Lahore on the tour of India in 1990–91, and he made 44 (at a highly critical time) and 5. He was on the tour of England in 1991 but was injured just when it looked as if he might make the Test side. His second appearance was in the historic first Test with South Africa after their return to Test cricket in 1991–92. He scored 17 and 64.

The following season he went to Australia, and in the third Test at Sydney announced his class to the world. After Australia had declared at 503 for 9, Lara went in at 31 for 2 and made 277, the fourth-highest at the time by a West Indian. He treated the Australian bowlers, who included McDermott, Hughes and Warne, with disdain, and was disappointed to be run out at 277, not afraid to admit he had his sights on Sobers' world-record 365. Lara topped the West Indies' batting averages. Later that season he helped the West Indies beat Pakistan in the three-match so-called "World Championship of Test Cricket" 1–0, averaging 43.20.

The following season England visited the West Indies. England had just reduced their deficit to 2–1 when the fifth Test began at St John's, Antigua. Lara went out to bat at 11 for 1, which soon became 12 for 2. In a rain-interrupted innings he advanced with first Adams, then Arthurton, then Chanderpaul to pass 300. As he went on and on, the talk at the start of the third day was of whether he could beat Sobers' 365. At 347 he was stuck for 18 minutes and was nearly yorked. Were nerves to deprive him? No: at 361 he smashed Caddick through the covers to equal the record, and next over he pulled Lewis to square leg for another boundary to beat the record. He accepted six minutes of congrat-ulations but was out through tired-

ness for 375 after 13 hours' batting. Sobers was one of the first to con-gratulate him.

Before this innings Lara had agreed to join Warwickshire for the 1994 season. Seven weeks after his great feat he went out to bat for Warwickshire against Durham at Edgbaston. Durham had declared at 556 for 8; Lara came in at 8 for 1. When 12, he was "bowled" from a no-ball, and he was dropped by the wicket-keeper at 18. But then he went on remorselessly and, with the match heading for a draw, went for another record. He was dropped at 238 and again at 413. When possibly the last over of the match began he was on 497 – Hanif Mohammad's world-record score was 499. He

> ## "Lara is the only batsman today who plays the game the way it should be played ... It's a pride and joy to watch him."
>
> *SIR GARFIELD SOBERS*

blocked three balls and was struck on the head by the fourth, but the next went for 4 and he ended 501 not out. It came from 427 balls.

Since then Lara has played several outstanding innings amid periods of apparent loss of motivation. When, after ten years, his Test record score was beaten by Matthew Hayden's 380 against Zimbabwe in 2003–04, Lara reclaimed it within six months with 400 not out against England at St Johns, Antigua. In November 2005, with 226 and 17 against Australia at Adelaide, he became the leading run-scorer in Tests, beating Allan Border's record by reaching 11,204 (average 53.86).

Lara replaced Courtney Walsh as West Indies captain in 1997–98, but has been an unsuccessful skipper, discarding or losing the role from time to time, as his batting brilliance was unable to halt West Indies' decline as a force in recent years.

CAREER FACT FILE

Born: May 2, 1969, Santa Cruz, Trinidad
Teams: Trinidad (1987–88 to 2003–04); Warwickshire 1994–98
Tours: Pakistan 1990–91, 1991–92 (not first-class), 1997–98; England 1991, 1995, 2000, 2004; Australia 1991–92, 1992–93, 1996–97, 2000–01, 2005–06; Sri Lanka 1993–94, 2001–02, 2002–03; New Zealand 1993–94; India 1994–95; Australia and New Zealand 1991–92 (World Cup); India and Pakistan 1995–96 (World Cup); England 1999 (World Cup); Sharjah (not first-class) 1991–92, 1997–98, 1999–00; South Africa 1998–99, 2002–03; Bangladesh 1999–00; Zimbabwe 2003–04; Canada (not first-class) 2000
First-class career: (1987–88 to 2005–06, 246 matches); **Batting:** runs 20,946; average 51.97; highest score 501 not out; centuries 60; **Bowling:** wickets 4; average 104.00; best 1–1; **Catches:** 300
Tests: (1990–91 to 2005–06, 121 matches); **Batting:** runs 11,204; average 53.86; highest score 400 not out; centuries 31; **Bowling:** runs 28; wickets 0; **Catches:** 148

LILLEE

The greatest fast bowler of his day, Dennis Lillee got a special kick from taking English wickets, and enjoyed the pleasure 167 times.

LILLEE *A smooth but menacing run-up.*

THE MENACE

CAREER FACT FILE

Born: July 18, 1949, Subiaco, Perth, Western Australia

Teams: Western Australia (1969–70 to 1983–84), Tasmania (1987–88), Northamptonshire (1988)

Tours: New Zealand 1969–70, 1976–77, 1981–82; England 1972, 1975, 1980, 1981, 1983 (World Cup); West Indies 1972–73; Pakistan 1979–80; Sri Lanka 1982–83; International Wanderers to South Africa 1975–76; Rest of World to England 1988

First-class career: (1969–70 to 1988, 198 matches)

Batting: runs 2,377; average 13.90; highest score 73 not out; centuries 0

Bowling: wickets 882; runs 20,695; average 23.46; best 8–29

Catches: 67

Tests: (1970–71 to 1983–84, 70 matches)

Batting: runs 905; average 13.71; highest score 73 not out; centuries 0

Bowling: wickets 355; runs 8,493; average 23.92; best 7–83

Catches: 23

Dennis Lillee, for a decade, was one of the most feared fast bowlers ever to play cricket. By the time he retired, he had taken more wickets than any Test bowler before him. He had done it with great technique and with courage, for he had to overcome severe back problems. He had also done it in the way of most fast bowlers: with a swagger, a belligerence and no fear whatever of offending the cricketing establishment.

With a fine physique and limitless stamina, he made his debut for Western Australia in 1969–70 and took 32 Sheffield Shield wickets. The following season he was in the Test team against England, taking eight wickets in the series dominated by England's John Snow. In 1971, he played for Haslingden in the Lancashire League, reaping the benefit when he toured England in 1972 and took 31 Test wickets at 17.87. It was the most wickets an Australian had taken in a series in England at the time.

However, his fine progress broke down in the West Indies in 1972–73 when he ended the first Test, in which he was wicketless, with stress fractures in the back, which kept him in plaster for six weeks. His return to Tests was in 1974–75 against England, when he was at his best. With new partner Jeff Thomson, he shattered the English batting, his and Thomson's names being joined as the fearsome "Lilian Thomson". Australia regained the Ashes 4–1, and retained them with a single win in England in 1975. Lillee took 46 English wickets in the two series.

The pair demolished the strong

> ## "After two Tests their names (Lillee and Thomson) had become synonymous with pain and terror or triumph and victory, depending on one's nationality."
>
> *DAVID FRITH on the 1974–75 Test series*

West Indians in 1975–76 when Australia were the strongest team in the world, largely thanks to Lillee and Thomson. Lillee took 11 wickets as Australia won the Centenary Test against England in 1976–77, but then joined Kerry Packer's World Series Cricket. With his black moustache, smooth 19-step run-up, perfect action and a delivery which threatened dismissal or injury to the batsman, he was not a man Packer could do without.

He returned to Tests in 1979–80, when, although less fast, he took 23 English wickets in three Tests, and went out to bat with an aluminium bat, actually scoring three runs with it before Brearley objected and the umpires ordered him to change it. Lillee held up the game for 10 minutes while he threw a tantrum. Later Brearley became his 100th English victim in Tests. In 1981, he took 39 wickets in a losing series in England, but did at least win a bet when backing England at 500–1 to win the Headingley Test

from an "impossible" position which, thanks to Botham, they did. His worst behaviour came in 1981–82 when, after impeding Javed Miandad, the Pakistani captain, a player he was pleased to dislike, he kicked him. This earned a suspension from two one-day matches.

That same season, against the West Indies, he returned his best innings analysis in Tests with 7 for 83. Australia won the match, but the series was drawn. When Lillee had Gomes caught, he passed Lance Gibbs' record of 309 Test wickets. By the end of the match, his 85 Test wickets in 1981 were a new record for a calendar year.

Lillee was by now battling against back problems once more, and played in only four more Test series, three of them disappointingly, but in his final series in 1983–84 he took 20 Pakistan wickets in a winning series. He, Greg Chappell and Rodney Marsh then retired from Tests together. If Thomson had been a great partner for Lillee, Marsh was more so, though less conspicuous. Both ended with a record 355 Test victims (Lillee's since passed) and their 95 shared dismissals (c Marsh b Lillee) was also a world record.

Lillee signed for Northamptonshire in 1988, but an ankle injury restricted his appearances to seven matches, and the popular warrior finally called it a day.

SHOUT IT OUT *Lillee appeals vociferously during the Tests in England in 1981.*

SOBERS

Sobers was a one-man cricket team, not only the world's best batsman but a bowler in three styles and a great fielder – the all-time all-rounder.

BEST OF THREE *Sobers had three styles of bowling, all effective.*

ALL-ROUND GREAT

SOBERS *plays hard through the slips.*

Sobers began his first-class career when he was not yet 17. Less than a year later, he was in the Test team against England, batting number 9. He made 14 not out and 26 and took 4 wickets. The following year against the Aussies he scored 231 runs and took six wickets – a promising start, as he was still only 18. All the time he was learning the craft that made him a master left-hand batsman on all types of

> ## "Sir Garfield St Aubrun Sobers was cricket's eighth knight and probably its greatest-ever player."
>
> *Cricketer and latterly writer*
> *PETER ROEBUCK*

wicket. At that time, he was bowling orthodox left-arm spin. He was always like lightning in the field and an outstanding catcher.

It was the visit to the West Indies of Pakistan in 1957–58 which really made Sobers' name. In the third

Test at Kingston, he made his first Test century, and then went on and on until captain Gerry Alexander declared at 790 for 3, the West Indies' highest score. Sobers himself had made 365 not out, the highest score ever made in a Test. In the next Test, he got 125 and 109 not out. His aggregate for the series was 824, his average 137.33.

Instantly famous, he cashed in at first by signing as a professional for Radcliffe and it was there that he developed a new bowling skill, left-arm medium-fast, or even sometimes fast, swing bowling. However, on tour in India during the English winter, he found the pitches unresponsive to his new quick style and tried out his left-arm off-breaks and googlies. His batting did not suffer with this preoccupation with bowling and, with centuries in the first three Tests, he took his record to six centuries in six successive Tests. As a batsman, he kept still as long as possible and then seemed to uncoil, launching himself into his shots and hitting the ball very hard. He was not merely an aggressive slinger of the bat, though – his shots were precise, occasionally delicate, and he could defend as well.

When England arrived in the West Indies in 1959–60, Sobers first

hit them for 154 when playing for Barbados, then in the first Test in his native Bridgetown, he scored 226, adding 399 for the fourth wicket with Frank Worrell (197 not out). It remains the West Indies' best stand in Tests. He amassed 709 runs in the series, averaging 101.28.

In the winter, he played in the famous series in Australia which began with the tied Test. He took 15 wickets in this series and from then on his bowling began to pay more dividends – in the 1961–62 series against India he took 23 wickets, his best in a single series. That year, he signed for South Australia, for whom he played 26 matches in three seasons.

After a successful tour of England in 1963, he was captain of the West Indies for the visit of Australia in 1964–65, and won the series 2–1. He had a superb tour of England in 1966, scoring 722 runs, average 103.14, and taking 20 wickets. The West Indies won 3–1 and three times Sobers passed 160. In the Lord's Test, with the West Indies 95 for 5 in their second knock, only 9 ahead of England, Sobers (163 not out) was joined by his cousin David Holford (105 not out) and the two added 274 unbeaten to turn the series. He had another spell in League cricket with Norton in the North Staffordshire League and then

agreed to play for Nottinghamshire in 1968, a spell which was to last seven years.

Meanwhile England won the 1967–68 series in the West Indies 1–0, after a generous Sobers' declaration at 92 for 2, leaving England to get 215. They did so, for which Sobers was much criticized.

Sobers announced his arrival in county cricket in typical fashion. At Swansea in August, against Glamorgan, he hit every ball of the six-ball over from Malcolm Nash for six, a new record for first-class cricket.

Sobers, who had played nearly non-stop for around 20 years, began to suffer injuries in 1972–73 and did not play in the home series against Australia, relinquishing the captaincy of the West Indies. He was back in the side for the tour of England in 1973, scoring 150 not out at Lord's. On England's visit in the winter, Sobers became the first batsman to pass 8,000 runs in Test matches during his innings in the second Test at Jamaica which was to be his last series. He was the second player (after Richie Benaud) to score 2,000 runs and take 200 wickets in Tests. He was knighted in 1975. He has suffered operations to knees and eyes in retirement, but retains his immense popularity.

CAREER FACT FILE

Born:	July 28, 1936, Bay Land, Bridgetown, Barbados
Teams:	Barbados (1952–53 to 1973–74), South Australia (1961–62 to 1963–64), Nottinghamshire (1968–74)
Tours:	England 1957, 1963, 1966, 1969, 1973; Australia 1960–61, 1968–69; New Zealand 1955–56, 1968–69; Ceylon and India 1966–67; India and Pakistan 1958–59; West Indian XI to England 1964; Rest of World to England 1965, 1967, 1968, 1970, to Pakistan 1970–71, to Australia 1971–72; Swanton to India 1963–64; Cavaliers to India 1962–63
First-class career:	(1952–53 to 1974, 383 matches)
Batting:	runs 28,315; average 54.87; highest score 365 not out; centuries 86
Bowling:	wickets 1,043; runs 28,941; average 27.74; best 9–49
Catches:	407
Tests:	(1953–54 to 1973–74, 93 matches)
Batting:	runs 8,032; average 57.78; highest score 365 not out; centuries 26
Bowling:	wickets 235; runs 7,999; average 34.03; best 6–73
Catches:	109

TENDULKAR

Tendulkar is more than arguably the best batsman in the world. In India he is an icon, with a status that transcends cricket.

TENDULKAR *already turning heads at age 12, he has evolved into a true legend.*

THE BOY MASTER

TENDULKAR *displaying his mastery in the 2003 World Cup*

In 1988 14-year-old Sachin Tendulkar, captain of his school cricket team, went out to bat 40 minutes before lunch with his side 84 for two. At the wicket was his friend, 16-year-old Vinod Kambli, who also would play for India. At lunch the next day the score was 748 for 2, Kambli 349 not out, Tendulkar 326 not out. Whereupon the school coach rang Tendulkar to tell him angrily that he must declare. The unbroken partnership of 664 is listed in Wisden as a record partnership for any cricket. One of the opposition bowlers, Sairaj Bahutule, also later played for India.

Tendulkar, who had made his first century aged 12, was soon known all over Bombay and crowds came to watch him. At 15, he made his first-class debut for Bombay, and scored 100. At the end of the season he averaged 64.77 and was disappointed, as were his public, when after much discussion, he was not picked to tour the West Indies and face the likes of Malcolm Marshall and Curtley Ambrose.

Truly, Tendulkar was a natural, a master batsman while still a boy. His Test debut was not too long delayed. In November 1989, he faced Imran Khan, Wasim Akram and Waqar Younis on tour in Pakistan. The fast men repeatedly bowled bouncers at the 16-year-old, once hitting him on the nose, but he responded with scores of 50 plus, becoming the youngest player to score a 50 in a Test. In the tour of England in 1990, the 17-year-old took a breathtaking catch at Lord's, and at Old Trafford saved India with his first Test century, an unbeaten 119. He was the youngest player to score a Test century in England, having six months earlier just failed with 88 to beat Mushtaq Mohammed's overall record. Two Test centuries followed in a losing series in Australia in 1990-91. A delightful 148 not out at Sydney, marked him out as a batsman of world class, but a century in the fifth Test also displayed his determination and spirit. Facing Australia's 346, the 18-year-old came in at 69 for two, but lost partners regularly, until India stood at 159 for eight. Tendulkar then cut loose, cutting savagely and driving on the up through the off-side, racing from 50 to 100 in 55 balls. By the time England toured India in 1992-93 the one-time boy wonder was showing his adult mastery with his fifth Test century, a career-best 165 made with perfect technique and strokes of text-book purity.

Tendulkar, like the other Indian Little Master before him, Gavaskar, is diminutive, but compact and muscular. He loves fast bowling, hitting the ball on the rise with a heavy bat with perfect timing so that the ball clatters into the boundary boards. He plays spinners with careful correctness, but is not afraid to sweep, and does not let any bowling subdue his aggression. Indeed, sometimes the best chance of getting him out is to hope his virtuosity runs away with him so that he plays the risky shots for the devil of it.

In 1992, the 19-year-old Tendulkar was the first overseas player to appear for Yorkshire. The young master coped well with the damp British conditions, making 1,070 runs.

Outstanding innings came regularly from Tendulkar. On a difficult patch at Edgbaston in 1996 his certainty and assurance in making 122 against England was in notable contrast to other players. It was followed by 177 at Trent Bridge. In 1996 he was appointed captain of India for the first time, aged 23. Such is Indian cricket politics, however, that this was only the first of at least three spells as captain.

Mohammed Azharuddin was captain when the Australians toured India in 1997-98, when the cricket world enjoyed the spectacle of the contest between the master batsman and the spin king, Shane Warne. Tendulkar was superb. An unbeaten 155 in the second innings of the first Test turned a first-innings deficit into a 179-run win, and an eventual 2-1 series win. Tendulkar made 336 runs in five innings for an average of 111.50. Warne's wickets cost 54 runs each, and he confessed to 'nightmares of Sachin running down the wicket to belt me'.

In the 1999 World Cup in England, Tendulkar's father died, and he went home to be with his mother. His family sent him back and he went out against Kenya to score 140 not out in an emotional

> ## "I never saw myself play, but I feel that this player is playing much the same as I used to play."
>
> *SIR DONALD BRADMAN*

display of batting that seemed to help him overcome his grief.

Tendulkar was captain again in 1999–2000, averaging 108.75 against New Zealand. Next season, his mastery of Warne and 126 in the deciding Test helped win an amazing series against Australia. Although he lost the captaincy again, he continued his dominance in all forms of cricket, and made 194 not out in the 2003–04 Test in Pakistan where India won for the first time in 20 attempts.

In December 2005 he became Test cricket's most prolific century-maker when he scored his 35th hundred, beating the record held by his countryman Sunil Gavaskar.

For all his adulation, Tendulkar remains a private man who is hard to know. He has two children and claims to like the records of Dire Straits. "I am a normal person who plays cricket," he says.

CAREER FACT FILE

Born: April 24, 1973, Bombay, India
Teams: Bombay/Mumbai (1988–89 to 2003–04); Yorkshire (1992)
Tours: Pakistan 1989–90, 1997–98, 2003–04; New Zealand 1989–90, 1993–94, 1994–95, 1998–99 2002–03; England 1990, 1996, 2002; Sharjah (not first-class) 1989–90, 1991–92, 1993–94, 1999–2000; Australia 1991–92, 1999–2000, 2003–04; Zimbabwe 1992–93, 1996–97, 1998–99, 2000–01, 2002–03; South Africa 1992–93, 1996–97, 2001–02, 2002–03; Sri Lanka 1993–94, 1996–97, 1997–98 2002–03; Singapore (not first-class) 1995–96, 1999–2000; West Indies 1996–97, 2001–02; Bangladesh 1997–98, 1998–99, 1999–2000, 2000–01; Kenya (not first-class) 2000–01
First-class career: (1988–89 to 2005–06, 222 matches); **Batting:** Runs 18,726; average 60.60; highest score 248 not out; centuries 59; **Bowling:** Wickets 61; average 60.34; best 3–10; **Catches:** 144; **Tests:** (1989–90 to 2005–06, 126 matches); **Batting:** 10,323 runs; average 56.71; highest score 248 not out; centuries 35; **Bowling:** 37 wickets; average 49.35; best 3–10; **Catches:** 77

WARNE

Warne showed that spin could be as effective a modern strike weapon as pace. He matched his wits with the batsman's and the better the batsman, the better he liked it.

SHANE WARNE *makes his leg breaks turn prodigiously.*

SPIN DOCTOR

Until Shane Keith Warne emerged in the 1990s it seemed that leg-spin and googly bowling was an art that had become more or less confined to the Indian sub-continent. By the turn of the century he had been celebrated as possibly the greatest practitioner the game has ever seen, and in the 137th edition of *Wisden Cricketers' Almanack* for the year 2000, he was named as one of the five cricketers of the century. Indeed, he was the only current player on the list.

Warne at first sight does not give the appearance of a world-class athlete, and has fought a tendency to tubbiness since his teenage days when he was an all-rounder in both senses. However, when he got into the Victoria side aged 21, he began working hard on his fitness, particularly after a stint at the Australian Cricket Academy in Adelaide, where he came under the tuition of the Test spinner Terry Jenner.

His Test debut came in the third Test of the 1991-92 series against India at Sydney, with Australia leading 2–0. It was an inauspicious beginning. Australia just avoided an

WARNE *appeals for another wicket.*

> ## "His ability to outthink a batsman sets him apart and makes him the best bowler I played against."
>
> *England captain*
> *MIKE ATHERTON*

innings defeat as Warne took one for 150 (a tired Shastri on 206) in 45 overs. He failed to take a wicket in the next Test, and although he "spun, toiled and grimaced", he was dropped, his two-match tally being one for 228.

Warne's first big success came in Sri Lanka the following season, when Sri Lanka needed only to score 181 in the fourth innings to win the first Test. Victory seemed assured until Warne came on and took the last three wickets without conceding a run for a 16-run win. Previously to that spell his one Test wicket had cost 346 runs.

It was when he was recalled for the second Test against West Indies starting in Melbourne on 26 December 1992 that Warne's career took off. He spun Australia to victory as the West Indies collapsed against him on the last day, when he claimed seven wickets for 21 in a final spell. That summer he came to England, and at Old Trafford bowled possibly the most famous ball in Test cricket, his first in a Test in England, an inswinging leg break which pitched outside the leg stump of Mike Gatting and hit the off stump. He was thus the first of 448 bowlers to clean bowl an opponent with his first ball in Ashes Tests.

Later, at Edgbaston, the England skipper Graham Gooch was bowled round his legs by a prodigious leg break trying to pad away.

Warne took a match-winning 34 wickets in the series and set the pattern for his career. In Melbourne in 1994-95 he took a brilliant hat-trick against England.

There have been hiccups. In 1995 Warne and Mark Waugh were fined by the Australian Cricket Board for selling information to an Indian bookmaker. The Board kept the incident secret, and it only came to light during the huge match-fixing scandals years later.

There was a finger operation in 1996, which afterwards gave him pain in both finger and arm whenever he bowled his big leg break, and caused him to rethink his strategies a little. Then in 1998 he suffered a shoulder injury, which meant that when the 1998-99 Ashes series started, he was in the commentary box rather than on the field. His replacement leg breaker was Stuart MacGill. MacGill was the leading wicket taker of the series with 27 at 17.70, Warne an "also bowled". They played together in the first three Tests in the following West Indies tour, but for the fourth, Warne, vice-captain and selector, was dropped, against his will. Australia won the match and the series was drawn 2–2. Warne was depressed after this, and the relationship with his friend and captain Steve Waugh was a little strained, but back in England for the World Cup he regained his enthusiasm, was leading wicket-taker and

Man of the Match in both semi-final and final.

In the series in New Zealand which followed, Warne passed Dennis Lillee's record of 355 Test wickets, becoming Australia's leading wicket-taker. Another finger injury caused another period of rest but he was back on Australia's losing tour to India in 2000-01, and then in England in 2001 he bagged his 400th Test wicket in the fifth Test at the Oval.

By February 2003 Warne, with 491 Test wickets, was on his way to Courtney Walsh's world record of 519. However, having declared that the 2003 World Cup would see his last one-day international appearances, he was sent home before a ball was bowled for being caught out for the "reckless act" of taking illegal substances. The ACB banned him for a year. Warne returned to the Test team in March 2004, on a tour of Sri Lanka. In the first Test, he secured the nine wickets needed to become the second bowler to reach 500 and at the series end he had 515. The exciting and attacking mixture of legspin, topspin, flipper, googly and backspin which so delighted spectators, and its blond, broad-shouldered purveyor, were back.

Warne was at his best on the tour of England in 2005, and became the first to take 600 Test wickets in the third Test at Old Trafford. With 40 wickets altogether and some spirited batting, he shared the Player of the Series award. And he finished 2005 by setting a new record for Test wickets in a year. His new mark of 96 beat Dennis Lillee's 1981 mark by 10.

CAREER FACT FILE

Born:	September 13, 1969, Ferntree Gully, Melbourne, Australia
Teams:	Victoria (1990–91 to 2004–05), Hampshire (2003–2005)
Tours:	Zimbabwe 1991–92 (Australia B), 1999–2000; Sri Lanka 1992–93, 1999–2000, 2002–03; New Zealand 1992–93, 1999–2000, 2004–05; England 1993, 1997, 2001, 2005; South Africa 1993–94, 1996–97; Pakistan 1994–95; West Indies 1994–95, 1998–99; India 1997–98, 2000–01, 2004–05
First-class career:	(1990–91 to 2005, 256 matches)
Batting:	runs 5,774; average 18.75; highest score 107 not out
Bowling:	wickets 1,134; runs 29,014; average 25.59
Catches:	218
Tests	(1991–92 to 2005–06, 134 matches)
Batting:	runs 2865; average 16.75; highest score 99
Bowling:	wickets 657; runs 16,423; average 25.00; best 8–71
Catches:	118

THE GREAT CRICKETERS

Although cricket is a statistician's delight, the great players are those who rise above figures and impress by personality, style and the excitement they generate. Thus any choice of nearly 200 of the greatest must be subjective. Those included here would be on many lists.

A

Abdul Qadir

Born: September 15, 1955, Lahore, Pakistan

Teams: Punjab (1975–76); Lahore (1975–76 to 1984–85); Habib Bank (1975–76 to 1995–96)

First-class: 208 matches; 3,740 runs, average 18.33; 960 wickets, average 23.22

Tests (1977–78 to 1990–91): 67 matches; 1,029 runs, average 15.59; 236 wickets, average 32.80

It was Abdul Qadir who announced the renaissance of the leg-break and googly bowlers in Test cricket when he played three Tests against England in Pakistan in 1977–78. He disappointed in England the following summer when he was troubled by injury, but by the time he returned in 1982 he was a potent force and his six wickets at Lord's played a significant part in Pakistan's victory.

In 1982–83, he took 22 wickets in three tests as Pakistan had a clean sweep against Australia, and he became the first bowler to take 100 wickets in a Pakistan season. The following season, he took 19 wick-ets in three Tests as Pakistan beat England in a rubber for the first time, and 10 wickets at the Oval in August 1987 ensured Pakistan's series victory in England. Three months later, Qadir produced an outstanding display of leg-spin and googly bowling when he took nine for 56 and four for 45 to bring Pakistan an innings victory over England at Lahore. His first-innings figures are a record for Pakistan in Test cricket, and he became only the second Pakistani bowler to take 200 Test wickets.

His bouncy run to the wicket, unquenchable enthusiasm and pas-sionate appeals established his character with the crowd. Often in disagreement with authority, he was a spin bowler with a fast bowler's attitude and temperament.

Bobby Abel

Born: November 30, 1857, Rotherhithe, Surrey

Died: December 10, 1936, Stockwell, London

Teams: Surrey (1881–1904)

First-class: 627 matches; 33,124 runs, average 35.46; 236 wickets, average 24.00

Tests (1888–96): 13 matches; 744 runs, average 37.20

A diminutive opening batsman, Bobby Abel became one of the great favourites at the Oval where he was dubbed "The Guv'nor". Surrey adopted a policy of recruit-ing young professionals in the late 1870s and engaged Abel as an off-break bowler. He was 23 before he made his first-class debut, and it was some years before he estab-lished himself. He did not score a century until 1886, and it was an innings of 144 against the Australians that season which really set him on this way, when he scored 1,000 runs in a season for the first time. He was to repeat that feat on 13 other occasions.

He toured Australia and South Africa with England sides, and, in Sydney, January 1892, he became the first England player to carry his bat through a completed Test innings. He was unbeaten for 132 out of 307. Three years earlier, he had hit 120 against South Africa in Cape Town.

In 1893, his career was threat-ened by an eye infection, but he recovered to exceed 2,000 runs every season between 1895 and 1902. In 1899, he made 357 not out against Somerset at the Oval, which remains the highest score ever made for Surrey. In the same season, he and Tom Hayward scored 448 for Surrey's fourth wicket against Yorkshire at the Oval, and this remained a world record for 50 years.

In 1901, he created another record when he scored 3,309 runs in first-class cricket. His team-mate Tom Hayward was to better this five years later.

Abel's eye problem came back, and his career ended abruptly in 1904. He coached Surrey in 1907. He also coached at Dulwich College and ran a sports shop.

Jimmy Adams

Born: January 9, 1968, Port Maria, Jamaica

Teams: Jamaica (1984–85 to 2000–01); Nottinghamshire (1994); Free State (2002–03)

First-class: 202 matches; 11,234 runs, average 39.69; 103 wickets, average 40.39

Tests (1991–92 to 2000–01): 54 matches; 3,010 runs, average 41.23; 27 wickets, average 49.48

Jimmy Adams is an all-round cricketer in every sense – a stylish left-handed batsman, a slow left-arm bowler and a wicket-keeper who has also played limited-over internationals as a wicket-keeper. He hit 79 and took four for 43 on his Test debut, against South Africa, and made his first Test century against England at Bouda, 1993–94. This was the second game of the series; in the first he had scored 95 not out and taken six catches to equal the Test record.

He played for several seasons in the Durham League, but assisted Nottinghamshire in 1994, and the following winter he hit two Test centuries against India. He toured England in 1995 and, at one time, was ranked number one batsman in the world, but he suffered a severe blow on the head at Taunton, from which it took him some time to recover.

He replaced Lara as captain of West Indies, but was himself replaced following the West Indies defeat, 5–0 against Australia in 2000–01. He played for Minor Counties cricket in England for Wiltshire in 2004.

Neil Adcock

Born: March 8, 1931, Sea Point, Cape Town, South Africa
Teams: Transvaal (1952–53 to 1959–60); Natal (1960–61 to 1962–63)
First-class: 99 matches, 451 runs, average 5.50; 405 wickets, average 17.25
Tests (1953–54 to 1961–62): 26 matches, 146 runs, average 5.40; 104 wickets, average 21.10

A tall fast bowler, Neil Adcock found his way into the South African side after only nine first-class matches. He was an immediate success, taking three wickets in the second innings as South Africa beat New Zealand in Durban, and following this with eight for 87 in the match as the Springboks triumphed in Johannesburg. He finished his first Test series with 24 wickets.. He was a hostile bowler, full of passion, but he was troubled by various injuries, and it was not until his second tour of England in 1960 that he showed himself at his

best. In five Tests, he took 26 wickets at 22.57 runs each, and his total for the tour was a record 108. These achievements were all the more remarkable when one considers that his new ball partner was no-balled out of Test cricket on this tour for his illegal action. Adcock is one of only five South African bowlers to have taken 100 wickets in Test cricket.

Following his retirement, he became a radio commentator.

Terry Alderman

Born: June 12, 1956, Subiaco, Perth, Western Australia
Teams: Western Australia (1974–75 to 1992–93); Kent (1984–86); Gloucestershire (1988)
First-class: 245 matches; 1,307 runs, average 8.32; 956 wickets, average 23.74
Tests (1981 to 1990–91): 41 matches; 203 runs, average 6.54; 170 wickets, average 27.15

Terry Alderman was a right-arm fast medium-pace bowler whose control and late movement proved too much for most English batsmen. He had not played Test cricket until he came to England in 1981, and nine wickets in the first match at Trent Bridge when he bowled unchanged through the second innings gave early indication of his worth. He finished the series, in which Australia were beaten, with a record 42 wickets in six Tests.

In 1982–83, Alderman's career suffered a severe setback when he dislocated a shoulder while tackling a pitch-invader during the first Test. The injury ended his season. He was due to tour England in 1985, but was withdrawn from the party when he revealed that he had signed to go to South Africa. He had enjoyed a good

ALDERMAN *40 series wickets twice.*

season for Kent in 1984 and was to have an outstanding one in 1986. He later assisted Gloucestershire with great success. He complemented his bowling with excellent slip fielding.

A key member of the overwhelmingly successful Australian side in 1989, he took 41 wickets in the series, five times capturing a wicket in his opening over. A modest and courteous man, fiercely competitive, he coached Western Australia in 1992–93.

Gubby Allen

Born: July 31, 1902, Bellevue Hill, Sydney, Australia
Died: November 29, 1989, St John's Wood, London
Teams: Middlesex (1921–1950); Cambridge University (1922–23)
First-class: 265 matches; 9,232 runs, average 28.67; 788 wickets, average 22.32
Tests (1930 to 1947–48): 25 matches; 750 runs, average 24.19; 81 wickets, average 29.37

"Gubby" Allen's career spanned 29 years, yet he was never able to play in more than a handful of games each season. He appeared in county cricket before he went up to Cambridge, and was probably the fastest bowler ever to play for Middlesex. He had the perfect action for a pace man, and became a stylish batsman.

In 1929, he became the only man to take all 10 wickets in an innings of a county match at Lord's, Lancashire being the opponents, and the following year he made his debut for England against Australia. His selection was opposed in some quarters as he had been born in Australia, and his uncle was an Australian Test cricketer.

He toured Australia with Jardine's side, 1932–33, and took 21 wickets in the "bodyline" series, although he himself refused to bowl leg-theory. He captained England against India in 1936 and was appointed to lead the side to Australia, 1936–37. Allen was not a county captain, and many believed his appointment was due to his Australian connections and had been made in an attempt to heal the wounds that existed following the "bodyline" tour. England won the first two Tests but lost the next three.

Allen played no more Test cricket before the Second World War but, astonishingly, was recalled to lead England in the West Indies, 1947–48, at the age of 45. He pulled a calf muscle on the boat on the way out, could not play in the first Test and, for the first time in history, the MCC went through a tour without a win to their credit.

Very close to his mentor Sir Pelham Warner, Allen succeeded him as the most influential administrator in the game, holding all the high offices. He was knighted for services to cricket in 1986.

Lala Amarnath

Born: September 11, 1911, Lahore, India
Died: August 5, 2000 New Delhi, India
Teams: Hindus (1929–30 to 1939–40); Southern Punjab (1933–34 to 1951–52); Patiala (1953–54 to 1957–58); Uttar Pradesh (1956–57); Railways (1958–59 to 1960–61)
First-class: 186 matches; 10,426 runs, average 41.38; 463 wickets, average 22.98
Tests (1933–34 to 1952–53): 24 matches; 878 runs, average 24.38; 45 wickets, average 32.91

Although his given name was Nanik, Amarnath, the father of two Test cricketers, was always known as

"Lala". By the time the MCC toured India, 1933–34, he was recognized as an accomplished batsman and was selected for the first Test match. He hit a century in the second innings, the first to be scored for India in a Test. It was during this season that his medium-pace bowling developed, for he had originally been a wicket-keeper, and he arrived in England in 1936 as an all-rounder of international standing, which was confirmed by 32 wickets and three centuries in the early part of the tour. His anger at the way in which the tour was being managed caused this instinctive and impetuous cricketer to erupt, and he was sent home for disciplinary proceedings. Later enquiries found him "not guilty".

He played in the Lancashire League, toured England in 1946 and took eight wickets at Old Trafford. He captained India in Australia, 1947–48 and was the leading wicket-taker in the series. He retained the captaincy for the home series against West Indies, 1948–49, and kept wicket in the fifth Test when Sen was injured, holding five catches.

Demanding more money and better travelling conditions, he was suspended from domestic cricket at the end of that series and was omitted from the side that toured England in 1952. The tour was a disaster, and he was reinstated as captain for the inaugural series against Pakistan, 1952–53, leading India to their first victory in a Test rubber. He enjoyed a fine series, but learned that he was to be replaced for the trip to the West Indies. He left the game an embittered man.

He has found consolation in the achievements of his sons. Mohinder scored more than 4,000 Test runs and was Man of the Match in the World Cup Final, 1983.

Curtly Ambrose

Born: September 21, 1963, Swetes Village, Antigua
Teams: Leeward Islands (1985–86 to 1999–00); Northamptonshire (1989–1996)
First-class: 239 matches; 3,448 runs, average 13.95; 941 wickets, average 20.24
Tests (1987–88 to 1996–97): 61 matches; 850 runs, average 12.50; 266 wickets, average 21.27
Standing 6ft 7in, Curtly Ambrose is

a fast bowler who presents an awesome sight for any batsman. He had to choose between cricket and basketball as a career, and, once he had made his choice, his advance was rapid. Successes in domestic cricket won him a place in the Test side against Pakistan. To their credit, Northamptonshire had recognized this potential and signed him, but the West Indies picked him for the tour of England, 1988, and his county debut was delayed. He played in all five Tests in England and never looked back.

In 1990, when England toured the Caribbean, he took eight for 45 in the second innings of the Barbados Test to bring off a sensational victory for the West Indies. Even more sensationally, he took six for 34 in the inaugural Test against South Africa, 1992, to bowl the West Indies to victory when the South Africans looked certain to win.

Ambrose took his 400th Test wicket at Headingley in August 2000. For the first time ever a Test attack comprised two bowlers, Ambrose and Walsh, both having reached the 400th mark. He played in one more Test, before retiring.

AMBROSE *Deadly when necessary.*

Leslie Ames

Born: December 3, 1905, Elham, Kent
Died: February 27, 1990, Canterbury, Kent
Teams: Kent (1926–51)
First-class: 593 matches; 37,248 runs, average 43.51; 24 wickets, average 33.37; caught 704, stumped 417
Tests (1929 to 1938–39): 47 matches; 2,434 runs, average 40.56; caught 74, stumped 23

AMES *Wicket-keeper with 100 100s.*

Les Ames was the outstanding wicket-keeper/batsman of the inter-war period, and he remains the only wicket-keeper to have scored a hundred hundreds in first-class cricket; eight of them came in Test matches. He joined Kent as a batsman in 1923, took up wicket-keeping and gained a regular place in the county side in 1927. This was the first of 17 seasons in which he scored 1,000 runs. In 1933, he made 3,058 runs.

In 1928, he created a new wicket-keeping record with 122 dismissals, but he beat this the following season with 128 dismissals. It is a record which is not likely to be beaten, nor is his record of 64 stumpings in 1932 when he claimed a hundred victims for the third time.

He holds another wicket-keeping record in that he made 417 stumpings in his career. Many of these came off "Tich" Freeman, the leg-spinner, with whom Ames had an almost supernatural understanding.

By 1938, he had begun to suffer from back trouble, and he did not keep wicket after the Second World War although he remained a prolific scorer. He was the first professional to become a selector, and he was both secretary and

manager of Kent during a very successful period for the county.

Dennis Amiss

Born: April 7, 1943, Harborne, Birmingham
Teams: Warwickshire (1960–1987)
First-class: 658 matches; 43,423 runs, average 42.86; 18 wickets, average 39.88
Tests (1966–1977): 50 matches; 3,612 runs, average 46.30
Any young player who wanted to know what was meant by correct technique had only to watch Dennis Amiss to find the answer. To see this right-handed opening batsman at the crease was in itself an aesthetic pleasure. He was associated with Warwickshire from the age of 15, and since leaving the playing staff he has become chief executive of the club, piloting them through a period of outstanding success. He took some time to establish himself in the England side, having a torrid time against the West Indies at the Oval on his debut. It was not until 1972–73, at Lahore, when he hit 112 against Pakistan, that he claimed a permanent place in the England side, and he followed his first Test century with 158 and 0 at Hyderabad and 99 and 23 in Karachi. A century against New Zealand followed, but he reached his peak in the Caribbean, 1973–74, when he hit three centuries in the rubber including a match-saving unbeaten 262 in Jamaica, the highest score of his career.

He also scored 206 against West Indies at the Oval, 1976, and, in all, made 102 centuries of which 11 were in Tests. He joined Packer's World Series and was later unfortunate not to be restored to the England side. He retired as Chief Executive of Warwickshire in 2006.

Warwick Armstrong

Born: May 22, 1879, Kyneton, Victoria, Australia
Died: July 13, 1947, Darling Point, Sydney, New South Wales, Australia
Teams: Victoria (1898–99 to 1921–22)
First-class: 269 matches; 16,158 runs, average 46.83; 832 wickets, average 19.71
Tests (1901–02 to 1921): 50 matches; 2,863 runs, average 38.69; 87 wickets, average 33.59

Warwick Armstrong was totally professional in his approach to the game. He was born to be a winner, and he showed no mercy to his opponents. He was a giant of a man who became known as "The Big Ship". He was a fine right-handed batsman and a medium-pace bowler who had turned to leg-breaks by 1905. His standing as an all-rounder can be seen from the fact that in three of his four tours of England – 1905, 1909 and 1921 – he completed the "double". In 1905, he scored 1,902 runs and took 122 wickets. His first visit to England had been three years earlier.

He was a mighty force in the Australian side of the Edwardian period, a good stroke-player and a relentlessly accurate bowler, but his relationships with the Australian Board were always strained. He was one of six players to refuse to take part in the Triangular Tournament of 1912.

He became captain of Australia when cricket resumed after the First World War and scored three centuries in the 1920–21 series which Australia won 5-0. They followed England back to England and won the first three Tests of the 1921 series at the end of which Armstrong retired.

There were those in authority who had not wanted Armstrong to lead the great 1921 side, but his players never wavered in their loyalty to him. His captaincy was shrewd, forthright, calculating, persistent and even ruthless, and in many ways he bridged the gap between the Golden Age and the ultra-professional approach of today. Ten Tests as captain, eight wins and two draws is a record to be envied.

Asif Iqbal

Born: June 6, 1943, Hyderabad, India
Teams: Hyderabad (1959–60); Karachi (1961–62 to 1968–69); PIA (1964–65 to 1979–80); National Bank (1976–77); Kent (1968–82)
First-class: 440 matches; 23,329 runs, average 37.26; 291 wickets, average 30.15
Tests (1964–65 to 1979–80): 58 matches; 3,575 runs, average 38.85; 53 wickets, average 28.33
Asif Iqbal began his career in India but emigrated to Pakistan in 1961.

ASIF IQBAL *Gallant all-rounder who always gave his best.*

He made his Test debut three years later, batting at number 10 and opening the bowling with his medium pace. An exciting batsman who could adapt his style according to the needs of the moment, he made his first Test century against England at the Oval, 1967, when he went in at number nine and scored 146 in 170 minutes, sharing a record stand of 190 with Intikhab Alam.

Asif was a dynamic cricketer with Kent whom he captained in 1968, and he played a major part in one of the most successful periods in that county's history. Between 1964 and 1977, he appeared in a record 45 consecutive Tests for Pakistan. He then announced his retirement from Test cricket, and a month later joined Kerry Packer's World Series. He had long pressed for better financial rewards for Pakistani players.

When the differences between Packer and the cricketing authorities were resolved, Asif returned to Test cricket and led Pakistan against India, 1979–80. It was the first time the two nations had met for almost 19 years, and this series marked the end of Asif's career. He has remained in the game mainly as an entrepreneur involved with Sharjah and as Pakistan's representative on the ICC for a time.

William Astill

Born: March 1, 1888, Ratby, Leicestershire
Died: February 10, 1948, Stoneygate, Leicestershire
Teams: Leicestershire (1906–39)
First-class: 733 matches; 22,731 runs, average 22.55; 2,431 wickets, average 23.76
Tests (1927–28 to 1929–30): 9 matches; 190 runs, average 12.66; 25 wickets, average 34.24
Ewart Astill was one of those great county professionals of the inter-war period whose achievements and abilities were never rewarded to the extent that they deserved. He made his debut in 1906, and he was ever-present in the next two seasons. As the First World War approached he lost form, but when he was demobilized after the war he was better than ever. A reliable middle-order batsman and a slow to medium-pace bowler who could turn the ball either way, he completed the all-rounder's "double" every season from 1921 until 1930 with the exception of 1927.

His consistency was finally rewarded when he was chosen to tour South Africa, 1927–28, and he made his Test debut at the age of 39. Two years later, he went to the West Indies and played in all four Test matches there.

He was a fine slip fielder and had a good cricket brain, and when he became the first professional to captain Leicestershire, 1935, the county enjoyed one of the most successful periods of their history.

Astill was a very good billiards player, an excellent pianist and vocalist, and a good ukulele player. He was an accomplished coach and did some fine work in this field.

Mike Atherton

Born: March 23, 1968, Manchester, Lancashire
Teams: Cambridge University (1987–89); Lancashire (1987–01)
First-class: 336 matches; 21,929 runs, average 40.03; 108 wickets, average 43.82
Tests: (1989–01) 115 matches; 7,728 runs, average 37.69; 2 wickets, average 151.00
Michael Atherton is a solid, dependable opening batsman who has enjoyed the longest of reigns as England captain. He made his Test debut in the Ashes series of 1989. He proved his worth a year later with Test centuries against India and New Zealand. A back operation and a loss of form against the West Indies and India brought one of the troughs of his career, but he returned in strength for the Ashes series of 1993. He had forged a good opening partnership with Gooch, and he made 80 and 99 in the Lord's Test and 55 and 63 at Headingley. Gooch stood down as captain when the Ashes were lost, and Atherton, 25 years old, succeeded him as captain. England won the last game in the series, their first success for 11 matches.

Although he did well in the Caribbean the following winter, England lost the series 3–1 and were bowled out for 46 in Trinidad. There was victory over New Zealand but problems against South Africa when television cameras spotted him ball-tampering, for which he was censured and fined. There was no success in Australia and his body-language did not inspire confidence or optimism, but he led England to victory over India, 1996, only to lose to Pakistan in the second half of the summer.

Attitude and performance in Zimbabwe brought heavy criticism of the England side, but redemption came in New Zealand where Atherton batted well, and he was reappointed England captain for the whole of the 1997 summer. He began by leading England to victory in the Texaco Trophy and scoring a century in the second match at the Oval.

Atherton captained England to West Indies in 1997–98, but resigned after England lost the series. He had led England in 52 Tests. He continued as a member of the England team and successfully opened the batting until the close of 2001, when he announced his retirement from top class cricket.

Mohammad Azharuddin

Born: February 8, 1963, Hyderabad, India

Teams: Hyderabad (1981–82 to 1999–00); Derbyshire (1991 and 1994)

First-class: 229 matches; 15,855 runs average 51.98; 17 wickets, average 46.23

Tests (1984–85 to 1999–00): 99 matches; 6,215 runs, average 45.03; no wickets for 12 runs

Mohammad Azharuddin created a record when he began his Test career with three centuries in successive matches against England, 1984–85. He proved that this was no temporary glory by being the leading run-scorer in England, 1986, as India took the series. His form lapsed a little, but he reasserted himself with an innings of 199 against Sri Lanka at Kanpur, December 1986. He was named as captain of the side to tour New Zealand, 1989–90, and to England, 1990. He hit hundreds at Lord's and Old Trafford.

Azharuddin became the most successful captain in Indian Test history, but a loss of form and poor results in South Africa, failure in the World Cup and eventually the loss of the series in England, 1996, cost him the leadership. He continued to hold his place in the side, but defeat in the Caribbean, coupled with indisciplined batting and a tumultuous private life, led to his being dropped from the side.

Azharuddin's final Test saw him make the only century in the 1999–00 series v South Africa. He also led Hyderabad to the Ranji Trophy final. These feats were soon forgotten when the Indian Board of Control banned him from cricket for life in December 2000 for taking money from bookies to fix cricket matches. Thus the career of one of India's greatest batsmen came to an end – he had captained his country in 47 of his 99 Tests.

Trevor Bailey

Born: December 3, 1923, Westcliff-on-Sea, Essex

Teams: Essex (1946-67); Cambridge University (1947–48); Prime Minister's XI, India (1963–64)

First-class: 682 matches; 28,641 runs, average 33.42; 2,082 wickets, average 23.13

Tests (1949 to 1958–59): 61 matches; 2,290 runs, average 29.74; 132 wickets, average 29.21

The best all-round cricketer to represent England in the post-war period until the arrival of Ian Botham, Trevor Bailey played a mighty role in England's rise from the depths to the recapturing of the Ashes in 1953 and their subsequent eminence in world cricket.

Educated at Dulwich College, he became known to audiences at Lord's during the war before joining the Royal Marines as soon as he left school. He served in Europe, but he was demobilized in time to play for Essex in 1946. He went up to Cambridge the following year, and by 1949 he was recognized as a bowler of genuine pace, a most reliable batsman and a brilliant close-to-the-wicket fielder. He was also a talented soccer player who got his blue and won an FA Amateur Cup medal with Walthamstow Avenue.

He had an excellent debut Test series against New Zealand, 1949, and when Hutton took over the captaincy of the England side Bailey was seen as an integral part of the plan to recapture the Ashes. At Lord's, 1953, he batted 257 minutes for 71 and added 163 with Willie Watson. This was one of the great rearguard actions of Test cricket. The partnership saved the match, and Bailey was a national hero. He bowled and batted well to help save the Headingley Test, and in the final victorious Test at the Oval, he hit 64 to complete a memorable series.

He went to the West Indies as Hutton's vice-captain, 1953–54, and had the remarkable bowling figures of seven for 34 in the first innings in Jamaica where Hutton made a double-century. Bailey's outstanding Test career continued until 1959, and even after that he continued to give fine service for Essex until 1967, captaining the county from 1955 until 1966. He performed the "double" eight times and is the only man to have scored 2,000 runs and taken 100 wickets in a post-war season, 1959.

Nicknamed "Barnacle" for his adhesive batting qualities in Test cricket, he could score quickly when needed. Since retirement, he has become a noted journalist, author and broadcaster. He is a man with a zest for life and a great generosity of spirit.

Warren Bardsley

Born: December 6, 1882, Nevertire, Warren, New South Wales, Australia

Died: January 20, 1954, Collaroy Plateau, Bondi, Sydney, New South Wales

Teams: New South Wales (1903–04 to 1925–26)

First-class: 250 matches; 17,025 runs, average 49.92; no wickets for 41 runs

Tests (1909–1926) 41 matches; 2,469 runs, average 40.47

Warren Bardsley was a stylish left-handed opening batsman of impeccable technique. He toured England four times and reached 2,000 runs on three of those trips.

He made his Test debut in 1909 and, in the fifth test, at the Oval, he scored 136 and 130, so becoming the first batsman to score a century in each innings of a Test match.

He made three hundreds against South Africa, but he was to wait until 1926 for his third and final century against England. He made 193 not out at Lord's which, at the time, was the highest score that had been made in a Lord's Test.

He captained Australia in the next two Tests, at Headingley and Old Trafford, when Herbie Collins was ill.

Eddie Barlow

Born: August 12, 1940, Pretoria, South Africa

Teams: Transvaal (1959–60 to 1967–68); Eastern Province (1964–65 to 1965–66); Western Province (1968–69 to 1980–81); Derbyshire (1976–78); Boland (1981–82 to 1982–83)

First-class: 283 matches; 18,212 runs, average 39.16; 571 wickets, average 24.14

Tests (1961–62 to 1969–70): 30 matches; 2,516 runs. average 45.74; 40 wickets, average 34.05

Eddie Barlow was a tenacious all-rounder, a right-handed batsman and right-arm medium-pace bowler of strength and determination. He was an integral part of a powerful South African side in the 1960s, but his Test career was cut short by his country's expulsion from international cricket. He had six Test centuries to his credit, including 201 against Australia at Adelaide, 1963–64.

He spent three seasons with Derbyshire, taking over the captaincy mid-way through the first year. A modest and warm man, he proved a belligerent leader who drove the county to new levels of fitness and attainment.

Barlow became a fine ambassador for his country and for the game. He coached Gloucestershire in 1990 and 1991.

Syd Barnes

Born: April 19, 1873, Smethwick, Staffordshire

Died: December 26, 1967, Chadsmoor, Staffordshire

Teams: Warwickshire (1894–96); Lancashire (1899–1903); Wales (1927–30)

First-class: 133 matches; 1,573 runs, average 12.78; 719 wickets, average 17.09

Tests (1901–02 to 1913–14): 27 matches; 242 runs, average 8.06; 189 wickets, average 16.43

Sydney Barnes played four games for Warwickshire and 46 for Lancashire, but he preferred league cricket to the county game. In spite of this fact, those who saw him and those who played against him considered him the greatest bowler of his time and, in the opinion of many, he remains the greatest bowler the game has known. He bowled at medium pace, was a master of length and of variations in flight and could turn the ball either way. He was able to adapt his bowling to any conditions.

Barnes was not an easy man. Gaunt, dark and brooding, he did not suffer fools gladly, and he needed handling carefully. He was virtually unknown when A.C. MacLaren invited him to tour Australia, 1901–02. He took five for 65 and one for 74 in the first Test and had match figures of 13 for 163 in the second after which injury hampered his tour. He played one Test against Australia in 1902 and took seven wickets, and thereafter spent most of his time in the leagues, issuing forth only to tour with England when invited.

In Australia, 1911–12, he took 34 wickets, average 22.38, in five Tests. In the Triangular Tournament of 1912, he took 39 wickets, average 10.3, and in South Africa, 1913–14, he took 49 wickets, average 10.93, in four Tests, which remains a world record. That marked the end of his Test career. After the First World War he confined himself to the leagues and to the Minor Counties with Staffordshire, for whom he played until 1935 when he was 62 years old. He is said to have taken all 10 wickets in an innings seven times and to have taken 6,229 wickets, average 8.33, in competitive matches in his long career.

Ken Barrington

Born: November 24, 1930, Reading, Berkshire
Died: March 14, 1981, Needham's Point, Barbados
Teams: Surrey (1953–68)
First-class: 533 matches; 31,714 runs, average 45.63; 273 wickets, average 32.62

BARRINGTON *Popular and determined.*

Tests (1955–68): 82 matches; 6,806 runs, average 58.67; 29 wickets, average 44.82

Stocky, with a pronounced nose and chin which suggested defiance, Ken Barrington was a very sound middle order batsman, a rock on which England so often depended. He had to fight his way into a strong Surrey side, but in two years he was in the England side – 1955, the same year in which he was capped. He made 0 against South Africa on his debut, but he was to make amends for this with 20 Test centuries, the first nine of them abroad. His first in England was his highest, 256 against Australia at Old Trafford, 1964, when he and Dexter put on 246 for the third wicket.

Barrington was a very difficult batsman to dislodge, and he proved the bane of Pakistan in 1967 when he hit centuries in three successive Tests. He played his last Test against Australia at Headingly in 1968. The following winter, playing in a double-wicket tournament in Australia, he suffered a mild heart attack and was forced to retire. He became a selector and managed England touring sides. He was assistant manager and coach to the England side in the Caribbean, 1981, when he died suddenly of a heart attack in the middle of a Test match. A most popular man, he is much missed.

Bishen Bedi

Born: September 25, 1946, Amritsar, India
Teams: Northern Punjab (1961–62 to 1966–67); Delhi (1968–69 to 1980–81); Northamptonshire (1972–77)
First-class: 370 matches; 3,584 runs, average 11.37; 1,560 wickets, average 21.69
Tests (1966–67 to 1979): 67 matches; 656 runs, average 8.98; 266 wickets, average 28.71

A slow left-arm bowler whose action was an aesthetic delight, Bishen Bedi was a most popular cricketer whose brightly coloured patkas became a feature of Test cricket and of the English county scene for several years. He was only 15 when he first played in the Ranji Trophy, and his Test debut came against the West Indies in Calcutta, December 1966. His Test career ended with the last match in the 1979 series in England. Surprisingly, he was not very successful in Tests in England although he enjoyed triumphs with Northamptonshire, whom he captained with flair. He also led India in 22 Tests, but he was outspoken and never far from controversy, being banned once for giving an unauthorized television interview and leading a move for improved payments.

He twice took 25 wickets in a series against England in India and took 21 wickets in Australia, 1969–70. Since his retirement he has managed Indian sides.

Alec Bedser

Born: July 4, 1918, Reading, Berkshire
Teams: Surrey (1939–60)
First-class: 485 matches; 5,735 runs, average 14.51; 1,924 wickets, average 20.41
Tests (1946–55): 51 matches; 714 runs, average 12.75; 236 wickets, average 24.89

BISHEN BEDI *Bowler of gentle guile but outspoken off the field.*

ALEC BEDSER *Soldier and cricketer.*

Alec Bedser played a handful of matches for Surrey in 1939, and then saw the early years of his career consumed by the war. He and his identical twin brother Eric were on the beaches at Dunkirk, but in the closing year of the war Alec Bedser came into prominence in matches at Lord's. He was a truly great right-arm medium fast bowler with a model action and an economic run to the wicket. A very strong man, he gave the impression that he could bowl all day and sometimes did. In the years immediately after the Second World War, he carried the England attack on his broad shoulders. He began his Test career with seven for 49 and four for 96 against India at Lord's, 1946, and followed with another 11 wickets at Old Trafford. In Australia, the following winter, he gained the respect of Bradman's men, but he was forced to plough a lonely furrow.

It was in 1953 that he finally gained the reward for his years of endeavour. When England regained the Ashes, Bedser was one of the heroes of the hour, claiming a record 39 wickets in five Tests. That outstanding achievement was almost the end of his Test career, for when he went to Australia with Hutton's side, 1954–55, he had an attack of

shingles and lost his place in the side after the first Test. He played his last Test against South Africa at Old Trafford in 1955. He took four wickets which brought his total to 236, at the time a record for Test cricket.

He was a major force in Surrey's run of seven consecutive championships, and he led the side on occasions. He was an England selector for over 20 years and was first awarded the OBE and then knighted for his services to cricket.

Richie Benaud

Born: October 6, 1930, Penrith, New South Wales, Australia
Teams: New South Wales (1948–49 to 1963–64)
First-class: 259 matches, 11,719, average 36.50; 945 wickets, average 24.73
Tests (1951–52 to 1963–64): 63 matches, 2,201 runs, average 24.45; 248 wickets, average 27.03

Richie Benaud has argued that he would not have won a place in the Australian side had he not learned to bat. He was an exciting batsman, but he was an even greater leg-break bowler, and he was a captain who must rank alongside Bradman and Armstrong as Australia's greatest. He, more than any other man, lifted Australian cricket from a period of tedium and gloom to a position of supremacy.

He made his Test debut against the West Indies, 1951–52, and played four Tests against South Africa the following season. He toured England in 1953 and made little impact, but he was an astute cricketer, and learned much. He was in the side that was shattered by Tyson and Statham, 1954–55, but he played a major part in Australia's revival weeks later when they won three Tests in the Caribbean. In the fifth match, at Sabina Park, he reached a maiden Test century in 78 minutes.

In 1956, he hit 97 at Lord's and when Australia went to India he took seven for 72 in Madras to set up his side's victory. He followed this with 11 wickets in the win in Calcutta. A year later, he dominated the series in South Africa with two centuries and 30 wickets.

He succeeded Craig as captain of Australia and immediately won

back the Ashes, 1958–59, found success in India and was victorious in a thrilling series against Worrell's West Indians.

In 1961, he was troubled by an injured shoulder, yet his Australian side retained the Ashes when, at Old Trafford, Benaud himself put in a remarkable spell of bowling on the last afternoon to take six for 70 and win the match. When he departed from Test cricket, he could claim that he had led Australia in six Test series of which five were won and one drawn. His contribution as player and captain had been incalculable.

He worked to establish Kerry Packer's World Series and became a journalist and commentator. His wit, charm, lucidity and deep knowledge of the game have made him an outstanding personality.

Colin Blythe

Born: May 30, 1879, Deptford, Kent
Died: November 8, 1917, Passchendaele, Belgium
Teams: Kent (1899–1914)
First-class: 439 matches; 4,443 runs, average 9.87; 2,503 wickets, average 16.81
Tests (1901–02 to 1909–10): 19 matches; 183 runs, average 9.63; 100 wickets, average 18.63

"Charlie" Blythe was one of the two great left-arm spinners of the Edwardian period, the other being Wilfred Rhodes. Blythe was rhythmic and graceful, a master of flight. He was a most intelligent bowler who made full use of his height. In 14 of his 15 full seasons in first-class cricket, he captured 100 wickets, and it is likely that he would have played more for England had he not been subject to epileptic fits.

Artistic (he played the violin) and highly strung, he had match figures of seven for 56 on his Test debut against Australia, 1901–02, and he was second only to Barnes among England bowlers for the series, and he enjoyed a fine tour of South Africa, 1905–06, taking 11 for 118 in Cape Town when England won their only match of the rubber. He had even greater success in 1907 when he took eight for 59 and seven for 40 against South Africa at Headingley, so becoming the only

bowler to take 15 South African wickets in a Test in England.

He was at the height of his powers in 1914 and had played in four championship-winning sides. When war broke out he enlisted and was killed in action in 1917.

David Boon

Born: December 29, 1960, Launceston, Tasmania
Teams: Tasmania (1978–79 to 1998–99), Durham (1997–99)
First-class: 350 matches; 23,473, average 44.00; 14 wickets, average 49.71
Tests (1984–85 to 1995–96): 107 matches; 7,422 runs, average 43,65; no wickets for 14 runs

Short, compact and strong, David Boon possesses a rock-like defence, but he also has a wide range of shots, specializing in a vicious square-cut. He played three Tests against the West Indies, 1984–85, and three on the tour of England a few months later, but it was not until he moved up to open the innings against India, 1985–86, that he recorded his first Test century. His partnership with Geoff Marsh became renowned, but when Mark Taylor came into the side Boon reverted to number three with equal success.

At first a slip fielder, he became a most capable short-leg, brave, reliable and most agile for a heavy man. He hit 200 against New Zealand at Perth, 1989–90, and runs flowed from him in every series. He was a foundation on which Australia built their success in the late 1980s and early 1990s. He announced his retirement from Test cricket before the World Cup, 1996, and scored a century against Sri Lanka in his penultimate appearance. It was his 21st Test hundred.

Boon captained Durham for three seasons 1997–99, and Tasmania from 1992–93 to 1998–99, retiring from first-class cricket at the end of 1999. He was awarded an MBE for his services to cricket.

Allan Border

Born: July 27, 1955, Cremorne, Sydney, New South Wales
Teams: New South Wales (1976–77 to 1979–80); Gloucestershire (1977): Queensland (1980–81 to 1995–96); Essex (1986–88)

First-class: 385 matches; 27,131 runs, average 51.38; 106 wickets, average 39.25

Tests (1978–79 to 1993–94): 156 matches; 11,174 runs, average 50.56; 39 wickets, average 39.10

BORDER *Success became a habit.*

No cricketer has appeared in more Test matches than Allan Border, no batsman has scored more runs in Test cricket and nobody has approached his record of captaining his country in 93 Tests. He allied a straightforward, sound technique to a concentration and determination which were exemplary, and few left-handed batsmen have been so free of faults as he. He was a useful left-arm slow bowler and a very fine close-to-the-wicket fielder. He took over the captaincy of Australia in troubled times and led them to the summit, winning the World Cup along the way. He was very determined and tactically sound and was worshipped by his men.

He first came to light as a most accomplished left-hander when Australia had been ravaged by defections to Packer's organization. Stocky, with cheerful, gleaming blue eyes, he never allowed his concentration to take away his delight in the game, and he learned in a tough school. His maiden Test hundred came against Pakistan in 1979, and he was soon established as his country's number three. In 1979–80, he

hit 150 not out and 153 against Pakistan in Lahore, the first batsman to hit 150 in each innings of a Test. In England, 1981, when Australia struggled, he batted 377 minutes with a broken finger to score an unbeaten 123 at Old Trafford.

He first became captain of Australia in 1984–85 and held the job until the end of the tour of South Africa, 1993–94. This marked the end of his Test career, but there was still one more world to conquer. He was a key member of the Queensland side that won the Sheffield Shield for the first time. He had also been part of an Essex side that won the county championship. His career was studded with 70 centuries of which 27 were in Tests, where his 156 catches were vital to Australia's success.

Bernard Bosanquet

Born: October 13, 1877, Bulls Cross, Enfield, Middlesex
Died: October 12, 1936, Wykehurst, Ewhurst, Surrey
Teams: Oxford University (1898–1900); Middlesex (1898–1919)
First-class: 235 matches; 11,696 runs, average 33.41; 629 wickets, average 23.80
Tests (1903–04 to 1905): 7 matches; 147 runs, average 13.36; 25 wickets, average 24.16

A tall, upstanding right-handed batsman who won his blue all three years at Oxford, Bosanquet was originally a medium-pace bowler. He played four Tests in Australia in 1903–04 and three against Australia in England in 1905. It was in the first of these Tests in England, at Trent Bridge, that Bosanquet took eight for 107 in the second innings and won the match. It is not as a player, however, that Bosanquet is best remembered, but as the perfecter of the googly, the off-break with the leg-break action – a delivery that is still known as the "Bosie" in Australia after its inventor.

Bosanquet developed the googly by playing billiards fives or "twisty grab". In the early part of the nineteenth century, it was feared that the googly would ruin the game, but it simply brought more mystery and vitality.

Bosanquet declined as a bowler after 1905, but advanced as a bats-

man and headed the national averages in 1908 when he hit 214 in 195 minutes for the Rest of England against the Champion County. He was an accomplished billiards player, ice hockey player and hammer thrower. He was father of the television news reader, the late Reginald Bosanquet.

Ian Botham

See Legends (pages 98–99)

Geoff Boycott

Born: October 21, 1940, Fitzwilliam, Yorkshire
Teams: Yorkshire (1962–86); Northern Transvaal (1971–72)
First-class: 609 matches; 48,426 runs, average 56.83; 45 wickets, average 32.42
Tests (1964 to 1981–82): 108 matches; 8,114 runs, average 47.72; 7 wickets, average 54.57

Geoffrey Boycott is one of the greatest opening batsmen that the game has known. He dedicated his life to the art of batting, practising assiduously and eschewing any shot that might even hint at threatening the loss of his wicket. When he walked out of Test cricket during the Tour of India, 1981–82, he had scored more runs than any other batsman in Test history and might well have scored more but for his own self-imposed exile from Test cricket for two years. His career was littered with controversy and he excited extremes of passion. A deeply sensitive man, he found that fame and success brought problems which were not always easy to cope with. His fans worshipped him; others saw his intense dedication as selfish.

His Test debut came against Australia at Trent Bridge, 1964, when he scored 48 and fractured a finger while fielding. In the last match of the series, he scored the first of his 22 Test centuries. The highest of these came at Headingley, 1967, when he made 246 not out against India, a

record for the series, but the innings occupied 573 minutes and he faced 555 balls. He was disciplined for slow scoring and was omitted from the next Test.

Headingley was his spiritual home, and he stirred great emotions when he scored his 100th hundred on the ground in 1977 during the Test match against Australia. He went on to make 191. In all, he scored 151 centuries in first-class cricket, and in 1971 and 1979 he averaged over 100 for the season.

BOYCOTT *A favourite scoring shot.*

No other English batsman has achieved this feat once.

His relationship with his own county was often tempestuous although he captained the side from 1971 to 1978. He has become a well known television summarizer since leaving the game. His comments are both intelligent and perceptive.

Donald Bradman

See Legends (pages 100–101)

Johnny Briggs

Born: October 3, 1862, Sutton-in-Ashfield, Nottinghamshire
Died: January 11, 1902, Heald Green, Cheadle, Cheshire
Teams: Lancashire (1879–1900)
First-class: 535 matches; 14,092 runs, average 18.27; 2,221 wickets, average 15.95
Tests (1884–85 to 1899): 33 matches; 815 runs, average 18.11; 118 wickets, average 17.75
Short, cheerful and immensely popular, Johnny Briggs made his first-class debut at the age of 16. He was a right-handed batsman and a fine fielder, but he developed into a slow left-arm bowler, although it was not until 1886 that he was truly recognized in that capacity.

In 1888–89, in South Africa, he took 21 wickets in two Tests, and his 15 for 28 at Cape Town constituted a record for one day in Test cricket as did his eight for 11, all bowled, in the second innings.

He had both a century and a hat-trick for England against Australia and was wonderfully consistent. At Headingley, 1899, he took three for 53 on the first day against Australia. That evening he had a violent epileptic fit and played no more cricket until the next season when he seems to have been as good as ever. He suffered another violent attack, however, and was confined to Cheadle Asylum where he died at the age of 39.

Basil Butcher

Born: September 3, 1933, Port Mourant, Berbice, British Guiana
Teams: British Guiana (1954–55 to 1970–71)
First-class: 169 matches; 11,628 runs, average 49.90; 40 wickets, average 30.42
Tests (1958–59 to 1969): 44 matches; 3,104 runs, average 43.11; 5 wickets, average 18.00
In a West Indian side studded with stars, it was sometimes all too easy to overlook the worth of Basil Butcher, yet he was among the most consistent batsmen in the world as a number four or five and was particularly successful in England. He was also a useful leg-break bowler and a fine fielder. He made his Test debut in India, 1958–59, and reached his first Test century in the third mach of the series which he followed with an innings of 142 in the fourth.

In the dramatic Lord's Test of 1963 he scored a magnificent 133, and three years later, at Trent Bridge, he saved the West Indies with the highest score of his career, an unbeaten 209, and shared in century partnerships for three wickets. The West Indies had trailed by 90 in the first innings, and Butcher's knock not only saved them when defeat looked probable, but set up a remarkable victory.

Greatly respected by his opponents, he was a professional in the Lancashire League for many years.

C

Bhagwat Chandrasekhar

Born: May 17, 1945, Mysore, India
Teams: Karnataka (1963–64 to 1979–80)
First-class: 246 matches; 600 runs, average 4.61; 1,063 wickets, average 24.03
Tests (1963–64 to 1979): 58 matches; 167 runs, average 4.07; 242 wickets, average 29.74
Chandrasekhar bowled his leg-breaks at a brisk pace, and he proved to be a match-winner in Test cricket when leg-break bowling seemed to be a dying art. He made an immediate impression when he made his Test debut against England 1963–64, and he bowled India to victory over Australia in Bombay a year later. By 1966–67, he was one of a trio of spinners who began to make India a formidable force in world cricket, and he took 18 wickets in three Tests against the West Indies. He bowled well in England in 1967, but the home side won the series. Four years later, he took six for 38 in the second innings at the Oval, and India beat England in England for the first time. His eight for 72 in the first innings at

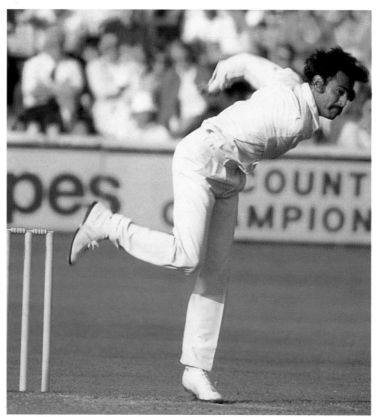

CHANDRASEKHAR *Quick leg-breaks brought more wickets than he scored runs.*

Delhi, 1972–73, was still unable to prevent England winning by six wickets, but he ended the rubber with a record 35 wickets and India took the series. He also bowled India to victory over Australia in Australia for the first time, 1977–78, taking 12 for 104 in the match and claiming his 200th Test wicket in the process. Thereafter he was handicapped by injury and lost form. He played his last Test in England, 1979, and retired the following year.

Greg Chappell

Born: August 7, 1948, Unley, Adelaide, South Australia
Teams: South Australia (1966–67 to 1972–73); Somerset (1968–69); Queensland (1973–74 to 1983–84)
First-class: 321 matches; 24,535 runs, average 52.20; 291 wickets, average 29.95
Tests (1970–71 to 1983–84): 87 matches; 7,110 runs, average 53.86; 47 wickets, average 40.70
Grandson of one Test captain, Victor Richardson, and brother of another, Ian, Greg Chappell was a tall, slim, elegant batsman who sharpened his technique with Somerset, hit the first century in the Sunday League and 18 months later scored a hundred on his Test debut against England in Perth. Now an integral part of the Australian side and of his brother's plans to revive Australian cricket, he hit centuries at Lord's and the Oval in the 1972 Ashes series and made 247 not out against New Zealand at Wellington, 1973–74. He made 133 in the second innings.

His brother groomed him to take over as captain of Australia, and in his first Test as captain, against the West Indies at Brisbane, 1975–76, he created a record by scoring a century in each innings. In 1972, he and Ian had provided the first instance of brothers scoring centuries in the same innings of a Test, against England at the Oval.

The Packer affair sapped the strength of the Australian side in 1977, but when it was resolved Greg Chappell was reinstated as captain, leading Australia for the last time against Sri Lanka, 1983. He seemed to select when he would play and this attitude, and his notorious tactics in a one-day international against New Zealand when he told his brother Trevor to bowl under-arm, brought him much criticism, but he had a dignified air and a desire to win, and he was a fine cricketer.

Ian Chappell

Born: September 26, 1943, Unley, Adelaide, South Australia
Teams: South Australia (1961–62 to 1979–80); Lancashire (1963)
First-class: 262 matches; 19,680 runs, average 48.35; 176 wickets, average 37.57
Tests (1964–65 to 1979–80): 75 matches; 5,345 runs, average 42.42; 20 wickets, average 65.80

The eldest of three brothers, all of whom played for Australia, Ian Chappell was a determined, gritty batsman, a brilliant slip fielder and an occasional leg-break bowler. Greg, too, turned to leg-breaks with some success after beginning as a medium-pacer. Ian made his Test debut against Pakistan in 1964, but he did not win a regular place in the Australian side until three years later. His first Test hundred came against India, 1967–68, and he did well in England the following summer. This was a low period in Australian cricket history, however, and when Illingworth's side got the upper hand in Australia, 1970–71, Lawry was dropped for the last Test and Ian Chappell appointed captain. Chappell immediately set about reshaping the Australian side, and they became a formidable, ruthless team. In 1972, he and his brother Greg scored centuries in the last Test at The Oval to win the match and draw the series against England. Wins over Pakistan, the West Indies and, in 1975, England followed. Ian Chappell then handed over the captaincy to Greg, while he himself set about establishing Packer's World Series, and in all that followed he proved a very tough negotiator.

His success as batsman and captain are undeniable, but he was abrasive to opponents and authority. His colourful language and tendency to run his side as a self-contained unit answerable to no one did cause controversy.

Brian Close

Born: February 24, 1931, Rawdon, Leeds, Yorkshire
Teams: Yorkshire (1949–70); Somerset (1971–77)
First-class: 786 matches; 34,994 runs, average 33.26; 1,171 wickets, average 26.42
Tests (1949–76): 22 matches; 887 runs, average 25.34; 18 wickets, average 29.55

Brian Close did the "double" in his first season in first-class cricket and played for England against New Zealand. He was a left-handed batsman who suited his mood to the occasion, a medium-pace or off-break bowler and a brave and brilliant close-to-the-wicket fielder. He was the youngest to gain a Yorkshire cap, but never quite lived up to that early promise, and his 22 Test caps were spread over a period of 27 years.

He was something of a cricketing eccentric, very popular with his players, and he captained Yorkshire from 1963 to 1970. With England outplayed by the West Indies, Close was appointed captain for the last Test, 1966, and England won. Honest, brave, and an astute tactician, he led England to more successes over India and Pakistan, but the tactics he adopted in a county match against Warwickshire caused an outcry, and his invitation to lead England in the Caribbean was withdrawn. At Tony Greig's insistence, he was recalled to the England side in 1976 at the age of 45 because he was such a tough fighter.

A brush with the Yorkshire committee caused him to move to Somerset whom he captained from 1972 until his retirement. He led England seven times, and won six and drew one of the matches in which he was captain.

Denis Compton

Born: May 23, 1918, Hendon, Middlesex
Died: April 23, 1997, Windsor, Berkshire
Teams: Middlesex (1936–58); Holkar (1944–45); Europeans (1944–45 to 1945–46)
First-class: 515 matches; 38,942 runs, average 51.85; 622 wickets, average 32.27
Tests (1937 to 1956–57): 78 matches; 5,807 runs, average 50.06; 25 wickets, average 56.40

DENIS COMPTON *A great entertainer.*

In the entire history of cricket, no player gave more pleasure nor entertained a crowd more fully than Denis Compton. By any standards he was a pure genius, and his delight in what he was doing, his passion for the game, was as transparent as it was infectious. The sun always seemed to shine when he played cricket. He was first picked for Middlesex as a slow left-arm bowler and was effective, if eccentric, in this area to the end of his career. He batted number eleven in his first match, but within weeks he was number four, and he completed 1,000 runs by the end of the season, a feat he accomplished 14 times in England and three times overseas. The following season, he was in the England side against New Zealand at the Oval, run out 65, and he scored a century in his first Test against Australia, 1938. He was unable to tour at this time, because he was under contract to Arsenal FC, winning an FA Cup winners' medal in 1950, a League Championship medal in 1948 and being capped for England in wartime internationals.

He went to Australia, 1946–47, and scored a century in each innings of the Adelaide Test. The following summer he broke all records. He made 3,816 runs, average 90.85, and hit 18 centuries. It seems likely that these records will never be beaten.

In five Tests against the South Africans, he hit 753 runs, average 94.12. That season he also took 73 wickets in all first-class matches.

In 1948, against the might of Bradman's Australians, he hit 184 at Trent Bridge and an unbeaten 145 at Old Trafford after he had been forced to retire hurt early in his innings. In South Africa, 1948–49, he hit 300 in 181 minutes for MCC against NE Transvaal. It remains the fastest triple-century ever recorded. By now, he was being troubled by an old knee injury sustained while playing football. It was to prove a severe handicap and to shorten his career. He had a kneecap removed, scored 278 against Pakistan, 1954, and two years later, minus his kneecap, hit 94 in his last Test against Australia at the Oval.

He worked as a PR consultant and as a journalist, and continued to charm all who met him. His one piece of advice to young cricketers was: "Enjoy it. It is over all too soon."

Learie Constantine

Born: September 21, 1901, Petit Valley, Diego Martin, Trinidad
Died: July 1, 1971, Brondesbury, Hampstead, London
Teams: Trinidad (1921–22 to 1934–35); Freelooters, India (1934–5); Barbados (1938–39)
First-class: 119 matches; 4,475 runs, average 24.05; 439 wickets, average 20.48
Tests (1928–39): 18 matches; 635 runs, average 19.24; 58 wickets, average 30.10

The game has known no more dynamic cricketer than Learie Constantine. His fielding was spectacular, his bowling fast and his batting violent. He was capable of turning the course of any match by a sensational act in one of these areas. He performed the "double" in 1928, and spent most of the 1930s playing in the Lancashire League where he was a tremendous favourite. He might even have qualified for Lancashire but for the colour prejudice which existed at the time.

He took 103 wickets on the 1939 tour of England, and, in the final Test at the Oval, the last before the outbreak of war, he hit 79 in an hour and took five for 75 in the first innings.

Constantine did welfare work among black people in Britain during the Second World War. Refused admission to a London hotel on one occasion, he took successful legal action over the matter. In the memorable words of C.L.R. James, Constantine "revolted against the revolting contrast between his first-class status as a cricketer and his third-class status as a man". His greatest joy came at the end of the war when England met the Dominions at Lord's. Constantine was the only black man in the side, but the rest of the team insisted that he should captain them. It was his last first-class match.

A barrister, a writer and an MP in the Trinidad parliament, he came back to London as High Commissioner for Trinidad and Tobago. He was awarded the MBE, knighted and finally created a Life Peer, Baron of Maraval and Nelson. He was posthumously awarded Trinidad's highest honour, the Trinity Cross.

Colin Cowdrey

Born: December 24, 1932, Bangalore, India
Died: December 4, 2000
Teams: Kent (1950–76); Oxford University (1952–54)
First-class: 692 matches; 42,719 runs, average 42.89; 65 wickets, average 51.21
Tests (1954–55 to 1974–75): 114 matches; 7,624 runs, average 44.06; no wickets for 104 runs
One of the very finest and most accomplished of post-war batsmen, Cowdrey was a prolific scorer who hit 107 centuries in first-class cricket and created a record by playing 114 times for England whom he captained on 27 occasions. He was a brilliant slip fielder, and, as a batsman, was a stylist who sought perfection. Had he been arrogant or ruthless, he would have scored many more runs.

He made his Test debut on Hutton's 1954–55 tour of Australia. He had been a surprise choice, but was an instant success, and his innings of 102 out of 191 in the third Test at Melbourne saved England from disaster in a match that they went on to win.

In 1957, at Edgbaston, he and Peter May shared a record partnership of 411 for the fourth wicket against the West Indies. It seemed inevitable that he would succeed May as England captain, but he was forced to give way to Dexter and M.J.K. Smith as the selectors believed his approach to be too benign. In 1966, he took over from Smith and then was replaced by Close. He was reinstated when Close was dropped for his misdemeanours, and he took England to the Caribbean, winning the series against all expectations.

An injury in a Sunday League game was to cost him the England captaincy again in 1969, and he could not be called the luckiest of players. In 1963 at Lord's he had his left arm broken by a ball from Wes Hall, but he went out to bat with his arm in plaster to save the day. Fortunately, he did not have to face a delivery. In 1974–75, he was called to Australia at the age of 42. It was an emergency, and he was needed to help combat the fast bowlers. It was his sixth tour of the country where he was very popular.

He was a surprisingly revolutionary President of the MCC and an active Chairman of the ICC. He was knighted for his services to cricket in the New Year's Honours List, 1992.

Martin Crowe

Born: September 22, 1962, Henderson, Auckland, New Zealand
Teams: Auckland (1979–80 to 1982–83); Central Districts (1983–84 to 1989–90); Somerset (1984–88); Wellington (1990–91 to 1994–95)
First-class: 247 matches; 19,608 runs, average 56.02; 119 wickets, average 33.70
Tests (1981–82 to 1995–96): 77 matches; 5,444 runs, average 45.36; 14 wickets, average 48.28
Not only one of the greatest batsmen of his generation, but one of the finest of all New Zealand batsmen, Martin Crowe made his Test debut in the rain-ruined match against Australia at Wellington in February 1982, when he was still seven months short of his 20th birthday. Tall, orthodox in style, elegant and powerful in execution, sound in temperament, he made his

MARTIN CROWE *Elegant stylist.*

first Test century against England at Wellington, 1983–84, saving a match which had looked lost. By the end of his Test career, he had 17 hundreds to his credit and had scored more Test runs than any other New Zealand batsman.

Initially, he bowled at a brisk medium pace, but a back injury, one of several which marred his career, effectively brought an end to his capacity as a bowler.

He made a great impact in his years with Somerset, encouraging young uncapped players and doing much for team spirit, but there was also controversy in that by offering him a new contract in 1987, Somerset brought to an end their association with Viv Richards and Joel Garner.

There was a reluctance to burden him with the captaincy of New Zealand too early in his career, but the decline in form of his elder brother Jeff and John Wright's unwillingness to do the job led to Martin Crowe being asked to take a young and inexperienced side to Pakistan, 1990–91. He battled bravely against the odds, and when he led New Zealand in New Zealand for the first time, he hit 299

against Sri Lanka at Wellington. This is the highest score ever made by a New Zealander in Test history, and he and Andrew Jones established a world record when they added 467 for the third wicket. Crowe scored centuries against all Test-playing nations with the exception of South Africa.

He developed a knee problem which necessitated an operation and caused him to play with a splint. He scored runs even though he was in pain, but following the tour of India, 1995–96, when he was in obvious trouble, he was asked to prove his fitness. Reluctantly, he was forced to retire, and a great player passed from the game.

D

Joseph Darling

Born: November 21, 1870, Glen Osmond, Adelaide, South Australia
Died: January 2, 1946, Hobart, Tasmania
Teams: South Australia (1893–94 to 1907–08)
First-class: 202 matches; 10,635 runs, average 34.52; 1 wicket, average 55.00
Tests (1894–95 to 1905): 34 matches; 1,657 runs, average 28.56
Son of a member of the Legislative Council who was responsible for introducing the bill which granted the lease on land that became Adelaide Oval, Joe Darling excelled as a left-handed batsman at college. First he worked in banking and then in wheat farming, so that it seemed he was lost to sport. But in 1893–94, he returned to Adelaide to open a sports store, and a year later, thickset with face burned by the sun, he was in the Australian side. He first toured England in 1896 and became an opening batsman. On his next three tours, 1899, 1902, and 1905, he captained the side.

Against MacLaren's side, 1897–98, he became the first batsman to hit three centuries in a Test rubber and the first to aggregate 500 runs in a series. In the third Test, at Adelaide, he made 178 and reached his century with the first six ever hit in Test cricket. To score six a batsman had to hit the ball out of the ground at that time. In the final Test, he hit 160 in 175 minutes.

A man of the utmost integrity, Darling was elected to the captaincy by his fellow players who revered him, and he worked hard on their behalf while maintaining strict discipline. He retired to help his wife raise their 15 children. He settled in Tasmania, reared merino sheep and became a successful politician.

Alan Davidson

Born: June 14, 1929, Lisarow, Gosford, New South Wales

Teams: New South Wales (1949–50 to 1962–63)

First-class: 193 matches; 6,804 runs, average 32.86; 672 wickets, average 20.90

Tests (1953 to 1962–63): 44 matches; 1,328 runs, average 24.59; 186 wickets, average 20.53

A left-handed fast bowler and a left-handed batsman who could hit the ball very hard, Alan Davidson made his Test debut in 1953, playing in all five matches. In 1958–59, he took 24 wickets against England, and two years later, he took 33 wickets and scored 212 runs against the West Indies. In the first match of that series, at Brisbane, he became the first player to score 100 runs and take 10 wickets in a Test.

In 25 Tests against England, he made 750 runs and took 84 wickets. He also held 23 catches to complete a fine record.

ARAVINDA DE SILVA *Wristy strength.*

He was President of the New South Wales Cricket Association for many years and was also Director of Rothman's National Sports Foundation.

Aravinda de Silva

Born: October 17, 1965, Colombo, Ceylon

Teams: Nondescripts (1988–89 to 2002); Kent (1995)

First-class: 220 matches; 15,000 runs, average 48.38; 129 wickets, average 29.17

Tests (1984 to 2002): 93 matches; 6,361 runs, average 42.97; 29 wickets, average 41.65

Right-handed, wristy, quick-footed, Aravinda de Silva might even have scored more Test runs had he not been so eager to score quickly. As it is, he has a host of records to his credit. His 267 against New Zealand at Wellington, 1990–91, is a national record. Twice he has reached a Test century with a six, and he became the first batsman to score an unbeaten century in each innings of a Test match, against Pakistan, 1997.

A useful off-break bowler, he played for Kent in 1995, scoring 1,781 runs, average 59.36, and in the Benson & Hedges Cup Final made 112 against Lancashire, one of the most thrilling and greatest innings ever seen at Lord's.

When Sri Lanka won the World Cup in 1996, de Silva took the Man of the Match award in the semifinal and in the final in which he scored an unbeaten century.

He is Sri Lanka's leading run scorer in Test cricket. In 2002–03 he appeared only in One-Day matches.

Ted Dexter

Born: May 15, 1935, Milan, Italy

Teams: Cambridge University (1956–58); Sussex (1957–68)

First-class: 327 matches, 21,150 runs, average 40.75; 419 wickets,

DONALD *One of the fastest bowlers of the 1990s.*

average 29.92

Tests (1958–68): 62 matches; 4,502 runs, average 47.89; 66 wickets, average 34.93

An exciting attacking batsman, classical in style, and a most capable medium-pace bowler, Ted Dexter made an immediate impact at Cambridge and played for England against New Zealand at Old Trafford in 1958. The following winter he was flown to Australia to boost a sagging England side. He was a right-handed batsman of regal splendour, authority and immense power. Imperious of manner, he

earned the nickname of "Lord Ted". He captained Sussex from 1960 to 1965, and he first led England in Pakistan and India, 1961–62, scoring 205, the highest innings of his career, against Pakistan in Karachi. He continued as England captain until the end of 1964, giving way to Cowdrey for just one "trial" Test in 1962.

For such an enterprising cricketer, he was a rather disappointing captain, being a great theorist and seemingly prone to lose interest. He was not the best handler of men, probably because he was so multi-talented. He was a very fine golfer.

He missed the tour of India, 1963–64, and stood as Conservative candidate against the future Labour Prime Minister, James Callaghan, in the autumn of 1964. He was unsuccessful and joined the England side in South Africa where he played under M.J.K. Smith. In 1965, he broke a leg and retired, but he continued to make infrequent appearances for Sussex and last played for England in 1968.

He was appointed chairman of the England committee in 1989 and held the job for four years. He did much good, intelligent work behind the scenes, but England's lack of success brought him unfair criticism. His contribution to the re-ordering of the game has never been fully appreciated.

Allan Donald

Born: October 20, 1966, Bloemfontein, South Africa

Teams: Orange Free State (1985–86 to 2003–04); Warwickshire (1987–2000); Worcestershire (2002)

First-class: 316 matches; 2,785 runs, average 12.05; 1,216 wickets, average 22.76

Tests (1991–92 to 2001–02): 72 matches; 652 runs, average 10.68; 330 wickets, average 22.25

A fast bowler of genuine pace, Allan Donald had proved his quality before South Africa's re-admission to Test cricket. His arrival at Warwickshire brought about a revival in the county's fortunes. He claimed 86 wickets in 1989, 83 in 1991 and 89 in 1995. Although his entry into Test cricket was late, he quickly became the fourth South African to take 100 Test wickets, and now only Hugh Tayfield with 170 wickets stands ahead of him.

He bowls with dedication and passion at all times, but he keeps a fuller length than most fast bowlers of his generation. He demolished Zimbabwe with eight for 71 and three for 42 at Harare, 1995–96, and his best bowling in domestic cricket is his eight for 37 for Free State against Transvaal at Johannesburg, 1986–87. Donald became the first South African to reach 300 Test wickets. He was his country's outstanding bowler in the two series against England in 1998 and in 1999–2000.

Martin Donnelly

Born: October 17, 1917, Ngaruawahia, Auckland, New Zealand
Died: October 22, 1999
Teams: Wellington (1936–37 to 1940–41) Canterbury (1938–39 to 1939–40); Middlesex (1946); Oxford University (1946–1947); Warwickshire (1948–1950)
First-class: 131 matches; 9,250 runs, average 47.43; 43 wickets, average 39.13
Tests (1937–1949): 7 matches; 582 runs, average 52.90; no wickets for 20 runs

A left-handed batsman of immense power and grace, Martin Donnelly was a natural athlete who represented Oxford University and England at rugby. His Test matches were for New Zealand against England, in England and, when he made his debut at Lord's in 1937, he was the second-youngest cricketer ever to represent New Zealand. He scored 1,414 runs on the tour.

He lost valuable years to the war in which he served as major in the Egyptian and Italian campaigns.

A graduate of University College, Canterbury, he went up to Oxford in 1946 and captained the eleven in 1947. He was a prolific run-scorer and hit 162 not out in three hours for the Gentlemen against the Players.

He played for Middlesex against the Indian tourists in 1946, but he went into business when he came down from Oxford and appeared for Warwickshire in 20 matches during the next three seasons.

In 1949 when New Zealand toured England, he excelled with 2,287 runs, average 61.81, which included 462 runs, average 77.00, in the Tests. At Lord's, he made 206, the first double-century in Test cricket by a New Zealand batsman.

His work took him to Australia and he settled in Sydney, leaving lovers of the game with a memory of charm and graciousness.

Jeffrey Dujon

Born: May 28, 1956, Kingston, Jamaica
Teams: Jamaica (1974–75 to 1991–92)
First-class: 194 matches; 9,308 runs, average 38.14; 1 wicket, average 45.00; caught 434, stumped 19;
Tests (1981–82 to 1991): 81 matches; 3,322 runs, average 31.94; caught 267, stumped 5

An elegant right-handed batsman and graceful, acrobatic wicket-keeper, Jeff Dujon established himself in the West Indian side on the tour of Australia, 1982–83, and the following season in the Caribbean hit his first Test century, against India in Antigua. He and Clive Lloyd put on 207 for the sixth wicket, and the West Indies won the series. Indeed, Dujon never played in a Test side which lost a series, and he was a member of the West Indian team which won a record 11 Tests in succession, 1984–85. He hit hundreds against England and Australia and claimed five Test centuries in all, a fine feat considering that he was invariably batting at number seven.

He had no serious rival for the position of West Indian keeper, and there was an outcry when he was finally omitted after an indifferent display against England in 1991.

E

John Edrich

Born: June 21, 1937, Blofield, Norfolk
Teams: Surrey (1958–78)
First-class: 564 matches; 39,790 runs, average 45.47; no wickets for 53 runs

Tests (1963–76): 77 matches; 5,138 runs, average 43.54; no wickets for 23 runs

A member of a famous Norfolk cricketing family, John Edrich was a solid, chunky, tough and dependable left-hand opening batsman who reached 1,000 runs in a season 21 times, including twice overseas. On six of those occasions he reached 2,000. He captained Surrey from 1973 to 1977, and led England in Sydney, 1974–75, when Denness dropped himself through lack of form. He had his ribs broken by the first ball he received from Lillee in the second innings and was forced to retire. Typically of Edrich, he returned to bat two and a half hours for an unbeaten 33.

He was one of that select group of batsmen who have scored a hundred hundreds, the highest of which was 310 not out against New Zealand at Headingley, 1965. He hit five sixes and 52 fours, the most boundaries ever hit in a Test innings.

Dogged by personal tragedies, he served as a Test selector and, more recently, as England batting coach.

Bill Edrich

Born: March 26, 1916, Lingwood, Norfolk
Died: April 24, 1986, Whitehill Court, Chesham, Buckinghamshire
Teams: Middlesex (1937–58)
First-class: 571 matches; 36,965 runs, average 42.39; 479 wickets, average 33.31

BILL EDRICH *Success in the ninth Test.*

Tests (1938 to 54–55): 39 matches; 2,440 runs, average 40.00; 41 wickets, average 41.29

Bill Edrich had three brothers and a cousin (John) who played county cricket, and there was a time when the Edriches could field a full eleven. Bill Edrich played for Norfolk from 1932 to 1936 when he should have made his debut for Middlesex, but his registration was delayed and he had to wait another year. He hit 2,154 runs in 1937, and the following season he scored 1,000 runs before the end of May and played for England against Australia. His first eight Tests were disastrous for him, but the ninth, against South Africa at Durban, 1938–39, saw him score 219.

A determined and aggressive batsman who finally settled at number three and a quick bowler off a shortish run who opened the England attack immediately after the Second World War, Edrich lived life to the full. He served in the RAF and was awarded the DFC and, pre-war, he played soccer for Tottenham Hotspur. He was a late selection for the England tour of Australia, 1946–47, but was named as senior professional. He turned amateur the following summer, probably hoping for the England captaincy, but his lust for living was not always in accord with the ideals of England selectors – which perhaps explains why he was often omitted from sides that he should have been in.

In 1947, he and his great friend Denis Compton rewrote the record books. The Middlesex "twins" excited a nation with their exploits as Edrich scored 3,539 runs, an aggregate beaten only by Compton that same summer, and hit 12 centuries, including his career-best 267 not out against Northamptonshire. The following season, he and Compton shared a Middlesex third-wicket record stand of 424 undefeated against Somerset. He captained Middlesex and, on retirement, returned to play for Norfolk. He was a man of intelligence and charm, and always good company.

Godfrey Evans

Born: August 18, 1920, Finchley, Middlesex
Died: May 3, 1999
Teams: Kent (1939–67)
First-class: 465 matches; 14,882 runs, average 21.22; 2 wickets, average 122.50; caught 816, stumped 250
Tests (1946–59): 91 matches; 2,439 runs, average 20.49; caught 173, stumped 46

One of the very greatest of wicket-keepers and an entertainer much loved by the crowd, Godfrey Evans appeared for Kent in a handful of matches in 1939 before succeeding Les Ames in 1946. Within a year he was England's first-choice keeper. He was an extrovert and he was spectacular, but he was eminently dependable, and his keeping standing up to Alec Bedser became one of the features of immediate post-war cricket. He was also a capable batsman who reached 1,000 runs in a season four times, and he hit seven centuries, two of them in Tests. Against India at Lord's, 1952, he made 105, and 98 of these runs came before lunch, yet in Adelaide, 1946–47, he created a world record when he batted 97 minutes before scoring his first run in the second innings. He could bat as the occasion demanded, but perhaps he never treated batting quite seriously enough in county matches.

He made four tours to Australia and two to South Africa and the West Indies, and he was popular everywhere. On his retirement, he was employed by Ladbrokes.

F

Aubrey Faulkner

Born: December 17, 1881, Port Elizabeth, South Africa
Died: September 10, 1930, Walham Green, London
Teams: Transvaal (1902–03 to 1909–10); MCC (1912–20)
First-class: 118 matches; 6,366 runs, average 36.58; 449 wickets, average 17.42
Tests (1905–06 to 1924): 25 matches; 1,754 runs, average 40.79; 82 wickets, average 26.58

Aubrey Faulkner was one of the earliest exponents of the googly when he delivered at a medium pace. He was also a very fine right-handed middle-order batsman. His Test debut came against England, 1905–06, and he played a significant part in South Africa winning four of the five Tests. He enjoyed a fine tour of England, 1907, and took nine wickets in the Headingley Test. When South Africa again beat England in a Test series in South Africa, 1909–10, he captured 29 wickets in the five Tests. In the first, he scored 78 and 123 and had match

figures of eight for 160. He hit 99 in the last Test.

In Australia the following year, he made South Africa's first double-century in a Test match, 204 at Melbourne, and followed this with 115 at Adelaide when South Africa beat Australia for the first time. He did the "double" on the tour of England, 1912, and a year later settled in England. He had a fine war record, being awarded the DSO, and he opened an indoor cricket school in London which benefited many cricketers and became world-famous. He was one of the heroes of MacLaren's side which overcame the mighty Australian side of 1921. He scored 153 and took six wickets.

Given to fits of melancholia, he died tragically by his own hand.

Fazal Mahmood

Born: February 18, 1927, Lahore, India
Died: May 30, 2005, Lahore, Pakistan
Teams: Northern India (1943–44 to 1946–47); Punjab (1951–52 to 1956–57); Lahore (1958–59)
First-class: 111 matches; 2,602 runs, average 23.02; 460 wickets, average 19.11
Tests (1952–53 to 1962): 34 matches; 620 runs, average 14.09; 139 wickets, average 24.70

Fazal Mahmood was a right-arm fast medium-pace bowler whose style was akin to Alec Bedser's. He was selected for India's tour of Australia, 1947–48, but stood down on the announcement of the Partition and waited for his international debut until 1952–53 when Pakistan entered Test cricket. In his country's second Test, against India at Lucknow, he took five for 52 and seven for 42 to bring Pakistan an historic victory. He had proved himself particularly devastating on matting, but he was equally effective in England in 1954. He captured four wickets at Lord's and Old Trafford, and at the Oval he took six for 53 and six for 46 to take Pakistan to victory over England.

A national hero, happy and popular, he was chosen to lead Pakistan when Kardar stepped down, but Fazal did not have Kardar's social status. With the added responsibility of being the main strike bowler, his captaincy suffered. It had begun sensationally when he put the West Indies in at Karachi and took seven

wickets to bowl his side to a 10-wicket victory. Thereafter, his bowling declined and his captaincy was criticized as factions developed. When he left Test cricket, he had a Pakistan record of 139 wickets to his credit.

Andrew Flintoff

Born: December 6, 1977, Preston. Lancashire
Teams: Lancashire (1995–2005)
First-class: 144 matches; 7,490 runs, average 35.83; 247 wickets, average 31.27
Tests (1998 to 2005): 54 matches; 2,747 runs, average 33.09; 158 wickets, average 30.91

The hero of England's team which recaptured The Ashes in 2005, the best description of "Freddie" Flintoff is big-hearted. That sums up his attitude to life as well as cricket. The final Test against Australia at the Oval in 2005 gives a fair demonstration of Flintoff's all round ability. First, his innings of 72 saved his side from collapse then, as the Australian batsmen got into their stride he took five wickets to keep their first innings advantage under control. Surely without those duel efforts, England would not have gained cricket's greatest prize.

Flintoff was capped by England in 1998, the youngest player to have that honour since Brian Close back in 1949. In 2000, chronic back problems seemed to threaten his bowling career and he was subjected to much media scrutiny over apparent weight issues. He missed the 2001 Test series against Australia, but returned to the fray in 2002 and has been a major player in England's great run of success since then.

Tich Freeman

Born: May 17, 1888, Lewisham, London
Died: January 28, 1965, Bearsted, Kent
Teams: Kent (1914–36)
First-class: 592 matches; 4,961 runs, average 9.50; 3,776 wickets, average 18.42
Tests (1924–25 to 1929): 12 matches; 154 runs, average 14.00; 66 wickets, average 25.86

His height earning him the nickname "Tich", Freeman took more wickets in county cricket than any other bowler in the history of the

game, and only Wilfred Rhodes took more wickets in all first-class cricket. In 1928, he became the only bowler to capture 300 wickets in a season, 304 at 18.05 runs each, and in the seven seasons that followed he took more than 200 wickets each season, so that between 1928 and 1935 he took 2,090 wickets. In 1936, he captured "only" 108 wickets for Kent and was not re-engaged.

Standing 5ft 2in, "Tich" Freeman was a leg-break and googly bowler who had immaculate control and posed difficulties with his flight which, because of his height, often had a low trajectory. That he played only 12 times for England and never against Australia in England is one of the unsolved mysteries of the game. In 1928, he took 22 wickets in three Tests against the West Indies, but he did not appear in a single Test on the tour of Australia that followed. Against South Africa, 1929, he captured 22 wickets in two matches, yet he did not play for England after that series.

He became a record wicket-taker in the Birmingham League after he left first-class cricket.

Charles Fry

Born: April 25, 1872, West Croydon, Surrey
Died: September 7, 1956, Child's Hill, Hampstead, London
Teams: Oxford University (1892–95); Sussex (1894–1908); London County (1900–1902); Hampshire (1909–1921); Europeans (1921–22)
First-class: 394 matches; 30,886 runs, average 50.22; 166 wickets, average 29.34
Tests (1895–96 to 1912): 26 matches; 1,223 runs, average 32.18; no wickets for 3 runs

Charles Fry made only one tour abroad with an England side, to South Africa, 1895–96, shortly after coming down from Oxford. He played in the first two Tests of the series, and his remaining 24 Test matches were all played in England. He would have been a regular choice for his country had he been able to spare the time. A first-class honours graduate in Classical Moderations, he won his blue in all four years at Oxford and also won blues for soccer and athletics. He would also have won a blue for rugby but for injury. In 1893 he equalled the world long-jump record. He was capped for England against Ireland at soccer in 1901 and played for Southampton in the FA Cup Final the following year. He was an author, journalist, broadcaster, fought three unsuccessful campaigns as a Liberal candidate, represented India at the League of Nations, captained Sussex from 1904 to 1908, edited a magazine and founded and directed the training ship *Mercury*. After the First World War, it was alleged that he was offered and declined the throne of Albania.

A correct batsman and great thinker on the game, he hit six centuries in succession in 1901 and made 3,147 runs, average 78.67, in the season. His list of activities and achievements gives ample reason why he did not play more for England. He captained England in the 1912 Triangular Tournament, winning four and drawing two of the six matches, but he was frequently the "kingmaker". He maintained that he was asked to replace Douglas as England captain in 1921, but could not spare the time and suggested Tennyson.

Joel Garner

Born: December 16, 1952, Enterprise, Christ Church, Barbados
Teams: Barbados (1975–76 to 1987–88); Somerset (1977–86)
First-class: 214 matches; 2,964 runs, average 16.74; 881 wickets, average 18.53
Tests (1976–77 to 1986–87): 58 matches; 672 runs, average 12.44; 259 wickets, average 20.97

6ft 8in tall, Joel Garner, "Big Bird", was a giant of a fast bowler. He used his height to the full, generated considerable pace off a comparatively short run and swung and cut the ball both ways. His first Test series was against Pakistan, 1976–77, and he took 25 wickets in five matches. He took 13 wickets in the first two Tests against Australia the following season, but missed the rest of the series because of his association with World Series Cricket. In the World Cup Final at Lord's, 1979, he took five for 38 to ensure the West

GARNER *Speed from a great height.*

Indies' victory over England, and he was a major factor in Somerset winning both the Sunday League and the NatWest Trophy the same year. The county had won no trophies before this time.

A shoulder injury handicapped him for a while, but he played a significant part in the West Indies' record 11 consecutive Test victories. He was not the least of a formidable quartet of fast bowlers. He was captain of Barbados when they won the Shell Shield, and, amidst controversy, was released by Somerset after the 1986 season. A genial man, he was popular wherever he went.

Mike Gatting

Born: June 6, 1957, Kingsbury, Middlesex
Teams: Middlesex (1975–98)
First-class: 551 matches, 36,549 runs, average 49.52; 158 wickets, average 29.76

Tests (1977–78 to 1994–95): 79 matches, 4,409 runs, average 35.55; 4 wickets, average 79.25

A batsman capable of taking apart any attack, and a medium-pace bowler, Mike Gatting was a dedicated professional who succeeded Mike Brearley as captain of Middlesex in 1983 and led them to every honour before standing down in 1997. A prolific scorer in county cricket, he made his Test debut in Pakistan, 1977–78, but did not score a Test hundred until his 54th innings at Bombay, 1984–85. He hit a double-century later in the same series.

When Gower fell out of favour after losing the first Test to India, 1986, Gatting was named as England captain. He could not reverse the trend against India and lost to New Zealand the same summer, but he led a harmonious side to victory in Australia the following winter. There was unease about his captaincy when Pakistan won in England in 1987 although Gatting himself hit two centuries in the series. A dreadful reverse sweep cost him his wicket in the World Cup Final later the same year and, according to some critics, also lost England the match. When the team went to Pakistan he had a notorious confrontation with umpire Shakoor Rana, and the following summer he was the subject of allegations in a newspaper regarding his social life. He was relieved of the captaincy and stood down after the third Test.

Gatting played against Australia when they toured in 1989, but it was revealed that he was to lead a side to South Africa, and he was automatically banned from Test cricket. He resumed his Test career in India, 1992–93, and was a controversial choice to tour Australia, 1994–95. He hit his 10th and last Test century at Adelaide, but he did not enjoy a successful tour.

Tough, rugged and honest, he became a Test selector in 1997.

He retired after the 1998 season, having hit 1,000 runs in a season for the 19th time. In 2000 he retired as Director of Coaching with Middlesex.

Sunny Gavaskar

Born: July 10, 1949, Bombay, India
Teams: Bombay (1967–68 to 1986–87); Somerset (1980)
First-class: 348 matches; 25,834

GAVASKAR: *Master batsman.*

runs, average 51.46; 22 wickets, average 56.36
Tests (1970-71 to 1956-87): 125 matches; 10,122 runs, average 51.12; 1 wicket average 206.00

Not quite 5ft 5in tall, Sunil Gavaskar was called "The Little Master". With a perfect batting technique, he overcame even the tallest, fastest West Indian bowlers, and on retirement had amassed a record number of Test runs and centuries. Outstanding from school, he became the best opening batsman in the world. His Test debut for India as a 21-year-old on a tour to West Indies in 1970–71 was sensational. He played in the last four Tests and scored four centuries, including 220 in the last Test when suffering from toothache. His 774 series aggregate is the highest for a debutant, and he helped India win their first match and first series against the West Indies. A reaction from this start set in, but after a fighting century at Old Trafford in 1974 he never looked back. In 1976 he became the first Indian to score 1,000 runs in a calendar year, a feat he repeated in 1978 and 1979, when he scored 1,555. In 1978–79 he beat Polly Umrigar's record Test aggregate for an Indian while scoring a century in each innings, a feat he became the only batsman to achieve three times. In 1982–83 he became the first Indian to carry his bat through a Test innings, scoring 127 not out against Pakistan. In the 1983–84 series against West Indies, he passed Bradman's record number of Test centuries and Boycott's record number of runs. He also made his highest Test score of 236 not out. His highest first-class score is 340, for Bombay against Bengal. He cap-

GIBBS *309 Test wickets with off-breaks.*

tained India 47 times in Tests, and played for the Rest of the World in MCC's bicentenary match at Lord's in 1987, scoring 188.

Lance Gibbs

Born: September 29, 1934, Queenstown, Georgetown, British Guiana

Teams: British Guiana/Guyana (1953–54 to 1974–75); Warwickshire (1967–73; South Australia (1969–70)

First-class: 330 matches; 1,729 runs, average 8.55; 1,024 wickets, average 22.72

Tests (1957–58 to 1975–76): 79 matches; 488 runs, average 6.97; 309 wickets, average 29.09

With his long fingers, Lance Gibbs was one of the greatest of off-spin bowlers and a very fine fielder in the gully. In his first Test series, against Pakistan, 1957–58, he took 17 wickets in four Tests, and in Australia he took 19 wickets in three Tests. At Sydney, he took three wickets in four balls, and in the next Test, at Adelaide, he performed the hat-trick. A year later, in Barbados, he bowled the West Indies to victory over India with eight for 38 in the second innings. In fact, he took eight for six in 15.3 overs, 14 of which were maidens. His success continued unabated and when he retired his 309 Test wickets was a record.

He enjoyed much success with Warwickshire and captured 131 wickets in first-class matches in 1971. He settled in the United

States, played for the USA. against Canada, 1983, and managed the West Indies in England, 1991.

Graham Gooch

Born: July 23, 1953, Whipps Cross, Leytonstone, Essex

Teams: Essex (1973–97): Western Province (1982–83 to 1983–84)

First-class: 581 matches; 44,846 runs, average 49.01; 246 wickets, average 34.37

Tests (1975 to 1994–95): 118 matches; 8,900 runs, average 42.58; 23 wickets, average 46.47

By the end of 1993, Graham Gooch stood surveying the game of cricket like an Alexander with no more worlds to conquer. He had scored more than a hundred hundreds, scored more runs in Test cricket than any other English batsman, more centuries for Essex than any other cricketer, played in more than 100 Tests, had captained England in victory and defeat, had made 333, the highest score by an England captain, and 123 against India at Lord's, 1990, had scored more runs in the Sunday League, Benson & Hedges Cup and sixty-over competition than any other batsman, had scored more runs in a season and more runs in a career than any other Essex batsman, and had captained his county to success

GOOCH *456 runs in one Test.*

in the championship as well as being an integral part of the side who had enjoyed a golden period winning every honour in the game.

His career, though, has not been without its share of upsets amd controversy. His Test career had begun with a "pair" against Australia in 1975, and he would have played more for England had he not excommunicated himself by

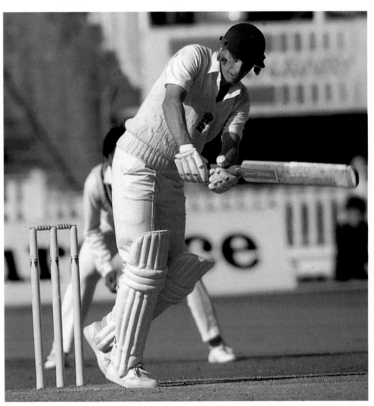

GOWER *Carefree elegance of a former age.*

joining a rebel tour in South Africa. He stands at the wicket suggesting a brooding melancholy, but he is a batsman of tremendous power, and he has been the scourge of attacks all over the world as 20 Test hundreds would testify. He is also a medium-pace bowler and a very fine slip fielder.

A fitness fanatic, he captained England in 34 Tests and went to Australia, 1994–95, under Mike Atherton, for his last Test series.

He retired from county cricket at the close of the 1997 season, but re-appeared in one first-class match in 2000.

David Gower

Born: April 1, 1957, Tunbridge Wells, Kent

Teams: Leicestershire (1975–89);

Hampshire (1990–93)

First-class: 448 matches; 26,339 runs, average 40.08; 4 wickets, average 56.75

Tests (1978–92): 117 matches; 8,231 runs, average 44.25; 1 wicket, average 20.00

An effortless left-hander who timed the ball with a sweetness that few have been able to match, David Gower made his Test debut against Pakistan at Edgbaston in 1978. The first ball he received in Test cricket he hit for four, and by the time his Test career finished 14 years later he had scored more runs in Test cricket than any other batsman. Tall and blond, he had a languid eloquence with the bat and so delicate was his timing that his batting always had a suggestion of human frailty which but added to its attraction. He had the style of the carefree amateur of the Golden Age, and with his looks and grace, he might have been better playing in that age as the mood took him and expenses allowed. He would have graced the Golden Age as he would have any era in which he batted.

He abandoned his degree studies at London University to

become a cricketer with Leicestershire in 1975, and if he took some time to prove himself statistically, his class was ever apparent. His first Test hundred came at the Oval in the second half of the 1978 summer. It was made against New Zealand, and it was followed by a century in Australia and 200 not out against India, 1979.

Gower first captained England against Pakistan, 1982–83, when he hit two centuries. He was unfortunate in being handed the poisoned chalice of captaining England against the powerful West Indies side, 1984, and England lost 5–0. The following winter, in India, he led with tact, shrewdness and calm, and England won the series which was played against the most tragic of backgrounds.

In 1985, his side regained the Ashes from a weakened Australian team, and he hit three centuries in the series, including 215 at Edgbaston. Then, in the winter, England lost 5–0 to the West Indies for the second time, and he took much blame for what many saw as his diffident approach. He was replaced when England lost to India, restored when England entertained Australia in 1989 and were soundly beaten, and not selected in the party to tour the West Indies the following winter. Back in the side in 1990 and chosen for the trip to Australia, he made two cen-

GRAVENEY *Style and grace.*

turies, but he upset skipper Gooch and the management when he and John Morris 'buzzed' their team mates with a pair of Tiger Moth aircraft while they were in the middle of a match against Queensland. When he was not selected for the tour of India, 1992–93, members of the MCC forced a special General Meeting to voice dissatisfaction at the way in which the game was being run.

Gower decided to retire and he became successful on television as a commentator.

W. G. Grace
See Legends (pages 104–105)

Tom Graveney
Born: June 16, 1927, Riding Mill, Northumberland
Teams: Gloucestershire (1948–60); Worcestershire (1961–70); Queensland (1969–70 to 1971–72)
First-class: 732 matches; 47,793 runs, average 44.91; 80 wickets, average 37.96
Tests (1951 to 69): 79 matches; 4,882 runs, average 44.38; 1 wicket, average 167.00

Tom Graveney scored 122 first-class centuries and reached 1,000 runs in an English season 20 times. He was one of the most attractive batsmen to have appeared since the war, full of grace and elegance. But, in spite of his complete command of stylish strokes and his consistency, he spent more than half his career unable to hold a regular place in the England side.

He began as the pride of Gloucestershire, whom he captained in 1959 and 1960, but he left the county following a disagreement over the captaincy and joined Worcestershire, whom he captained 1968–70. He first played for England against South Africa in 1951, and the following winter he hit the first of his 11 Test centuries, 175 against India at Bombay. His highest Test score was his 258 against the West Indies at Trent Bridge in 1957 when he and Peter Richardson added a record 266 for the second wicket. Graveney had an outstanding record against West Indies and played a major part in the series victory in the Caribbean, 1967–68, hitting 118 in Trinidad. He

GREENIDGE *Power and aggression.*

made 75 against the West Indies at Old Trafford, 1969, but was banned for appearing in a benefit game on the Sunday and never played Test cricket again.

He was appointed President of the MCC for 2004–05

Gordon Greenidge
Born: May 1, 1951, Black Bess, St Peter, Barbados
Teams: Hampshire (1970–87); Barbados (1972–73 to 1990–91)
First-class: 523 matches; 37,354 runs, average 45.88; 18 wickets, average 26.61
Tests (1974–75 to 1990–91): 108 matches; 7,558 runs, average 44.72; no wicket for 4 runs

A brilliantly aggressive right-handed opening batsman, Gordon Greenidge was brought to England at the age of 12 and lived and was educated in Reading. He could have played for England but chose the West Indies instead, and with Desmond Haynes formed one of the most successful opening partnerships Test cricket has known. They shared 16 century partnerships in 89 Tests together. In county cricket, he had another formidable opening partnership with the South African Barry Richards. Greenidge was prolific in all forms of cricket, and at one time

he held the record for the highest score in all three one-day competitions in England.

He hit double-centuries against England, Australia and New Zealand and made 19 Test centuries in all. Perhaps his most memorable innings came at Lord's in 1984 when the West Indies were set to score 342 runs in just over five hours. Greenidge made 214 not out off 241 balls with two sixes and 29 fours, and the West Indies won by nine wickets.

Greenidge captained the West Indies on one occasion when Richards was unfit.

Syd Gregory
Born: April 14, 1870, Moore Park, Randwick, Sydney, New South Wales, Australia
Died: August 1, 1929, Moore Park, Randwick, Sydney, New South Wales, Australia
Teams: New South Wales (1889–90 to 1911–12)
First-class: 369 matches; 15,190 runs, average 28.25; 2 wickets, average 195.00
Tests (1890–1912): 58 matches; 2,282 runs, average 24.53; no wickets for 33 runs

Known as "Little Tich" because he was only 5ft 4in tall, Syd Gregory was a quick-scoring, middle-order, right-handed batsman whose consistency and, above all, brilliant fielding at cover kept him in the Australian side for 22 years. He made the first of his eight tours to England in 1890, and on four of his tours he exceeded 1,000 runs. The first of his four Test hundreds came at Sydney in December 1894, when he hit 201 in 244 minutes. This was the first double century to be scored in a Test in Australia. He made a century at Lord's, 1896, and at the Oval three years later.

When Clem Hill and five other leading players refused to play in the Triangular Tournament in England, 1912, Syd Gregory was recalled to captain the side after an absence of three years from Test cricket. The side was woefully weak and ill-disciplined and, at 42, Gregory was past his best.

Tony Greig
Born: October 6, 1946, Queenstown, South Africa

Teams: Border (1965–66 to 1969–70); Sussex (1966–78); Eastern Province (1970–71 to 1971–72)
First-class: 350 matches; 16,660 runs, average 31.19; 856 wickets, average 28.85
Tests (1972–77): 58 matches; 3,599 runs, average 40.43; 141 wickets, average 32.20

Son of a Scottish RAF officer with a distinguished war record who was posted to South Africa at the end of the war, Tony Greig excites the same conflicting passions as Jardine. Standing 6ft 7in tall, with blond hair and an engaging smile, he was a brave, attacking batsman and a right-arm medium pace bowler who also bowled off-breaks to good effect. A dominant and attractive personality, he qualified for Sussex and made an impact with 156 against Lancashire in his first championship match, 1967. He played for England against Rest of the World, 1970, and two years later made his Test debut, hitting 57 and 62 and taking one for 21 and four for 53 against Australia at Old Trafford. It was the first of an unbroken sequence of 58 Tests.

The first of his eight Test centuries came against India the following winter, and a year later, as vice-captain on the tour of the Caribbean, he hit a century in the third Test and bowled England to a sensational victory and a draw in the series in the last Test when he took eight for 86 and five for 70 with his off-breaks. His outstanding match analysis in this game remains a record for

GREIG *Over-charismatic, under-rated.*

England against the West Indies.

He was also involved in a controversial incident with Kallicharan in this series and deprived of the vice-captaincy in Australia. Having led Sussex since 1973, when Denness was sacked in 1975 he became captain of England. Immensely popular, he instilled self-belief and a fighting spirit into a flagging England side. He would smile even when beaten, but there were always those ready to remind him he was South African.

He inspired England to a memorable series victory in England, 1976–77, and English cricket was respectful and joyful, but in the Centenary Test in Melbourne, it was learned that he had been recruiting players for Packer's World Series. Regarded by some as a traitor, he was sacked as captain and did not play Test cricket after 1977. He had been the first man to score 3,000 runs and to take 100 Test wickets for England, and his record stands comparison with anyone's.

He settled in Australia and worked as a commentator and in insurance. His actions brought sponsorship and more money into cricket, and he shook the establishment out of complacency. It would be difficult to find a professional cricketer who has anything but praise and affection for him. It was revealed that he suffered from a mild form of epilepsy.

Clarrie Grimmett

Born: December 25, 1891, Caversham, Dunedin, New Zealand
Died: May 2, 1980, Kensington Park, Adelaide, South Australia
Teams: Wellington (1911–12 to 1913–14); Victoria (1918–19 to 1923–24); South Australia (1924–25 to 1940–41)
First-class: 248 matches; 4,720 runs, average 17.67; 1,424 wickets, average 22.28
Tests (1924–25 to 1935–36): 37 matches; 557 runs, average 13.92; 216 wickets, average 24.21

Clarrie Grimmett was the first bowler to take 200 Test wickets. He was a leg-break and googly bowler who was born in New Zealand and moved to Australia at the start of the First World War. A sign-writer by trade, he worked hard at his bowling and became a prolific wicket-taker in the Sheffield Shield, but he was 33

before he made his Test debut against England at Sydney, 1924–25. He took five for 45 and six for 37. On the tour of England, 1926, he took over 100 wickets, and he and fellow leg-spinner Arthur Mailey were the main Test wicket-takers.

Mailey had departed by 1928–29, and Grimmett bore the burden of the Australian attack, capturing 23 wickets but sending down nearly 400 overs in the Tests. In 1930, when he again captured more than 100 wickets in England, including all 10 for 37 in an innings against Yorkshire, he took 29 Test wickets, and the following winter he mesmerized the West Indies in Australia, claiming 33 wickets in the series. He repeated this feat in only four Tests against South Africa the following season. He was again successful in England, 1934, and in South Africa, 1935–36, he broke all records with 44 wickets, average 14.59, in five Tests. Astonishingly, he never played Test cricket again although many thought he should have come to England in 1938 even at the age of 46.

George Gunn

Born: June 13, 1879, Hucknall Torkard, Nottinghamshire
Died: June 29, 1958, Tylers Green, Cuckfield, Sussex
Teams: Nottinghamshire (1902–32)
First-class: 643 matches; 35,208 runs, average 35.96; 66 wickets, average 35.68
Tests (1907–08 to 1929–30): 15 matches; 1,120 runs, average 40.00; no wickets for 8 runs

A small, slim right-handed opening batsman, George Gunn was one of a cricketing family, and for a period he and his son played alongside each other in the Nottinghamshire side. George Gunn was a batsman in the classical mould, but he was an eccentric and played as the mood took him, which is probably why his only Test in England was against Australia at Lord's in 1909. The previous series, 1907–08, he had been in Australia and was called into the England side in an emergency. He made 119 and 74 in his first Test, hit another century in the last Test and headed the batting averages for the series. He reached 1,000 runs in a season

20 times and had a fine opening partnership with W.W. Whysall. His last Test was against the West Indies in Jamaica, April, 1930. He scored 85 and 47 run out. He was just short of his 51st birthday.

H

Richard Hadlee

See Legends (pages 104–105)

Wes Hall

Born: September 12, 1937, St Michael, Barbados, West Indies
Teams: Barbados (1955–56 to 1970–71); Trinidad (1966–67 to 1969–70); Queensland 1961–62 to 1962–63)
First-class: 170 matches; 2,673 runs, average 15.10; 546 wickets, average 26.14
Tests (1958–59 to 1968–69): 48 matches; 818 runs, average 15.73; 192 wickets, average 26.38

After beginning his career as a wicket-keeper/batsman, the 6ft 2in Wes Hall developed into one of the great fast bowlers of the early 1960s. He took a very long run and brought the ball down from a great height, his smooth run-up foreshadowing that of Michael Holding in its athleticism and grace. He made his Test debut for the West Indies on a tour of India and Pakistan in 1958–59, taking 46 wickets in the eight Tests at a cost of less than 18 runs. He took 22 wickets against the English tourists the following year, and 21 in the great tour of Australia in 1960–61, nine of them in the famous tied

HALL *Speed and stamina.*

Test. With Charlie Griffith as his partner, he was formidable when the West Indies beat England 3–1 in 1963 and bowled throughout the 200 minutes of the last day at Lord's, including the last over when England drew needing six to win with the last pair together, and Cowdrey batting with a broken arm in plaster. He was a slogging tail-ender, although at Trinidad in 1967–68 he batted throughout the last two hours with Sobers to save the match against England. On retiring he went into politics and became Sports Minister in Barbados.

Walter Hammond

Born: June 19, 1903, Dover, Kent
Died: July 1, 1965, Kloof, South Africa
Teams: Gloucestershire (1920–51); South African Air Force (1942–43)
First-class: 634 matches; 50,551 runs, average 56.10; 732 wickets, average 30.58
Tests (1927–28 to 1946–47): 85 matches; 7,249 runs, average 58.45; 83 wickets, average 37.80

Hammond was the outstanding English cricketer of the 1930s, topping the batting averages for each of the eight seasons between 1933 and 1946. No English batsman has beaten his total of 36 double-centuries, and his highest score of 336 not out, made for England against New Zealand in 1932–33, was at the time a Test match record. His average for the two-match series was 563. His county championship debut was delayed because of objections about his qualification and he returned from a tour of the West Indies in 1925–26 with a mystery illness which made him miss the 1926 season altogether. He came back so well in 1927 that he made his Test debut in South Africa the following winter.

He was a majestic batsman, whose off-drive was regarded as one of the classic shots of cricket, a more than useful fast-medium bowler and a brilliant fielder at slip, where for Gloucestershire against Surrey in 1928 he held a world record 10 catches. Against Australia, in the 1928–29 series, he made 905 runs, then a record, averaging 113.12.

HAMMOND *with rival Bradman.*

Hammond turned amateur in 1938 and was immediately given the England captaincy, which he retained until the first tour after the war, in 1946–47, when his powers at last began to decline. He was a strange, aloof man, not popular as a captain, and played rarely after his Test career ended, finally going to live in South Africa. Of his many records his total of 7,249 runs in Tests stood for nearly 25 years.

Hanif Mohammad

Born: December 21, 1934, Junagadh, India
Teams: Bahawalpur (1953–54); Karachi (1954–55 to 1968–69); PIA (1960–61 to 1975–76)
First-class: 238 matches; 17,059 runs, average 52.32; 53 wickets, average 28.47
Tests (1952–53 to 1969–70): 55 matches; 3,915 runs, average 43.98; 1 wicket, average 95.00

Hanif Mohammad was a small batsman with an immaculate defence and limitless concentration. He was called "The Little Master". He made his first-class debut for Karachi and Bahawalpur in 1951–52 when only 16 years old, and after the partition of India made his Test debut for Pakistan against India in 1952–53, in Pakistan's first-ever Test. At 17 years 300 days, he was the world's youngest Test wicket-keeper. He also opened the batting, scoring 51 in his first innings, and he soon

dropped wicket-keeping to become a specialist batsman. His Test career comprised 55 of Pakistan's first 57 Tests. In the first Test against the West Indies in Bridgetown in 1957–58, when Pakistan followed on 473 behind, he made the then second-highest Test score of 337 to save the match, batting for 16 hours, 10 minutes, the longest Test innings. In 1958–59, batting for Karachi against Bahawalpur at Karachi, he was run out off the last ball of the day for 499, the highest score in first-class cricket until Brian Lara beat it in 1994. He captained Pakistan in 11 Tests from 1964–65 to 1967. He is the brother of Wazir, Mushtaq and Sadiq, and the father of Shoaib, all Pakistani Test players.

Neil Harvey

Born: October 8, 1928, Fitzroy, Melbourne, Victoria, Australia
Teams: Victoria (1946–47 to 1956–57); New South Wales (1958–59 to 1962–63)
First-class: 306 matches; 21,699 runs, average 50.93; 30 wickets, average 36.86
Tests (1947–48 to 1962–63): 79 matches; 6,149 runs, average 48.41; 3 wickets, average 40.00

Neil Harvey was a brilliant left-handed middle-order batsman, an occasional off-break bowler and an outstanding fielder at cover point or slip. He was particularly good on difficult pitches. He had just turned 18 when he first played for Victoria and a year later made his Test debut against India. In his second Test be became the youngest Australian to score a century, at 19 years 121 days. He came to England with Bradman's great side in 1948, and became the first Aussie left-hander to make 100 on his debut against England. He was at the wicket in the second innings with Bradman as Australia scored 404 for three on the last day to win. For the next 15 years Harvey was Australia's leading batsman. In 1949–50 in South Africa, he hit four centuries and averaged 132.00, including a magnificent 152 not out to win on a crumbling pitch after Australia had made 75 in the first innings and were 59 for three in the second. He made four centuries against South Africa in 1952–53 (average 92.66) and three in the

West Indies in 1954–55 (average 108.33). He captained Australia once, in Benaud's absence at Lord's in 1961, and Australia won. Twenty-one of his 67 centuries were in Tests, the highest, 205, against South Africa in Melbourne in 1952–53, and his Test aggregate was at the time second only to Bradman for Australia.`

Lindsay Hassett

Born: August 28, 1913, Geelong, Victoria, Australia
Died: June 16, 1993, Bateman's Bay, New South Wales, Australia
Teams: Victoria (1932–33 to 1952–53)
First-class: 216 matches; 16,890 runs, average 58.24; 18 wickets, average 39.05
Tests (1938–53): 43 matches; 3,073 runs, average 46.56; no wicket for 78

The 17-year-old Lindsay Hassett made 147 not out against the touring West Indians two years before he made his first-class debut for Victoria. Only 5ft 6in, he was a neat, quick-footed batsman with all the strokes, and a polished fielder. In 1938 he toured England, making his debut in the first Test. After the war, he captained the Australian Services team in the unofficial Victory Tests in England and India. He was vice-captain to Bradman on the tour of England in 1948 and took over the captaincy of Australia for the tour of South Africa in 1949–50. He was an excellent captain with a well-known sense of humour – perhaps his most public joke coming after he had twice dropped Washbrook on the boundary from hooks in a Test at Old Trafford, when he borrowed a policeman's helmet in preparation for the next one. He retired after Australia lost the series in England in 1953. He made eight double-centuries, but the highest of his 10 Test centuries was 198 not out against India at Adelaide in 1947–48.

Matthew Hayden

Born: October 29, 1971, Kingaroy, Queensland, Australia
Teams: Queensland (1991–92 to 2004–05); Hampshire (1997); Northants (1999–2001)
First-class: 259 matches; 21,749 runs, average 53.69; 17 wickets,

average 39.47

Tests (1990 to 2005): 74 matches; 6,382 runs, average 53.18; 0 wickets

Matthew Hayden was a run-maker from childhood, but was perceived to have a faulty technique. Nevertheless on his debut for Queensland he made 149 in an all-out aggressive display. His first Test came in 1993–94 in South Africa, but by March 2000, when recalled

HASSETT *Dapper batsman.*

against New Zealand, he had made only seven appearances. He blossomed spectacularly in India in 2000–01, finishing the calendar year 2001 with 1,391 Test runs, then third highest of all time. From February 2001 to January 2003 he scored 2,560 in 25 Tests, with 11 centuries, and an average of 67.36. He changed the style of Test opening batsmen by attacking from the first ball, and against Zimbabwe in Perth in 2003–04 played the then highest Test innings of 380.

Desmond Haynes

Born: February 15, 1956, St James, Barbados, West Indies

Teams: Barbados (1976–77 to 1994–95); Middlesex (1989–94)

First-class: 360 matches; 25,027 runs, average 46.17; 7 wickets, average 28.71

Tests (1977–78 to 1993–94): 116 matches; 7,487 runs, average 42.29; 1 wicket, average 8.00

Desmond Haynes was a sound but aggressive opening batsman who made over 100 Test appearances for the West Indies, 89 in a prolific part-

nership with Gordon Greenidge, with whom he shared a record 16 century opening partnerships. Including World Cups, he made seven tours to England and eight to Australia, as well as tours to Pakistan, India, New Zealand and Zimbabwe. His first tour to England as a Test player, in 1980, was his most successful, when he averaged 51.33 in the Tests. In 1984 his 125 at the Oval in the fifth Test guaranteed the West Indies' "blackwash" – the first side to win all five in a rubber in England. A hamstring injury in 1988 ended a run of 78 consecutive Tests. He captained the West Indies in four Tests in 1990. He played county cricket for Middlesex from 1989 and in 1990 he hit 2,346 runs, average 69.00, including his career highest of 255 not out against Sussex at Lord's. His highest in Tests was also at Lord's, 184 against England in 1980. He was immensely successful in international one-day cricket, with a record number of runs, 8,649 (average 41.38) and centuries, 17.

Tom Hayward

Born: March 29, 1871, Cambridge

Died: July 19, 1939, Cambridge

Teams: Surrey (1893–1914)

First-class: 712 matches; 43,551 runs, average 41.79; 481 wickets, average 22.95

Tests (1895–96 to 1909): 35 matches; 1,999 runs, average 34.46; 14 wickets, average 38.64

One of a famous cricketing family, Tom Hayward was a most reliable right-handed opening batsman, who, in 1906, scored 3,518 runs in an English season, which stood as a record until 1947. In 1913, he became the first professional to score 100 hundreds in first-class cricket, and he reached 1,000 or more runs in a season for 20 consecutive seasons beginning in 1895. In 1900, he scored 1,000 runs before the end of May. He was also a useful medium-pace bowler, and in 1897 he completed the "double". The following year, he scored an unbeaten 315 against Lancashire at the Oval.

His Test debut came against South Africa, 1895–96, and he hit 122 at Johannesburg in his second match. He was a tremendous

influence on Jack Hobbs, who followed him from Cambridge to the Oval, and he was Hobbs's first great opening partner, the pair sharing 40 partnerships of 100 or more. Hayward was also involved in six century first-wicket stands for England.

He was coach at Oxford after his retirement.

Vijay Hazare

Born: March 11, 1915, Sangli, Maharashtra, India

Died: December 12, 2004, Baroda, India

Teams: Maharashtra (1934–35 to 1940–41); Central India (1935–36 to 1938–39); Baroda (1941–42)

First-class: 238 matches; 18,740 runs, average 58.38; 595 wickets, average 24.61

Tests (1946 to 1952–53): 30

matches; 2,192 runs, average 47.65; 20 wickets, average 61.00

A small, right-handed batsman with the full complement of wristy strokes and a medium-pace bowler, Vijay Hazare made two scores of over 300 in his career, and he and Gul Mahomed created a world record when they put on 577 for Baroda's fourth wicket against Holkar in 1946–47. In 1939–40, he had established himself with 316 not out for Maharashtra against Baroda and had hit another triple-century the same season.

Duleepsinhji apart, who played his cricket in England, Hazare was the first Indian to hit a triple-century, and certainly the first to hit two. Coached by Clarrie Grimmett, he made his Test debut in England in 1946, and, at Adelaide, 1947–48, he became the first batsman to score a century in each innings of a Test for India. He was to go on to score centuries against each of the four countries against whom he played.

He was named captain of the side to tour England in 1952. His team was weak, and despite his consistent batting, the tour was a disaster. He was deposed as captain for the inaugural series against Pakistan, but he still managed a century in Bombay. He was reinstated for the tour of the West Indies in 1952–53, but India lost and that marked the end of his international career. Nevertheless, he can proudly boast that he scored two centuries against England, 1951–52, and captained his country to their first-ever Test victory in the same series.

George Headley

Born: May 30, 1909, Colon, Panama

Died: November 30, 1983, Meadowbridge, Kingston, Jamaica

Teams: Jamaica (1927–28 to 1953–54)

First-class: 103 matches; 9,921 runs, average 69.86; 51 wickets, average 36.11

Tests (1929–30 to 1953–54): 22

HAYNES *Reliable opener.*

matches; 2,190 runs, average 60.83; no wickets for 230 runs

In the 1930s George Headley was nicknamed the "Black Bradman", and his Test record still shows him to have been one of the greatest batsmen in the history of the game. He announced his quality in his first Test match, hitting 176 against England in the second innings at Bridgetown. In the third Test, in Georgetown, he became the first West Indian to score a century in each innings, and this feat was followed by 223 in the fourth and final Test in Kingston. He remains the only batsman to score four Test hundreds before the age of 21, and, until the record was beaten by Javed Miandad, he was the youngest batsman to score a double-century in Test cricket.

The West Indies toured Australia, 1930–31, and lost the Test series by four to one, but Headley hit two centuries. He scored 169 against England at Old Trafford, 1933, and headed the first-class averages, and he took an unbeaten 270 off the England bowlers at Kingston in 1935. In 1939, he became the first man to score a century in each innings in a Test match at Lord's.

Headley had a fine cricket brain, but was denied the West Indian captaincy until 1948, and then led the side for only one Test. He was the first black man to captain them.

He was a professional in the Lancashire League and both his son and grandson became Test cricketers, his grandson for England.

Patsy Hendren

Born: February 5, 1889, Turnham Green, Middlesex
Died: October 4, 1962, Tooting Bec, London
Teams: Middlesex (1907–37)
First-class: 833 matches; 57,611 runs, average 50.80; 47 wickets, average 54.76
Tests (1920–21 to 1934–35): 51 matches; 3,525 runs, average 47.63; 1 wicket, average 31.00

"Patsy" Hendren, a great entertainer and one of the most loved characters the game has known, hit 170 first-class hundreds in his career. For a decade after the First World War, he was an integral part of England's middle order, and he was a fine outfielder.

He did not have the easiest of Test baptisms against Armstrong's Australians, and it was not until Headingley, 1924, that he scored the first of his seven Test centuries, 132 against South Africa. He hit his second in the same series. He was part of Chapman's side which regained the Ashes in 1926, and he thrived in the West Indies, 1929–30, when he hit four double-centuries during the tour. His aggregate for the tour was 1,765 runs, average 135.76, which remains a record, and it included his highest Test innings, 205 not out in Trinidad. He hit 301 not out for Middlesex against Worcestershire in 1933, and three times he exceeded 3,000 runs in a season.

He coached Sussex and at Harrow following his retirement, and he was the Middlesex scorer, 1953–59.

Graeme Hick

Born: May 23, 1966, Salisbury, Rhodesia
Teams: Zimbabwe (1983–84 to 1985–86); Worcestershire (1984–2005); Northern Districts (1987–88 to 1988–89); Queensland (1990–91)
First-class: 486 matches; 38,437 runs, average 52.96; 232 wickets, average 44.43
Tests (1991–01): 65 matches; 3,383, average 31.32; 23 wickets, average 56.78

Before they attained Test status, Zimbabwe invested much money and hope in Graeme Hick, a right-handed batsman of phenomenal potential and great power. He is also a capable off-break bowler and fine slip fielder. Hick decided to play league cricket, to qualify for Worcestershire and, ultimately, for England. Tall, confident, Hick appeared to be realizing the potential all had recognized during the seven years of county cricket he played prior to qualifying for England. He was the youngest cricketer to score 2,000 runs in a season; in 1986, he scored 1,000 runs before the end of May 1988, and became the youngest player to reach 50 first-class centuries. While reaching his thousand before the end of May he hit an astonishing 405 against Somerset. He was equally effective in New Zealand, and, after a slow start, scored well for Queensland although the Australians were

never so enthusiastic about him as the English press.

Able to play Test cricket in 1991, he was looked upon as England's saviour, but he found international cricket a tough proposition. In his 22nd Test innings, he scored 178 against India in Bombay, and there was a century against South Africa at Leeds, 1994, but in 1996 he was vulnerable to both the guile of Mushtaq and the speed of Waqar. In the last five years, Hick has been in and out of the England Test side. He was given yet another opportunity on the winter tour of 2000–01 to Pakistan and Sri Lanka, but failed to produce any worthwhile innings. He was therefore excluded for the Tests of 2001. In contrast his overall form in One Day Internationals has been quite acceptable. In first-class cricket he continues – in 1998 he became the second youngest player ever to score 100 centuries in first-class matches. He was captain of Worcestershire from 2000 to 2002.

Clem Hill

Born: March 18, 1877, Hindmarsh, Adelaide, South Australia
Died: September 5, 1945, Parkville, Melbourne, Victoria, Australia
Teams: South Australia (1892–93 to 1922–23)
First-class: 252 matches; 17,213 runs, average 43.57; 10 wickets, average 32.30
Tests (1896 to 1911–12): 49 matches; 3,412 runs, average 39.21

A short, powerful left-handed batsman with a crouched stance, Clem Hill delighted crowds with his sound defence and explosive attack. He had the right temperament for the big occasion and rarely failed although he was always at his best on the hard wickets in Australia. He was a magnificent fielder in the deep where he took some memorable catches, notably one to dismiss Lilley in the Old Trafford Test of 1902 which Australia won by three runs.

Not included in the side to tour England in 1896, he scored a double-century against New South Wales, and a public outcry caused him to be added to the party. His first Test century came at Melbourne, 1897–98, when he hit

188, the highest score made by an under-21 in an Ashes Test. In 1900–01, he made an unbeaten 365 for South Australia against New South Wales. In three successive Test innings the following season he scored 99, 98, and 97. In 1902, he hit 119 in the only Test match ever to be played at Bramall Lane, Sheffield.

His relations with the Australian Board were uneasy, and he twice refused to tour England. He captained Australia to success against South Africa, 1910–11, but lost heavily to Douglas's side the following season, and that defeat by England ended his Test career. It was alleged that he was involved in a fight with a selector.

George Hirst

Born: September 7, 1871, Kirkheaton, Yorkshire
Died: May 10, 1954, Lindley, Huddersfield, Yorkshire
Teams: Yorkshire (1891–1929); Europeans (1921–22)
First-class: 826 matches; 36,356 runs, average 34.13; 2,742 wickets, average 18.73
Tests (1897–98 to 1909): 24 matches; 790 runs, average 22.57; 59 wickets, average 30.00

In the years before the First World War, there were those who believed that if you needed a man to die for you on the cricket field, you would choose George Hirst. He was loyal, tough and kind, and he lived and breathed Yorkshire and the game itself. He bowled medium-fast left-arm, and he batted right-handed with skill and aggression. He performed the "double" 14 times, and he is the only man in the history of the game to have taken 200 wickets and scored 2,000 runs in the same season – 2,385 runs and 208 wickets, 1906. The previous year he had made 341 against Leicestershire, which remains a Yorkshire record.

Hirst's achievements for his native county are legion, yet his Test record was surprisingly moderate. Perhaps his most famous exploit was when he and Rhodes brought England victory over Australia at the Oval in 1902 by scoring the 15 runs needed in a tense last-wicket stand. Hirst, who had match figures of six for 84, was unbeaten on 58.

He coached at Eton for many years on his retirement.

Jack Hobbs

See Legends (pages 106–107)

Michael Holding

Born: February 16, 1954, Half Way Tree, Kingston, Jamaica
Teams: Jamaica (1972–73 to 1988–89); Lancashire (1981); Tasmania (1982–83); Derbyshire (1983–89); Canterbury (1987–88);
First-class: 222 matches; 3,600 runs, average 15.00; 778 wickets, average 23.43
Tests (1975–76 to 1986–87): 60 matches; 910 runs, average 13.78; 249 wickets, average 23.68

A right-arm fast bowler, Michael Holding made the art look easy, and it is not hard to understand why batsmen referred to him as "Whispering Death". Initially, he lacked control, but soon his considerable pace was allied with accuracy and remarkable stamina, and by 1976 he was the most formidable of the West Indies' pace quartet. At Old Trafford that year, he took five for 17 as England were hurried out for 71. In the final Test, at the Oval, he produced an astonishing display of fast bowling. On a benign pitch on which Amiss made a double-century and England scored 435, he took eight for 92, the best figures by a West Indian bowler against England, and when he took six for 57 in the second innings to win the game he became the first West Indian to take more than two wickets in a Test.

A man of education and charm, he fell from grace when he reacted angrily against an umpire's decision in New Zealand by kicking over the stumps. This was not characteristic. He performed well for Derbyshire and for Tasmania. He is now a popular commentator.

Conrad Hunte

Born: May 9, 1932, Shorey's Village, St Andrew, Barbados
Died: December 3, 1999, Sydney Australia
Teams: Barbados (1950–51 to 1966–67)
First-class: 132 matches; 8,916 runs, average 43.92; 17 wickets, average 37.88

HOLDING *Silent, gliding menace.*

Tests (1957–58 to 1966–67): 44 matches; 3,245 runs, average 45.06; 2 wickets, average 55.00

Conrad Hunte was a most reliable and sound opening batsman and an excellent fielder. He scored 142 on his Test debut against Pakistan, 1957–58, and in the third Test of the same series he made 260, sharing a second-wicket stand of 446 with Sobers. A third century came in the fourth Test, and he had a different kind of record in the last when he became the first West Indian to be out to the first ball of a Test match. In England, 1966, he began the series with a flourishing 135, but three years earlier he had done even better with 182 followed by an unbeaten 108 in the final Test.

Hunte was a natural batsman who liked to attack, but who played to the needs of his side, and consistency was his trade mark. Following his retirement, he worked for the Moral Rearmament movement and coached in South African townships.

Len Hutton

Born: June 23, 1916, Fulneck, Pudsey, Yorkshire
Died: September 6, 1990, Norbiton, Kingston-upon-Thames, Surrey
Teams: Yorkshire (1934–55)
First-class: 513 matches; 40,140 runs, average 55.51; 170 wickets, average 29.51
Tests (1937 to 1954–55): 79 matches; 6,971 runs, average 56.67; 3 wickets, average 77.33

Len Hutton was one of the greatest opening batsmen that cricket has seen, and, in the opinion of many, England has never had a better captain. He batted in the classical mould. There was time to spare, and he had the mastery of every shot without resorting to brutality. In the years before the war, he was also a useful leg-break bowler. He was reared in the hard and eminently successful Yorkshire side of the 1930s and gained early guidance from his opening partner Herbert Sutcliffe.

Chosen for England against New Zealand in 1937, he was out for 0 and 1 on his Test debut, but he made the first of his 19 Test hundreds in the next match. The following season, he scored a century in his first Test against Australia, and, at the Oval, he made history by batting 13 hours 17 minutes to score 364, which was to remain the highest score in Test cricket for nearly 20 years. He was 22 years old. Against the West Indies in 1939, he played innings of 196 and 165 not out to bring his aggregate to 1,109 runs in his last eight Tests before the outbreak of war.

An injury sustained in an accident early in the war led to him being invalided out of the army in 1942, and his left arm was now two inches shorter than his right. If, in the post-war years, he was not quite the batsman he had been in 1939, he was still as good as anyone in the world.

He had his bad periods, but when England faced a crisis of captaincy they turned to Hutton. When he led England against India at Leeds in 1952 he was the first professional to captain England. He scored two centuries in the series which England won resoundingly. Traditionalists were still opposed to his appointment, but he regained the Ashes, 1953, led England to a draw in the Caribbean after they had been two Tests down and retained the Ashes in Australia, 1954–55.

His own form did not falter, but a back problem and, one feels, weariness caused him to retire. He was, and remains, a national hero, knighted in 1956 for his services to cricket. He had led England out of the wilderness.

Raymond Illingworth

Born: June 8, 1932, Pudsey, Yorkshire
Teams: Yorkshire (1951–83); Leicestershire (1969–78)
First-class: 787 matches; 24,134 runs, average 28.06; 2,072 wickets, average 20.28
Tests (1958–73): 61 matches; 1,836 runs, average 23.24; 122 wickets, average 31.20

Ray Illingworth had a most eventful career, during and after his playing days. A right-handed, solid middle-order batsman and off-break bowler, he completed the "double" six times and won a place in the England side between 1958 and 1969, experiencing modest success. He had been a vital member of the Yorkshire side, but a contractual dispute led him to leave his native county and become captain of Leicestershire. His success with his new county was phenomenal, for they won all the domestic competitions bar the Gillette Cup during the period when he was their captain. But he had led the side in only eight first-class matches when he was called upon to lead England in place of the injured Colin Cowdrey in 1969. There was immediate success over the West Indies, and he both regained and defended the Ashes. He did not suffer defeat in a Test match until his twentieth game in charge, and there are those who say that he was the best captain they ever played under. The defeat by India followed by heavy defeats at the hands of the West Indies, 1973, ended his Test career.

In 1979, he retired from first-class cricket and became manager of Yorkshire, but problems at the club forced him to assume the captaincy in 1982 at the age of 50. He finally stood down in 1983.

In 1993, he became chairman of selectors, but his three years in charge were neither happy nor good for the game.

Imran Khan

See Legends (pages 108-109)

Inzaman-ul-Haq

Born: March 3, 1970, Multan, Pakistan
Teams: Multan (1995–86 to 2003–04); United Bank (2004–05
First-class: 223 matches; 15,565 runs, average 51.03; 39 wickets, average 33.20
Tests (1992 to 2004–05): 103 matches; 7,746 runs, average 50.95; 0 wickets

The outstanding Pakistani batsman of his generation, Inzaman will soon, unless unforeseen circumstances intervene, overtake Javed Miandad as his country's highest Test run getter. A protégé of Imran Khan, he burst on the international stage in the 1992 World Cup. Inzaman did much to help Imran bring the trophy home. The timing and power in his batting during the Final gave Pakistan the edge over Australia. From that season onwards his scoring in One Day Internationals has been phenomenal and he became only the second batsman in the world to reach the 10,000 run mark in ODIs.

Inzaman is a resolute cricketer who knows his own mind, despite his rather baby face, these qualities have enabled him to survive and indeed swim successfully in the shark-infested waters of international cricket. Even his weakness when it comes to trying to avoid run outs has not told against him. As Pakistan's current captain he is a suitable successor to the great Imran Khan.

J

Archie Jackson

Born: September 5, 1909, Rutherglen, Lanark, Scotland
Died: February 16, 1933, Clayfields, Brisbane, Queensland, Australia
Teams: New South Wales (1926–27 to 1930–31)
First-class: 70 matches; 4,383 runs, average 45.65
Tests (1928–29 to 1930–31): 8 matches; 474 runs, average 47.40

Archie Jackson was a right-handed batsman of grace and beauty who seemed destined for greatness, but who was the stuff of tragedy. He played his first Test match against England at Adelaide in February, 1929, and made 164, becoming the youngest player to score a century in an Ashes series. He arrived in England in 1930 with a reputation higher than Bradman's. He scored a thousand runs, but he appeared in only two Tests. He played four times against the West Indies the following winter, but his health was failing. He moved to Brisbane to be near his girlfriend and in the hope that a better climate would improve matters, but he died at the age of 23.

F. S. Jackson

Born: November 21, 1870, Allerton Hall, Chapel Allerton, Leeds, Yorkshire
Died: March 9, 1947, Knightsbridge, London
Teams: Cambridge University (1890–93); Yorkshire (1890–1907)
First-class: 309 matches; 15,901 runs, average 33.83; 774 wickets, average 20.37
Tests (1893–1905): 20 matches; 1,415 runs, average 48.79; 24 wickets, average 33.29

Educated at Harrow and Cambridge where he won his blue all four years and was captain for two seasons, Sir Stanley Jackson was rarely able to play regularly although he was an all-rounder of outstanding ability, a right-handed stylish batsman and fast medium-pace bowler, who did the "double" in 1898. He had made his Test debut at Lord's in 1893, scoring 91 and 5. At the Oval, he made 103, but he was unable to play in the third and final Test. All his Test matches were in England against Australia.

He served in the Boer War, was invalided home with enteric fever and was persuaded to play for the Gentlemen against the Players at Scarborough while convalescing. He hit 13 and 42 against an attack which included Hirst and Rhodes, and then he went back to the Boer War. He was an MP for 11 years, was Financial Secretary to the War Office and Party Chairman, but as soon as Baldwin became Prime Minister, Jackson was sent to India as Governor of Bengal where he narrowly escaped assassination.

Jackson was chosen for England whenever available and captained the side in 1905 when two Tests were won and three drawn. Jackson topped both the England batting and bowling averages for the series.

He was president of the MCC, a Test selector and president of Yorkshire CCC from 1939 until his death.

Douglas Jardine

Born: October 23, 1900, Malabar Hill, Bombay, India
Died: June 18, 1958, Montreux, Switzerland
Teams: Oxford University (1920–23); Surrey (1921–33)
First-class: 262 matches; 14,848 runs, average 46.83; 48 wickets, average 31.10
Tests (1928 to 1933–34): 22 matches; 1,296 runs, average 48.00; no wickets for 10 runs

Few captains of England have excited as much passion and controversy as Douglas Jardine; none has been more successful. His father, Malcolm, captained Oxford in 1891 and scored a century in the Varsity match the following year before embarking on a highly successful legal career in India. Douglas returned to Britain at the age of nine and was sent to Winchester. He played in three Varsity matches in his four years at Oxford where he was regarded as a rather cool intellectual and a batsman of outstanding ability with great powers of concentration and immense courage. He never bowed to pain.

He played for Surrey while still at Oxford and won his first Test caps against the West Indies in 1928. He went with Chapman's side to Australia, 1928–29, played in all five Tests and averaged 46.62. He also raised the passions of the Australian crowd who saw him as cold and aloof. He batted in a brightly coloured Harlequin cap and was regarded as symbolic of the Imperial order, the British establishment.

Jardine could well have captained England against Australia in 1930, but he had no independent means and had to give his time to business. He took no part in the series. But he led England against New Zealand in 1931 and against India in 1932, and was the obvious choice to take the side to Australia, 1932–33. There were those among the hierarchy who were worried about what they saw as his arrogance, but he prepared for the tour meticulously and, though amateur in status, he was professional in approach. He asserted that all things being equal he would select a Northerner before a Southerner because the Northerner's attitude and determination were akin to his own.

Jardine discussed tactics with Arthur Carr, the Nottinghamshire and former England skipper, and he evolved leg-theory, fast bowling on the leg side to a leg side field. It was later dubbed "bodyline". In Larwood, and to a lesser extent Voce, he had the bowlers to make the theory effective. England won the series four to one. He was the subject of fierce criticism, but he was worshipped by his men.

In 1933, he captained England against the West Indies – who employed leg-theory at Jardine. He countered with a century. He took the side to India the following winter, but announced that he would not play against Australia in 1934. There were those who believed that he had been let down by the administration. He was only 33 years old when he retired from cricket and was, arguably, the best number five in the world. In 15 Tests as captain, he won nine and lost only once. He averaged 50 with the bat.

Javed Miandad

Born: June 12, 1957, Karachi, Pakistan
Teams: Karachi (1973–74 to 1975–76); Sind (1973–74 to 1975–76); Sussex (1976–79); Habib Bank (1976–77 to 1995–96); Glamorgan (1980–85)
First-class: 402 matches; 28,647 runs, average 53.44; 191 wickets, average 33.48
Tests (1976–77 to 1994–95): 124 matches; 8,832 runs, average 52.57; 17 wickets, average 40.11

One of the most exciting batsman of his day, Javed Miandad towers over other Pakistani batsman in his achievements. He has 23 Test centuries to his credit, and he is 3,000 runs ahead of the field. His 280 not out against India at Hyderabad, 1982–83, is second only to Hanif Mohammad's triple-century in the Caribbean, but Javed has also hit

271 against New Zealand at Auckland, 1988–89, and 260 against England at the Oval, 1987. A strong aggressive right-handed batsman with every shot at his command, Javed has captained Pakistan with distinction although he has never been far from controversy, and he has retired, been replaced and reinstated. He was also highly successful in county cricket.

Certainly his exploits helped to take Pakistan to an eminence in world cricket, and he played a major part in the winning of the World Cup, 1992. He returned to play in the 1996 World Cup and then in 1997–98 played in the Wills Cup for Karachi Blues, but has not been seen in first-class matches since 1995–96. He remains Pakistan's most capped player.

Sanath Jayasuriya

Born: June 30, 1969, Matara, Ceylon

Teams: Colombo (1988–89 to 1996–97); Bloomfield (1996–97 to 2004–05); Somerset (2005)

First-class: 240 matches; 13,864 runs, average 40.06; 187 wickets, average 32.10

Tests (1990–91 to 2004–05): 100 matches; 6,580 runs, average 42.17; 92 wickets, average 32.78

Jayasuriya won his first Test cap for Sri Lanka in New Zealand, 1990–91. A forceful left-handed batsman and slow left-arm bowler, he was slow to establish himself in the Sri Lankan side. It was in the 1996 World Cup that he sprang to prominence.

Used as an opener and in his all-round capacity, he was voted the most valuable man of the tournament, and he devastated England in the quarter-final with 82 off 44 balls, a brilliant innings. In August 1997 he made the fourth highest Test score when making 340 against India at Colombo, sharing in a record Test stand for any wicket of 576 with Roshan Mahanama.

Appointed to succeed Ranatunga as Sri Lanka's captain in 1999–2000, he began by beating Australia in a one day series, then won the Test series which followed.

JAYASURIYA *World Cup hero.*

Gilbert Jessop

Born: May 19, 1874, Cheltenham, Gloucestershire

Died: May 11, 1955, Fordington, Dorset

Teams: Gloucestershire (1894–1914); Cambridge University (1896–99); London County (1900–03)

First-class: 493 matches; 26,698 runs, average 32.63; 873 wickets, average 22.79

Tests (1899–1912): 18 matches; 569 runs, average 21.88; 10 wickets, average 35.40

Gilbert Jessop was the stuff of legend. Known as "The Croucher" because of his stance at the wicket, he was the most consistent fast

JAVED MIANDAD *Controversial run-getter.*

scorer the game has known, capable of hitting all round the wicket, and a most exciting figure. He batted right-handed and was a fast right-arm bowler who opened the attack on his Test debut against Australia, Lord's, 1899. He went to Australia, 1901–02, but he was too adventurous a player to be a total success in Test cricket. One of his 53 centuries came in 40 minutes, another in 42. He twice performed the "double", and he scored 1,000 runs in a season on 14 occasions, twice going on to 2,000. He captained both Cambridge University and Gloucestershire, and he was a secretary of that county for five years.

His name is most remembered for his 104 for England against Australia at the Oval, 1902. Going in at 48 for five, he reached his century in 75 minutes, the fastest century in Test history at that time, and England went on to win by one wicket.

Ian Johnson

Born: December 8, 1917, North Melbourne, Victoria, Australia

Died: October 9, 1998, Melbourne, Australia

Teams: Victoria (1935–36 to 1955–56)

First-class: 189 matches; 4,905 runs, average 22.92; 619 wickets, average 23.30

Tests (1945–46 to 1956–57): 45 matches; 1,000 runs, average 18.51; 109 wickets, average 29.19

Ian Johnson was a rare product for Australia, an off-break bowler. He

relied more on variations in flight than in vicious turn, and he was a good lower-order batsman. He first played Test cricket in New Zealand, 1945–46, but he did not bowl. Indeed, he did not bowl until his third Test match, against England at Sydney, 1946–47, when he took six for 42 and two for 92. He did well against India, 1947–48, and he had a good tour of England, 1948, but had little effect in the Tests. He was not selected for the 1953 tour so it was very surprising when he was named as captain of Australia in succession to Hassett.

Victory in the first Test was followed by destruction at the hands of Tyson and Statham. There was surprising success in the West Indies where Johnson took seven for 44 to bring victory in Georgetown. In England, 1956, on pitches which aided spin, Johnson failed. When Laker took 19 wickets at Old Trafford Johnson had four for 151, which disappointed him bitterly. He took the side to India, but it was the magic of Benaud which won the series. In his last match, Johnson completed the "double" in Test cricket. He later became secretary of Melbourne CC.

Bill Johnston

Born: February 26, 1922, Beeac, Victoria, Australia

Teams: Victoria (1945–46 to 1954–55)

First-class: 142 matches; 1,129 runs, average 12.68; 554 wickets, average 23.35

Tests (1947–48 to 1954–55): 40 matches; 273 runs, average 11.37

Bill Johnston was a tall, strongly built left-arm fast medium-pace bowler who swung and cut the ball appreciably. He was quietly effective against India, 1947–48, but he took England by storm a few months later. He took nine for 183 in the first Test, and he shared the new ball with Lindwall when Miller was injured. He finished the series with 27 wickets in the five Tests, and he took 102 on the tour. His first Test against South Africa, 1949–50, brought his best figures, six for 44, in the second innings. His took 23 wickets in the series as Australia won four of the five Tests, drawing in Johannesburg.

In successive home series, he scourged England with 22 wickets and West Indies with 23. At the time, he had reached 100 Test wickets faster than any other bowler in history. In 1952–53, he took 21 wickets against South Africa, but there were signs of wear and tear, and he had a persistent knee injury which hampered him on the 1953 tour of England when, being dismissed only once, he had the experience of averaging 102 with the bat, top score 28. He did well in four Tests against England, 1954–55, while all about him fell, but that marked the end of his career. His son played for South Australia.

Alvin Kallicharran

Born: March 21, 1949, Paidama, British Guiana

Teams: Guyana (1966–67 to 1980–81); Warwickshire (1971–90); Queensland (1977–78); Transvaal (1981–82 to 1983–84); Orange Free State (1984–85 to 1987–88)

First-class: 505 matches; 32,650 runs, average 43.64; 84 wickets, average 47.97

Tests (1971–72 to 1980–81): 66 matches; 4,399 runs, average 44.43; 4 wickets, average 39.50

A most attractive left-handed batsman and a useful right-arm leg-break bowler, Alvin Kallicharran graced county cricket for several seasons, eventually being registered as an English qualified player. He hit 1,000 runs in an English season 12 times, and he scored 100 not out on his Test debut for the West Indies against New Zealand in Georgetown. This was followed by 101 in his next match in Trinidad. He was the second West Indian to accomplish this feat. He batted consistently against Australia and on his first tour of England, 1973, and in the Caribbean, 1973–74, he scored 158, 21, 93, and 119 in the first three Tests against England. He was equally successful in India the following year.

With the rest of the West Indian side, he signed to join Packer's World Series but withdrew when he found he was in breach of contract with a Queensland radio

station. Left as senior player, he captained the West Indies against Australia and India, making centuries in both series, but this was not a happy time for him. When Clive Lloyd returned, Kallicharran's form declined, and he elected to play in South Africa so exiling himself from Test cricket.

Jacques Kallis

Born: October 16, 1975, Pinelands, Cape Town. South Africa

Teams: Western Province (1993–94 to 2004–05); Middlesex (1997); Glamorgan (1999)

First-class: 180 matches; 13,456 runs, average 53.82; 318 wickets, average 30.55

Tests (1995–96 to 2004–05): 93 matches; 7,337 runs, average 56.87; 183 wickets, average 31.60

With an ideal temperament for Test cricket – he was said to be surprised when a reporter asked him if "sledging" in Australia affected him – Jacques Kallis has proved himself a brilliant all-rounder for South Africa. He appears equally at home in Tests as in One Day

KALLICHARRAN *Neat Test batsman.*

Internationals, winning several Man of the Match awards in World Cup competitions. His Test debut came against England in 1995–96 where his determination as a batsman was often commented upon. In the subsequent One Day series

he really flourished. With Middlesex in 1997 he averaged 40 with the bat and 20 with the ball, making him among the most prominent all-rounders that summer. Opponents claimed that he, on occasion, could deliver the ball as fast as Allan Donald. Due to factors beyond his control his 1999 season with Glamorgan was fairly brief, but he shone in One Day games. His international career continues to blossom and in the summer of 2003 he passed Gary Kirsten to become the highest scoring batsman in South African Test history.

Rohan Kanhai

Born: December 26, 1935, Port Mourant, British Guiana

Teams: British Guiana–Guyana (1954–55 to 1973–74); Western Australia (1961–62); Trinidad (1964–65); Warwickshire (1968–77); Tasmania (1969–70)

First-class: 416 matches; 28,774 runs, average 49.01; 18 wickets, average 56.05

Tests (1957 to 1973–74): 79 matches; 6,227 runs, average 47.53; no wickets for 85 runs

Rohan Kanhai believed in the power of bat over ball, and he would have been at home in the Golden Age, for he was a master in all he did. One of the most thrilling sights of the 1960s was that of Kanhai on his backside as the ball thundered over the boundary at square-leg after a pull so vicious that it had swept the batsman off his feet.

He made his Test debut in the first Test of the West Indies' tour of England in 1957. Unwisely, he was asked to keep wicket in the first three Tests, but thereafter he was allowed to concentrate on his batting. His maiden Test hundred came against India, at Calcutta, 1958–59, when he scored 256. He was to make 15 more Test centuries.

Kanhai played in many parts of the globe, and his contribution to Warwickshire cricket was immense. In 1974, at Edgbaston, he and John Jameson shared an unbroken second-wicket stand of 465 against Gloucestershire, which was, at the time, a world record.

In 1972–73, with Sobers recovering from an operation, Kanhai captained the West Indies against

Australia. He was then 37 years old. He led West Indies in two series against England, both of which were tinged with controversy. In 1973, at Edgbaston, umpire Fagg refused to take the field at the start of the third day because of Kanhai's reaction to one of his decisions while the following winter, in Port of Spain, he was captain when Tony Greig ran out Kallicharran "after the close of play". Kallicharran was reinstated. In spite of these incidents, Kanhai was respected for having brought a sense of discipline to a West Indies side which had become very lax in the last years of Sobers' captaincy.

Kapil Dev

Born: January 6, 1959, Chandigarh, India

Teams: Haryana (1975–76 to 1994–95); Northamptonshire (1981–1983); Worcestershire (1984–1985)

First-class: 275 matches; 11,356 runs, average 32.91; 835 wickets, average 27.09

Tests (1978–79 to 1993–94): 131 matches; 5,248 runs, average 31.05; 434 wickets, average 29.64

The greatest all-round cricketer that India has ever produced, Kapil Dev appeared in more Test matches than any other Indian. Only three Indian batsmen scored more Test runs, and, with 434 Test wickets, he holds a world record which is likely to stand for many years. He made his Test debut against Pakistan in October 1978, and in his 25th Test, with Pakistan again the opponents, he completed 1,000 runs and 100 wickets. At 21 years 27 days, he was the youngest cricketer to perform the "double" in Test matches.

In his first Test as India's captain, 1982–83, he completed 2,000 Test runs, and in the next match he became the youngest player to complete the double of 2,000 Test runs and 200 Test wickets. He led India to victory over England in England and, memorably, to triumph in the World Cup, 1983. In that competition, with India 17 for five and then 78 for seven against Zimbabwe at Tunbridge Wells, Kapil Dev played one of the most astonishing innings ever seen in international cricket, an unbeaten 175.

Some months later, he took nine for 83 in the West Indies' second

KAPIL DEV *Youngest to Test "double".*

innings of the Test in Ahmedabad, but India lost. He overtook Hadlee's record number of wickets in his last series, against Sri Lanka, 1993–94.

Alan Knott

Born: April 9, 1946, Belvedere, Kent
Teams: Kent (1964–85)
First-class: 511 matches; 18,105 runs, average 29.63; 2 wickets, average 43.50; caught 1,211, stumped 133
Tests (1967–81): 95 matches; 4,389 runs, average 32.75; caught 250, stumped 19

A truly great wicket-keeper, Alan Knott was recognized as outstanding from the moment he first played for Kent and forced his way into the England side within three years. In his first two Tests, against Pakistan, he held 12 catches and made a stumping, and an illustrious career was launched. Meticulous and fastidious to the point of eccentricity, he maintained a strict diet and a disciplined programme of exercise. Through constant application, he made himself into a batsman cap-able of scoring five Test centuries and defying any attack. His batting was unorthodox, but it was a style he evolved to suit his needs and abilities.

In both Test and county cricket, he fashioned a wonderful partnership with the left-arm spinner

Derek Underwood, and they became a telling combination.

Knott's involvement with World Series Cricket and a tour of South Africa curtailed his Test career. He has aided England's coaching and selection, and his son James played occasionally for Surrey from 1995 to 1998, as reserve wicketkeeper.

C. J. Kortright

Born: January 9, 1871, Furze Hall, Fryerning, Ingatestone, Essex
Died: December 12, 1952, Brook Street, South Weald, Essex
Teams: Essex (1894–1907)
First-class: 170 matches; 4,404 runs, average 17.61; 489 wickets, average 21.05

Although he never appeared in Test cricket, Kortright is regarded by many as the fastest bowler ever to play county cricket. He first played for Essex before the county attained first-class status, and his

KNOTT *Dedicated wicket-keeper.*

best season was 1895 when he claimed 76 wickets at under 16 runs each. He was an amateur with a good private income, and he captained Essex in 1903, but by then his bowling had declined, and he played as a batsman.

Anil Kumble

Born: October 17, 1970, Bangalore, India
Teams: Karnataka (1989–90 to 2004–05); Northamptonshire (1995);

Leicestershire (2000)
First-class: 198 matches; 4,643 runs, average 22.87; 928 wickets, average 24.74
Tests (1990 to 2004–05): 97 matches; 1,670 runs, average 17.04; 465 wickets, average 28.38

A leg-break bowler, Anil Kumble was one of the three spinners who destroyed England in India, 1992–93. He had made little impact when he had toured England in 1990, playing in one Test and capturing three expensive wickets, but as he matured, he became a potent force in any attack. He bowls at a brisker pace than most spinners and is relentlessly accurate. Bespectacled and gentle, he is a most effective bowler in limited-over internationals as well as Test cricket.

He played for Northamptonshire in 1995 and, with 105 wickets in 17 games, he came close to taking them to the championship. In 1996, he failed to find form on India's tour of England, but he remains a vital part of India's attack.

In February 1999 he became the second man in Test history to capture all ten wickets in a single innings. The feat was for India v Pakistan in Delhi. His first eight overs cost 37 runs without a wicket; his next 19 overs again cost 37 runs, but included ten wickets. Another record fell to Kumble in December 2004 when he passed Kapil Dev as India's all-time leading wicket-taker in Tests and in the same season he crossed the 450 wicket threshhold.

L

Jim Laker

Born: February 9, 1922, Frizinghall, Bradford, Yorkshire
Died: April 23, 1986, Putney, London
Teams: Surrey (1946–59); Essex (1962–64); Auckland (1951–52)
First-class: 450 matches; 7,304 runs, average 16.60; 1,944 wickets, average 18.41
Tests (1947–48 to 1958–59): 46 matches; 676 runs, average 14.08; 193 wickets, average 21.24

The world of cricket has not seen a better off-spinner than Jim Laker, and his achievements stand as testimony to his greatness. A Yorkshireman who came south to follow his career with Surrey, for

whom he made his debut shortly after the Second World War, he toured the West Indies, 1947–48, and was a success in a series that was mostly disastrous for England. Indeed, on his Test debut, he took seven for 103 and two for 95. He took four wickets in his first Test against Australia a few months later, but it was some time before he could claim a regular place in the England side.

He was a vital member of the Surrey side which won the county championship seven years in succession, and when Australia toured England in 1956 he took all 10 of their wickets for 88 runs at the Oval. More sensational events were to follow. He took 11 for 113 in the Headingley Test, and in the next encounter, at Old Trafford, he performed the greatest bowling feat in cricket by taking nine for 37 and 10 for 53. He finished the rubber with a record 46 wickets to his credit. His last Test was on the tour of Australia, 1958–59, when a great England side finally began to disintegrate. He wrote a book which caused him to

LAKER *19 wickets in a Test.*

part from Surrey in acrimony although wounds were later healed and he served on the cricket committee. He played for Essex as an amateur, helping to bring on young bowlers, and he earned fame as a commentator and journalist.

Allan Lamb

Born: June 20, 1954, Langebaanweg, Cape Province, South Africa
Teams: Western Province (1972–73 to 1982–82); Northamptonshire (1978–1995); Orange Free State (1987–88)
First-class: 467 matches; 32,502 runs, average 48.94; 8 wickets, average 24.87
Tests (1982–92): 79 matches; 4,656 runs, average 36.09; 1 wicket, average 23.0

Allan Lamb learned his cricket in South Africa and played for Western Province before coming to England to assist Northamptonshire. His English parentage and residence allowed him to qualify for England in 1982, and he was immediately selected to play against India. He scored the first of his 14 Test hundreds in his third match.

A stocky, belligerent batsman, he took three centuries off the West Indian attack in 1984, and he played 45 successive Tests for England before being dropped after failures against India, 1986. He bounced back with a brave century against the West Indies, 1988, and he scored heavily for Northamptonshire whom he captained from 1989 until 1995, taking them to success in the NatWest Trophy, 1992, and coming close to claiming the championship three years later.

A witty man and a joyful companion, he was an excellent batsman in limited-over matches, and he and his friend Ian Botham toured venues with their "Lamb and Beef" show.

Brian Lara

See Legends (pages 110–111)

Harold Larwood

Born: November 14, 1904, Nuncargate, Nottinghamshire
Died: July 22, 1995, Sydney, Australia
Teams: Nottinghamshire (1924–38); Europeans (1936–37)
First-class: 361 matches; 7,289 runs, average 19.91; 1,427 wickets, average 17.51

Tests (1926 to 1932–33): 21 matches; 485 runs, average 19.40; 78 wickets, average 28.35

Harold Larwood's name will for ever be linked with the term "bodyline", and for all too brief a period he was regarded as the fastest and the best bowler in the world. He was right-arm, bowled off an 18-yard run and, although of only medium height, leapt into a high, classical, explosive delivery. He made his England debut during his first full season, 1926, toured Australia in 1928–29 and played against them in 1930, but it was the tour of Australia, 1932–33, that is best remembered. Bowling very fast and with unerring accuracy, he often attacked the line of the leg stump to a packed leg side field. He took 33 wickets in the series which England won 4–0, but he and Jardine were accused of intimidation and deliberately attacking the batsman's body. Larwood never played Test cricket again, and he retired from county cricket owing to injury in 1938. He emigrated to Australia in 1949.

Bill Lawry

Born: February 11, 1937, Thornbury, Melbourne, Victoria, Australia
Teams: Victoria (1955–56 to 1971–72)
First-class: 249 matches; 18,734 runs, average 50.90; 5 wickets, average 37.60
Tests (1961 to 1970–71): 67 matches; 5,234 runs, average 47.15; no wickets for 6 runs

A tall, lean, left-handed opening batsman with immense powers of concentration and infinite patience, Bill Lawry enjoyed an excellent first

LARWOOD *"Bodyline" scapegoat.*

Test series in England, 1961, when he hit two centuries and topped the batting averages in both the Test series and all first-class matches. His was not the style, however, to win over spectators at a time when cricket was in crisis and accused of dullness. He was not well treated by the press who continued to hound him when, as senior player, he automatically succeeded Simpson as captain, 1967–68. He won a series against India, drew with England and won a crushing victory in the West Indies after losing the first Test. In the second, he and Ian Chappell added 298 in 310 minutes for the second wicket, and Lawry made 205. He also hit 151 in the last Test. He led Australia to victory over India, but they were crushed in South Africa and when things began to go wrong against Illingworth's side, 1970–71, he was relieved of the captaincy and dropped for the final Test. He has since worked as a commentator.

Maurice Leyland

Born: July 20, 1900, New Park, Harrogate, Yorkshire
Died: January 1, 1967, Scotton Banks, Harrogate, Yorkshire
Teams: Yorkshire (1920–1947); Patiala (1926–27)
First-class: 686 matches; 33,660 runs, average 40.50; 466 wickets, average 29.31
Tests (1928–1938): 41 matches; 2,764 runs, average 46.06; 6 wickets, average 97.50

A tough left-hander whose fighting qualities epitomized Yorkshire cricket during the county's period of dominance in the 1930s, Leyland was also a fine outfielder and a very useful left-arm bowler who specialized in "Chinamen", the slow left-armer's off-break.

He was eight seasons in the Yorkshire side before winning his first Test cap, against the West Indies, 1928. He failed to score, but he was a controversial choice ahead of Woolley for the tour of Australia the following winter. He played only in the last Test, scoring 137 and 53 not out. He was now a virtual regular in the England side and was invaluable to Jardine on the "bodyline" tour, providing what the captain wanted, "con-

LAWRY *Concentration and patience.*

crete" in the middle of the order.

His last Test was at the Oval against Australia in 1938 when he and Hutton put on a record 382 for the second wicket and Leyland made his highest Test score, 187.

He was 46 when cricket resumed after the war, but he played for two seasons and later coached Yorkshire.

Dennis Lillee

See Legends (pages 112–113)

Ray Lindwall

Born: October 3, 1921, Mascot, Sydney, New South Wales, Australia
Died: June 23, 1996, Brisbane, Australia
Teams: New South Wales (1941–42 to 1953–54); Queensland (1954–55 to 1959–60)
First-class: 228 matches; 5,042 runs, average 21.82; 794 wickets, average 21.35
Tests (1945–46 to 1959–60): 61 matches; 1502 runs, average 21.15; 228 wickets, average 23.03

Ray Lindwall had a beautiful fast bowler's action, and he had no peer in the decade immediately following the Second World War. His Test debut was against New Zealand, 1945–46, and in the last two Tests against England the following season, he took 15 wickets. Against India, at Adelaide, 1947–48, he took seven for 38 in the second innings, which were to remain his best figures in Test cricket, but it was in England weeks later that he was to prove most devastating, taking 27 wickets in the series, which included six for 20 at the Oval as England were bowled out for 52. He continued to dominate batsmen, and he played Test cricket until he was 38, finishing with what was then a record number of wickets for an Australian.

He was a very useful, hard-hitting lower-order batsman and hit centuries against both England and the West Indies. He captained Australia once when Ian Johnson was unfit against India in Bombay, 1956–57.

Clive Lloyd

Born: August 31, 1944, Queenstown, Georgetown, British Guiana
Teams: British Guiana/Guyana (1963–64 to 1982–83); Lancashire (1968–86)
First-class: 490 matches; 31,232 runs, average 49.26; 114 wickets, average 36.00
Tests (1966–67 to 1984–85): 110 matches; 7,515 runs, average 46.67; 10 wickets, average 62.20

A hard-hitting, left-handed batsman, fine fielder and medium-pace bowler, Clive Lloyd captained the West Indies in 74 Tests and won 36 of them; both figures are records. He moved with the silkiness of a cat and began his long Test career with innings of 82 and 78 not out in the West Indies victory over India in Bombay, 1966–67. In his next series, he hit two centuries against England.

In 1974–75, he took over as captain of the West Indies for the tour of India. In his first match in charge, he reached 100 off 85 balls and finished with 163. In the fifth Test, he hit a career-best 242 not out. As well as his successes in Test matches, he took the West Indies to World Cup triumphs in 1975 and 1979.

He was criticized in that he simply rotated his four fast bowlers, and there were times when his sides appeared to lack discipline, but he won a record 11 Tests in a row between 1984 and 1985, and when he lost his last match as captain, in Sydney, January 1985, it was his first defeat in 26 matches.

He gave magnificent support to Lancashire, particularly when they dominated the one-day game, and

LLOYD *Outstanding skipper.*

he was immensely popular. He settled there in retirement, although he still retains a great interest in West Indian cricket and has managed several West Indian touring parties.

M

Charles Macartney

Born: June 27, 1886, West Maitland, New South Wales, Australia
Died: September 9, 1958, Little Bay, Sydney, New South Wales, Australia
Teams: New South Wales (1905–06 to 1926–27)
First-class: 249 matches; 15,019 runs, average 45.78; 419 wickets, average 20.95
Tests (1907–08 to 1926): 35 matches; 2,131 runs, average 41.78; 45 wickets, average 27.55

Known as the "Governor General", Charles Macartney was a dominant batsman, never afraid to improvise and ever on the lookout for runs. There was artistry in his right-handed batting, but when he first came to England in 1909 he was primarily a slow left-arm bowler. His seven for 58 and four for 27 won the Headingley Test on that first tour, but against South Africa, 1910–11, it was his batting that flourished. In the fifth Test, he opened the innings for the first time and made 137 and 56. In the second innings, he reached 50 in 35 minutes.

In 1920–21, at Sydney, he scored 170, his highest Test score, in 244 minutes against England, and when Australia came to England in 1921

he hit the only Australian century of the rubber. It happened to be his fourth century in consecutive innings and followed his 345 in a day against Nottinghamshire.

In 1926, in England, he scored three hundreds in successive Test innings, becoming the first man to score three hundreds in a rubber in England. He retired from Test cricket after this tour.

Archie MacLaren

Born: December 1, 1871, Whalley Range, Manchester
Died: November 17, 1944, Warfield Park, Bracknell, Berkshire
Teams: Lancashire (1890–1914)
First-class: 424 matches; 22,236 runs, average 34.15; 1 wicket, average 267.00
Tests (1894–95 to 1909): 35 matches; 1,931 runs, average 33.87

As a batsman, Archie MacLaren was one of the brightest jewels of the Golden Age, but as captain of England in 22 Tests against Australia and of Lancashire for 12 seasons his credentials are less impressive. A majestic right-handed batsman, rich in classical strokes, he came into the Lancashire side in 1890 straight from Harrow and made 108 against Sussex at Hove in his first match.

He hit 424 against Somerset at Taunton, 1895, the highest score in first-class cricket in England until Brian Lara's 501 in 1994. He went to Australia, 1894–95, and scored 120 in the fifth Test; all of his Tests were against Australia. Four of his five Test hundreds were made in Australia where the warmer climate was kinder to his lumbago. In his second tour of Australia, 1897–98, he became the first English batsman to hit two centuries in a rubber. The five Test series in which he captained England all ended in defeat, but he was a reluctant skipper in 1909 when, at 37, he felt that he was no longer up to standard. In 1921, he fielded an all-amateur side against the conquering Australians and beat them in a match which has passed into legend. He took a side to New Zealand, 1922–23, and hit 200 not out in his last first-class match. He was 53 years old.

Stan McCabe

Born: July 16, 1910, Grenfell, New South Wales, Australia
Died: August 25, 1968, Beauty Point, Mosman, Sydney, New South Wales, Australia
Teams: New South Wales (1928–29 to 1941–42)
First-class: 182 matches; 11,951 runs, average 49.38; 159 wickets, average 33.72
Tests (1930–38): 39 matches; 2,748 runs, average 48.21; 36 wickets, average 42.86

Short, stocky and strongly built, Stan McCabe was an attacking middle-order batsman and medium-pace bowler who played one of Test cricket's great innings when he hit 232 out of 300 at Trent Bridge in 1938. He batted heroically against Larwood and Voce at Sydney, 1932–33, to make an unbeaten 187, and he was consistently successful on his three tours of England, 1930, 1934 and 1938.

He made his first-class debut at the age of 18 and was the "baby " of the side on his first tour of England. He did not return to cricket after the Second World War, setting up a successful sporting equipment business.

Craig McDermott

Born: April 14, 1965, Ipswich, Queensland, Australia
Teams: Queensland (1983–84 to 1995–96)
First-class: 174 matches; 2,856 runs, average 16.32; 677 wickets, average 28.10
Tests (1984–85 to 1995–96): 71 matches; 940 runs, average 12.20; 291 wickets, average 28.62

Craig McDermott was forced to retire in 1997 because of persistent injury problems, but he could point to the fact that only Dennis Lillee had taken more wickets in Test cricket for Australia than he had. A red-headed, right-arm fast bowler, he took 10 wickets in his first two Tests, against the West Indies, and in England, 1985, he claimed 30 wickets in the series to give him a sensational start to his Test career. At Old Trafford, he took eight for 141 to become the youngest Australian ever to take eight wickets in a Test innings.

There were troughs as well as heights in his career, but he

destroyed India, 1991–92, with 31 wickets, average 12.83, in five Tests. He had agreed to play for Yorkshire the following summer but he was in need of an operation and was forced to withdraw. His tour of England, 1993, was blighted by the need for an operation on an intestinal complaint. Despite this, he returned in 1994–95 to take 32 English wickets and be the major force in the Ashes series. His last Test matches were against Sri Lanka. Capable of hitting hard and often, he was sometimes sent in early in one-day internationals to help lift the scoring-rate.

Ted McDonald

Born: January 6, 1891, Launceston, Tasmania, Australia
Died: July 22, 1937, Blackrod, Bolton, Lancashire
Teams: Tasmania (1909–10 to 1910–11); Victoria (1911–12 to 1921–22); Lancashire (1924–31)
First-class: 281 matches; 2,663 runs, average 10.44; 1,395 wickets, average 20.76
Tests (1920–21 to 1921–22): 11 matches; 116 runs, average 16.57; 43 wickets, average 33.27

Tall and strong, "Ted" McDonald was a natural athlete whose bowling was rhythmical and graceful. He had exceptional pace and could move the ball either way. He played in the last three Tests against England, 1920–21, making little impact, but the following summer, he and Jack Gregory destroyed England. McDonald finished the series with 27 wickets in the three-Test rubber in South Africa, 1921–22. He then joined Nelson in the Lancashire League and qualified for the Red Rose county. He was a key reason for Lancashire winning the champion-ship four times in five seasons, beginning in 1926. He took 205 wickets in 1925 and 190 in 1928. He had no standing as a batsman, but he made a century in 100 minutes against Middlesex at Old Trafford, 1926. He was killed in the aftermath of a road accident. Signalling for help, he was knocked down by another car.

Jackie McGlew

Born: March 11, 1929, Pietermaritzburg, South Africa
Died: June 9, 1998, Pretoria, South Africa
Teams: Natal (1947–48 to 1966–67)
First-class: 190 matches; 12,170 runs, average 45.92; 35 wickets, average 26.62
Tests (1951 to 1961–62): 34 matches; 2,440 runs, average 42.06; no wickets for 23 runs

An obdurate opening batsman with infinite patience, Jackie McGlew was an outstanding cover fielder and a respected and successful captain of Natal for several seasons. He first toured England in 1951 and made his Test debut at Trent Bridge. He was dropped after the second Test and accomplished little in four Tests in Australia, 1952–53, but when the team moved on to New Zealand he hit 255 not out at Wellington. This was then the highest score for South Africa in Test cricket, and he became only the second player to be on the field for the whole of a Test match.

Vice-captain for the tour of England in 1955, he led the side in the third and fourth Tests when Cheetham was injured, scored centuries in both and took South Africa to two victories. Appointed captain for the home series against England, 1956–57, he was able to play only in the second Test because of a shoulder injury. His replacement, van Ryneveld, did well and kept the job for the tour of Australia. McGlew, captain in the first Test when van Ryneveld was unavailable, hit two centuries in the series and was reinstated as captain when van Ryneveld retired.

McGlew led South Africa to England in 1960, but the series was painfully dull and he drew much of the criticism. In 1961–62, New Zealand surprisingly drew the series in South Africa. McGlew's last match ended in defeat, and he finished with a thumb in splints and a shoulder in plaster.

He continued to play for Natal, and he never lost the reputation or nickname of being "Sticky".

Glenn McGrath

Born: February 9, 1970, Dubbo, New South Wales, Australia
Teams: New South Wales (1992–93 to 2004–05); Worcestershire (2000); Middlesex (2004)
First-class: 179 matches; 936 runs, average 7.80; 797 wickets, average 20.57
Tests: (1993–94 to 2005): 114 matches; 600 runs, average 7.40; 525 wickets, average 21.27

Tall, lean and mean, Glenn McGrath is the equal of any present-day fast bowler. On the 2001 Australian tour to England McGrath, who is 6ft 5ins tall, was a splendid complement to the spin of Shane Warne. McGrath relies almost entirely on a perfect line and length, always waiting for the batsman to lose patience and make a false move. He has been known to lose his temper and let fly the odd bumper, but the wrath soon evaporates and he returns to calmly execute the opposing batsman.

His first summer in County cricket – 2000 with Worcestershire – was an outstanding success. Not only did he take the most first-class wickets in England that summer (80), but even more incredibly, he beat a bowling record in the Sunday League, which had stood since 1969. The accurate Derek Shackleton had then set the record for the least runs conceded per over in the season. McGrath in 2000 managed a miserly 2.16 runs per over. On Australia's 2001 tour of England, McGrath topped both the Test bowling table and that of the first-class table too.

He became the eighth bowler to reach 400 wickets in 2002 and the fourth to pass 500 in the opening Test of the 2005 Ashes series. McGrath's absence with injuries coincided with Australia's two defeats in the lost series. The two facts could not be considered in any way unconnected.

Graham McKenzie

Born: June 24, 1941, Cottesloe, Perth, Western Australia
Teams: Western Australia (1959–60 to 1973–74); Leicestershire (1969–75)
First-class: 383 matches; 5,662 runs, average 15.64; 1,219 wickets, average 26.96
Tests: (1961 to 1970–71): 60 matches; 945 runs, average 12.27; 246 wickets, average 29.78

"Garth" McKenzie had a superb physique and bowled fast with a smoothness and economy of style that were a model for younger players. At the time, he was the youngest cricketer to reach 100, 150 and 200 runs in Test cricket, and he was Australia's main strike bowler for a decade. His Test debut came at Lord's in 1961, and his five for 37 in the second innings set up Australia's victory. He captured 20 wickets when the Ashes were retained against Dexter's side, 1962–63, and he had 29 in England in 1964, which equalled Grimmett's record at that time. In the Old Trafford Test, he gave a remarkable performance, taking seven for 153 as England scored 611. His final Test came at Sydney, 1970–71, when he took his 246th wicket, just two short of Benaud's record, and was forced to retire hurt when struck in the mouth by a ball from Snow.

He gave fine service to Leicestershire for seven seasons, and they won the championship for the first time in his last season with them.

Roy McLean

Born: July 9, 1930, Pietermaritzburg, South Africa
Teams: Natal (1949–50 to 1965–66)
First-class: 200 matches; 10,969 runs, average 36.88; 2 wickets, average 61.00
Tests (1951 to 1964–65): 40 matches; 2,120 runs, average 30.28; no wickets for 1 run

A delightfully aggressive right-handed stroke-maker, Roy McLean was also a brilliant out-fielder. His eagerness to score and to entertain was not always to the liking of the South African selectors, and his 11 "ducks" in his Test career was a sign of his impetuosity. He first played Test cricket during the 1951 tour of England, making 67 run out at Headingley. He topped 1,000 runs in 1955 and 1960, and he scored 142 in the Lord's Test on the first of those tours, hitting a brisk 50 at Old Trafford as South Africa successfully chased a target of 145 in 135 minutes. Not unnaturally, he was an immense favourite with crowds who warmed to his fielding.

Majid Khan

Born: September 28, 1946, Ludhiana, India

Teams: Lahore (1961–62 to 1982–83); Punjab (1964–65 to 1967–68); PIA (1968–69 to 1980–81); Glamorgan (1968–76); Cambridge University (1970–72)
First-class: 410 matches; 27,444 runs, average 43.01; 223 wickets, average 32.14
Tests (1964–65 to 1982–83): 63 matches; 3,931 runs, average 38.92; 27 wickets, average 53.92

Son of Jahangir Khan who played cricket for India with distinction, Majid was born in the year before Partition, but his cricket has been played in Pakistan. A highly gifted all-rounder, Majid was an attacking right-handed batsman, confident, calm and cultured, and a medium-pace or off-break bowler. His Test debut came against Australia in Karachi when he was out for 0 and opened the Pakistan bowling, claiming Bill Lawry as his first Test victim. He toured England in 1967 and, although he did little in the series, he hit an astonishing 147 not out in 89 minutes against Glamorgan. His innings included five sixes in an over off Roger Davis, and Glamorgan were prompted to engage him. He was a fine acquisition for the county and captained them for three years before finally leaving in acrimony and discord. He was a highly successful captain of Cambridge University.

His highest score against England was 99, but he hit eight Test centuries, three of them against Australia and two, including his highest, 167, against the West Indies. He was something of an amateur spirit, not totally at home in the new commercialism that was sweeping the game, and, as a captain, he was shabbily treated by authorities in Pakistan and at Glamorgan. He now has the most powerful position in cricket administration in Pakistan.

Vinoo Mankad

Born: April 12, 1917, Jamnagar, India
Died: August 21, 1978, Bombay, India
Teams: Western India (1935–36); Nawanagar (1936–37 to 1941–42); Hindus (1936–37 to 104–46); Maharashtra (1943–44); Gujarat (1944–45 to 1950–51); Bengal (1948–49); Bombay (1951–52 to 1955–56); Rajasthan (1956–57 to 1961–62)
First-class: 233 matches; 11,591 runs, average 34.70; 782 wickets, average 24.53
Tests (1946 to 1958–59): 44 matches; 2,109 runs, average 31.47; 162 wickets, average 32.32

"Vinoo" Mankad began his career with aspirations of becoming a fast bowler, but under the tutelage of the Sussex all-rounder A. F. Wensley, he became a left-arm spinner and a tenacious right-handed batsman who often opened the innings. He was India's first great spin bowler and the best all-rounder of his generation. His Test debut did not come until 1946 when he performed admirably in all three Tests and completed the "double" in all matches. He hit two centuries against Australia, 1947–48, and remained an automatic choice for India for the next decade. His first great moment came against England at Madras, 1951–52, when he took eight for 55 and four for 53 to bowl India to an innings victory, their first win in Test cricket. He captured 34 wickets in the series, a record at that time.

He received an offer to play in the Lancashire League, but said that he would not accept if the Indian Board assured him he would be picked to tour England, 1952. Insanely, they refused to give that assurance, but the side was so overwhelmed that Haslingden, his club, released him to play in three of the four Tests. He responded heroically. At Lord's, he hit 72 and then bowled 73 overs to take five for 196 as England made 537. Mankad then scored 184 out of 378 before sending down another 24 overs.

In 1952–53, India won their first rubber, beating Pakistan. Mankad was again the hero with 25 wickets in four Tests. In all, he hit five Test centuries, his highest being 231 against New Zealand at Madras, 1955–56, when he and Pankaj Roy scored 413 for the first wicket which remains a world Test record.

Rodney Marsh

Born: November 11, 1947, Armadale, Perth, Western Australia
Teams: Western Australia (1968–69 to 1983–84)
First-class: 257 matches; 11,067, average 31.17; 1 wicket, average 84.00; caught 803, stumped 66
Tests (1970–71 to 1983–84): 96 matches; 3,633 runs, average 26.51; no wickets for 54 runs; caught 343, stumped 12

No wicket-keeper had accounted for more batsmen in Test cricket than Rodney Marsh, until Ian Healy took his record. Had he not spent a period with World Series cricket, Marsh's record would have been even greater for he had no rival during the time that he was Australia's keeper. He first appeared on the Test scene in 1970–71 when Illingworth's side regained the Ashes, and was treated with contempt by English critics who dubbed him "iron gloves", but he made three stumpings during the series and scored an unbeaten 92 in his fourth match. His keeping improved dramatically and, when he hit 118 against Pakistan at Adelaide, 1972–73, he became the first Australian wicket-keeper to score a hundred in Test cricket. Two more were to follow before the end of his career, and he had made a century on his first-class debut.

Marsh became a folk hero, epitomizing the aggressive and determined cricket of the conquering Australians of the Chappell brothers' era, and, off the field, he was a great favourite as he mingled warmly with people at social events. Having been Director of the Australian Cricket Academy, he switched sides and held a similar post in English cricket. In 2005 he became ICC Director of Coaching.

Malcolm Marshall

Born: April 18, 1958, Bridgetown, Barbados
Died: November 4, 1999, Bridgetown, Barbados
Teams: Barbados (1977–78 to 1990–91); Hampshire (1979–93); Natal (1992–93 to 1995–96)
First-class: 408 matches; 11.004 runs, average 24.83; 1,651 wickets, average 19.10
Tests (1978–79 to 1991): 81 matches; 1,810 runs, average 18.85; 376 wickets, average 20.94

Malcolm Marshall was possibly the greatest of a great battery of West Indian fast bowlers of the 1980s. Remarkably, he stood only 5ft 10in tall, but he made his lack of height an advantage. With his whippy action he could make his fastest deliveries skid off the wicket rather than dig in, making him a dangerous bowler to face in both senses. His assets were dedication, skill, ambition and fitness. He was in the Barbados side at 19, and in the Test side touring India at 20.

MCGRATH *A cornerstone of Australia's recent dominance of world cricket.*

The following summer he arrived at Hampshire as an overseas replacement for Andy Roberts and, beginning with nine wickets in his first match, he became one of the most successful of all imported cricketers. He played for Hampshire for 14 seasons, taking 100 wickets twice, including 134 (44 more than the next bowler) in 1982, when he recorded his best figures, eight for 71 against Worcestershire.

In the 1984 Test at Headingley he suffered a double fracture of his left thumb after only six overs, but came in to bat as last man with Gomes on 96, staying till Gomes got his hundred. Marshall then took seven for 53 in England's second innings, his best Test figures at the time. He also took a catch. From then on he blossomed, becoming the leading strike bowler in the world. He loved bowling in England, and his best Test innings analysis was at Old Trafford in 1988 – seven for 22. The following winter in Australia, he passed Lance Gibbs' total of 309 Test wickets to become the leading West Indian wicket-taker.

When his Test career finished, he went to play for Natal in South Africa, where he improved his highest first-class score to 120 not out. He made seven first-class centuries in all. In 1996-97 he was appointed the West Indies coach. Although one of the world's most hostile and dangerous bowlers (he famously squashed England captain Mike Gatting's nose) he was a sunny and considerate man off the field, and liked by all. Sadly he died of cancer when only 41.

Peter May

Born: December 31, 1929, Reading, Berkshire
Died: December 21, 1994, Liphook, Hampshire
Teams: Surrey (1950–63); Cambridge University (1950–52)
First-class: 388 matches; 27,592 runs, average 51.00; no wickets for 49 runs
Tests (1951–61): 66 matches; 4,537 runs, average 46.77

The finest English batsman of the post-war era, Peter May first appeared for Surrey during his first year at Cambridge, and his England

MURALITHARAN *Bamboozles opponents with his wristy off-spin action.*

debut came the following season, against South Africa at Headingley. He made 158. He had a successful series against India, 1952, but a failure in the first Test of the Ashes series, 1953, led to his being dropped until the final Test when he returned to play a part in England's victory. From that point on, he was an automatic choice for England.

A tall, elegant batsman with the full range of classical stroke-play, he was immediately recognized as the natural successor to Hutton as England's captain. He learned the art of captaincy under the two outstanding leaders of his time, Hutton and Surridge, whom he succeeded as Surrey's captain during the period of that county's greatest glory. Gentle and well-mannered as he was, and greatly admired and respected by his men, May had a ruthless, professional streak which served him well in Test cricket. He became captain of England in 1955 and led the side on a record 41 occasions with a record 20 victories to his credit. In 1957, he ended the West Indian supremacy over England when he and Colin Cowdrey defied Ramadhin in a fourth-wicket stand of 411, a record. May made 285 not out in that innings.

The disappointment came in Australia, 1958–59, when a great England side broke up and was surprisingly and heavily defeated. A year later, May was forced home from the Caribbean for medical

treatment and, although he returned briefly in 1961, he announced his retirement. Illness and pressure had taken their toll. He was still short of his 32nd birthday.

He later held every high office in the game, but his period as chairman of selectors was not a happy one. He was dealing with players who no longer spoke his language. Values had changed.

Vijay Merchant

Born: October 12, 1911, Bombay, India
Died: October 27, 1987, Bombay, India
Teams: Hindus (1929–30 to 1945–46); Bombay (1933–34 to 1950–51)
First-class: 150 matches; 13,470 runs, average 71.64; 65 wickets, average 32.12
Tests (1933–34 to 1951–52): 10 matches; 859 runs, average 47.72; no wickets for 40 runs

Merchant was small and compact, and there was a delicacy in his movement as he built an innings. A right-handed opener, he was India's first great batsman, and he gave evidence of his greatness on his two tours to England, scoring 1,745 runs in 1936 and 2,385 runs in 1946. His Test career began against Jardine's side, 1933–34, when he batted in the middle order, but he opened on the 1936 tour and scored 114 in the second innings at Old Trafford when he and Mushtaq Ali put on 203 for the first wicket and saved the Test. In 1946, he scored 128 at the Oval. His third Test hundred was his highest, 154 against England in Delhi, 1951–52, when he and Hazare established an Indian record for the series by scoring 211 for the third wicket. This was Merchant's last Test, for he sustained a shoulder injury which ended his career. He held high office in the administration of Indian cricket after his retirement.

In domestic cricket he bowled medium-pace and hit 359 not out for Bombay against Maharashtra, 1933–34.

Keith Miller

Born: November 28, 1919, Sunshine, Melbourne, Victoria, Australia
Died: October 11, 2004, Mornington, Victoria, Australia.
Teams: Victoria (1937–38 to 1946–47); New South Wales (1947–48 to 1955–56);

Nottinghamshire (1959)
First-class: 226 matches; 14,183 runs, average 48.90; 497 wickets, average 22.30
Tests (1945–46 to 1956–57): 55 matches; 2,958 runs, average 36.97; 170 wickets, average 22.97

Keith Miller was a glorious all-round cricketer. He was a tremendous hitter of the ball, powerful and brilliant in his stroke-play, and a magnificent fielder and a fast bowler whose partnership with Ray Lindwall became legendary. His lust for life was transmitted into his cricket, and he thrilled crowds with all that he did on the field.

He served in England during the war, played for the Australian Services, was outstanding in the Victory Tests and scored a memorable 185 in 165 minutes for the Dominions against England in 1945, an innings that was studded with gigantic sixes. He made his Test debut against New Zealand, 1945–46, and in his first Test against England a year later he took seven for 60 in the first innings. In the fourth Test of the series he made 141 not out. In 1948, in England, he and Lindwall swept all before them initially, but injury prevented Miller from bowling for much of the time. His batting was still integral to Bradman's great side.

Tall and physically strong, Miller was a beautiful athlete, but he was a man of moods and he never found fun in destroying weak opposition. He relished a contest, and in the Caribbean, 1954–55, he hit three Test centuries and took 20 wickets in the series. He never captained Australia but he led New South Wales with a characteristic casual air that gave rise to many amusing stories. He retired in 1956, but he appeared for Nottinghamshire against Cambridge University in 1959 and scored 62 and 102 not out. An author, journalist, commentator and bon viveur, he never lost his desire to live life to the full.

Bruce Mitchell

Born: January 8, 1909, Ferrierer Deep Gold Mine, Johannesburg, South Africa
Died: July 2, 1995, Johannesburg, South Africa
Teams: Transvaal (1925–26 to 1949–50)
First-class: 173 matches; 11,395

runs, average 45.39; 249 wickets, average 25.63

Tests (1929 to 1948–49): 42 matches; 3,471 runs, average 48.88; 27 wickets, average 51.11

Bruce Mitchell retains the record of having scored more runs in Test cricket than any other South African batsman. He was a stylish, right-handed opening batsman of infinite patience, a leg-break bowler and an outstanding slip fielder. He came to England in 1929, scored 88 and 61 not out on his Test debut at Edgbaston, and played in all five matches in the series. Against Chapman's team, 1930–31, he hit 123 at Cape Town and shared a record opening stand of 260 with Siedle. The following season, in New Zealand, he shared an opening partnership of 196 with Christy which remains a record for the series. Mitchell made 113. When South Africa beat England in England for the first time, 1935, Mitchell hit two centuries, one of which was an unbeaten 164 in the Lord's Test where South Africa gained their famous victory.

He remained a dominant force, and when South Africa came to England in 1947, he hit 120 and 189 not out at the Oval and was on the field for the entire match bar eight minutes – 12 balls. There was a century and 99 against England, 1949–50, but, astonishingly, he was omitted when Australia went to South Africa a year later and so he retired.

Arthur Morris

Born: January 19, 1922, Bondi, New South Wales, Australia

Teams: New South Wales (1940–41 to 1954–55)

First-class: 162 matches; 12,614 runs, average 53.67; 12 wickets, average 49.33

Tests (1946–47 to 1954–55): 46 matches; 3,533 runs, average 46.48; 2 wickets, average 25.00

A century in each innings on the occasion of his first-class debut for New South Wales against Queensland heralded the career of Arthur Morris, one of the most graceful of left-handed opening batsman to have charmed the Test arena. In his first series against England, 1946–47, he scored three centuries in succession, including

one in each innings at Adelaide. In England, 1948, he had an outstanding tour and topped the Test matches' batting averages. His three centuries in the series included a match-winning 182 at Headingley where he and Bradman put on 301 in 217 minutes for the second wicket. He followed this with 196 run out at the Oval. He hit centuries in successive innings against South Africa in South Africa, 1949–50 and made 206 against Freddie Brown's side at Adelaide the following season.

He had a poor series in England, 1953, and his last series was against Hutton's side, 1954–55, when he hit 153 in the first Test.

A delightful man, he captained Australia on two occasions.

Muttiah Muralitharan

Born: April 27, 1972, Kandy, Sri Lanka

Teams: Tamil Union (1991–92 to 2003–04); Lancashire (1999–2005); Kent (2003)

First-class: 186 matches; 1,898 runs, average 11.64; 1,087 wickets, average 18.76

Tests (1992–93 to 2004–05): 96 matches; 1025 runs, average 12.81; 568 wickets, average 22.23

A bowler of extraordinary off spinners, Murali has a remarkably flexible wrist, which enables him to conjure with the ball and baffle the best batsmen. He made his Test debut at the age of twenty and was soon hitting the headlines.

However between the lines came hints that his action was unfair. The hints exploded into controversy when in December 1995, Darrell Hair, the Australian umpire no-balled Murali for throwing during the Melbourne Test, Sri Lanka v Australia. He was "called" again in the following Test. After long study, the ICC experts agreed with the Sri Lankan Board that the problem was an optical illusion caused because he had a slightly bent arm from birth. Resuming his Test career Murali had great success in the 1996 World Cup. When Sri Lanka came to England for a single Test in 1998, he captured 16 wickets in the match at The Oval, giving Sri Lanka their first win over England in England.

1999 saw him playing county cricket for Lancashire. Available for just seven Championship contests, Murali took no less than 66 wickets at 11.77 runs each. He was pipped at the post so far as topping the first-class averages was concerned by a margin of 0.40 from Saqlain. He returned again to Lancashire for seven matches in 2001 and again reached 50 wickets. He is by a large margin Sri Lanka's leading Test wicket-taker.

N

Monty Noble

Born: January 28, 1873, Sydney, New South Wales, Australia

Died: 22 June, 1940, Randwick, Sydney, New South Wales, Australia

Teams: New South Wales (1893–94 to 1919–20)

First-class: 248 matches, 13,975 runs, average 40.74; 624 wickets, average 23.14

Tests (1897–98 to 1909): 42 matches, 1,997 runs, average 30.25; 121 wickets, average 25.00

Banker, dentist, manufacturer's agent, writer, broadcaster, right-handed batsman with a sound defence and an ability to hit hard when necessary, a medium pace off-break bowler and a brilliant fielder, Monty Noble stood over 6ft tall and was a master of many trades, especially cricket. He took six for 49 on his Test debut against England, 1897–98, and he followed this with eight wickets in his next Test. He first captained Australia in the 1903–04 series and hit his only Test century in his first match as captain. He also led the side in 1907–08 and 1909.

He scored 1,000 runs on all of his four visits to England, making more than 2,000 in 1905. His highest score was 284 against Sussex at Hove, 1986. A strong disciplinarian, he rebuked his players for talking to spectators and urged abstinence during a Test match. Dedicated to the ethics of the game, he was deeply respected by his opponents.

Dudley Nourse

Born: November 12, 1910, Durban, South Africa

Died: August 14, 1981, Durban,

South Africa

Teams: Natal (1931–32 to 1952–53)

First-class: 175 matches; 12,472 runs, average 51.53; no wickets for 124 runs

Tests (1935–1951): 34 matches; 2,960 runs, average 53.81; no wickets for 9 runs

Son of "Dave" Nourse, a Test player of the Edwardian era, Dudley Nourse was a sound right-handed batsman who must rank among the most gifted produced by South Africa. In the years either side of the Second World War, he could lay claim to a place in a World XI. He came to England in 1935 and was in the side that won at Lord's – South Africa's first win in England– but it was against Australia the following winter that he truly revealed his international class. He hit 91 in the first Test and 231 in 289 minutes in the second at Johannesburg. Two centuries followed against England, 1938–39, and he was vice-captain to Melville on the 1947 tour when he hit centuries at Trent Bridge and Old Trafford. He led South Africa against England and Australia, scoring two hundreds in the first series and one in the second.

He captained the party to England, 1951, and, batting with a broken thumb and in considerable pain, he hit 208 in 550 minutes at Trent Bridge to equal the record of seven centuries against England. He was 40 years old.

O

Norm O'Neill

Born: February 19, 1937, Carlton, New South Wales, Sydney, Australia

Teams: New South Wales (1955–56 to 1966–70)

First-class: 188 matches; 13,859 runs, average 50.95; 99 wickets, average 41.01

Tests (1958–59 to 1964–65): 42 matches; 2,779 runs, average 45.55; 17 wickets, average 39.23

Norman O'Neill was an unlucky cricketer in that he suffered from being dubbed "the new Bradman" when he first broke upon the scene. In spite of having only a moderate time in the Ashes series, 1958–59, he arrived in England two years later with an immense reputation. He had scored a century against Pakistan and two against India, 1959–60, and had made 181 against the West Indies in the famous tied Test of December, 1960, but he found English conditions difficult in 1961 and did not score a century until the final Test, at the Oval. On the tour as a whole, though, he did well.

O'Neill was a highly entertaining right-handed batsman, rich in strokes, a useful leg-break bowler and brilliant fielder. He was a warm and generous man but he was a rather nervous starter and, although he hit six Test centuries, never quite accomplished all that had been expected of him. It should be said, though, that he was hampered by recurring knee trouble which eventually caused his retirement.

He appeared to become less enamoured of the game, and at the end of the series against the West Indies in the Caribbean, 1964–65, articles appeared under his name criticizing the action of Griffith, the West Indian fast bowler. His Test career was at an end, but he continued to score heavily in domestic cricket.

Bill O'Reilly

Born: December 20, 1905, White Cliffs, New South Wales, Australia
Died: October 6, 1992, Sutherland, Sydney, New South Wales
Teams: New South Wales (1927–28 to 1945–46)
First-class: 135 matches; 1,655 runs, average 13.13; 774 wickets, average 16.60
Tests (1931–32 to 1945–46): 27 matches; 410 runs, average 12.81; 144 wickets, average 22.59
In the years immediately before the Second World War, "Tiger" O'Reilly was described as one of the greatest bowlers of all time. He bowled leg-breaks and googlies and had the ability to vary his pace and to make the ball rear awkwardly.

His Test debut came against South Africa, 1931–32. In the "bodyline" series a year later, he captured 27 wickets, including 10 for 129 at Melbourne where Australia gained their only victory of the rubber. In England, 1934, he was a huge success, heading the first-class averages and topping the Test averages with 28 wickets at 24.92 runs each. In his first Test in England, at Trent Bridge, he had

four for 75 and seven for 54, his best in Test cricket. He claimed 28 wickets in South Africa, 1935–36, and 25 against Allen's side the following year. In a full Test series, he never failed to take at least 20 wickets, and, in four Tests in England, 1938, he captured 22 wickets at 27.72, a remarkable performance considering England's 903 for seven at the Oval where he sent down 85 overs to take three for 178. At Headingley, he bowled Australia to victory with his third 10-wicket haul in Test cricket. His last Test was in New Zealand shortly after the war, with match figures of eight for 33. He became a well-respected cricket writer.

Eddie Paynter

Born: November 5, 1901, Oswaldtwistle, Lancashire
Died: February 5, 1979, Keighley, Yorkshire
Teams: Lancashire (1926–45)
First-class: 352 matches; 20,075 runs, average 42.46; 30 wickets, average 45.70
Tests (1931–39): 20 matches; 1,540 runs, average 59.23
Eddie Paynter scored 322 for Lancashire at Hove in 1937, and was a most loyal servant to the Red Rose county. An attacking left-handed batsman and brilliant fielder, he made his Test debut against New Zealand, 1931, and went to Australia with Jardine's team, 1932–33. He did not play until the third Test when he scored 77 as England staged a recovery, and, in the next Test, became the stuff of legend when he rose from his sickbed to hit 83 at number eight when England were in some trouble. He scored a century in each innings of the first Test in South Africa, 1938–39, and made his highest Test score, 243, in the third match.

He had not gained a regular place in the Lancashire side until 1931, and his career was effectively ended by the outbreak of the Second World War.

Robert Peel

Born: February 12, 1857, Churwell, Leeds, Yorkshire

Died: August 12, 1941, Morley, Leeds, Yorkshire
Teams: Yorkshire (1882–98)
First-class: 436 matches; 12,191 runs, average 19.44; 1,775 wickets, average 16.20
Tests (1884–85 to 1896): 20 matches; 427 runs, average 14.72; 101 wickets, average 16.98
In the great Yorkshire tradition of slow left-arm bowlers, Bobby Peel maintained the principles of line and, especially, length. He was a most capable, punishing left-arm batsman who scored 210 not out against Warwickshire in 1896, the year he did the "double". He took 100 wickets in a season on seven other occasions. He was regarded as the best bowler of his type in England and made three trips to Australia. In his first Test, 1884–85, he took eight wickets at Sydney and finished the series with 21 to his credit. He was triumphant at Sydney again three years later when he had match figures of 10 for 58, and he and Lohmann bowled Australia out for 42 in the first innings.

Peel took 24 wickets in three Tests against Australia, 1888, including seven for 31 and four for 37 in the final match at Old Trafford. Rarely, if ever, did he fail, and in his last Test, against Australia at the Oval, 1896, he took two for 30 and six for 23 to bowl England to victory. Australia were all out for 44 in their second innings.

The following year he took the field for Yorkshire in an inebriated state and, according to some reports, urinated against the sightscreen. Lord Hawke dismissed him immediately from the Yorkshire XI.

Graeme Pollock

Born: February 27, 1944 Durban, South Africa
Teams: Eastern Province (1960–61 to 1977–98); Transvaal (1978–79 to 1986–87)
First-class: 262 matches; 20,940 runs, average 54.67; 43 wickets, average 47.65
Tests (1963–64 to 1969–70): 23 matches; 2,256 runs, average 60.97; 4 wickets, average 51.00
Only Don Bradman ended a Test career with an average higher than Graeme Pollock's. One of the

greatest of all batsmen, he was at his peak at a time when South Africa was banned from international cricket.

A schoolboy prodigy, when not quite 17 he became the youngest player to score a century in the Currie Cup. Less than two years later he became the youngest South African to score a double century and, when just past 20, he was made captain of Eastern Province. Although right-handed in all other things, Pollock batted left-handed.

He made his Test debut in Australia in 1963-64. An early century on that tour led Don Bradman to congratulate the 19-year-old on one of the best innings he'd seen. In the third Test he scored 175 in 283 minutes, becoming the third player to score two Test centuries before he was 20. Later in a Test at Trent Bridge he scored 125 from 145 balls, becoming the youngest ever to score 1,000 runs in Tests. In 1966-67 in South Africa he averaged 76.51 against Australia, South Africa winning the series 3-1, although before then they'd not beaten Australia in a match at home for 64 years. His last series was also against Australia, South Africa winning 4-0 by huge margins, Pollock topping the averages with 73.85, and playing South Africa's highest Test innings of 274. After that South Africa were banned because of the apartheid policy.

Peter Pollock

Born: June 30, 1941, Pietermaritzburg, Natal, South Africa
Teams: Eastern Province (1958–59 to 1971–72)
First-class: 127 matches; 3,028 runs, average 22.59; 485 wickets, average 21.89
Tests (1961–62 to 1969–70): 28 matches; 607 runs, average 21.67; 116 wickets, average 24.18
Tall, fair-haired and a bowler of genuine pace, Peter Pollock comes from a cricketing family. On his Test debut, 20 years old, he took three for 61 and six for 38, his best Test figures, against New Zealand, and he finished the series with 17 wickets from three matches.

When South Africa drew the

rubber in Australia, 1963–64, he confirmed his standing as a leading strike bowler with 25 wickets in the series. In 1965, in the three-match series in England, he claimed 20 wickets, and his 10 for 87 in 47.5 overs in the match at Trent Bridge brought South Africa victory and clinched the rubber.

In 1969–70, Australia were trounced in all four Tests in South Africa. The South African opening attack of Procter and Peter Pollock was lethal. Pollock had 15 wickets in the series, but he pulled a hamstring and could bowl only seven balls in the last innings of what was to be his final Test, for South Africa's exile from international cricket followed. When the exile ended in 1992, Pollock was chairman of selectors.

Shaun Pollock

Born: July 1973, 1973, Port Elizabeth, South Africa
Teams: Natal (1991–92 to 2004–05); Warwickshire (1996–2002)
First-class: 169 matches; 6,275 runs, average 32.85; 616 wickets, average 22.28
Tests (1995–96 to 2004–05): 94 matches; 3,133 runs, average 31.33; 377 wickets, average 22.64

The son of Peter Pollock and nephew of Graeme, Shaun is a genuinely fast right arm bowler, who swings the ball both ways. He possesses a good bouncer and can produce a well-disguised slower ball. In addition he is no mean batsman – going in at No. 9 against West Indies at Bridgetown in March 2001 he hit 106 not out.

His Test debut came against England in 1995–96 and he was even then the pick of his side's bowlers in a rain affected game, then ended that initial series topping his country's bowling averages. He formed a most dangerous partnership with Allan Donald.

He appeared in county cricket only in 1996, when he effectively stood in for Donald in the Warwickshire side. Pollock created a sensation in his first competitive game by capturing four wickets in four balls in the Benson & Hedges match v Leicestershire.

His first taste as South African captain came in the 1998 Commonwealth games in Malaysia

– South Africa won the Gold Medal, but several countries failed to send their top players. In the famous tied semi-final, South Africa v Australia, in the World Cup in 1999 he returned the best bowling figures of five for 36, but unfortunately Australia went through to the Final. He has been consistently ranked in the top three in the Test Bowling tables.93 matches; 7,337 runs, average 56.87; 183 wickets, average 31.60game had known. He made 429 against Tasmania at Melbourne, 1922–23, and five years later, on the same ground, he hit 437 against Queensland. He was a right-handed opening batsman whose defence looked impenetrable and who had a wide range of shots. He hit 110 on his Test debut, against England, 1924–25, and when he hit 128 at Melbourne he became the first batsman to score centuries in his first two Tests. He was hampered by illness in England in 1926 and appeared only in the last two Tests. In Australia, 1928–29, he had his hand broken by a ball from Larwood in the second Test and did not play again in the series.

By 1930, his opening partnership with Woodfull was established, and the pair set up Australia's victory at the Oval with a stand of 159. Ponsford scored 110, and he followed this with two centuries against the West Indies a few months later. Two unsuccessful home series cast doubts on his ability at the top level, but, at Headingley, 1934, he made 181, and in the next match, at the Oval, he and Bradman scored 451 in 316 minutes for a world-record partnership for the second wicket – Ponsford hit 266. His Test career ended with that Test.

Ricky Ponting

Born: December 19, 1974, Launceston, South Africa
Teams: Tasmania (1992-93 to 2002-03)
First-class: 189 matches; 15,993 runs, average 59.01; 14 wickets, average 53.57
Tests (1966–67 to 1969–70): 95 matches; 7,662 runs, average 56.75; 5 wickets, average 44.80

Described, shortly after he had started out on his professional career, as the golden boy of Australian cricket, Ponting made his first-class debut at the age of 17. Three seasons later, he had entered the Test arena, being a gifted middle-order batsman and a fielder in the Rhodes class.

Problems however occurred during the 1998–99 Ashes series. Ponting lost his place in the Australia side. He took to drink and was involved in a nightclub brawl. This earned him a three-match ban. He soon mended his ways. No incidents of a similar nature have occurred, indeed two years later he was being spoken of as Steve Waugh's successor to lead Australia. In March 2002, he was given the One Day captaincy and in 2003–04 he assumed the Test match mantle. Ponting brings the same aggression to his leadership as he has done to his batting and fielding.

In 2005 he became only the second Australian to reach 8,000 One Day International runs and as this book was going to press, Ponting became Australia's leading ODI run-maker. On the Test match scene, his batting average at the end of the 2005 Ashes series was only exceeded – among Australians – by the incomparable

Sir Donald Bradman. A place in the top-ten of run-scorers in both Tests and ODIs is likely in the not too distant future.

Mike Procter

Born: September 15, 1946, Durban, South Africa
Teams: Gloucestershire (1965–81); Natal (1965–66 to 1988–89); Western Province (1969–70); Rhodesia (1970–71 to 1975–76); Orange Free State (1987–88)
First-class: 401 matches; 21,936 runs, average 36.01; 1,417 wickets, average 19.53
Tests (1966–67 to 1969–70): 7 matches; 226 runs, average 25.11; 41 wickets, average 15.02

One of the most dynamic performers the game of cricket has known, Mike Procter played only seven Test matches because his career only began to flower just as South Africa were excluded from international cricket.

Procter made his Test debut against Australia in South Africa during 1966–67, and took a total of 15 wickets in three matches. Three years later, against the very same opposition, he took 26 wickets in four Tests, finishing with his best, six for 73, at Port Elizabeth. In seven Test matches, he was never on a losing side, and South Africa won six of them.

MIKE PROCTER *Great all-rounder whose Test career was sadly short.*

His energies then had to be concentrated on domestic cricket. In 1970–71, he hit six hundreds in consecutive innings for Rhodesia, and he will ever be remembered for his achievements with Gloucestershire and the influence he had on that county. He was a ferocious batsman, a fielder of brilliance, and a fast bowler who occasionally turned to off-breaks. Gloucestershire won trophies when he was in the side, for he always seemed to be scoring runs, taking wickets or making a catch. He captained the county from 1977 to 1981. He hit 1,000 runs in a season nine times and took 100 wickets in a season twice. He was cricket manager at Northamptonshire, 1990–91, and held a similar position with the South African national side from 1992 to 1994.

R

Sonny Ramadhin

Born: May 1, 1929, Esperance Village, Trinidad

Teams: Trinidad (1949–50 to

RAMADHIN *An instant sensation.*

1952–53); Lancashire (1964–65)

First-class: 184 matches; 1,092 runs, average 8.66; 758 wickets, average 20.24

Tests (1950 to 1960–61): 43 matches; 361 runs, average 8.20;

158 wickets, average 28.98

Sonny Ramadhin came to England in 1950 with a handful of first-class matches behind him and nothing known of him save that he was a spin bowler. Within months he had become the talk of the cricket world. Having been beaten in cold weather at Old Trafford, the West Indies won the remaining three Tests of the series, and Ramadhin took 26 wickets. He headed the first-class averages for the tour with 135 wickets, average 14.88. It was at Lord's that he and his spin partner Valentine bowled the West Indies to their first win in England. Ramadhin took five for 66 and six for 86. He had a perfect control of length, flighted the ball well, and bowled both off-breaks and leg-breaks – he was truly a "mystery" bowler. He was less successful in Australia but he devastated the New Zealand batsmen.

He continued to trouble England in the Caribbean with 23 wickets, 1953–54, and when he arrived in England in 1957 and took a Test-best seven for 49 in the first encounter at Edgbaston it seemed that England would again fall under his spell, but he was destroyed by May and Cowdrey in the second innings. He sent down 98 overs and took two for 179, and he was never quite the same again.

He played Lancashire League cricket, but his venture into county cricket came late in his career and was not a success. He became a publican.

Arjuna Ranatunga

Born: December 1, 1963, Colombo, Ceylon

Teams: Sinhalese SC (1988–89 to 1996–97)

First-class: 146 matches; 7,941 runs, average 42.33; 90 wickets, average 32.65

Tests (1981–82 to 1996–97): 61 matches; 3,471 runs, average 35.41; 14 wickets, average 67.28

A chunky, aggressive, left-handed batsman and a right-arm medium-pace bowler, Arjuna Ranatunga played in Sri Lanka's inaugural Test against England, February 1982. He was 18 years 78 days old and still attending Anada College. He hit 54, Sri Lanka's first 50 in Test cricket. A

year later, he made 90 against Australia, and, at Lord's, August 1984, hit a splendidly entertaining 84. He revealed himself as a joyous and enthusiastic cricketer, and his love of the game was infectious.

He hit centuries against India and Pakistan, and remains a consistent scorer. He first captained Sri Lanka in Australia, 1989–90 – it was not an easy time, but he battled on happily. Greatness awaited him, though. Sri Lanka became most adept at the one-day game, and, in 1996, Ranatunga led them to victory in the World Cup. His own contribution was immense – he averaged 120.50 from the six matches and topped the batting averages for the competition.

K. S. Ranjitsinhji

Born: September 10, 1872, Sarodar, Kathiawar, India

Died: April 2, 1933, Jamnagar, India

Teams: Cambridge University (1893–94); Sussex (1895–1920); London County (1901–04)

First-class: 307 matches; 24,692 runs, average 56.37; 133 wickets, average 34.59

Tests (1896–1902): 15 matches; 989 runs, average 44.95; 1 wicket, average 39.00

A batsman of feline grace and Eastern mystery, "Ranji" was a cricket legend. With exceptionally keen eyesight and supple and powerful wrists, he played shots that others could only imagine, and his leg-glance was breathtaking in audacity, beauty and execution. He had moderate success at Cambridge, but from 1899 to 1904 he was supreme among batsmen in England. He hit 3,159 runs in 1899, and followed this with 3,065 runs, average 87.57 in 1900. In three other seasons he reached 2,000 runs and in six more 1,000. He also reached 1,000 runs on a tour of Australia, 1897–98.

He was the first Indian to play Test cricket and the second batsman, after Grace, to hit a century on his Test debut. He was also the first batsman to score a hundred before lunch in a Test. He made 62 and 154 not out at Old Trafford, 1896, and he went from 41 to 154 in 130 minutes before lunch on the third day. In 1897–98, he hit 175 in

his first Test in Australia.

Ranjitsinhji captained Sussex from 1899 to 1903 and then returned to India. He made infrequent appearances thereafter. As the Maharaja Jam Sahib of Nawanagar, he became involved in administration of his state and was a delegate to the League of Nations.

John Reid

Born: June 3, 1928, Auckland, New Zealand

Teams: Wellington (1947–48 to 1964–65); Otago (1956–57 to 1957–58)

First-class: 246 matches; 16,128 runs, average 41.35; 466 wickets, average 22.60

Tests (1949–1965): 58 matches; 3,428 runs, average 33.28; 85 wickets, average 33.35

John Reid was a complete all-round cricketer, a hard-hitting middle-order batsman, a brisk bowler of off-cutters and a wicket-keeper of no mean ability. He made 50 and 25 on his Test debut at Old Trafford, 1949, and in his next match, at the Oval, he kept wicket and scored 93. He did not really blossom until the 1953–54 series in South Africa when, at Cape Town, he hit his maiden Test century.

New Zealand cricket had reached a low ebb by the mid-1950s, and, following a crushing defeat by the West Indies at Dunedin, 1955–56, Reid was appointed captain. In the last match of the series, he top-scored with 84 and New Zealand won a famous victory. His side suffered badly in England, 1958, but in South Africa, 1961–62, against all expectations, New Zealand drew the series, each side winning two Tests. It was the first time New Zealand had won two Tests in a rubber, and Reid topped the batting and bowling averages, hitting 142 in Johannesburg.

He led New Zealand in 34 consecutive Tests, but retired after the disappointing 1965 tour of England, feeling his side had made no real advance. In all, he hit six Test centuries.

Wilfred Rhodes

Born: October 29, 1877, Kirkheaton, Yorkshire

Died: July 8, 1973, Branksome Park, Dorset

JOHN REID *A good all-rounder and inspiring captain of New Zealand.*

Teams: Yorkshire (1898–1930); Patiala (1926–27); Europeans (1921–22 to 1922–23)
First-class: 1,110 matches; 39,969 runs, average 30.81; 4,204 wickets, average 16.72
Tests (1899 to 1929–30): 58 matches; 2,325 runs, average 30.19; 127 wickets, average 26.96

When Lord Hawke dismissed Robert Peel from the Yorkshire team in 1897 the county were left in need of a slow left-arm bowler. The vacancy was filled by Wilfred Rhodes who took six for 63 in the first match of the 1898 season and, by the end of the season, he had claimed 154 wickets. So began one of the most illustrious and record-breaking careers in cricket. He was to take 100 or more wickets 23 times, and in three of those seasons he exceeded 200 wickets. He achieved the "double" in 16 seasons, a record that is never likely to be beaten, and, in all, he reached 1,000 runs 20 times. His total of 4,024 wickets is a world record.

He made his Test debut at Trent Bridge in 1899. It was the first Test to be played at the ground, and it also marked the end of W.G. Grace's Test career. Rhodes had match figures of seven Australian wickets for 118. He also played in the first Test staged at Edgbaston, 1902, when Australia were bowled out for 36 – Rhodes took seven for 17. Better was to come. On his first tour of Australia, 1903–04, he took seven for 56 and eight for 68 to bowl England to victory in the Melbourne Test. When he went to Australia eight years later, he was Hobbs's opening partner, and the pair established an Ashes record at Melbourne in the fourth Test when they put on 323, Rhodes making 179. The record stood for 77 years.

Barry Richards

Born: July 21, 1945, Morningside, Durban, South Africa
Teams: Natal (1964–65 to 1982–83); Gloucestershire (1965); Hampshire (1968–78); South Australia (1970–71); Transvaal (1970–71)
First-class: 339 matches; 28,358 runs, average 54.74; 77 wickets, average 37.48
Tests (1969–70): 4 matches; 508 runs, average 75.57; 1 wicket, average 26.00

In the opinion of many, Barry Richards was unquestionably the finest batsman of his generation. An aggressive right-handed opening batsman with total command of every shot, he adorned county cricket for a decade, and his first-wicket partnership with Gordon Greenidge was largely instrumental in bringing Hampshire the county championship and two Sunday League titles.

If he had a fault, it was that it all seemed to come so easily to him that at times he appeared lackadaisical. A thrilling batsman, he hit 325 on the opening day of the match between South Australia and Western Australia at Perth, 1970–71. He finally made 356. He scored 1,000 runs in a season five times in South Africa and nine times in England. He was also a useful off-break bowler.

His Test debut in 1969–70 saw him score two centuries in seven innings against Australia and average 75.57 for the series. That was to be both the beginning and end of his Test career, for these were South Africa's last Tests before their exclusion.

Viv Richards

Born: March 7, 1952, St John's, Antigua
Teams: Leeward Islands (1971–72 to 1990–91); Somerset (1974–86); Queensland (1976–77); Glamorgan (1990–93)
First-class: 507 matches; 36,212 runs, average 49.33; 223 wickets, average 45.15
Tests (1974–75 to 1991): 121 matches; 8,540 runs, average 50.23; 32 wickets, average 61.37

Viv Richards scored more runs and played in more Test matches than any other West Indian cricketer. A brilliant, natural right-handed attacking batsman and a right-arm bowler of medium pace or spin, he was capable of destroying any attack in the world in all

BARRY RICHARDS *Careless genius.*

forms of cricket. Apart from his mighty Test record, he scored 6,721 runs in limited-over internationals, including 11 centuries.

He first played for Somerset in 1974 and made his Test debut in India the following winter, scoring 192 not out in his second match, the first of 24 Test centuries. A fine natural athlete who played World Cup soccer as well as World Cup cricket, he led a violent assault on the England bowling in the World Cup Final 1979, and the following year he captained the West Indies for the first time.

In 1976, he appeared in only four Tests in the series against England but hit 232, 63, 4, 135, 66, 38 and 291 to give him 829 runs, average 118.42. It brought his aggregate of Test runs for the calendar year to a record 1,710. His second tour of England was an equal triumph, and when he came for his fourth tour, 1988, he was captain. He retired from Test cricket after the 1991 series, having led the West Indies 50 times.

The first West Indian to score a hundred hundreds, he dominated in county cricket. He was associated with Somerset in their glory years when they won all the one-day trophies. His highest innings for Somerset was 322 against Warwickshire, 1985. He left Somerset with some acrimony, but returned to county cricket with Glamorgan and helped them win the Sunday League in his last season in cricket. He was knighted for services to cricket in 1998.

Richie Richardson

Born: January 2, 1962, Five Islands Village, Antigua
Teams: Leeward Islands (1981–82 to 1995–96); Yorkshire (1994); Windward Islands (1997–98); Northern Transvaal (1996–97)
First-class: 217 matches; 13,950 runs, average 42.40; 6 wickets, average 39.66
Tests (1983–84 to 1995–96): 86 matches; 5,949 runs, average 44.39; no wickets for 18 runs

A shy, modest and courteous man, Richie Richardson succeeded Viv Richards as captain of Leeward Islands and of the West Indies. A right-handed batsman of immense talent and great eagerness to hit

VIV RICHARDS *Dismissive arrogance of a master batsman.*

the ball, he took some time to prove himself at Test level. He hit two centuries against Australia, 1983–84, but he failed to do himself justice in England the following summer although his ability was apparent. When he made his third trip to England, 1991, he showed that he had mastered the slower wickets and topped the Test batting averages. He now began to thrive, and hit his eighth Test hundred against Australia, 1992–93, and led the West Indies to victory in the series. In all, he now has 16 Test hundreds to his credit.

He was hugely successful in one-day internationals, but the pressures began to tell on him. He left Yorkshire because he was exhausted and ordered to rest for six months. He was reinstated as the West Indies' captain far too quickly and failure in the World Cup, 1996, led to him relinquishing the captaincy and leaving Test cricket. He played for Northern Transvaal in 1996–97, but averaged only 23.09, then the following season joined Windward Islands, whose side had fallen on hard times. Again he failed to reproduce his old form and Windwards failed to win a single game.

Andy Roberts

Born: January 29, 1951, Urlings Village, Antigua
Teams: Leeward Islands (1969–70 to 1983–84); Hampshire (1973–78); New South Wales (1976–77); Leicestershire (1981–84)
First-class: 228 matches; 3,516 runs, average 15.69; 889 wickets, average 21.01
Tests (1973–74 to 1983–84): 47 matches; 762 runs, average 14.94; 202 wickets, average 25.61

Andy Roberts was the third West Indian to claim 200 Test wickets and, at his peak, he was considered to be one of the two or three best fast bowlers in the world. He reached 100 Test wickets more quickly than any bowler had done before, although his record was later beaten by Botham. He was a great favourite with Hampshire, and he played a major part in their Sunday League triumphs. In 1974, he took 119 wickets, average 13.62, in 21 matches for the county in first-class cricket and was the most feared bowler in the land.

His Test debut had come against England the previous winter, but it was in India, 1974–75, that he really established himself as an international cricketer. He captured 32 wickets in the series, and at Madras he had match figures of 12 for 121. His best bowling came in Perth a year later when he took seven for 54 in the second innings to give the West Indies their only victory of the series.

He joined Packer's World Series along with the other West Indian cricketers, and he was never quite the same afterwards. He assisted Leicestershire on a part-time basis, appearing in 36 matches, and later coached the West Indian team.

S

Salim Malik

Born: April 16, 1963, Lahore, Pakistan
Teams: Lahore (1978–79 to 1985–86); Habib Bank (1982–83 to 2000–01)
First-class: 269 matches; 16,586 runs, average 45.94; 93 wickets, average 41.58
Tests (1981–82 to 1998–99): 103 matches; 5,768 runs, average 43.69; 5 wickets, average 82.80

An exquisite stroke-maker, Salim Malik is a right-handed batsman and leg-break bowler who caught the eye as soon as he appeared in international cricket.

He became the youngest player to score a hundred in his first Test match, and 100 not out against Sri Lanka, March 1982. He did not play in any of the Tests in England the following summer, but on his second trip to England, 1987, scoring 99 at Headingley and 102 at the Oval, he was a huge success and proved the linchpin of the side. He was even more successful five years later.

He assisted Essex for two seasons and scored heavily in 1991, sharing in a fourth-wicket record stand of 314 with Nasser Hussain at the Oval and ending the season with 1,972 runs to his credit. He was less prolific in 1993, but remained highly entertaining.

Salim's career has had its troughs, and, having been made captain of Pakistan in South Africa and Zimbabwe, he faced allegations of bribery which led to his suspension for some time. He was deemed innocent and regained his place in the Pakistan side where he showed that he had lost none of his ability to

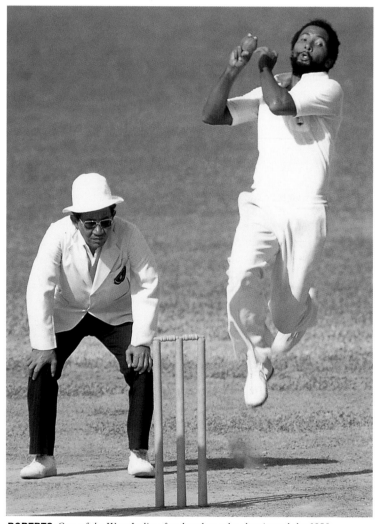

ROBERTS *One of the West Indian fast bowlers who dominated the 1980s.*

play as his side required.

Justice Qayyam's enquiry into match fixing recommended a life ban on Salim in May 2000.

Sarfraz Nawaz

Born: December 1, 1948, Lahore, Pakistan

Teams: Lahore (1967–68 to 1984–85); Punjab University (1968–69 to 1971–72); Northamptonshire (1969–1982); Punjab (1974–75); Railways (1975–75); United Bank (1976–77 to 1977–78)

First-class: 299 matches; 5,709 runs, average 19.35; 1,005 wickets, average 24.62

Tests (1968–69 to 1983–84): 55 matches; 1,045 runs, average 17.71; 177 wickets, average 32.75

Sarfraz Nawaz was a high-class, fast medium-pace bowler who was only the third Pakistani cricketer to take 100 Test wickets and score 1,000 Test runs. He had an impressive Test career, but it was punctuated by injury and arguments with the Pakistan Board of Control. He was never far from controversy, and the last such incident was when he refuted Allan Lamb's assertion that he was the bowler who taught others how to scratch one side of the surface of the ball. Sarfraz took legal action but did not pursue the case to the full.

In March 1979, at Melbourne, Pakistan celebrated their 100th Test by beating Australia. It was a most unlikely victory, for Australia needed 77 to win and had seven wickets in hand with time to spare. Sarfraz then produced one of the greatest spells of bowling in Test history taking those seven wickets in 33 balls while he conceded one run. He finished with nine for 86, and Pakistan won by 71 runs. In the next Test, he caused a furore when he successfully appealed for "handled ball" against Hilditch when the batsman picked up the ball and tossed it back to him.

He helped Northamptonshire during a successful period although he was once not re-engaged. He went into politics when he left cricket.

Ravi Shastri

Born: May 27, 1962, Bombay, India

Teams: Bombay (1979–80 to 1993–94); Glamorgan (1987–91)

First-class: 245 matches; 13,202 runs, average 44.00; 509 wickets, average 32.89

Tests (1980–81 to 1992–93): 80 matches; 3,830 runs, average 35.79; 151 wickets, average 40.96

Ravi Shastri is the only batsman other than Gary Sobers who has hit six sixes in one over. He scored 200 not out for Bombay against Baroda, 1984–85, and hit 13 sixes, six of them in one over. It was the fastest double-century on record, 113 minutes, and the runs came off 123 balls.

A tall, calm and composed right-handed batsman, he won his first Test cap as a slow left-arm bowler. He was flown to New Zealand as a replacement in February 1981, and just short of his 19th birthday, took six wickets in the match including three with his last four balls in the second innings. In spite of these achievements, he never quite reached the peak expected of him. His bowling lacked variety and subtlety in flight, but he became a reliable opening batsman. He was seen as captain-elect of India, but, in the event, led his country in only one Test. He played a fine innings of 187 against England at the Oval, 1990, and made 206 against Australia at Sydney, 1991–92.

He did well with Glamorgan and was immensely successful in one-day internationals.

Alfred Shaw

Born: August 29, 1842, Burton Joyce, Nottinghamshire

Died: January 16, 1907, Gedling, Nottinghamshire

Teams: Nottinghamshire (1864–1897); Sussex (1894–95)

First-class: 404 matches; 6,585 runs, average 12.44; 2,026 wickets, average 12.13

Tests (1876–77 to 1881–82): 7 matches; 111 runs, average 10.09; 12 wickets, average 23.75

Alfred Shaw sent down the first ball to be bowled in Test cricket and appeared in seven of the first eight Test matches. He made two tours to North America and was involved with four tours of Australia, captaining the 1881–82 side. For a long period during his career he was, without question, supreme among slow bowlers, so relentlessly accurate that he bowled more overs in his career than he conceded runs.

A natural leader of men, with a strong personality, Shaw captained Nottinghamshire to four successive championship titles, 1883 to 1886, after which his connection with his native county virtually ended and he was employed to coach young Sussex cricketers. After six years' absence from county cricket, he reappeared for Sussex in 1894 at the age of 50.

He was a strong upholder of the rights of the professional cricketer and did much to help his fellow men. He refused to tour Australia with Grace's side in 1875 because the professionals were to be allowed only second-class facilities, and he led a strike of Nottinghamshire professionals six years later. His faction demanded a formal contract of employment which would guarantee an automatic benefit at the end of an agreed span of years. This was seen as anarchy by the Nottinghamshire committee who dropped the offenders, confirmed in their belief that it would be better to have an amateur captain. There was a reconciliation eventually, but Shaw's team-mates pointed out that the county went into rapid decline when he was no longer at the helm.

Bobby Simpson

Born: February 3, 1936, Marrickville, New South Wales, Australia

Teams: New South Wales (1952–53 to 1977–78); Western Australia (1956–57 to 1960–61)

First-class: 257 matches; 21,029 runs, average 56.22; 349 wickets, average 38.07

Tests (1957–58 to 1977–78): 62 matches; 4,869 runs, average 46.81; 71 wickets, average 42.26

A most dependable right-handed opening batsman, useful leg-break and googly bowler and one of the finest slip fielders the game has known, Bobby Simpson had a Test career that was divided into two distinct parts. When he became captain of Australia, 1963–64, he had not recorded a Test match century, and it was not until his second tour of England, 1964, in the fourth Test at Old Trafford, that Simpson reached three figures; it was his 52nd Test innings. He and Lawry put on 201 for the first wicket, and Simpson went on to score 311, the highest score by an Australian Test captain and the longest innings played against England, 762 minutes. He followed this with a century in each innings against Pakistan at Karachi, 1964–65. Three years later, he announced that he would retire at the end of the season. He scored hundreds in the first two Tests against India and stood down. Recalled for the fourth Test as a farewell gesture, he had match figures of eight for 97.

He became director of a successful public relations business, and it was believed his career was over. In 1977–78, however, Australian cricket was ravaged by the Packer affair and the defection of the leading players. Simpson came out of retirement to lead Australia against India. Superbly fit in his forties, he hit two Test centuries and won the series. He was less successful in the Caribbean, and with the war with Packer resolved, the Australian Board no longer had need of him.

He held strict, traditional values in attitude, fitness, dress and behaviour, and he became coach to Allan Border's side of the late 1980s. He also coached Leicestershire for two seasons.

John Snow

Born: October 13, 1941, Peopleton, Worcester

Teams: Sussex (1961–77)

First-class: 346 matches; 4,832 runs, average 14.17; 1,174 wickets, average 22.72

Tests (1965–76): 49 matches; 772 runs, average 13.54; 202 wickets, average 26.66

Among the greatest of English post-war fast bowlers, John Snow was also among the most moody and most prone to brushes with authority. While not possessing a classical action, he was rhythmical and intelligent. He was raw when he first played for England in 1965, and did not go to Australia the following winter. He took 12 wickets in three Tests against the West Indies, 1966, and played a major part in England's victory in the final Test, not least because he scored his maiden first-class fifty and shared a last-wicket stand of 128 in 140 minutes with Higgs.

In the West Indies, 1967–68, he was outstanding, taking seven for 79 at Kingston, 10 for 142 in the match at Georgetown, and finishing the series with 27 wickets in four Tests. Yet perhaps his greatest performance was in Australia with Illingworth's side, 1970–71, when England regained the Ashes and he took 31 wickets, including a Test-best seven for 40 at Sydney. Controversy struck the following summer when he barged into Gavaskar in the Lord's Test and was banned for one match. He lost his appetite for county cricket, joined World Series Cricket, published two volumes of poetry and an autobiography called *Cricket Rebel*. He played Sunday League cricket for Warwickshire in 1980.

Garfield Sobers

See Legends (pages 114.115)

F R Spofforth

Born: September, 1853, Balmain, Sydney, New South Wales, Australia
Died: June 4 1926, Ditton Hill Lodge, Long Ditton, Surrey
Teams: New South Wales (1874-75 to 1884-85); Victoria (1885-86 to 1887-88)
First-class: 155 matches; 1,928 runs, average 9.88; 853 wickets, average 14.95
Tests (1876-77 to 1886-87): 18 matches; 217 runs, average 9.43; 94 wickets, average 18.41

Tall, intelligent, able to vary speed, cut and swerve, Spofforth was basically a fast medium pace bowler. He refused to play in the first Test match of all in 1876-77 because his wicketkeeper Murdoch was not chosen, but he appeared in the second. It was in the third Test, January 1879, at Melbourne that he really made his mark, taking six for 48 and seven 62 as Australia won by 10 wickets. This came as no surprise, for "The Demon" had routed the MCC at Lord's in 1878, taking six for 4 and five for 16 as the Australians won in a day. His record in England was phenome-

nal, and in 1884 he took 207 wickets, averageing 12.82.

He had lost some of his demon by 1887 and emigrated to England the following year. He played for Derbyshire from 1889-91, captaining the side in 1890, but the county did not have first-class status at that time.

Brian Statham

Born: June 17, 1930, Gorton, Manchester, Lancashire
Died: June 10, 2000
Teams: Lancashire (1950–68)
First-class: 559 matches; 5,424 runs, average 19.80; 2,260 wickets, average 16.37
Tests (1950–51 to 1965): 70 matches; 675 runs, average 11.44; 252 wickets, average 24.84

For a period of more than 10 years, Statham was one of England's great opening bowlers, forming lethal partnerships with both Trueman and Tyson. He bowled right-arm with a fluid, easy action and was relentlessly accurate. He was honest, loyal and reliable, a great teamman who, reluctantly, captained Lancashire from 1965 to 1967.

Flown to Australia as a reinforcement, 1950–51, he made his Test debut in New Zealand and claimed Bert Sutcliffe as his first Test wicket. He did not really establish a regular place in the England side until the tour of the Caribbean, 1953–54, and it was in Australia a year later that he and Tyson bowled England to victory. A few months later, he showed the English public his prowess with a Test-best seven for 39 against South Africa at Lord's. He played for England until the Oval Test against South Africa, 1965, and in this last match took five for 40 and two for 105.

A left-handed batsman, he was capable of useful tail-end innings, and was a fine fielder in the deep. He took 100 wickets in a season 13 times and performed the hat-trick on three occasions.

Alec Stewart

Born: April 8, 1963, Merton, Surrey
Teams: Surrey (1981–03)
First-class: 447 matches; 26,165 runs, average 40.06; caught 721, stumped 32

Tests (1989–90 to 2003): 133 matches; 8,463 runs, average 39.54; caught 263, stumped 13

The son of Surrey and England opening batsman Mickey Stewart, Alec comes from an all-round sporting family. He joined the Surrey staff in 1981 as a wicket-keeper/batsman, making his debut that season and also developing his game during the winter in Western Australian grade cricket. A superb timer of the ball, he relied on a good eye, and scored heavily through the covers and off the back foot. It was not until he was nearly 27, however, that he forced himself into the Test team, touring the West Indies in 1989-90. With Surrey colleague Jack Richards established behind the stumps, he was picked as a batsman, although was deputy wicket-keeper on the tour to Australia and New Zealand in 1990-91.

He was slow to get going in Tests, and was picked only for the fifth Test against West Indies in 1991, when he was also asked to keep wicket. In the Test with Sri Lanka which followed, he was chosen as a batsman and made his first Test century at number three. He was vice-captain to Gooch on the tour to New Zealand in 1991-92, then after an excellent World Cup he made 190 in the first Test against Pakistan and in the second at Lord's became the sixth Englishman to carry his bat in a Test. When Gooch was ill, he captained England in a Test in India in 1992-93, and for the following Test in Sri Lanka. The selectors, how-

ever, could never decide whether to play Stewart as a pure batsman or as wicket-keeper batsman, at which times his form with the bat slightly declined, and it was uncertainty over his role which led to Atherton, not him, replacing Gooch as captain. Played as an opener only in West Indies in 1993-94 he was superb, scoring 118 and 143 at Bridgetown to enable England to inflict a first defeat on West Indies there in 59 years. Stewart improved his Test average to an excellent 46 before reverting once again to becoming England's regular keeper, since when his average has steadily dropped to just below 40.

Long captain of Surrey, Alec Stewart became captain of England in 1998 and retained the highest standards in all three of his roles. After being succeeded by Nasser Hussain, he was named Man of the Match in his 100th Test, coming in on a hat-trick and scoring 105 against West Indies at Old Trafford in August 2000. Whether ranked as a batsman or as a wicket-keeper/batsman, Alec Stewart is among the best the world has seen.

Bert Sutcliffe

Born: November 17, 1923, Ponsonby, Auckland, New Zealand
Died: April 20, 2001, Auckland, New Zealand
Teams: Auckland (1941–42 to 1948–79); Otago (1946–47 to 1961–62); Northern Districts (1962–63 to 1965–66)
First-class: 233 matches; 17,447 runs, average 47.41; 86 wickets, average 38.05

SNOW *Poet who destroyed Australia with fast bowling in 1970–71.*

Tests (1946–47 to 1965): 42 matches; 2,727 runs, average 40.10; 4 wickets, average 86.00

Bert Sutcliffe was the finest New Zealand cricketer of his generation and must rank as one of the best left-handed batsmen of the period. He had a cheerful disposition, and was a thing of beauty with a bat in his hands. He was stylish, correct and joyful. He made his Test debut in March 1947, when he shared an opening stand of 133 with Walter Hadlee against England. Sutcliffe made 58, and his class was obvious. He was an outstanding success in England in 1949, scoring 2,627 runs on the tour and averaging 60.42 in the Tests with a century at Old Trafford. In 1952–53 he hit 385 for Otago against Canterbury, and three years earlier had hit 355 for Otago against Auckland. These remain the two highest individual scores to be made in New Zealand.

He captained New Zealand in four Tests between 1951 and 1954, but captaincy was not a job he relished, and it is significant that his best Test score, 230 not out against India in Delhi, 1955–56, came after he had relinquished the leadership.

Sutcliffe retired from Test cricket in 1958–59, but was persuaded to return in 1967. He made 151 against India in Calcutta, but was 42 years old. He proved to be a fine coach.

Herbert Sutcliffe

Born: November 24, 1894, Summerbridge, Harrogate, Yorkshire
Died: January 22, 1978, Cross Hills, Yorkshire
Teams: Yorkshire (1919–45)
First-class: 754 matches; 50,670 runs, average 52.02; 14 wickets, average 41.21
Tests (1924–35): 54 matches; 4,555 runs, average 60.73

Herbert Sutcliffe's career fits neatly into the period between the two wars, and he averaged 1,000 runs in a season every year from 1919 to 1939. He made only a brief appearance in 1945. He was unquestionably one of the greatest opening batsman of all time with an outstanding Test record. Technically sound, neat, determined and totally unflappable, he batted right-handed, was at home on any wicket and shaped his game

to the occasion. His opening partnership with Hobbs in the England side is legendary, and his county partnership with Holmes was equally famous. He was mentor to the young Len Hutton.

The first of his 15 three-figure Test opening partnerships with Hobbs came in his debut Test against South Africa, in 1924. In the next match, they put on 268, and Sutcliffe made 122, the first of his 16 Test centuries. He scored a century in his first match against Australia, a century in each innings in his second, and in the fourth match of the series became the first batsman to hit four centuries in a rubber. Most famously, at the Oval, 1926, when England regained the Ashes, Hobbs and Sutcliffe made 172 on a sticky wicket. Sutcliffe ended with 161.

In 1930, at Leyton, Sutcliffe and Holmes scored a world-record 555 for the first wicked against Essex. Sutcliffe made 313. His last Test was against South Africa at Lord's in 1935, although many felt he should have been retained longer. Once offered the captaincy of Yorkshire, he refused, unwilling to break the amateur tradition.

T

Maurice Tate

Born: May 30, 1895, Brighton, Sussex
Died: May 18, 1956, Wadhurst, Sussex
Teams: Sussex (1912–1937)
First-class: 679 matches; 21,717 runs, average 25.04; 2,784 wickets, average 18.16
Tests (1924–35): 39 matches; 1,198 runs, average 25.48; 155 wickets, average 26.16

Son of a Sussex cricketer who played one match for England, Maurice Tate was a great medium-pace right-arm bowler and a great character. He began as an off-break bowler, but became a seam bowler of brisk pace after the Second World War. Some insisted his deliveries gathered pace off the wicket. Few bowlers have used the seam to such good effect; very few have been as popular. He was also a most capable lower middle-order batsman, good enough, in fact, to score 100 not out against South Africa at Lord's in 1929.

Tate's Test debut was sensational. At Edgbaston, 1924, he and Arthur Gilligan bowled South Africa out for 30 in 12.3 overs. Tate took four for 12 and had five for 83 in the second innings. He took 30 wickets in the series, and created a record with 38 wickets in Australia the following winter. He was England's leading bowler of the time before the pace of Larwood.

He completed the "double" eight times, and in three of those seasons his 1,000 runs were coupled with 200 wickets. He was held in great affection by the public.

Hugh Tayfield

Born: January 30, 1929, Durban, South Africa
Died: February 25, 1994, Pietermaritzburg, South Africa
Teams: Natal (1945–46 to 1946–47); Rhodesia (1947–48 to 1948–49); Transvaal (1956–57 to 1962–63)
First-class: 187 matches; 3,668 runs, average 17.30; 864 wickets, average 21.86
Tests (1949–50 to 1960): 37 matches; 862 runs, average 16.90; 170 wickets, average 25.91

Hugh Tayfield was a very fine off-break bowler whose 170 wickets in Test cricket remains a South African record. He played in all five Tests against Australia 1949–50, and took seven for 23 at Durban when he and Mann bowled the opposition out for 75. Surprisingly not chosen for the tour of England in 1951, he was flown out as a replacement but did not play in a Test. In Australia in 1952–53 he thrived with a record 30 wickets, and at Melbourne he bowled South Africa to victory with 13 for 165 in the match.

Success continued unabated, and when South Africa came to England in 1955 he became the first bowler from that country to take 100 Test wickets. He took 26 wickets in the series and had astonishing figures in the second innings at the Oval when he took five for 60 in 53.4 overs of which 29 were maidens. England suffered more at his hands in South Africa, 1956–57, when he established a record with 37 wickets in the rubber, including his career-best nine for 113 in Johannesburg.

HERBERT SUTCLIFFE *Imperturbable.*

Mark Taylor

Born: October 27, 1964, Leeton, New South Wales, Australia
Teams: New South Wales (1985–86 to 1998–99)
First-class: 253 matches; 17,415 runs, average 41.95; 2 wickets, average 38.50
Tests (1988–89 to 1998–99): 104 matches; 7,525 runs, average 43.49; 1 wicket, average 26.00

A left-handed opening batsman and brilliant slip fielder, he forced his way into the Australian side against the West Indies in 1988–89, and scored 136 in his first Test against England the following summer. He and Geoff Marsh became a formidable opening pair and, at Trent Bridge, they established a record with a stand of 329. Taylor hit 219. He finished the series with 839 runs, an aggregate exceeded only by Bradman and Hammond in rubbers between England and Australia.

When Marsh retired, Taylor continued to flourish with Slater as his partner, and he succeeded Border as Australia's captain. He helped maintain Australia's supremacy in world cricket with home and away series victories against the West Indies and triumph over Atherton's side, 1994–95.

After a period of bad form – whilst captain of the 1997 Australian side to England, he actually dropped himself from the One Day squad – he ended his Test career in a blaze of glory, whilst captaining the country to Pakistan. Australia won the series and Taylor hit 334 not out in the second Test at Peshawar. Returning to Australia he announced his retirement and took a job promoting the Sydney Olympics.

Sachin Tendulkar

See Legends (pages 116–117)

Jeff Thomson

Born: August 16, 1950, Greenacre, Sydney, New South Wales, Australia
Teams: New South Wales (1972–74); Queensland (1974–75 to 1985–86); Middlesex (1981)
First-class: 187 matches; 2,065 runs, average 13.58; 675 wickets, average 26.46
Tests (1972–73 to 1985): 51 matches; 679 runs, average 12.81; 200 wickets, average 28.00

Jeff Thomson made an inauspicious start in Test cricket when he played against Pakistan, 1972–73, but two years later, after he had moved to Queensland, the selectors recalled him. The result was devastating as he and Lillee, with whom his name was to be permanently associated, demolished England. Thomson, bowling at a great pace, took three for 59 and six for 46. He finished the series with 33 wickets in nine innings. A few weeks later he was in England for the World Cup and a four-match series, and, if not quite so potent as in Australia, he and Lillee again destroyed England. Back in Australia the following winter, 1975–76, he and Lillee outbowled their West Indian counterparts and swept Australia to a 5–1 series victory.

Thomson joined World Series Cricket, then retracted, and then rejoined. He played for Middlesex in 1981, but injury restricted him to eight matches. He was recalled to the Test scene in 1985 after three years' absence, but the old bite had gone.

Graham Thorpe

Born: August 1, 1969, Farnham, Surrey
Teams: Surrey (1988–2005)
First-class: 341 matches; 21,937 runs, average 45.04; 26 wickets, average 53.00
Tests (1993–2005): 100 matches; 6,744 runs, average 44.66; no wickets for 37 runs

A left-handed batsman and right-arm medium-pace bowler who has repaid the faith shown in him initially by chairman of selectors, Ted Dexter, and county captain, Ian Greig, Graham Thorpe made his Test debut against Australia, 1993, and hit 114 not out.

He was the veteran of several "A" tours before winning his first Test cap, and held his place in the Surrey side because his bowling was considered useful even when he was not scoring runs. Once in the Test side, he displayed admirable temperament and confirmed that he was the most reliable of batsmen. He hit 123 against Australia at Perth, 1994–95, and was England's leading run-scorer against the West Indies the following summer. An indifferent run throughout 1996 was ended with centuries in successive Tests in New Zealand early in 1997.

His Test career was rather hampered by injury, but he maintained his batting form. Against Pakistan in the 2001 series in England he topped the averages, only to miss all but one Test in the series immediately following versus Australia.

Frederick Trueman

Born: February 6, 1931, Stainton, Yorkshire
Teams: Yorkshire (1949–68)
First-class: 603 matches; 9,231 runs, average 15.56; 2,304 wickets, average 18.29
Tests (1952–65): 67 matches; 981 runs, average 13.81; 307 wickets, average 21.57

A genuine, whole-hearted fast bowler whose belligerence made him feared by batsmen and whose outspokenness and reputation caused him to clash with authority more than once and to miss tours and Tests he might have played in, Freddie Trueman was one of the game's great bowlers, fit to rank alongside Hadlee, Lillee and the rest.

Initial raw pace was augmented by subtlety, and he made a dramatic entry into Test cricket, 1952. He took three Indian wickets for 89 in the first innings and four for 27 in the second. Three of these came in eight balls and left India 0 for 4. This was on his home ground of Headingley, and there were eight wickets at Lord's and nine at Old Trafford where his first-innings eight for 31 remains the best analysis against India and was the best of Trueman's Test career. Another five wickets in a rain-ruined final Test gave 29 for the series.

Thereafter things did not go so smoothly. He helped England regain the Ashes, 1953, with four for 86 in the deciding match of the series, but it was the only Test in which he appeared. He fared poorly in the Caribbean and gained adverse publicity, with the result that he missed the tour of Australia, 1954–55, and it was not until 1957 that he re-established himself and was a permanent fixture in the England side.

For Yorkshire, Trueman was a leading force throughout his career. He took 100 wickets in a season 12 times and did the hat-trick four times. He was in seven championship-winning sides, and Yorkshire did not take the title again until 2001. He was a very useful aggressive batsman and a brilliant close-to-the-wicket fielder.

At the Oval, 1964, Neil Hawke, the Australian, was caught at slip by Cowdrey off Trueman who thereby became the first bowler in Test history to take 300 wickets. His international career ended the following season.

Trueman played Sunday League matches for Derbyshire, 1972, and became a noted commentator and much in demand as an after-dinner speaker.

Hugh Trumble

Born: May 12 1867, Abbotsford, Melbourne, Australia
Died: August 14 1938, Hawthorne, Melbourne, Australia
Teams: Victoria (1887-88 to 1903-04)
First-class: 213 matches; 5,395 runs, average 19.47; 929 wickets, average 18.44
Tests (1890 to 1903-04): 32 matches; 851 runs, average 19.79; 141 wickets, average 21.78

Hugh Trumble was a right-arm medium pace off-break bowler and sound middle order batsman. He had prominent ears and a large nose, and he usually wore a large stetson. Grace said he was the best bowler Australia had ever sent to England, and Fry believed him to be not only one of the greatest bowlers but a master of ield placing and a wonderful judge of the game. The first of his five tours to England was in 1890 when he did little, but thereafter he was immensely successful. In 1901-02 he performed the hat trick at Melbourne against England, and two years later, on the same ground, he again did the hat trick when he took seven English wickets for 28 in what proved to be his last first class match.

At the Oval, 1902, he took eight for 65 and four for 108, and scored 64 not out and 7 not out to become the first Australian to take 10 wickets and score 50 runs in a Test. He captained Australia in two Tests.

Victor Trumper

Born: November 2, 1877, Darlinghurst, Sydney, New South Wales, Australia
Died: June 28, 1915, Darlinghurst, Sydney, New South Wales, Australia
Teams: New South Wales (1894–95 to 1913–14)
First-class: 255 matches; 16,939 runs, average 44.57; 64 wickets, average 31.37
Tests (1899 to 1911–12): 48 matches; 3,163 runs, average 39.04; 8 wickets, average 39.62

Trumper's figures cannot compare with those of Bradman, yet there is a unanimity of opinion that he was the greatest batsman Australia produced before the arrival of Don. Right-handed, effortless, perfectly balanced, supple, he moved into his shots with a grace that bewitched all who saw him. He was modest, kindly and immensely popular. Arthur Mailey described the effect that Trumper had on people when he recalled, as a junior, bowling the great man and feeling he that he had killed a dove. He scored 0 and 11 in his first Test, and in his second, at Lord's, he made a chanceless unbeaten 135. He was 21.

By the end of that tour, he was opening the innings, and when Australia arrived in England in 1902 he was supreme. At Old Trafford, he reached his century in 108 minutes before lunch on the first day.

In 1903–04, at Sydney, he reached his century in 94 minutes and, batting number five, he got 185 not out. He made another century in the same series. Seven years later, South Africa visited Australia, and Trumper scored 159 at Melbourne and 214 not out, a Test record for Australia at the time, at Adelaide. He died of Bright's disease in 1915, and a country mourned.

Charles Turner

Born: November 16, 1862, Bathurst, New South Wales, Australia
Died: January 1, 1944, Manly, Sydney, New South Wales, Australia
Teams: New South Wales (1882–83 to 1909–10)
First-class: 155 matches; 3,856 runs, average 15.54; 993 wickets, average 14.25
Tests (1886–87 to 1894–95): 17 matches; 323 runs, average 11.53; 101 wickets, average 16.53

Short and thick-set, Turner bowled fast-medium and shot to fame when he took 17 wickets against Alfred Shaw's England side in 1881–82. This feat was for Twenty-two of Bathurst, and by the following season he was in the state side. On the occasion of his Test debut at Sydney, 1887, he took six for 15 as England were bowled out for 45, their lowest-ever score against Australia. From this moment, the legend of "Turner the Terror" was born. In his next two Tests against England, he took nine wickets and 12 wickets, and his first three Tests in England, 1888, brought him 21 wickets in four innings. Yet England won the series.

He formed a lethal partnership with Ferris, and on that 1888 tour they took 534 wickets between them in all matches. In 1887–88, Turner had become the first bowler to take 100 wickets in an Australian season.

In 1894–95, having taken 11 wickets in two Tests against England, he was dropped. Reinstated for the fourth Test, he took seven wickets as Australia won by an innings, but he was dropped again. Belatedly receiving an invitation to tour England, 1896, he declined through pressure of business and passed from Test cricket.

Glenn Turner

Born: May 26, 1947, Dunedin, New Zealand
Teams: Otago (1964–65 to 1982–83); Northern Districts (1976–77); Worcestershire (1967–82)
First-class: 455 matches; 34,346 runs, average 49.70; 5 wickets, average 37.80
Tests (1968–69 to 1982–83): 41 matches; 2.991 runs, average 44.64; no wickets for 5 runs

Glenn Turner is arguably the greatest batsman New Zealand has ever produced - and certainly the country's best professional. He is the only New Zealand batsman to have scored more than 30,000 runs in his career and the only New Zealand batsman to have scored a hundred centuries (103). His 100th hundred came in his last season with Worcestershire, 1982, when he hit the highest score of his career, 311 not out against Warwickshire at Worcester.

Turner was the total professional cricketer. He dedicated himself to cricket, working tirelessly to earn his fare to England and joining Worcestershire to learn the game in the hard round of county cricket. He never forgot a lesson, and he developed from the "strokeless wonder" of his early days to a free-scoring opening batsman capable of making runs as quickly as anybody.

TRUEMAN *First to 300 Test wickets.*

He began his Test career with a "duck" against the West Indies, 1968–69, but in his second Test he hit 74, and New Zealand won. His first Test century came in Pakistan in November 1969, when he batted over seven hours for 110.

It was in the 1971–72 series in the Caribbean that Turner established himself as one of the most accomplished batsmen in world cricket. He hit 672 runs in the series, including two double-centuries, average 96.

On the tour of England, 1973, he reached a thousand runs by the end of May, the only New Zealander to have achieved the feat, but he disappointed in the Test series. He led New Zealand in the World Cup, 1975, and in the series against India which followed.

In 1978, he decided to give all his efforts to Worcestershire, and the first rift occurred between Turner and the New Zealand authorities. He did return to Test cricket, but his relationship with the New Zealand Board was never an easy one. He saw them as amateurs in a professional world.

He subsequently managed and coached New Zealand sides, but he was replaced in 1997, mainly because many considered him too authoritarian and too demanding while stinting with praise.

Whatever his failings as a coach,

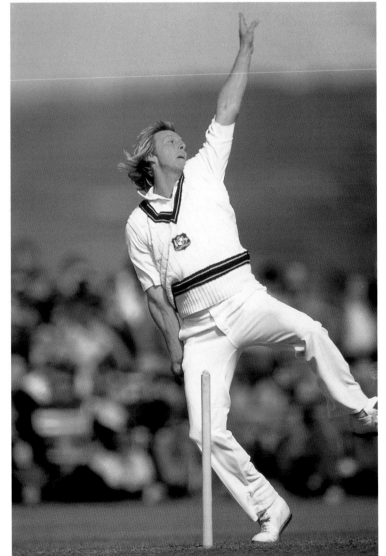

JEFF THOMSON *With Lillee he formed a devastating partnership.*

Glenn Turner remains one of the most dedicated, most professional and most successful cricketers in New Zealand's history, and it is unlikely that his records will ever be beaten.

Frank Tyson

Born: June 6, 1930, Farnworth, Lancashire

Teams: Northamptonshire (1952–60)

First-class: 244 matches; 4,103 runs, average 17.09; 767 wickets, average 20.89

Tests (1954 to 1958–59): 17 matches; 230 runs, average 10.95; 76 wickets, average 18.56

Tall and strong, "Typhoon" Tyson was, for all too brief a period, the most aggressive and lethal fast bowler in the world. His exceptional speed was recognized from the start of his career, but his run-up was excessive and his accuracy was not always to be relied upon. He was chosen to tour Australia in 1954–55 ahead of Freddie Trueman, and made his Test debut against Pakistan shortly before the party left for the southern hemisphere. He took four wickets in the first innings, but England lost.

In the first Test, at Brisbane, he took one for 160, and England lost by an innings, but, in the second match, at Sydney, he had four for 45 and six for 85. He bowled with amazing stamina and great speed, and England won a remarkable victory. He took seven for 27 and his place in history was assured when England went on to win their first rubber in Australia for 22 years and so retain the Ashes. He bowled with considerable success against South Africa the following summer, but wear and tear and injuries took their toll, and he played in only a handful of Tests before his retirement.

An English graduate from Durham University, he settled in Australia where he taught, coached, wrote and commentated.

Polly Umrigar

Born: March 28, 1926, Sholapur, Maharashtra, India

Teams: Parsees (1944–45 to 1945–46);

Bombay (1946–47 to 1962–63); Gujarat (1950–51 to 1951–52)

First-class: 243 matches; 16,155 runs, average 52.28; 325 wickets, average 25.68

Tests (1948–49 to 1961–62): 59 matches; 3,631 runs, average 42.22; 35 wickets, average 42.08

A tall, forceful batsman, medium-pace bowler and splendid fielder, "Polly" Umrigar was a dashing cricketer who led Bombay to five successive Ranji Trophy triumphs at the beginning of their period of dominance in the competition. He was the leading Indian batsman of his generation and made his Test debut in 1948, but he had to wait until the last match of the series against England, 1951–52, for his second cap. He hit 130 not out, India won by an innings and Umrigar's international career was launched.

He had a wretched time in England, 1952, as did other Indian batsmen, but he topped the averages in the inaugural series with Pakistan, 1952–53. In the first Test against New Zealand at Hyderabad, 1955–56, he made India's first double-century in Test cricket, 223. He later took over the captaincy and won the series. He led India in eight Tests, and hit 12 Test centuries.

Derek Underwood

Born: June 8, 1945, Bromley, Kent

Teams: Kent (1963–87)

First-class: 676 matches; 5,165 runs, average 10.12; 2,465 wickets, average 20.28

Tests (1966 to 1981–82): 86 matches; 937 runs, average 11.56; 297 wickets, average 25.83

Derek Underwood was the leading spin bowler in England for nearly 20 years. Left-arm, he bowled at a pace quicker than most spinners, but he combined accuracy with variety and was a danger to batsmen on any wicket. His career began sensationally for he was the youngest player to take 100 wickets in his debut season, but he was wicketless on his Test debut, against the West Indies, three years later. The following year, 1967, he had his first five-wicket Test haul, against Pakistan, and in the final match of the Ashes series, 1968, bowled England to victory at the Oval with seven for 50 in the second innings.

He continued to thrive, and on a damp wicket he was unplayable. He established records against New Zealand, and at Lord's, 1974, became the only English bowler to take 13 wickets in a Test against Pakistan. His eight for 51 in the second innings was a record.

His partnership with wicket-keeper Knott was vital and, but for the fact that Underwood became involved with World Series Cricket and a rebel tour to South Africa, he might well have become the leading wicket-taker in Test cricket.

V

Alf Valentine

Born: April 28, 1930, Kingston, Jamaica

Died: May 11, 2004, Orlando, Florida, USA

Teams: Jamaica (1949–50 to 1964–65)

First-class: 125 matches; 470 runs, average 5.00; 475 wickets, average 26.21

Tests (1950 to 1961–62): 36 matches; 141 runs, average 4.70; 139 wickets, average 30.32

Tall and slim, Alf Valentine was a slow left-arm spinner who arrived in England in 1950 with little experience of first-class cricket. He was to take 123 wickets on the tour, 33 of them in Tests. He began with eight for 104 and three for 100 at Old Trafford, but the West Indies lost. The sensation came at Lord's when he and Ramadhin bowled the West Indies to a famous victory and were celebrated in a calypso.

He showed his real quality with 24 wickets in Australia, 1951–52, when his six for 102 in the second innings in Adelaide gave West Indies their sole victory in the series. He was equally successful against India, 1952–53, but he had declined by the time England went to the Caribbean the following year, and he was ineffective in England in 1957 and 1963.

Michael Vaughan

Born: October 29, 1974, Manchester, Lancashire

Teams: Yorkshire (1993–2005)

First-class: 225 matches; 14,289 runs, average 38.41; 114 wickets,

average 45.10

Tests (1999–2000 to 2005): 62 matches; 4,513 runs, average 43.81; 6 wickets, average 89.50

Because Vaughan's family moved from Manchester to Sheffield it was with Yorkshire that he became a gritty, unspectacular middle-order batsman. Although he won an Under-15 Cricketer of the Year award and was England Under-19 captain, the unfriendly pitches at Headingley formed a cautious style which probably delayed his Test debut until 1999–2000. He was encouraged to develop a more aggressive style by Yorkshire's Australia player Darren Lehmann, transforming his batting and success, especially after he first opened for England in New Zealand in 2001–02. In 14 Tests in 2002 he was England's most reliable batsman, scoring 1,481 runs, average 61.70, with six centuries. Another century in the final Ashes match at Sydney early in 2003 gave him 633 runs for the series, average 58.20, and the Player of the Series award.

He took over from Nasser Hussain as England captain after the first Test of the 2003 season, and led England to a 3–0 series win in the West Indies in 2003–04. In 2005, he captained England in the victorious Ashes series.

Dilip Vengsarkar

Born: April 6, 1956, Rajapur, Bombay, India

Teams: Bombay (1975–76 to 1991–92)

First-class: 260 matches; 17,868 runs, average 52.86; 1 wicket, average 126.00

Tests (1975–76 to 1991–92): 116 matches; 6,868 runs, average 42.13; no wickets for 36 runs.

For a decade only Sunil Gavaskar stood ahead of Dilip Vengsarkar as India's most prolific run-scorer in Test history, and only Gavaskar had scored more Test centuries for India than Vengsarkar's 17. He was a batsman of true quality, an artist and fluent stroke-maker who was rushed into the Test side as an opener before his 20th birthday, but who settled to become India's regular number three. In 1976–77, he had his hand broken by a ball from Bob Willis, but he established himself in Australia the following season. In

1978–79, he scored two Test centuries against the West Indies, and, in Calcutta, where he made an unbeaten 157, he and Gavaskar shared a record unbroken stand of 344 for the second wicket.

In 1979, he made a century in the Lord's Test, and was to repeat this feat in 1982 and 1986 to establish a record. India won the Lord's Test in 1986, and Vengsarkar followed his century with 61 and 102 not out in difficult conditions at Headingley to help India clinch the series. He captained India in 10 Tests and scored centuries against all nations he faced, with the exception of New Zealand.

S. Venkataraghavan

Born: April 21, 1945, Madras, India
Teams: Madras/Tamil Nadu (1963–64 to 1984–85); Derbyshire (1973–75)
First-class: 341 matches; 6,617 runs, average 17.73; 1,390 wickets, average 24.14
Tests (1964–65 to 1983–84): 57 matches; 748 runs, average 11.68; 156 wickets, average 36.11
An intelligent off-break and fine close-to-the-wicket fielder, Venkataraghavan made his Test debut against New Zealand, 1964–65, and in the fourth and final Test of the series he produced his best performance in international cricket, taking eight for 72 and four for 80 to bowl India to victory. For much of his Test career he vied with Prasanna for the off-spinner's spot in the Indian side, but Venkataraghavan bowled well on the 1971 tour of England and played an important role in India's victory in the series. He captained India in the World Cup, 1975, and on the tour of England, 1979.

He had productive years with Derbyshire, taking 68 wickets in 1975. He took up umpiring after retiring, and is now recognised as one of the world's leading umpires.

Hedley Verity

Born: May 18, 1905, Headingley, Leeds, Yorkshire
Died: July 31, 1943, Caserta, Italy
Teams: Yorkshire (1930–39)
First-class: 378 matches; 5,605 runs, average 18.08; 1,956 wickets, average 14.90
Tests (1931–1939): 40 matches; 669 runs, average 20.90; 144 wickets, average 24.37
The strength of Yorkshire cricket was founded on sound batting and on great slow left-arm bowlers – Peate, Peel, Rhodes and, in the 1930s, Hedley Verity. Quicker than many of his type, Verity was relentlessly accurate and could spin the ball viciously. He was an intelligent cricketer, dignified and equable of temperament, who took 100 wickets in a season nine times. In 1935, 1936 and 1937, he exceeded 200 wickets.

On a damp pitch at Lord's in 1934, he took 14 Australian wickets in a day, 15 for 104 in the match, and bowled England to an innings victory. He was a key member of the England side for seven years.

At Headingley, in 1932, he took all 10 Nottinghamshire wickets for 10 runs, a world record which remains unequalled. He had taken all ten Warwickshire wickets on the same ground the previous season.

On September 1, 1939, he took 7 for 9 as Yorkshire beat Sussex at Hove. During the war, he was commissioned in the Green Howards and was wounded leading his men in an 8th Army attack in Sicily during the invasion of Italy in 1943, and died of his wounds some days later.

Gundappa Viswanath

Born: February 12, 1949, Bhadravati, Mysore, India
Teams: Mysore/Karnataka (1967–68 to 1987–88)
First-class: 308 matches; 17,970 runs, average 40.93; 15 wickets, average 48.60
Tests (1969–70 to 1982–83): 91 matches; 6,080 runs, average 41.93; 1 wicket, average 46.00
Brother-in-law to Sunil Gavaskar, Viswanath was a most attractive and attacking middle-order batsman who hit 230 in 340 minutes on the occasion of his first-class debut for Mysore against Andhra. In 1969–70, he made his Test debut for India against Australia at Kanpur. He was out for 0 in the first innings and made 137 in the second. It was the first of 14 Test hundreds, and only against Sri Lanka did he fail to score a century. He played in a record 87 consecutive Tests for India and captained them on two occasions.

A kind and gentle man, characteristics reflected in his delightful batting, he toured England four times and played in all the Tests on those tours, but his highest Test score came at Madras, 1981–82, when he hit 316 with Yashpal Sharma. His 222 was, at the time, the highest score made by an Indian batsman against England. After retiring as a player, Vishwanatah became chairman of the Indian selectors.

VALENTINE *11 wickets on Test debut.*

Clyde Walcott

Born: January 17, 1926, New Orleans, St Michael, Barbados
Teams: Barbados (1941–42 to 1955–56); British Guiana (1954–55 to 1963–64)
First-class: 146 matches; 11,820 runs, average 56.55; 35 wickets, average 36.25; caught 174, stumped 33
Tests (1947–48 to 1959–60): 44 matches; 3,798 runs, average 56.68; 11 wickets, average 37.00; caught 53, stumped 11
In the years immediately after the Second World War, the West Indies were powered by three great batsmen: the Three Ws, Worrell, Weekes, and Walcott. In 1945–46, Walcott and Worrell added an unbroken 574 for Barbados's fourth wicket against Trinidad. It was just a sample of what was to come. Walcott was a giant of a man who could hit with tremendous power and could play all the shots. He was also a capable wicket-keeper who kept to Ramadhin and Valentine, an excellent slip and a useful medium-pace bowler.

At Lord's, 1950, he scored 168 not out in the second Test and shared a record stand of 211 with Gomez for the sixth wicket. He also dominated the series against England, 1953–54, and against Australia, 1954–55. He made three centuries against England, the highest being 220 at Bridgetown, and against Australia

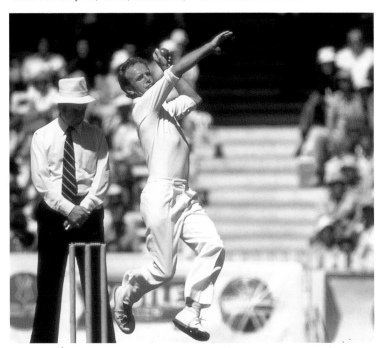
UNDERWOOD *Sometimes unplayable spinner whose pace approached medium.*

he hit five centuries in the series, scoring a century in each innings of the second and fifth Tests, even though Australia took the rubber by three matches to nil. In all, he hit 15 Test centuries, and his highest score in first-class cricket was the 314 not out he scored during his record partnership with Worrell, 1945–46, when he was 20 years old.

He played in the Lancashire League in the 1950s, managed several West Indian sides after his retirement and was awarded the OBE for his services to the game. He coached and commentated and was President of the West Indian Board for some years. He became Chairman of the International Cricket Council and was knighted in 1994.

Courtney Walsh

Born: October 30, 1962, Kingston, Jamaica

Teams: Jamaica (1981–82 to 2000–01); Gloucestershire (1984–98)

First-class: 429 matches; 4,530 runs, average 11.32; 1,807 wickets, average 21.71

Tests (1984–85 to 2000–01): 132 matches; 936 runs, average 7.54; 519 wickets, average 24.44

A right-arm fast bowler with a high-action and economic style, Courtney Walsh has enhanced his talent as a bowler by remaining consistent and durable over a number of years, and he not only overtook Malcolm Marshall as West Indies' leading Test wicket-taker, but went on to top Kapil Dev's all-time Test record. Deeply respected as a player, he has become, in turn, captain of Jamaica, Gloucestershire and the West Indies. He toured England in 1984 without playing in a Test, but appeared in all five matches in Australia the following winter. With the West Indies having such a battery of fast bowlers at their disposal, it was hard for Walsh to maintain a regular place in the side, but he had an outstanding tour of India, 1987–88, with 26 wickets in four Tests. Initially, he rarely had use of the new ball, but he took wickets regularly.

Walsh became the first player in Test cricket to reach 500 wickets. This milestone came in the Second Test v South Africa at Port of Spain in March 2001. He retired at the end of the series; once more he had been the leading wicket taker for his country. On his final tour to England in 2000 he also headed the bowling with the magnificent figures of 40 wickets, average 11.42. Just as he served the West Indies he was a brilliant player in county cricket. In 1998, his last season for Gloucestershire he took 106 Championship wickets, average 17.31 and topped the English first-class averages.

Doug Walters

Born: December 21, 1945, Marshdale, Dungog, New South Wales, Australia

Teams: New South Wales (1962–63 to 1980–81)

First-class: 258 matches; 16,180 runs, average 43.84; 190 wickets, average 35.69

Tests (1965–77 to 1980–81): 74 matches; 5,357 runs, average 48.26; 49 wickets, average 29.08

Doug Walters was an attacking right-handed batsman who delighted with his stroke-play and his sense of adventure. He was also a successful medium-pace bowler. He triumphed in Australia, but crowds in England and South Africa never saw the best of him. He burst upon the scene with 155 on his debut against England at Brisbane, 1965–77, and made 115 in his second Test, at Melbourne. On leave from national service, 1967–68, he made 93, 62 not out, 94 and run out 5 against India. Released for the tour of England, 1968, he was not a success, and made three more trips without doing himself justice. He was impetuous, a weakness that bowlers exploited by attacking his off-stump. Elsewhere he thrived.

Against the West Indies in Australia, 1968–69, he scored 118, 110, 50, 242 and 103 in successive Test innings to become the first to score four centuries in a rubber against the West Indies. At Christchurch, 1976–77, he made 250 against New Zealand, his highest Test score. In all, he made 15 Test hundreds.

Waqar Younis

Born: November 16, 1971, Vehari, Pakistan

Teams: Multan (1987–88 to 1990–91 and 1997–98); United Bank (1988–89 to 1996–97); Rawalpindi (1998–99); Redco (1999–00); Surrey (1990–93); Glamorgan (1997–98); National Bank (2001–02); Warwickshire (2003)

First-class: 228 matches; 2,972 runs, average 13.38; 956 wickets, average 22.33

Tests (1989–90 to 2002–03): 87 matches; 1,010 runs, average 10.20; 373 wickets, average 23.56

Many believe Waqar Younis is the best fast bowler to have appeared in Test cricket since the Second World War. He is able to move the ball late both ways at great pace and possesses a deadly yorker. In 1991, playing for Surrey on the unresponsive wickets at the Oval, he was the leading bowler in England with 113 wickets. His Test debut against India at Karachi, 1989–90, had seen him take four for 80, and by the time he had played 10 Tests he had 50 victims to his credit. With Wasim Akram, he formed a lethal partnership for Pakistan which is now accepted as one of the great fast-bowling duos of all time. Waqar took a record 29 wickets in a three-match series against New Zealand, 1990–91, and his 100th victim came in his 20th Test. He routed England with a record 22 wickets, 1992, and was devastating again in 1996.

He had a second spell in Championship cricket, for Glamorgan in 1997 and 1998, but in the latter season, he played only four matches before being sent home with an elbow injury. Since then he has not been so successful for Pakistan, though he did play in the 1999 World Cup and captained his country on their 2001 tour of England – his seven wickets in that Test series cost 35 runs each.

Johnny Wardle

Born: January 8, 1923, Ardsley, Yorkshire

Died: July 23, 1985, Hatfield, Doncaster, Yorkshire

Teams: Yorkshire (1946–58)

First-class: 412 matches; 7,333 runs, average 16.08; 1,846 wickets, average 18.97

Tests (1947–48 to 1957): 28 matches; 653 runs, average 19.78; 102 wickets, average 20.39

Johnny Wardle was the best left-arm wrist spinner of his generation, one in a long line of great Yorkshire slow left-arm bowlers. He had an infinite variety of deliveries in his armoury and was a wicket-taker on any surface. He was a hard-hitting later-order batsman and a keen fielder. He made his Test debut on the 1947–48 tour of the West Indies, but was poorly used by G.O. Allen, and his Test appearances were to remain intermittent for some seasons as he vied first with Jack Young and then with Tony Lock. He played in the first three Tests in 1953 when England regained the Ashes and captured 13 wickets, but he gave way to Lock for the last two Tests.

He was outstanding in South Africa, 1956–57, taking 23 wickets in four Tests, and he played in one Test against the West Indies the following summer, but that marked the end of his international career. He put his name to newspaper articles criticizing the Yorkshire captain and some of his colleagues. He was sacked by his county, and the MCC withdrew the invitation he had been sent to tour Australia in 1958–59. To the crowd he had seemed a jolly prankster; many of his team-mates saw a different character. It was a sad end to a fine career.

Shane Warne

See Legends (pages 118–119)

Cyril Washbrook

Born: December 6, 1914, Barrow, Clitheroe, Lancashire

Died: April 27, 1999

Teams: Lancashire (1953–59)

First-class: 592 matches; 34,101 runs, average 42.67; 7 wickets, average 44.14

Tests (1937–56): 37 matches; 2,569 runs, average 42.81; 1 wicket, average 33.00

A right-handed opening batsman and brilliant cover fielder, Washbrook captained Lancashire from 1954 to 1959, the first professional to hold that post. He was later president of the club he served so well as a player. His Test debut came against New Zealand in 1937, but it was not until 1946 that he played his second match. In the years immediately after the Second World War, he formed a successful opening partnership with Hutton, and they shared three consecutive century partnerships in Australia, 1946–47, when Washbrook hit the first of his six Test hundreds. His second came against Australia at Leeds in 1948, but it was on the tour of South Africa the following winter that he excelled. He made 195 at Johannesburg, and he and Hutton put on 359 for the first wicket.

It was believed that his Test career had ended with the tour of Australia, 1950–51, but he was a Test selector in 1956, and his fellow selectors persuaded him to return to play against Australia at Leeds at the age of 41. He scored 98, and England won by an innings.

Wasim Akram

Born: June 3, 1966, Lahore, Pakistan
Teams: PACO (1984–85); Lahore (1985–86); Lancashire (1988–1997); PIA (1995–03); Hampshire (2003)
First-class: 257 matches; 7,161 runs, average 22.73; 1,042 wickets, average 21.64
Tests (1984–85 to 2001–02): 104 matches; 2,898 runs, average 22.64; 414 wickets, average 23.62

Wasim Akram has developed into one of the great all-rounders of world cricket. A left-arm fast bowler with a capacity to swing the ball late either way, in 1996 at the Oval he became the second Pakistani bowler to take 300 wickets in Test cricket. Two months later, against Zimbabwe in Sheikhupura, he hit 257 not out batting at number eight, a Test record, and shared a record eighth-wicket stand of 313 with Saqlain Mushtaq in the match against Zimbabwe. Left-handed, he is a ferocious hitter of the ball, unwinding like a spring.

Wasim Akram formed, with Waqar Younis, one of the most feared fast-bowling partnerships cricket has known. He was captain of Pakistan for 25 Tests, during which time he enjoyed a run of nine wins and two draws, including a 2–0 series win in England. He was a wonderful In 1999–2000 – his final season as captain – he became the first Pakistan bowler to capture 400 wickets in Tests.

He was a fine acquisition for Lancashire, particularly effective in the one-day game, helping them to four limited-over trophies. Wasim's final season in Championship cricket for Lancashire came in 1997, when he broke down after just one game.

WALCOTT *Powerful and prolific.*

Mark Waugh

Born: June 2, 1965, Canterbury, Sydney, New South Wales, Australia
Teams: New South Wales (1985–86 to 2003–04); Essex (1988–90, 1992 and 2002)
First-class: 368 matches; 26,855 runs, average 52.04; 208 wickets, average 40.98
Tests (1990–91 to 2002-03): 128 matches; 8,029 runs, average 41.81; 59 wickets, average 41.16

When English crowds first saw Mark Waugh play for Essex they wondered how on earth he had not claimed a place in the Australian side alongside his twin brother.

He was at last rewarded with a Test cap against England at Adelaide, 1990–91, and made an outstanding 138. Since that time, he has been a regular member of the Australian side He and his twin brother Steve established a world-record fifth-wicket partnership for New South Wales against Western Australia, in 1990–91, with an unbroken stand of 464. Mark Waugh himself made 229 not out, his highest-ever score.

He has continued his successful Test career into the 21st century and on the 2001 tour of England, played in all five Tests, averaging 86.00 with the bat. If he has a fault, it is that he sometimes gives his wicket away in a careless or languid manner.

Steve Waugh

Born: June 2, 1965, Canterbury, Sydney, New South Wales, Australia
Teams: New South Wales (1984–85 to 2002-03); Somerset (1987–88); Kent (2002)
First-class: 356 matches; 24,052 runs, average 51.94; 249 wickets, average 32.75
Tests (1985–86 to 2003–04): 168 matches; 10,927 runs, average 51.06; 92 wickets, average 37.14

Steve Waugh won a place in the Australian side five years ahead of his twin brother with whom, in 1990–91, he shared a stand of 464, the highest recorded in Australia. A lean, clean hitter of the ball, with great determination and concentration, he has proved himself a top-class all-rounder with his medium-pace bowling.

His Test debut came against India, 1985–86, but it was not until his 27th Test that he first notched a century. He had made two 90s against the West Indies, 1988–89, but in England the following summer he scored 177 not out at Leeds and 152 not out at Lord's. He was the player of the series, but there were doubts as to his ability against the fastest bowling. Briefly, he lost his place in the Australian side, but then returned to dismiss any doubts as to his courage and technique. Subjected to a barrage of short-pitched bowling, he scored 200 against the West Indies in Jamaica, 1994–95, when Australia won a famous series. He was appointed Australia's vice-captain for the tour of England, 1997.

He has been captain of Australia since 1998–99. Under his leadership Australia won the 1999 World Cup and have had a tremendous record in Test cricket. In 2001 he successfully skippered the side in the Ashes series and topped the batting averages into the bargain.

He led Australia to another successful Ashes series in 2002-03 and made his 29th Test century in the final match, equalling Donald Bradman's record.

He was a surprise omisson from

WALSH *Fine fast bowler and captain.*

Australia's 2003 World Cup-winning squad, despite captaining the side to victory four years earlier, but was recalled for the tour to the West Indies in April 2003.

DOUG WALTERS *Exciting stroke-maker.*

Everton Weekes

Born: February 26, 1925, Westbury, St Michael, Barbados

Teams: Barbados (1944–45 to 1963–64)

First-class: 152 matches; 12,010 runs, average 55.34; 17 wickets, average 43.00

Tests (1947–48 to 1957–58): 48 matches; 4,455 runs, average 58.61; 1 wicket, average 77.00

Everton Weekes was a brilliant, attacking right-handed batsman, glorious to watch, and one of the legendary Three Ws – along with Frank Worrell, and Clyde Walcott. The first of his 15 Test centuries came in his fourth match, against England at Kingston, Jamaica. This was followed by centuries in his next four Test innings, against India a year later. These included a century in each innings in Calcutta. He was close to hitting six hundreds in successive Test innings but was run out for 90 in Madras. He established a record in the final Test when he made 56 in the first innings, so becoming the only batsman to hit seven consecutive 50s in Test cricket. He enjoyed a fine tour of England, 1950, and made 206 against them in 1953–54, and had made 207, his highest Test score, a year earlier.

Troubled by sinus problems, he left the Test scene earlier than expected. Like the other two Ws, he was knighted for his services to the game.

Bob Willis

Born: May 30, 1949, Sunderland, County Durham

Teams: Surrey (1969–71); Warwickshire (1972–84); Northern Transvaal (1972–73)

First-class: 308 matches; 2,690 runs, average 14.30; 899 wickets, average 24.99

Tests (1970–71 to 1984): 90 matches; 840 runs, average 11.50; 325 wickets, average 25.20

Tall, with an unorthodox open-chested action, Bob Willis made himself one of England's greatest fast bowlers, and only Ian Botham has taken more wickets for England. He first played for Surrey in 1969 and within 18 months was on his way to Australia as replacement for the injured Alan Ward. Surrey's reluctance to give him his county cap persuaded him to join Warwickshire, whom he captained from 1980 to 1984. In truth, he was never a great performer in county cricket, but in Tests no man has given more for his country. At Headingley in 1981, he took eight for 43 in Australia's second innings to give England victory by 18 runs. He operated with amazing concentration, as if he were a man possessed. The Test arena has rarely seen a better or more passionate display of fast bowling.

He captained England from 1982 to 1984 having been vice-captain on several tours. He has since acted as a commentator and as head of the National Sporting Club.

Bill Woodfull

Born: August 22, 1897, Maldon, Victoria, Australia

Died: August 11, 1965, Tweed Heads South, New South Wales, Australia

Teams: Victoria (1921–22 to 1933–34)

First-class: 174 matches; 13,388 runs, average 64.99; 1 wicket, average 24.00

Tests (1926–34): 35 matches; 2,300 runs, average 46.00

Bill Woodfull was a right-handed opening batsman with so solid and stout a defence that he was deemed "unbowlable". His Test career began on the tour of England in 1926, and he scored centuries in his third and fourth Tests. He was a surprising and somewhat controversial choice to lead Australia to England in 1930, but he hit 155 at Lord's and Australia won the series. He was equally successful as captain against both the West Indies and South Africa, but against Jardine's side in the "bodyline" series the outcome was very different.

The son of a clergyman, a teacher, Woodfull was highly respected by his players, but he was a traditionalist in a changing world. His reaction to Jardine's tactics in 1932–33 was to accuse England of not playing the game, and his attitude virtually assured Australia that they would not be opposed by Jardine and Larwood in 1934. Australia duly regained the Ashes when confronted by a toothless attack and an ill-led side.

A true assessment of Woodfull as a captain is difficult to make, for the achievements of Bradman intrude, but apart from 1932–33 he was successful, and his record as a batsman is impressive.

Frank Woolley

Born: May 27, 1887, Tonbridge, Kent

Died: October 18, 1978, Halifax, Nova Scotia, Canada

Teams: Kent (1906–38)

First-class: 978 matches; 58,959 runs, average 40.77; 2,066 wickets, average 19.87

Tests (1909–34): 64 matches; 3,283 runs, average 36.07; 83 wickets, average 33.91

"There was all summer in a stroke by Woolley, and he batted as is sometimes shown in dreams." So said Robertson-Glasgow, and none who saw the great left-handed all-rounder would disagree with him. He was an exquisite batsman, a slow left-arm bowler and a brilliant slip fielder whose 1,018 catches remain a world record. He scored his runs quickly and gracefully, and he ended his career with 132 centuries to his credit, five of them in Tests. His bowling was a feature of the first part of his career, and he completed the "double" eight times. In four of those seasons, he took 100 wickets and scored 2,000 runs. No other cricketer has achieved this feat on four occasions. He reached 1,000 runs in a season 28 times and, in 1928 went on to reach 3,352. The substance of his Test career came between 1912 and 1926, although he played last against Australia in 1934 at the age of 47.

Frank Worrell

Born: August 1, 1924, Bank Hall, Bridgetown, Barbados

Died: March 13, 1967, Mona, Kingston, Jamaica

Teams: Barbados (1941–42 to 1946–47); Jamaica (1947–48 to 1963–64)

First-class: 208 matches; 15,025 runs, average 54.24; 349 wickets, average 28.98

Tests (1947–48 to 1963): 51 matches; 3,860 runs, average 49.48; 69 wickets, average 38.72

After years of discussion and controversy, Frank Worrell was, in 1960–61, the first black man to be appointed captain of the West Indies for more than a single match. He began his career regarded primarily as a left-arm bowler of great pace and movement. He quickly climbed the batting order, for his elegant right-handed batting was stamped with class. He made his maiden century in his second season and scored 131 in his second Test, against England, 1947–48. From that point, he was linked with two other great batsmen, Weekes and Walcott, as a triumvirate, the Three Ws. He and Walcott had already shared an unbroken stand of 574 for Barbados against Trinidad, and Worrell had made 308 not out for Barbados against Trinidad, 1943–44, when he and John Goddard put on 502 for the fourth wicket. Worrell was 19 years old.

Before he became captain of the West Indies, he had led a Commonwealth side in India, and was admired as a man of character and dignity, all grace and charm on and off the field. When he was appointed captain of the West Indies in Australia, 1960–61, the pressure upon him was immense for the campaign on his behalf had been strong and involved issues outside cricket. His response to the situation was heroic, and the outcome romantic.

The first Test was tied and, although the West Indies eventually lost the series, Worrell and his side left Australia amid tumultuous acclaim. He led the West Indies in two more series and won them both. He had united the side which had once been a group of individuals from different islands vying for supremacy. At the end of the 1963 tour of England, mission accomplished, he retired.

He became a senator in the Jamaican parliament, was knighted and continued as a cricket administrator. Three years after being knighted, he died of leukaemia at the age of 42 and was honoured by a memorial service in Westminster Abbey, the first sportsman to be so recognized.

Doug Wright

Born: August 21, 1914, Sidcup, Kent
Died: November 13, 1998
Teams: Kent (1932–57)
First-class: 497 matches; 5,903 runs, average 12.34; 2,056 wickets, average 23.98
Tests (1938 to 1950–51): 34 matches; 289 runs, average 11.11; 108 wickets, average 39.11

Doug Wright bowled leg-breaks and googlies at medium pace. He had a kangaroo-like approach to the wicket, and he was unique among bowlers. He first played for England against Australia in 1938 and took five wickets on his debut, but he was woefully erratic. The selectors kept faith with him over a number of years because he was capable of producing the unexpected that could turn a match. He took 100 wickets in a season 10 times, with 177 in 1947 as his best, but a greater measure of his ability to change the course of a game is the fact that he performed the hat-trick on no fewer than seven occasions.

A professional cricketer and a man of warmth and honesty, he captained Kent from 1954 to 1956, a difficult time in the county's history.

John Wright

Born: July 5, 1954, Darfield, Christchurch, New Zealand
Teams: Northern Districts (1975–76 to 1983–84); Derbyshire (1977–88); Canterbury (1984–85 to 1988–89); Auckland (1989–90 to 1992–93)
First-class: 366 matches; 25,073 runs, average 42.35; 2 wickets, average 169.50
Tests (1977–78 to 1992–93): 82 matches; 5,334 runs, average 37.82; no wickets for 5 runs

A man of the utmost courtesy and charm, John Wright was a left-handed opening batsman who became the first New Zealander to pass 4,000 runs in Test cricket. Only Richard Hadlee played in more Test matches for the Kiwis, and only Martin Crowe scored more runs. Wright had great powers of concentration and was an elegant strokemaker, exceptionally strong off the back foot, ever popular and always a delight to watch.

He gave Derbyshire outstanding service for 12 seasons, and was a mainstay of the New Zealand side during the finest period of that country's cricketing history. When, in 1987–88, Jeff Crowe lost form and confidence, Wright took over the captaincy of New Zealand, but only on the understanding that Crowe should return as soon as he wished. In all, Wright led New Zealand in 14 tests but, in truth, he was captaining a great side that was already in decline.

Wright's Test record was exemplary in that he scored centuries against all six countries against whom he played and maintained a consistent average.

A graduate of Otago University, he was appointed the coach and manager of Kent in 1997, before moving to India to coach the national side in 2000.

India won their first three series under Wright, including a 2-1 defeat of Australia, but the Indian Cricket Board demanded he write to explain subsequent poor performances against Sri Lanka and South Africa.

His side reached the World Cup finals in 2003, when they were beaten by Australia, and Wright extended his contract by two years soon after.

Bob Wyatt

Born: May 2, 1901, Milford, Surrey
Died: April 20, 1995, Truro, Cornwall
Teams: Warwickshire (1923–39); Worcestershire (1946–51)
First-class: 739 matches; 39,405 runs, average 40.04; 901 wickets, average 32.84
Tests (1927–28 to 1936–37): 40 matches; 1,839 runs, average 31.70; 18 wickets, average 35.66

A consistent and determined batsman and useful medium-pace bowler, Bob Wyatt captained Warwickshire from 1930 to 1937 and Worcestershire from 1949 until 1951. He also captained England in 16 Tests, but he was never fortunate as England's captain nor was his selection as captain a popular one.

He had made his Test debut in South Africa, 1927–28, and made the first of his two Test centuries against the same opposition in 1929. The following year he captained England against Australia in controversial circumstances. Percy Chapman, a national hero, the England captain who had brought back and retained the Ashes, was dropped for the Oval Test and Wyatt appointed in his place. It was not a popular move.

Wyatt served under Chapman in South Africa and was vice-captain to Jardine in Australia, 1932–33. When Jardine stood down, Wyatt was named as captain against Australia in 1934 but was unable to play in the first Test because of injury. England were heavily beaten in the final Test and surrendered the Ashes.

He led England to the West Indies, 1934–35, where he made some rather bizarre decisions which turned the tour into something of a disaster. The West Indies won a series for the first time and Wyatt had his jaw broken in the final Test.

In spite of this, he captained England against South Africa in 1935. The South Africans won a Test and a series in England for the first time, and Wyatt's unfortunate career as England skipper was at an end. He played under Allen against India in 1936 and was a late call-up for the Australian tour that followed, but, in 1938, he announced that he was contracted to write for the *Daily Mail* and was not available for Test cricket.

Never at ease with authority, he resigned the captaincy of Warwickshire when he disagreed with the committee. He became a Test selector for several years and was 56 when he played his last game of cricket. He died less than two weeks from his 94th birthday.

Z

Zaheer Abbas

Born: July 24, 1947, Sialkot, India
Teams: Karachi (1965–66 to 1975–76); PWD (1968–69); PIA (1969–70 to 1986–87); Gloucestershire (1972–85); Sind (1975–76 to 1976–77); Dawood Club (1975–76)
First-class: 459 matches; 34,843 runs, average 51.54; 30 wickets, average 38.20
Tests (1969–70 to 1985–86): 78 matches; 5,062 runs, average 44.79; 3 wickets, average 44.00

The first Pakistani batsman to hit 100 centuries in a first-class career, Zaheer Abbas was a player of rare quality with an infinite capacity to entertain with his vast repertoire of beautiful strokes. Initially, he batted in glasses, later changing to contact lenses, but this never handicapped his batting nor his fine slip fielding. He made a spectacular entrance into Test cricket, scoring 274 at Edgbaston in 1971, his first Test in England and only his second in all. He made 240 at the Oval in 1974 and 235 not out against India at Lahore in 1978. His fourth double-century in a Test match was the most historic, in that he emulated Boycott by scoring his 100th hundred in a Test, 215 against India, again at Lahore. In that series, he became the first Pakistani batsman to score centuries in three successive innings, and he was also the first Pakistani batsman to score 5,000 Test runs. Zaheer set two career records: eight times he scored a century in each innings of a match and four times he made 200 and 100 in a match.

A modest, gentle man, he was immensely popular in his years with Gloucestershire when the county enjoyed a successful time, particularly in limited-overs cricket.

Zaheer captained Pakistan in 14 Tests, taking over from Imran in 1983–84, acting as a buffer between Javed and his critics before relinquishing the job to Javed in 1984–85. He stood down from the national side after the second Test against Sri Lanka in 1985, intimating that he had been forced to retire by certain senior players. It was a sad end to an outstanding career.

THE CATHEDRALS OF CRICKET

Whilst Lord's Cricket Ground in London is considered the world headquarters of cricket, Test Matches were played at both The Oval and Old Trafford before such games took place at Lord's. Over 70 venues have now staged Test matches.

It is impossible to say with any certainty which is the oldest ground still used for cricket, if only because early references give such descriptions as Richmond Green, Kennington Common, Dartford Heath, Moulsey Hurst, Penhurst Park, Kew Green, Hyde Park and Clapham Common, but there is no information as to where exactly in these parks, commons or greens the matches took place.

The oldest ground where we have definite knowledge of a match being played approximately where cricket is still played is the Artillery Ground on City Road, Finsbury, London. The match in question was London v Surrey played on August 30, 1730. The following year the first definite reference to a specific match on a current ground is Mitcham v Ewell on Mitcham Green on October 2, 1731.

The Sevenoaks Vine Ground is first mentioned in July 1740, when Sevenoaks opposed London, but it is most probable that the ground had been used some years earlier when Kent played Sussex in Sevenoaks. Extracts from the diary of Thomas Marchant, written between 1717 and 1727, indicate that cricket was played regularly in the Henfield and Hurstpierpoint areas of Sussex between the various villages, and references in documents to matches in Kent and Surrey would seem to imply that similar inter-village matches were being played in those counties. It would therefore come as no surprise if evidence emerged proving that a number of village greens in the south-east of England, on which cricket is still played, were used for cricket prior to 1730.

THE CLASSIC *Lord's Cricket Ground.*

ENGLISH GROUNDS

LORD'S

Of the cricket grounds in the British Isles in use today for first-class cricket, Lord's ground is the oldest. The first match on the ground was MCC v Hertfordshire on June 22, 1814 and the first first-class match was MCC v St John's Wood on July 13 to 15 the same year.

The present site was the third ground laid out by Thomas Lord. The first, which is now Dorset Square, London, was opened in 1787. Lord had laid out the ground at the behest of the Cricket Club, which met at the Star and Garter in Pall Mall and had in recent years played its matches on White Conduit Fields, Islington. The ground was used until 1810, by which time Lord had already set out an alternative ground at Lisson Grove not far away. However, the building of the Regent's Canal meant that within a few years Lord had to seek a third site off St John's Wood Road, a few hundred yards north-east of the second ground.

The Cricket Club of the Star and Garter adopted the name Marylebone Cricket Club from the district of London in which Lord's was situated and in 1866 the club bought the freehold of the ground. At this time, the ground was used by the MCC and for such set-piece matches as had traditionally been staged there – Eton v Harrow, Oxford v Cambridge, Gentlemen v Players and North v South. In 1877, the MCC agreed to allow Middlesex County Cricket Club to use the ground for their home fixtures.

The first Test match to take place there was staged on the ground on July 21 to 23, 1884, England beating Australia by an innings and five runs.

In recent years, considerable modernisation of Lord's has taken place, culminating in the total refurbishment of the historic Pavilion in 2004–05.

TRENT BRIDGE

This ground, situated in the Nottingham suburb of West Bridgford, was laid out in 1838 by William Clarke. Clarke was the landlord of the Trent Bridge Inn, the ground being in the field at the rear of the Inn; he was also the captain and effective manager of the Nottinghamshire county team. The first first-class match was played on the ground in 1840 when Nottinghamshire opposed Sussex.

The county had previously played their matches on the Nottingham racecourse, but as this was owned by the town council, no entrance money could be charged to spectators, hence the move to the new ground. In the nineteenth century, the ground was also used at various times by both Nottingham Forest Football Club and Notts County FC. The latter did not leave until 1910 and, in the meantime, two England soccer internationals were staged at the venue in the 1890s.

The first Test Match staged on the ground was on June 1 to 3, 1899 when England drew with Australia. Tests were played in Nottingham intermittently until 1939, and since the Second World War Test matches have been held on the ground in most seasons.

THE OVAL

William Baker, treasurer of the Montpelier Cricket Club, took a lease on 10 acres of ground, then used as a market garden and situated at the Oval, Kennington. He converted the land to a cricket ground and the first match was played on the new ground on May 13, 1845. In August of the same year, the Gentlemen of Surrey opposed the Players of Surrey on the ground, and after the match a meeting was arranged, at which it was proposed to form a Surrey County Cricket Club. The formation duly took place and the Surrey Club played the first first-class match at the Oval on May 25 and 26, 1846. The Surrey Club created an organization for south London similar to the Marylebone Club at Lord's.

The Oval was to become a centre of more than just cricket. The first Association Football match played on the ground was England v Scotland on November 19, 1870. Within two years, the Oval was recognized as the major football ground in London and in 1872 the Football Association Cup Final, between Royal Engineers and Wanderers, took place there. To soccer were added regular rugby union matches, with the University Rugby Union match being played at the Oval from 1873. England met Ireland in a rugby union match in 1875, but in 1891 it was decided that the scrummages were damaging the turf too much and rugby ceased to be played there. Soccer ceased to be staged on the ground as a regular event after 1895.

The first Test match to be played in England was at the Oval on September 6 to 8, 1880, when England beat Australia by five wickets. It is still a tradition that the final Test in a five- or six-match series in England takes place at the Oval.

A new stand, costing £24 million, was opened in 2005.

FENNER'S, CAMBRIDGE

F.P. Fenner, the Cambridge Town Club all-rounder, took the lease of a field in Cambridge and opened

TRENT BRIDGE *Sir Garfield Sobers opening the new stand at Trent Bridge in 1998.*

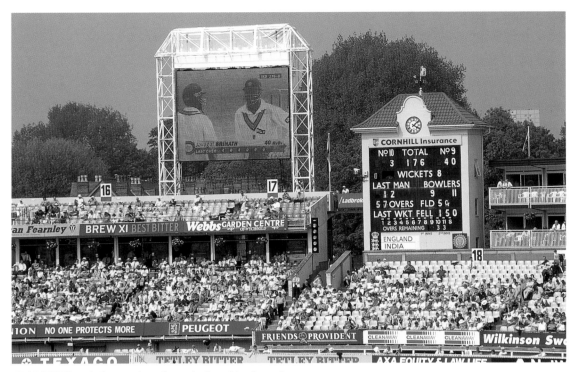

EDGBASTON *with the scoreboard overshadowed by the replay screen.*

undertaken when the war ended and it was possible to play one of the Victory Tests there in August 1945. Appropriately, the new press box, opened in 1987, was named after Neville Cardus, whose reputation had been made through the columns of the *Manchester Guardian*.

EDGBASTON, BIRMINGHAM

The present Warwickshire County Cricket Club was founded in 1882 and it soon became apparent that the club would not flourish until it established a good ground in the Birmingham area. William Ansell, the honorary secretary of the county club, was the driving force behind the search for and the acquisition of a suitable site in Edgbaston. The Warwickshire Cricket Ground Co. Ltd was founded in 1885 to raise the necessary capital, and the ground staged its first match on June 7, 1886, Warwickshire opposing the MCC. The first first-class game came late on in the same season when the Australian touring team played an England XI.

Warwickshire were promoted to first-class status in 1894 and the ground has been the headquarters of the County Championship playing side since it commenced in the competition in 1895.

The first Test match to be played at Edgbaston was on May 29 to 31, 1902, England opposing Australia in a remarkable match which saw the touring side all out for 36, their lowest total ever – this in reply to England's 376 for 9 declared. Rain on the last day prevented an England victory. The next Test was in 1909 – again Australia failed badly, being all out for 74. Edgbaston, however, was rarely used for international matches after that until 1957 when the West Indies played England. Since that date, it has been one of the six Test grounds in regular use.

HEADINGLEY, LEEDS

In 1887, a group of sports enthusiasts set up the Leeds Cricket, Football and Athletic Co. Ltd,

1846. In 1848, having created what was described as perhaps the smoothest ground in England – being in fact too easy, causing too much run-getting – he sublet the ground to Cambridge University Cricket Club and the first first-class match was staged on the ground on May 18 and 19, 1848, the university playing the MCC. It has remained the university ground ever since, the university buying the freehold in 1894. Prior to 1848, the university played on Parker's Piece, the first notable match there being against the town club in 1871. A cinder running track was laid out round Fenner's cricket area in the mid-1860s and was used by the University Athletics Club – athletics were staged there until the 1950s.

ST LAWRENCE GROUND, CANTERBURY

The headquarters of Kent County Cricket Club, the St Lawrence ground, was officially opened on May 16, 1847. Immediately prior to 1847, Kent had played on the Beverley Cricket Club ground in Canterbury, but for six years from 1835 the centre of the county club had been at West Malling. The Kent County Cricket Club, on its reformation in 1870, announced

that the St Lawrence ground would in future be the official county ground. The club purchased the freehold of the ground in 1896. In 1876, W.G. Grace scored 344 for MCC v Kent at Canterbury, this being the highest individual first-class score at the time, and it remains the ground record. By coincidence, the bowling record for the ground is held by W.G.'s brother, E.M. Grace, who took 10 for 69 for the MCC in 1862.

More than anything else the ground was famous for the Canterbury Festival, which for many years involved an MCC-selected England team opposing Kent, followed by two more fixtures; apart from cricket, theatrical performances were an integral part of the festival.

Kent by no means confined their matches to Canterbury, though, and since the Second World War have staged matches on the following other grounds: Rectory Field, Blackheath; Hesketh Park, Dartford; Crabble ground, Dover; Cheriton Road, Folkestone; Garrison ground, Gillingham; Bat and Ball ground, Gravesend; Mote Park, Maidstone; Lloyds Bank ground, Beckenham; and the Nevill ground, Tunbridge Wells. In recent years, of these only

Maidstone and Tunbridge Wells have still found favour.

OLD TRAFFORD, MANCHESTER

The ground was formed in 1857 as the home of Manchester Cricket Club; when the present Lancashire Club was formed in 1864, the county made Old Trafford its home. Until recent years the official name of the major club was the Lancashire County and Manchester CC.

The first major inter-county game on the Old Trafford ground was staged on July 20 to 22, 1865, when Lancashire played Middlesex. Old Trafford became the second ground in England to hold a Test match, when England played Australia in the first of a series of three Tests in 1884. The ground began to build its reputation for rain interruptions immediately – the first day of the first Test was completely washed out.

As the name implies, the ground was at one time owned by the de Trafford family, but was acquired by the Manchester Club in 1898.

It was the one major English cricket ground to be badly affected by bombing in the Second World War, but repairs were quickly

Football and Athletic Co. Ltd, chaired by Lord Hawke, in order to buy land in the Leeds area for use as a sports field. A 22-acre site was purchased and divided into portions for a variety of sports. The cricket area was officially opened on May 27, 1890 when the local Leeds Cricket Club used the grounds; the first first-class match was in September 1890, a North-of-England side playing the Australians. In 1891, Yorkshire County Cricket Club played its first first-class game at Headingley and the first Test was on June 29 and 30, 1899, England opposing Australia.

At that time, the headquarters of Yorkshire County Cricket Club were in Sheffield. In fact Sheffield had always been considered the centre of Yorkshire cricket – two grounds had been laid out, one following the other in Darnall, then another appeared in Hyde Park. It was on Sheffield Hyde Park ground that Yorkshire opposed Norfolk in 1833. In the 1840s, the Hyde Park ground became run down and M.J. Ellison, a keen supporter of Sheffield cricket, organized a meeting to discuss the foundation of a new ground. This materialized in April 1855 as Bramall Lane Cricket Ground. Some eight years later Ellison was instrumental in founding Yorkshire County Cricket Club and naturally Sheffield and Bramall Lane were the headquarters of the new club. In 1862, the first soccer match was played at Bramall Lane, which led to the foundation of Sheffield United, and the ground was shared by the cricket and football clubs. The first first-class match at Bramall Lane was Yorkshire v Sussex in August 1855. The first, and only, Test match was played on July 3 to 5, 1902 when England played Australia. Bramall Lane continued to stage county matches with success through to 1939, but after the Second World War the football club became more and more dominant and the last county match was Yorkshire v Lancashire, August 4 to 7, 1973.

Headingley, like Bramall Lane, has suffered because of its football connections, but its Test-match status has been maintained to the present day. However, Yorkshire County Cricket Club, at the time of writing, have bought the ground and entered into a deal with a local college for naming rights. It will be known as the Headingley Carnegie Stadium until 2015.

Yorkshire have had, and indeed do have, a number of other famous grounds. Scarborough has been staging an important cricket festival for more than 100 years at its North Marine Road ground. The first first-class match was on September 7 to 9, 1874: Yorkshire v Middlesex. For many years, the September Festival comprised a Gentlemen v Players match and a match involving the current touring side.

Another major cricketing centre is Bradford. The Park Avenue ground was opened in July 1880. The football club which shared the venue fell on hard times in the 1950s and left the Football League, as a result of which the accommodation became increasingly dilapidated. In 1980, the grandstand had to be demolished and in 1985 the pavilion followed suit. Friends of Park Avenue formed an association to restore the ground and first-class cricket returned in 1992 after a gap of some years. Other grounds which were used by Yorkshire for first-class cricket in 1996 were Acklam Park, Middlesbrough (first used in 1956), Abbeydale Park, Sheffield (first used in 1946, by Derbyshire) and St George's Road, Harrogate (first used in 1882).

COUNTY GROUND, HOVE

The cricket ground in Eaton Road, Hove has been the headquarters of Sussex County Cricket Club since 1872. The first match played by Sussex on the ground was, appropriately, against Kent, the home county's oldest rivals, commencing June 6, 1872.

Sussex have been as unfortunate as Thomas Lord in their battle with building development. Their original ground had been set out at the behest of the Prince of Wales in the 1790s, when he made Brighton a fashionable resort. This ground was taken over in the 1820s by a Brighton businessman, James Ireland, and he was responsible for organizing what is now considered the first match to decide the Champion County of England, in 1825 against Kent. The Prince's ground then became known as Ireland's Gardens. The builders took over the site in the 1840s and it is now Park Crescent, Brighton. Sussex then moved to a new

	NOTABLE BATTING RECORDS ON SOME CURRENT ENGLISH FIRST-CLASS GROUNDS		
	Edgbaston	501*	B.C. Lara, Warwickshire v Durham, 1994
	Taunton	424	A.C. MacLaren, Lancashire v Somerset, 1895
	The Oval	366	N.H. Fairbrother, Lancashire v Surrey, 1990
	Trent Bridge	345	C.G. MacCartney, Australians v Nottinghamshire, 1921
	Canterbury	344	W.G. Grace, MCC v Kent, 1876
	Chesterfield	343*	P.A. Perrin, Essex v Derbyshire, 1904
	Gloucester	341	C.M. Spearman, Gloucestershire v Middlesex, 2004
	Headingley	334	D.G. Bradman, Australia v England, 1930
	Hove	335*	M. W. Goodwin, Sussex v Leicestershire, 2003
	Lord's	333	G.A. Gooch, England v India, 1990
	Worcester	331*	J.D.B. Robertson, Middlesex v Worcestershire, 1949
	Northampton	329*	M.E.K. Hussey, Northants v Essex, 2001
	Cheltenham College	318*	W.G. Grace, Gloucestershire v Yorkshire, 1876
	Scarborough	317	K.R. Rutherford, New Zealand v D.B. Close's XI, 1986
	Cardiff	313*	S.J. Cook, Somerset v Glamorgan, 1990
	Old Trafford	312	J.E.R. Gallian, Lancashire v Derbyshire, 1996
	Eastbourne	310	H. Gimblett, Somerset v Sussex, 1948
	Colwyn Bay	309*	S.P. James, Glamorgan v Sussex, 2000
	Fenner's	304*	E. de C. Weekes, West Indies v Cambridge University, 1950
	Bristol	302*	W.R. Hammond, Gloucestershire v Glamorgan, 1934

	NOTABLE BOWLING RECORDS ON SOME CURRENT ENGLISH FIRST-CLASS GROUNDS		
	Headingley	10–10	H. Verity, Yorkshire v Nottinghamshire, 1932
	The Oval	10–28	W.P. Howell, Australians v Surrey, 1899
	Lord's	10–38	S.E. Butler, Oxford University v Cambridge University, 1871
	Bristol	10–40	E.G. Dennett, Gloucestershire v Essex, 1906
	Taunton	10–42	A.E. Trott, Middlesex v Somerset, 1900
	Edgbaston	10–51	H. Howell, Warwickshire v Yorkshire, 1923
	Worcester	10–51	J. Mercer, Glamorgan v Worcestershire, 1936
	Old Trafford	10–53	J.C. Laker, England v Australia, 1956
	Cheltenham College	10–66	A.A. Mailey, Australians v Gloucestershire, 1921
	Chesterfield	10–66	J.K. Graveney, Gloucestershire v Derbyshire, 1949
	Fenner's	10–69	S.M.J. Woods, Cambridge University v C.I. Thornton's XI, 1890
	Canterbury	10–129	Jas. Lillywhite, South v North, 1872
	Trent Bridge	9–19	J. Grundy, Nottinghamshire v Kent, 1864
	Scarborough	9–28	J.M. Preston, Yorkshire v MCC, 1888
	Hove	9–35	J.E.B.B.P.Q.C. Dwyer, Sussex v Derbyshire, 1906
	Gloucester	9–44	C.W.L. Parker, Gloucestershire v Essex, 1925
	Cardiff	9–57	P.I. Pocock, Surrey v Glamorgan, 1979
	Eastbourne	9–62	A.G. Nicholson, Yorkshire v Sussex, 1967

ground in Hove, close to the sea front and known as the Brunswick ground. This opened in 1848, but in 1871 the builders took over and the site of this ground is Third and Fourth Avenues, Hove. The county's next move was to their present ground, but to further complicate the story another ground was in operation between 1834 and 1844 which was generally known as Lillywhite's ground and situated where Montpelier Crescent now stands.

Sussex have also played on various other grounds in the county, but by 1996 only two of the old established county venues remained in use for first-class cricket: Horsham (the current ground there has been used by the county since 1908) and Eastbourne (The Saffrons, which Sussex have used since 1897). In addition, the county has been playing matches at Arundel Castle since 1975, when a Sunday League game was staged there. More recently, championship games have come to Arundel.

COUNTY GROUND, BRISTOL

Gloucestershire County Cricket Club have used the ground at Ashley Down since 1899. It has, however, had a somewhat chequered history – in 1916 the county club had to sell the ground to Fry's, the chocolate manufacturers, in order to pay off the club's debts. The club regained ownership of the ground in 1932.

In its earliest days, the county club played many of its matches on two school grounds. The one at Clifton College was used from 1871 to 1932, whilst the one at Cheltenham College, which came into county use the year after Clifton College, has long been established as a ground for an annual cricket festival. In 1882, the County staged its first match on the Spa ground at Gloucester, but this has not been used for county matches since 1923. After that year, the majority of county matches played in the city have been at what is still known, though incorrectly, as the Wagon Works ground.

AUSTRALIAN GROUNDS

MCG, VICTORIA

The first home inter-colonial match played by Victoria was staged at Emerald Hill on the south side of the Yarra River on March 29 and 30, 1852, in the district now known as South Melbourne, and Victoria's opponents were Tasmania. Within a few years of this game, the ground had disappeared, with a railway line

SYDNEY CRICKET GROUND *under lights during the 1992 World Cup.*

through its centre.

When Victoria faced New South Wales for the first time at home on March 26 and 27, 1856, the match was staged on what is still Melbourne Cricket Ground. It was on March 15, 1877 that what is now considered to be the first Test match was commenced. The English touring team, under James Lillywhite, opposed Australia. Australia won this historic first match by 45 runs and a return match was immediately arranged on the same ground; this time England won by four wickets. Some spectators accused the England team of deliberately losing the initial match in order to

raise the odds on England winning the second so that, with betting a major feature of cricket, the England players could make a killing!

SCG, NSW

The first first-class match to be played in Sydney took place on January 14 and 15, 1857, when New

South Wales played Victoria. This game was played on the Domain, the ground having been used for the first time in the previous month. In 1870–71, the New South Wales v Victoria fixture was moved to the much better ground of the Albert Club. Here spectators had to pay, whereas previously the inter-colonial matches in Sydney could be viewed free of charge.

However, in the 1870s, the New South Wales Cricket Association wished to find a new ground and, after various discussions and some objections from the Albert Cricket Ground Company, took over the Garrison ground in Sydney, whose name was then changed to the

Association ground. The first first-class match on the Association ground was New South Wales v Victoria on February 22 to 25, 1878. The Albert ground itself was sold off as a building site. The Association ground, now known as Sydney Cricket Ground, is still the major ground in New South Wales. The first Test match to be staged there took place on February 17 to 21, 1882, when Australia beat England by five wickets.

ADELAIDE OVAL, SOUTH AUSTRALIA

The Adelaide Oval has been the principal cricket ground in South Australia since the introduction of first-class cricket to the colony. In 1871, the South Australian Cricket Club had set about finding suitable land to create a ground for inter-colonial matches and a South Australian Cricket Association was set up to pursue that aim. Land was found in North Park, Adelaide, and the first game was played there on November 11, 1872. It was between British-born and Colonial-born. The first first-class match was against Tasmania in November 1877 – the first time that South Australia opposed another colony on even terms. It was not until 1881 that Victoria played South Australia even-handed at Adelaide and the first Test match on the ground commenced on December 12, 1884, when England beat Australia by eight wickets.

GABBA, QUEENSLAND

Queensland was created as a separate colony in 1859 and played its first first-class match on April 1 to 4, 1893 when the home team defeated New South Wales by 14 runs. The match was played on the Exhibition ground in Brisbane which was situated in Bowen Hills. The ground had first been used for a match when the 1887–88 English team had visited Brisbane.

However, in 1896 a new ground was opened at Woolloongabba (more commonly known as Gabba). The first first-class match was played there on February 19 to 22,

1898, when A.E. Stoddart's team opposed a combined Queensland and Victoria XI. Queensland played its first Shield match there against South Australia in 1898–99 and the Gabba, as it is familiarly called, remains the principal cricket venue in Queensland. The first Test match in the state was not staged at the Gabba, but on the Exhibition ground on November 30 to December 5, 1928, when England beat Australia by 675 runs. The first Test at the Gabba was Australia v South Africa, commencing November 27, 1931, and every subsequent Brisbane Test has been played on that ground.

WACA, WEST AUSTRALIA

The Western Australian Cricket Association was formed by the leading clubs of Perth specifically to create a good-quality ground within the city. A suitable site was secured in East Perth in 1899, but it took several years to form a practical cricketing surface and the first match on the ground did not take place until the 1893–94 season. The first first-class match was on April 3 to 6, 1899, when South Australia beat Western Australia by four wickets.

In addition to cricket, football was played on the ground and a cycle track was laid round the perimeter.

Western Australia did not join the Sheffield Shield until 1947–48. It was not until December 1970 that the first Test match was played in Perth, Australia opposing England.

TASMANIAN GROUNDS

The two major cricket centres on the island are at Hobart and Launceston. The first first-class match in Australia was staged at Launceston on February 11 and 12, 1851, Tasmania playing Victoria – the game was billed at the time as XI of Port Philip against XI of Van Diemen's Land. The cricket ground used was part of the local racecourse at the time and the Northern Tasmanian Cricket Association, on its formation, took over the ground in 1886–87 – adjacent to the ground cycling, tennis and bowling also took place. A limited-overs international was staged at Launceston in 1985–86 but, since the Second World War, the ground at Hobart has usually taken precedence.

The first first-class match in Hobart was played on March 4 and 5, 1858: Tasmania v Victoria. It was staged on the Lower Domain ground which was taken over by the Southern Tasmanian Cricket Association in 1869. The building

BELLERIVE GROUND *in Tasmania.*

of a railway ended cricket on the ground in 1873 and a new one opened in 1881–82. The first first-class game on the new ground was on January 8 and 9, 1890, Tasmania v Victoria. This ground is usually referred to as the Upper Domain ground or TCA ground.

A limited-overs international match was played on the ground in 1984–85, but the State Government were trying to bring Test cricket to Tasmania and decided that the best prospective venue was the Bellerive Oval. Cricket had been played in

Bellerive Park from the 1880s, but the cricket area did not become enclosed until 1947. Major redevelopment of the ground began in 1985 and the first first-class game took place from January 23 to 25, 1987, Tasmania playing the West Indies. Continued improvements to the ground led to the first Test match at Bellerive and in Tasmania in December 1989, when Australia opposed Sri Lanka.

In 2003 Test matches were staged in Darwin and Cairns for the first time.

WACA *the home of Western Australia.*

NOTABLE BATTING FEATS ON AUSTRALIA'S MAJOR GROUNDS

BATTING

Sydney
452* D.G. Bradman, NSW v Queensland, 1929–30

Melbourne
437 W.H. Ponsford, Victoria v Queensland, 1927–28

Brisbane
383 C.W. Gregory, NSW v Queensland, 1906–07

Adelaide
369 D.G. Bradman, S Australia v Tasmania, 1935–36

Perth
356 B.A. Richards, S Australia v W Australia, 1970–71

Hobart
305* F.E. Woolley, MCC v Tasmania, 1911–12

* not out

NOTABLE BOWLING FEATS ON AUSTRALIA'S MAJOR GROUNDS

BOWLING

Perth
10–44 I.J. Brayshaw, W Australia v Victoria, 1967–68

Melbourne
10–61 P.J. Allan, Queensland v Victoria, 1965–66

Sydney
10–36 T.W. Wall, S Australia v NSW, 1932–33

Launceston
9–2 G. Elliott, Victoria v Tasmania, 1857–58

Adelaide
9–41 W.J. OReilly, NSW v South Australia, 1937–38

Brisbane
9–45 G.E. Tribe, Queensland v Victoria, 1945–46

SOUTH AFRICAN GROUNDS

The first Test matches played in South Africa both occurred in March 1889, the first being on St George's Park, Port Elizabeth, and the second on the Newlands ground, Cape Town. These two matches are also considered to be the first two first-class matches played in South Africa. Both of the grounds used are still venues for Test and first-class cricket.

Port Elizabeth Cricket Club has played at St George's Park from its earliest days and in 1876 the first major South African cricket competition – the Champion Bat Tournament – was staged in St George's Park, between Kingwilliamstown, Grahamstown, Capetown and Port Elizabeth. Eastern Province, whose base is Port Elizabeth, played in the Currie Cup for the first time in 1893–94, but the first Currie Cup game at St George's Park was not until 1902–03.

The Newlands ground is the base for Western Province. WPCC was formed in 1864 and originally played on Southey's Field, now part of Plumstead, due to city expansion. They moved to Newlands in 1888, the first match being Mother Country v Colonial-Born on January 2, 1888.

Western Province entered the Currie Cup in 1892–93 and the first Currie Cup games were played at Newlands in 1893–94, when Western Province, who had won the trophy in 1892–93, retained the title.

NEWLANDS GROUND in Cape Town, South Africa, under floodlights.

Johannesburg was the third South African city to stage a Test match, commencing on March 2, 1896 – with South Africa playing England on what is now termed the Old Wanderers ground. The Old Wanderers ground was required for an expansion of the railway and in 1948–49 Test cricket was transferred to the rugby stadium at Ellis Park, Johannesburg. In 1956–57, the present Wanderers Stadium at Kent Park, Johannesburg, saw its first Test match, South Africa playing England. The ground is also the headquarters of the Transvaal side.

The first first-class match staged in Durban was in April 1885, when Transvaal played Western Province on the Oval, Albert Park. The second was on the Lord's ground in March 1898, and on this ground Durban saw its first Test in January 1910 when South Africa played England. The Lord's ground is now long gone and since 1923 Test matches in Durban have been played on the Kingsmead ground.

In 1995–96, South Africa played for the first time at Centurion, formerly Verwoerdburg. Centurion Park is the headquarters of Northern Transvaal Cricket Union.

East London and Potchefstroom staged tests in 2002–03.

WEST INDIAN GROUNDS

The first first-class match in the West Indies was played on the Garrison Savannah ground in Bridgetown, Barbados, on February 15 and 16, 1865, when the island opposed Demerara. It was not until 1883–84 that a second first-class match took place, and

	NOTABLE BATTING FEATS ON SOUTH AFRICA'S MAJOR GROUNDS
B A T T I N G	**Johannesburg** **337*** D.J. Cullinan, Transvaal v N Transvaal, 1993–94 **306*** E.A.B. Rowan, Transvaal v Natal, 1939–40 **304*** A.W. Nourse, Natal v Transvaal, 1919–20 **Worcester, Cape Province** **307*** T.N. Lazard, Boland v W. Province, 1993–94

	NOTABLE BOWLING FEATS ON SOUTH AFRICA'S MAJOR GROUNDS
B O W L I N G	**Johannesburg** **10–26** A.E.E. Vogler, E Province v Griqualand West, 1906–07 **Cape Town** **10–59** S.T. Jefferies, W Province v OFS, 1987–88

SABINA PARK in Kingston, Jamaica.

this time at the Wanderers CC ground at Bay Pasture, Bridgetown. The Pickwick CC ground at Kensington Oval saw first-class cricket in 1894–95, when R.S. Lucas's Team visited Barbados. It is appropriate that the first Test in the West Indies should have taken place on the Kensington Oval ground against England in January 1930. Test matches and first-class cricket have been staged regularly on the ground since then.

Georgetown, Guyana, saw its first first-class game on the Eve Leary Parade ground in 1865–66. The present ground, Bourda, was first used for first-class matches in September 1887–88 and the first Test played there was in February 1930, West Indies v England. This remains the principal ground in what was British Guiana, now Guyana.

The Queen's Park Oval in Port of Spain is the major Trinidad ground, whilst Sabina Park is the main venue in Kingston, Jamaica. Both these grounds were first used for Test cricket during the 1929–30 series against England.

The fifth ground in the West Indies to hold a Test match was the Recreation Ground in St John's, Antigua. St Lucia saw its first Test match at Beausejour Stadium in June 2003.

NEW ZEALAND GROUNDS

New Zealand first-class cricket commenced in Dunedin on January 27, 1864, when Otago played Canterbury. The venue was the South Dunedin recreation ground. In 1879–80, the Caledonian ground in Dunedin was used by Otago, but in 1883–84 the Province played on the Carisbrook ground. It was not, however, until March 1955 that a Test match was played at Carisbrook, when New Zealand played England. This ground remains the main venue in Otago.

The ground at Hagley Park, Christchurch, has staged first-class matches, commencing February 1865, but the present main Christchurch ground for Test and for Canterbury first-class games is Lancaster Park. The reason for the switch from Hagley Park to Lancaster Park was that no admission charges could be levied at the former ground. Lancaster Park saw its first first-class match in 1882–83 and its first Test in 1929–30, when New Zealand played England.

The first first-class match at Wellington was Wellington v Auckland on November 28 and 29, 1873. The principal ground is the Basin Reserve which has staged Test matches since January 1930.

The Domain was the major ground in Auckland from 1853, but in the season 1912–13 Eden Park superseded the Domain as the principal first-class venue. The first Test at Eden Park was in February 1930. The ground is used for both cricket and rugby.

McLean Park, Napier, where Central Districts play some of their first-class matches, staged its first Test in February 1979, when New Zealand played Pakistan.

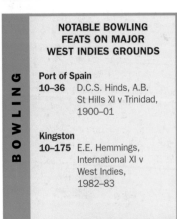

<table>
<tr><td rowspan="2" style="writing-mode:vertical-rl">BATTING</td><td>

NOTABLE BATTING FEATS ON MAJOR WEST INDIES GROUNDS

St John's
400   B.C. Lara, West Indies v England, 2003–04

Kingston
365* G.St A. Sobers, West Indies v Pakistan, 1957–58

Bridgetown
337   Hanif Mohammad, Pakistan v West Indies, 1957–58
308* F.M.M. Worrell, Barbados v Trinidad, 1943–44

Port of Spain
324   J. B. Stollmeyer, Trinidad v British Guiana, 1946–47

* not out
</td></tr>
</table>

NOTABLE BOWLING FEATS ON MAJOR WEST INDIES GROUNDS

Port of Spain
10–36   D.C.S. Hinds, A.B. St Hills XI v Trinidad, 1900–01

Kingston
10–175 E.E. Hemmings, International XI v West Indies, 1982–83

NOTABLE BATTING FEATS ON MAJOR NEW ZEALAND GROUNDS

Christchurch
385   B. Sutcliffe, Otago v Canterbury, 1952–53

Dunedin
355   B. Sutcliffe, Otago v Auckland, 1949–50

Auckland
336* W. R. Hammond, England v New Zealand, 193233

* not out

NOTABLE BOWLING FEATS ON MAJOR NEW ZEALAND GROUNDS

Christchurch
10–28 A.E. Moss, Canterbury v Wellington, 1889–90

Auckland
9–36   A.F. Wensley, Auckland v Otago, 1929–30

Wellington
9–43   T. Eden, Nelson v Wellington, 1875–76

Napier
9–47   T.H. Dent, Hawkes Bay v Wellington, 1900–01

Dunedin
9–50   A.H. Fisher, Otago v Queensland, 1896–97

BASIN RESERVE in Wellington, New Zealand.

INDIAN GROUNDS

Something in the region of 300 separate grounds have staged first-class cricket in India, but in a number of towns and cities it is not totally clear which ground was used, mainly because the names of grounds have changed in many cases.

This brief piece on Indian grounds is therefore confined to the major Test match grounds – there have been 19 Test venues so far. The oldest and senior ground for Test cricket is Eden Gardens, Calcutta, where India played England in 1933–34. The Gymkhana ground in Bombay and the Chepauk ground in Madras were also used for Test matches that same season. When the West Indies toured India in 1948–49, the Feroz Shah Kotla ground in Delhi and the Brabourne Stadium in Bombay hosted Tests for the first time. Neither of the two Bombay grounds mentioned is now used for Tests, the current ground being the Wankhede Stadium, first used in

1974–75. The two grounds not so far mentioned which have seen most Test cricket are Green Park, Kanpur (first match played 1951–52) and Karnataka CA ground, Bangalore (first match 1974–75).

PAKISTANI GROUNDS

The first home Test match by Pakistan was played at the Dacca Stadium in 1954–55 – but Dacca is now in Bangladesh. Four other venues were used in the same season for Tests: Dring Stadium, Bahawalpur; Lawrence Gardens, Lahore; Services ground, Peshawar; and National Stadium, Karachi. Only the last has remained a regular Test venue. Lawrence Gardens in Lahore was superseded by the Gaddafi Stadium. The other venue that has regularly seen Test cricket is the Iqbal Stadium, Faisalabad.

Since 1980, other cities which have hosted Tests are Rawalpindi, Gujranwala, Sialkot and Multan. The Services Ground at Peshawar has been superseded by the Arbab Niaz Stadium. The Defence Stadium at Karachi was used in 1993.

SRI LANKAN GROUNDS

Since Sri Lanka was raised to Test-match status in 1981–82, four different grounds in Colombo have been used for Test matches, namely Saravanamuttu Stadium, Sinhalese Sports CC, Colombo CC and Premadasa Stadium. Tests have also been played at Kandy and at Moratuwa.

The highest innings in Sri Lanka is 340 by S.T. Jayasuriya for Sri Lanka v India in Colombo in 1997–98 and the best bowling feat is 10–41 by G.P. Wickramasinghe for Sinhalese SC in 1991–92.

ZIMBABWEAN GROUNDS

Three grounds have been used for Test matches in Zimbabwe: Harare Sports Club in Harare and two in Bulawayo, namely Bulawayo Athletic Club and the Queen's Sports Club. The highest score in Zimbabwe is 266 by D.L. Houghton in 1994–95 and the best bowling feat is 9–71 by M.J. Procter in 1972–73.

NOTABLE BATTING FEATS ON PAKISTANI GROUNDS	
Karachi	
499	Hanif Mohammad, Karachi v Bahawalpur, 1958–59
Karachi	
428	Aftab Baloch, Sind v Baluchistan, 1973–74
Lahore	
350	Rashid Israr, Habib Bank v National Bank, 1976–77
Peshawar	
334*	M.A. Taylor, Australia v Pakistan, 1998–99

NOTABLE BOWLING FEATS ON PAKISTANI GROUNDS	
Peshawar	
10–28	Naeem Akhtar, Rawalpindi B v Peshawar, 1995–96
Karachi	
10–58	Shahid Mahmood, Karachi Whites v Khairpur, 1969–70
Faisalabad	
10–92	Imran Adil, Bahawalpur v Faisalabad, 1989–90

NOTABLE BATTING FEATS ON INDIAN GROUNDS	
Poona (Pune)	
443*	B.B. Nimbalkar, Maharashtra v Kathiawar, 1948–49
Bombay (Mumbai)	
377	S.V. Manjrekar, Bombay v Hyderabad, 1990–91
Secunderabad	
366	M.V. Sridhar, Hyderabad v Andhra, 1993–94
Bangalore	
353	V.V.S. Laxman, Hyderabad v Karnataka, 1999–00

NOTABLE BOWLING FEATS ON INDIAN GROUNDS	
Jorhat	
10–20	P.M. Chatterjee, Bengal v Assam, 1956–57
Bombay (Mumbai)	
10–78	S.P. Gupte, President's XI v Combined XI, 1954–55
Jodhpur	
10–78	P. Sunderam, Rajasthan v Vidarbha, 1985–86
Kotla	
10–74	A. Kumble, India v Pakistan, 1998–99

CHEPAUK GROUND *in Madras (Chennai), India.*

ADMINISTRATION & BUSINESS

The administration of cricket is founded on tradition. The Cricket Club at the Star and Garter Tavern in London set out the Laws of the game, and the MCC has continued to revise and update them. Regulations concerning the qualification of players and teams for Test and first-class cricket have not been so adroitly handled. Much of the history of administration has been about trying to shut the door after the horse has bolted.

After several years of consultation and one false dawn, the controllers of English cricket created a new governing body, the England and Wales Cricket Board, which was officially established on January 1, 1997 and succeeded the Cricket Council, nominally the ruling body since 1969. The new board's objective was closer co-operation between the first-class professional game and the amateur game, and to this end each first-class county has a cricket board which includes representatives of the county club and the County Cricket Association.

The England and Wales Cricket Board is run directly by a management board of 14 plus a non-voting chief executive. Its first chief executive is T.M. Lamb, former Middlesex and Northamptonshire bowler and, until his appointment, Cricket Secretary of the now disbanded Test and County Cricket Board. Its first chairman is Lord MacLaurin of Knebworth, former Chairman of the Tesco supermarket chain.

The reason behind the change is the poor performance of the England Test team during the last five or so years. It was felt that the old regime failed to develop enough cricketers of real international standard. It is clearly several years too early to assess the merits of the new set-up

MCC DOMINANT

The foundations for cricket administration seem to have been laid in the Star and Garter Tavern, Pall Mall, the dinner venue for the Cricket Club – akin to the Jockey Club, another sporting organization based at the Star and Garter. The Laws of cricket were made and revised on several occasions by this club, whose membership was drawn from the aristocracy and landed gentry of the day. In 1787, the club persuaded Thomas Lord to set out a private cricket ground in Marylebone for the use of the club's members, and the press dubbed the organization the Marylebone Cricket Club. Prior to this it had been known as the White Conduit Cricket Club, since it had played its matches on White Conduit Fields in Islington, and on occasion it was also referred to as the Star and Garter Cricket Club. But it is as the Marylebone Cricket Club that it has achieved worldwide fame.

Through the first half of the nineteenth century English cricket, apart from the Laws which were adjusted from time to time by the MCC Committee, was allowed to grow unchecked by any controlling body. In 1861, the secretary of Surrey, William Burrup, wrote to the MCC asking if a meeting of county officers and the MCC could be convened to sort out the qualifications for county players and the boundary between North and South – the match between North of England and the South being the major fixture of the day. The MCC ignored the request for a meeting and simply replied giving the definition the MCC used in both cases for matches at Lord's. Democracy didn't raise its ugly head.

Three years later, when the problems of legalizing over-arm bowling were being resolved by the MCC Committee, a meeting in London sparked discussion about a "cricket parliament". The MCC allowed the arguments for and against to run their course in the press and the idea drifted away.

COUNTIES CONVENE

In 1872, eight counties were represented at a meeting held in London to define the qualification of county cricketers. One of the regulations which it passed stated that, in case of a dispute regarding residential qualification, the MCC should make the final decision. The matter was then debated at the MCC Annual General Meeting in May 1873 and a final set of regulations agreed on July 1, 1873. Earlier in the same year, the MCC had attempted to offer a cricket Challenge Cup to be competed for by the counties. Five counties entered, but two then withdrew and only one match, Kent v Sussex, was actually played – the idea that all the matches be staged at Lord's did not seem attractive to some counties.

The next question which needed to be resolved was the arrangement of inter-county fixtures. Surrey took the initiative by inviting all the county clubs to a fixtures meeting in December 1875. The man who instigated this meeting, which was thereafter an annual event, though from 1877 at Lord's rather than at the Oval, was Charlie Alcock, the greatest of all sports administrators. One story about him recalls when he became secretary to Surrey in 1872 only to find an unbusiness-like organization paying its players haphazardly. Alcock told one of the senior pros that, in future, payment would be made on a set day each month, and was surprised that the player seemed not to like the arrangement. Apparently the previous year Mr Burrup (Alcock's predecessor) had paid him three times for the Lancashire match!

Because counties only played 10 or 12 matches a season in the 1870s, the professionals were paid by the match and usually had a summer engagement with a local club, with a clause releasing them if they were selected by the county. After 1895, when the County Championship expanded and increased fixtures to perhaps 20, the counties took to employing players for the season, seconding them to local league clubs when they were not needed.

Although the Australians toured England every other year throughout the 1880s, the top players were not greatly inconvenienced by England call-ups. The 1880 Test was not played until September 6, and the 1882 match in late August. Three Tests were arranged per season in 1884, 1886, 1888 and 1890, but each was scheduled for three days. There was no England selection committee – the committee which ran the home ground picked the England side.

BOARD OF CONTROL

Everything was rather casual until Lord Harris, the captain of Kent, decided to put cricket's house in order. At the Secretaries' Meeting of December 1887, he proposed the setting-up of a committee to look at the feasibility of a County Cricket Council – the motion was passed by 14 votes to 9. The council was duly set up and held meetings in 1888. Unfortunately, Lord Harris, its first chairman, was appointed Governor of Bombay and, in his absence, the council effectively collapsed when in December 1890 A.J. Webbe (Middlesex) proposed and W.H.C. Oates seconded that this meeting of the County Cricket Council be suspended *sine die*.

It was a very sad end to a laudable venture. The problem was

LORD HARRIS *Power at Lord's for 30 years.*

that the individual county committees had grown too strong and were wary of giving power to a central body.

Once Lord Harris's stint as Governor of Bombay was over he began moves to create an English Board of Control and finally succeeded in 1898. The board comprised six members of the MCC and six county representatives, all also members of the MCC. It agreed to stage five Tests in 1899 against the Australians (compared to three in the recent past) and, more importantly, to distribute the profits among all the county clubs.

The board would also appoint a selection committee and raise the fees paid to England players

MACLAREN *Outstanding captain.*

selected for the Tests. What the board did not decide to control were English Test teams going overseas. These touring parties remained private speculations, at least for the present.

In 1903, Archie MacLaren, with the backing of the Australians, was trying to gather an England team to tour Australia. He failed to get the players he wanted and gave up, but at the last minute the MCC offered to organize the tour. The professionals were to be paid £300 and the amateurs just their expenses. The pros would receive bonuses if the tour made a profit. Although England won the Test series, the venture lost £1,500. There would be more successful trips, however, in the future. The MCC also embarked on frequent tours to other countries, normally with the host country guaranteeing the MCC against loss.

AUSTRALIAN RULES

The principal Australian cricketing colonies – New South Wales, Victoria and South Australia – were an independent trio, and the first two were divided within themselves. New South Wales Cricket Association had to co-operate with the trustees of the Sydney Cricket Ground for the staging of New South Wales' representative games. Similarly Victoria Cricket Association needed Melbourne Cricket Club, because the latter controlled the Melbourne ground. The only English equivalent was the MCC, which, of course, controlled Lord's ground, and Middlesex County Cricket Club, but in this case the relationship was almost invariably amiable.

The NSWCA were very much the junior partner and had to do what the Sydney ground authorities wanted during the last years of the nineteenth century, but common sense later prevailed and both sides benefited. The Melbourne Cricket Club was the most powerful body in Australian cricket, responsible for organizing touring teams overseas, both to England under the Australia banner and to New Zealand under its own name. The Victorian Cricket Association

staggered from one crisis to another and had very little financial clout.

From these divisions a central Australian body had to be formed to represent Australian interests in the growing arena of international cricket. The first attempt was the Australasian Cricket Council founded in March 1892, a feeble body which soon disappeared. The present Australian Board of Control first met in May 1905, despite the fact that South Australia, who were in the original discussions, withdrew. Queensland were admitted almost at once; South Australia came into the fold within two years; Tasmania joined in 1907; and Western Australia in 1914. From 1909, this representative board was responsible for all Test tours to and from Australia.

The Australian administration and its English counterpart were very different in approach. The Australian system involved virtually every active cricketer on a democratic basis. Each cricket club which belonged to a colony (now state) cricket association elected representatives to the association; in its turn the association elected members to the Board of Control. In England, local cricketers and local cricket clubs had no say in the government of the game. Even for paid-up members of a first-class county club the link with the Board of Control was tenuous. The only people with any real say were members of the MCC, and membership was not easy to obtain.

SOUTH AFRICAN DEMOCRACY

The only other country to achieve by the turn of the century a similar standard of cricket administration to England and Australia was South Africa. The South African Cricket Association was formed in April 1890 and was run on the same lines as the Australian Board. South African local cricket was organized into a number of Provincial Unions. Each union was managed by delegates from local affiliated clubs and sent two representatives to the meetings of the South African CA.

South Africa sent its first team to

CRICKET CONFLICT *The Calcutta Club from India.*

England in 1894. It was a far-sighted South African who took it upon himself to complete the administrative pyramid by creating in 1909 the Imperial Cricket Conference, with delegates from England, Australia and South Africa. The architect was Sir Abe Bailey. Behind his plan was the idea of a Test Tournament, staged in England, between the three countries. After some problems raised by Australia, the scheme came off in 1912. Unfortunately for Sir Abe, the weather that summer was dreadful, and open war was being waged in Australia between the major cricketers and their Board of Control, leaving the 1912 Australian side without their stars. It would be a good many years before another triangular contest between the top cricketing nations would be tried.

On the first-class domestic front in England, the MCC had been embarrassed twice – in 1902 and 1903 – when suggested alterations to the Laws, which had been expected to be passed without controversy, provoked outcries. The MCC secretary realized that

some sort of discussion with the world outside Lord's was needed if this type of awkwardness were to be avoided in the future. He therefore set up in 1904 the Advisory County Cricket Committee which included members of the first-class counties and could act as a sounding board before legislation was debated by the MCC Committee itself. By this odd arrangement, first-class county cricket was governed until 1969.

ICC EXPANSION

Between the two World Wars, the major change in administration came at the top. Lord Harris, almost single-handedly, decided to expand the Imperial Cricket Conference. At one fell swoop, he brought in New Zealand, the West Indies and India, despite the apparently insuperable problem that India did not have a governing body.

New Zealand had had such a body – the New Zealand Cricket Council – since December 1894. It was somewhat dominated by Christchurch, its base, but was a representative organization. West

Indian cricket in the 1920s was very much under the thumb of H.B.G. Austin (later Sir Harold Austin) of Barbados. He had captained two West Indian sides to England and effectively created the West Indian Board of Control in 1926, with the help of R.H. Mallett. The Indian Board of Control was set up in December 1928.

In India there was a conflict of interest between the powerful Calcutta Club and the factions which ran the Bombay Quadrangular Tournaments. One of the thorny problems was whether Englishmen long resident in India should play Test cricket for India – there was already the precedent of Ranjitsinhji representing England rather than India and soon his path would be followed both by his nephew Duleepsinhji and by the Nawab of Pataudi. The other thorn was even sharper – who should be the leader of Indian cricket? In 1931, Lord Willingdon, a former Sussex cricketer, was appointed Viceroy. He was not in favour of the Maharaja of Patiala, an extremely enthusiastic patron of the game and on the surface an obvious

choice. A second candidate was the Maharajkumar of Vizianagram. Considerable intrigue and machin-ations went on between the interested parties. Somehow Anthony De Mello, as secretary of the Cricket Board, kept the organization afloat and Test tours to and from India went ahead. Just as importantly, the Ranji Trophy was launched. To have achieved these things in a country as vast and diverse as India is an enormous tribute to De Mello's efforts.

With each Test country now having an established system of rules for its cricket and the ICC set on a firm base, the game continued with no major administrative problems until after the Second World War. The creation of Pakistan in 1947 established another strong cricketing entity. Having joined the ICC, Pakistan in 1952–53 became the seventh Test-playing country, their first series being against neighbouring India. The idea of Pakistan remaining as part of India for cricketing purposes had been suggested briefly, but this soon faded away.

In 1961 international cricket administration went awry when South Africa left the British Commonwealth. By the then rules of the Imperial Cricket Conference, South Africa were now automatically debarred from Test cricket. England, Australia and New Zealand simply ignored the ruling and Test matches by those countries continued against South Africa as if nothing had happened.

It was not a situation which could continue, and in 1965 the world body changed its name to the International Cricket Conference and created a new class of membership for non-Test-playing countries. Ceylon (now Sri Lanka), Fiji and the United States joined as associate members. The following year Bermuda, Denmark, East Africa and the Netherlands became members. More countries joined throughout the 1970s and in 1981 Sri Lanka was moved up to full membership and Test Match status. Zimbabwe became the ninth full member in 1992. Bangladesh were added in 2001 and Kenya were recognized as a country to play official one-day internationals.

South Africa's Test Matches ceased in 1969–70 because of pressure from anti-apartheid campaigners, and did not resume until 1991, when South Africa's race laws were abolished.

In order to produce some competitive inter-national cricket below Test level, John Gardiner devised the ICC Trophy. This limited-overs competition was first staged in 1979 in England and involved the following countries: Bermuda, East Africa, Fiji, Papua New Guinea, Singapore, Argentina, Denmark, Canada, Bangladesh, Malaysia, Sri Lanka, USA, Wales, the Netherlands and Israel. Wales only played because Gibraltar dropped out at the last minute. Sri Lanka beat Canada in the final.

In 1984, the ICC created a third category of membership for the very minor cricketing nations. Italy became the first affiliate. The world organization had a second change of title in 1989 and since then has been known as the International Cricket Council. From being little more than an annual talking shop, the ICC now has a chief executive and a permanent office based at Lord's.

Over the last few years, governing bodies in the countries belonging to the ICC have been radically overhauled due to the revolution of televising matches and the advertising revenues this generates.

The ICC moved its headquarters to Dubai in 2005. Twelve associate members took part in the Intercontinental Cup in 2004. The ICC ruled that all the matches in the competition would be first-class.

ENGLAND CATCHES UP

English cricket remained run by the MCC, in the guise of the MCC-dominated Board of Control and the MCC Advisory County Cricket Committee, until 1969, when a new governing body, the Cricket Council, was set up with two administrative bodies directly under it – the Test and County Cricket Board (dealing, as its name implies, with England Test teams and the County Championship), and the National Cricket Association, which ran amateur cricket below county level. The 1997 foundation of the England and Wales Cricket Board swept all this away.

The previous 27 years had also seen the financial side of English cricket radically transformed, as the table below shows.

INDIAN ENGLISHMAN
The Nawab of Pataudi.

ENGLISH COUNTY CLUB FINANCES: Comparison of revenue	
1969	
Match receipts	17%
Membership	25%
Supporters' association	28%
Broadcasting, Test matches and sponsors	29%
1996	
Match receipts	01%
Membership	11%
Catering	06%
Broadcasting, Test matches and sponsors	81%

HISTORY OF THE LAWS OF CRICKET

No game can operate without a set of rules, written or unwritten. Cricket's earliest laws are apparently lost, but the code of 1744, which survives, contains the basic elements which are still in operation today.

The basic Laws of today are almost a book in their own right, yet it would be perfectly possible to stage a game using the simple laws of 1744 and scarcely notice the difference between a 1744 game and a game played under current laws.

The 1744 Laws were merely a revision of an earlier version, now apparently lost. This is not supposition because a document exists of 1727 which is entitled *Articles of Agreement between His Grace the Duke of Richmond and Mr Brodrick for two cricket Matches concluded the eleventh of July 1727.* These articles discuss points of possible controversy and not the basic rules for cricket and therefore constitute an agreed appendix laid down for the two specific matches – it was vital that disputes did not arise since large sums of money were wagered on the match result.

A study of the 1744 Laws does reveal some interesting detail. For instance, although the size of the wicket, the length of the pitch, the weight of the ball and the number of balls per over are all given, there is no mention of the number of players required for each team. The magical number of eleven which seems sacred to cricket therefore does not go back even as far as the earliest known laws. It is not until 1884 – after Test matches had been established for seven years and the County Championship for more than half a century – that a law is introduced: "A match is played between two sides of eleven players each, unless otherwise agreed to".

The one 1744 Law which has been repeatedly changed relates to the size of the wickets: in 1798 this was increased to 24 inches by 7 inches; around 1819 it was increased again to 26 inches by 7 inches; about four years later there was another increase, to 27 inches by 8 inches; and in 1931 the size became 28 inches by 9 inches. These changes were made because pitches improved and batsmen again and again came to dominate bowlers.

Many of the newer laws that are not in the original 1744 version have been added simply because players have tried to subvert the spirit of the game. The first of these attempts came in 1771. The 1744 Laws give no ruling on the size of a cricket bat. In September 1771, a certain Thomas White of Reigate arrived at the wicket with a bat which was the same width as the wicket. A law was passed there and then limiting the width of a bat to 4¼ inches, and the law specifying this dimension has remained in force to the present time.

In 1774, the first law specifically ruling that a batsman could be out leg before wicket was introduced. Again, this was made law because batsmen began to deliberately put their legs in front of the wicket to prevent themselves being bowled, though the 1744 code does include a note about umpires judging

GENTLEMANLY CONDUCT *A game of cricket as played when the 1744 Laws were in force.*

Ye Laws of Ye Game of Cricket

Ye pitching of ye first Wicket is to be determined by
ye cast of a piece of Money.
When ye first Wicket is pitched and ye popping Crease cut, which
must be exactly 3 Foot 10 Inches from ye Wicket, ye other Wicket
is to be pitched, directly opposite, at 22 Yards distance,
and ye other popping Crease cut 3 Foot 10 Inches before it.
Ye bowling Creases must be cut, in a direct line, from each Stump.
Ye Stumps must be 22 inches long, and ye Bail 6 inches.
Ye Ball must weigh between 5 and 6 ounces.
When ye Wickets are both pitched and all ye Creases cut,
ye Party that wins the toss up may order which Side
shall go in first at his option.

Laws for ye Bowlers 4 Balls and Over

Ye bowler must deliver ye Ball with one foot behind ye Crease
even with ye Wicket, and When he has bowled one ball or
more shall bowl to ye number 4 before he changes wickets,
and he shall change but one in ye same innings.
He may order ye Players that is in at his Wicket to stand on
which side of it he pleases at a reasonable distance.
If he delivers ye Ball with his hinder foot over ye bowling Crease ye
Umpire shall call No Ball, though she be struck, or ye Players bowled
out, Which he shall do without being asked, and no Person shall have
any right to ask him.

Laws for ye Strikers, or Those that are in

If ye Wicket is Bowled down, it's Out.
If he strokes, or treads down, or falls himself upon
ye Wicket in striking, but not in over running, it's Out.
A stroke or nip over or under his Batt, or upon his hands, but not
arms, if ye Ball be held before she touches ye ground,
though she be hug'd to the body, it's Out.
If in striking both his feet over ye popping Crease and his Wicket put
down, except his Batt is down within, it's Out.
If he runs out of his ground to hinder a Catch, it's Out.
If a Ball is nipp'd up and he strikes her again, wilfully,
before she comes to ye Wicket, it's Out.
If ye Players have cross'd each other, he that runs for
ye Wicket that is put down is out. If they are not cross'd,
he that returns is out.

Batt Foot or Hand over Ye Crease

If in running a notch ye Wicket is struck down by a throw, before his
foot hand or Batt is over ye popping Crease, or a stump hit by ye Ball
though ye Bail was down, it's Out. But if ye Bail is down before, he
that catches ye Ball must strike a Stump
out of ye ground, Ball in hand, then it's Out.
If ye Stroker touches or takes up ye Ball before she is lain quite still,
unless asked by ye Bowler or Wicket-keeper, it's Out.

When ye Ball has been in hand by one of ye Keepers or Stopers, and
ye Player has been at home, He may go where he pleases
till ye next ball is bowled.
If either of ye Strikers is cross'd in his running ground, designedly,
which design must be determined by the Umpires, N. B. the umpire(s)
may order that Notch to be scored.
When ye Ball is hit up, either of ye Strikers may hinder ye catch in
his running ground, or if she's hit directly across ye wickets, ye other
Player may place his body any where within ye swing of his Batt, so
as to hinder ye Bowler from catching her, but he must
neither strike at her nor touch her with his hands.
If a Striker nips a ball up just before him, he may fall before his
Wicket, or pop down his Batt before she comes to it, to save it.
Ye Bail hanging on one Stump, though ye Ball
hit ye Wicket, it's not Out.

Laws for Wicket Keepers

Ye Wicket Keepers shall stand at a reasonable distance behind ye
Wicket, and shall not move till ye Ball is out of ye Bowler's hand, and
shall not by any noise incommode ye Striker, and if his hands, knees,
foot or head be over or before ye Wicket,
though ye Ball hit it, it shall not be Out.

Laws for Ye Umpires

To allow 2 Minutes for each Man to come in when one is out,
and 10 Minutes between each Hand.
To mark ye Ball that it may not be changed.
They are sole judge(s) of all Outs and Ins, of all fair and unfair play,
of frivolous delays, of all hurts, whether real or pretended,
and are discretionally to allow what time they think
proper before ye Game goes on again.
In case of a real hurt to a Striker, they are to allow another to come
in and ye Person hurt to come in again but are not to allow a fresh
Man to play, on either Side, on any Account. They are sole
judge(s) of all hindrances, crossing ye Players in running,
and standing unfair to strike, and in case of hindrance
may order a Notch to be scored.
They are not to order any Man out unless appealed
to by (any) one of ye Players.

(These Laws are to ye Umpires Jointly)

Each Umpire is ye sole judge of all Nips and Catches, Ins and Outs,
good or bad Runs, at his own wicket, and his determination shall
be absolute, and he shall not be changed for another
Umpire without ye consent of both Sides.
When ye 4 Balls are bowled he is to call Over.

(These Laws are Separately)

When both Umpire(s) (shall) call Play, 3 times, 'tis at ye peril
of giving ye Game from them that refuse (to) Play.

THE CODE OF 1744

These laws of cricket were, in all probability, written to control the conduct of the players in the match between Kent and All England, which was staged on the Artillery Ground in 1744.

whether a batsman was standing unfair to strike. At that time batsmen were firm-footed, not moving their feet to the ball.

In 1788 came the law giving a penalty of five runs if the fieldsman stops the ball with his hat. It would seem that the information about the fielder who kept doing this and thus forced a change in the law is lost. A similar type of law is that relating to a lost ball – about 1805 a fielder was allowed to claim lost ball and the batting side would be credited with a given number of runs. One visualizes an important match sometime prior to this law being introduced, with a pair of batsmen scurrying forever between the wickets as the fieldsmen search a field of wheat for the ball.

The law stating that bowling must be under-arm was brought in during the early years of the nineteenth century when bowlers, frustrated that the batsmen had mastered their attack, raised their bowling arm above shoulder height in order to deliver the ball at a faster pace. The law to permit bowling with the hand up to shoulder height was finalized in 1835. In 1864, over-arm bowling was legalized.

It is worth noting that boundaries did not appear in the Laws until 1884.

The first total revision of the Laws was not undertaken until 1883–84, when the MCC set up a sub-committee whose task it was to revise the Laws by defining terms, supplying omissions, and better wording, but without altering the spirit of the game. The sub-committee produced draft copies which were sent to all the major county clubs, to Oxford and Cambridge, to Victoria and New South Wales, and to New York and Philadelphia. No vast alterations were made in the course of this revision and it was a very good attempt to put the laws into a logical sequence. The success of this new version can be judged by the fact that it was to last for over 60 years.

With regard to the pitch and its location, in the 1744 Laws the side which won the toss selected the piece of ground on which the wickets should be pitched. In 1774, the law stated that the visitors could select the ground for the pitch, but it had to be within 30 yards of the spot chosen by the home team. Thirty years later, the law stated that the umpires had the task of selecting the ground to be used for the pitch.

There was no mention in the earliest Laws of the way the pitch should be maintained during the match, but in the 1788 version rolling, watering, covering, mowing and beating of the pitch could take place by mutual consent. About 1823, a clause was added to say that the pitch could be changed after rain. In 1860, the side next to bat could order the pitch to be rolled, and in 1883 a clause was added to allow rolling for 10 minutes before the start of play. In 1931, this was reduced to seven minutes. The most controversial topic now concerning

the pitch is the question of whether matches should be played on covered or uncovered pitches.

A period of three years was spent during the 1940s drafting a totally revised set of Laws to remove any ambiguities. The man who rationalized the draft was Colonel R.S. Rait Kerr and the new code came into effect in April 1948.

Throughout the 1950s the chief concern of the officials in relation to the Laws was connected with bowling. The problem of drag caused by the fast bowler's back foot being over the bowling crease when the ball was delivered was highlighted by the increasing improvement in camera techniques. Therefore, a rule governing the front foot's position was eventually passed. There was also a spate of throwing whereby a number of bowlers no-balled in first-class cricket. The famous case of the South African, Geoff Griffin, who was no-balled in the 1960 Lord's Test brought matters to a head – the various countries agreed to clamp down on bowlers with dubious actions. The number of bouncers bowled in an over was also limited.

Over the years minor additions were required as players tried to bend the Laws – the appearance of a metal bat, for example, required a law stating that bats should be wooden – and the wearing of helmets required another change. In autumn 1974, Billy Griffith was asked to redraft the 1947 code and in 1980 the present Laws came into force.

INTIMIDATORY BOWLING

The Laws, however, are not set in concrete, and the regulations which govern the game are under constant review. The front-foot law which, as stated, is the present method of determining a no-ball is a case in point. This law is unpopular with bowlers and with many commentators, but the authorities have tried to ensure that a batsman has only to face a ball propelled at him from the full 22 yards. In a positive attempt to reduce the number of no-balls bowled, the Australian Board of Control began to penalize bowlers

two runs for each no-ball in the 1990–91 season, and England adopted the same penalty in 1993, although these strictures have only applied in first-class domestic competitions not Test matches.

The war against intimidatory bowling, the direct attack on the batsman's body, was waged by MCC in 1935 in the wake of the "bodyline" tour. Umpires were instructed to take action against such bowling, and umpires remain the sole arbiters of what is fair and unfair play. It is the bowling of fast, short-pitched deliveries that is considered unfair if, in the opinion of the umpire at the bowler's end, such deliveries are an attempt to intimidate the batsman. The International Cricket Council has decreed that a bowler may not bowl more than two fast, short-pitched deliveries an over, but great responsibility has been placed upon the umpire and the way in which he interprets the law. Umpires and captains have certainly disagreed over its implementation, and West Indian sides under Clive Lloyd and Viv Richards opposed the

restriction as a deliberate attempt to reduce the effectiveness of attacks which consisted of four bowlers of considerable pace.

Bowlers would argue that all laws and regulations which have been introduced in the past 20 years have been introduced in an attempt to reduce their potency and to give greater advantages to the batsman. The decision in the early 1980s to have complete, unconditional covering for all pitches meant that never again would a bowler operate on a pitch severely affected by the weather. The decision certainly took some romance from the game. Hobbs and Sutcliffe had become part of legend when, on a pitch made treacherous by overnight rain, they scored 172 for England's first wicket against Australia at the Oval in 1926, and, six years later, at Headingley, Hedley Verity exploited a drying wicket to take all 10 Nottinghamshire wickets for 10 runs to establish a record that is not likely to be beaten. On the reverse side, Morris Sievers took five for 21 as Australia bowled out England

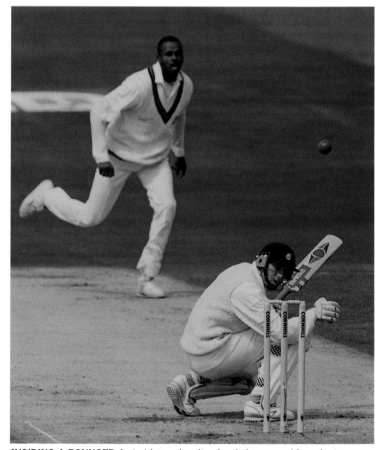

AVOIDING A BOUNCER *Intimidatory bowling has led to several law changes.*

NO BALL *Griffin, the South African fast bowler, was no-balled for throwing in the 1960 Lord's Test.*

for 76 on a Melbourne "gluepot" in 1937, but he never played Test cricket again, for the Australian selectors decided that he was only a "bad wicket" bowler.

LBW

Certainly the complete covering of pitches has made life easier for the batsman and harder for the bowler, but the batsman would argue that the changes in the lbw law have been in favour of the bowler. Until 1935, a ball had to be pitched straight in line between wicket and wicket to obtain a leg before decision, but in 1935, a new law was introduced which embraced balls pitched outside the off-stump although the ball had to strike the batsman in line between wicket and wicket.

In 1970, the law was amended again so that a batsman could be adjudged leg before if he offered no stroke to a ball which struck him outside the off stump and which, in the opinion of the umpire, would have hit the wicket. Mike Gatting was to be forgetful of this law at Lord's in 1984 when he succumbed twice to Malcom Marshall in the England-West Indies Test.

These changes in the law regarding lbw had tended to encourage the off-break or in-slant bowler while the leg-break bowler can gain no decision for a ball pitched outside leg stump which the batsman is still at liberty to pad away. This fact, and lush outfields

which enable the ball to retain its shine longer, made leg-break bowling virtually extinct by the 1960s, but top performers like Abdul Qadir, Anil Kumble and Shane Warne have resurrected the art and became the most potent match-winners in Test cricket, not least because batsmen were at a loss as to how to play them.

Although several batsmen argued against the "new" lbw law in 1935 and again against its extension in 1970, none really saw a reduction in his run-getting powers, and the bowler would continue to argue that all legislation has been against him, especially in the restrictions set upon him in the limited-over game where the length of his run-up is often bounded by regulations and his allowed number of overs is invariably determined as a fifth of the innings quota.

ONE-DAY FIELDING

Following a pattern of defensive fields in the early days of one-day competitions which began domestically in England in 1963 and internationally in Australia in 1970–71, a circle was drawn some 30 yards from the pitch and fielders had to be within the circle at certain times during the innings. By the time of the 1996 World Cup, only two fieldsmen were permitted to be outside the circle during the first 15 overs of the innings, and for the remaining overs only five fieldsmen were permitted to be

outside the circle. This ruling was brilliantly exploited by Sri Lanka whose opening batsmen, Jayasuriya and Kaluwitharana, were never afraid to hit over the heads of fielders and scored at a devastating rate.

Limited-over cricket became exceedingly popular when Kerry Packer introduced his break-away World Series Cricket in 1978–79. It was in this era that coloured clothing and floodlit games became the norm, and the limited-over game has proliferated to such an extent that, internationally, it outnumbers Test cricket by five to one. Coloured clothing has been adopted for Sunday League games in England and a white ball is also used although, until 1997, there were not even plans for a day/night game.

It could be said that the one-day game has transformed the attitude of both players and spectators, yet it moves at a pace and excites attention. The first-class game stands accused of reducing itself to a crawl. Where once 20 overs an hour was the expectation, the ICC now recognizes 15 overs an hour as being the requirement for a Test match, and few Test sides have been able to maintain the rate, so anxious are players to preserve their stamina. Even heavy fines have failed to solve the problem just as they have problems of behaviour.

SUBSTITUTES

It has now become a regular occurrence for bowlers to leave the

field to change shirts or to receive some form of treatment after finishing a spell, and the substitute is increasingly in evidence. Indeed, South Africa has experimented with allowing sides to name 14 players and to use eleven of them in whatever capacity they wish during the course of a game while, in New Zealand, 1996–97, as many as 15 players appeared for one side in an inter-provincial game because four of the original 11 had to be released midway through the match to appear in an international fixture.

In 2000 the MCC completely redrafted the Laws. In fact the number of changes were minor, but, with lawyers checking each dot and comma, the numbers of words used increased by 25%.

A new section 'The Spirit of Cricket' was added as a kind of foreword. This made the captains responsible for the conduct of all their players. The umpires can now give the batting side five extra runs if the fielding side infringes the Laws in a certain number of ways. The other scoring change was that wides and no-balls count as one run, in addition to any made by the batsman.

More than one commentator pointed out that as the new laws are designed to combat obscure points found only in cricket at top level, the Laws should not have been fundamentally altered for ordinary matches, but the extra clauses should have been an appendix applying just at top level.

EQUIPMENT

To play cricket requires a bat, a ball and a set of wickets – the three basic necessities since records began. The bat has changed only once, from a hockey-stick type to the present one. The ball has scarcely altered. The stumps have simply grown in size as the pitch has altered from rough meadow to billiard table. The one major change has been the armour demanded by the batsman.

The three essential elements of cricket are the bat, the ball and the wicket. Everyone is familiar with the appearance, size and material of these three pieces of cricket equipment as used in present-day cricket matches, but originally they must have been nothing more than a thick wooden stave to use as a bat, probably a rounded lump of wood as a ball and two thin sticks stuck in the ground as a wicket.

The first mention of the bat comes in a court case of 1613, when Nicholas Hockley assaulted Robert Hewett with a stick called a "cricket staffe" value one penny. In 1622, several youths were in court for playing at cricket in a churchyard because, for one reason, their ball might have broken the church windows. Unfortunately for the historian, the man presiding over the court didn't ask for a description of the ball, so we can only assume it was a hard object!

The price of bats seems to have halved between 1613 and 1624, since in the latter year, in a court case there is a reference to a small staff called a "cricket batt", worth half a penny.

In 1658, the writer Edward Phillips, a nephew of Milton, states in a piece:

"Would my eyes had been beat out of my head with a cricket-ball, the day before I saw thee."

The cricket ball thus remains a hard and dangerous object, but its exact nature is still a mystery.

INDISTINGUISHABLE *In this cricket match, painted in about 1744, the batsman and the fielders are equally unprotected.*

These lines written in a bible about 1680 are the first to refer to the wicket:

*"All you that do delight
in Cricket
Come to Marden, Pitch
your wickets"*

At the start of the eighteenth century there is no evidence as to the sizes of the bat, ball or wickets and there are no pictorial representations. No actual bats, balls or wick-

ets from the seventeenth century are preserved in any museum or pavilion.

The first detailed description of a match, published in 1706, throws no further light on the matter. The Articles of Agreement for the two matches between the Duke of Richmond's side and Mr Brodrick's side say nothing on the subject, though they state that the pitch should be 23 yards long and that there should be 12 players per side.

The first dim light to be shed on

the nature of bat, ball and wicket comes with a lithograph of 1739 showing young children, eight or nine years old, playing cricket. The bat is very much like a modern hockey stick; the wicket, two stumps and a cross-piece. The Laws of 1744 only help in two aspects: firstly that the stumps should be 22 inches high and six inches wide, and secondly that the ball should weigh between five and six ounces. The bat is not mentioned. However, in or about 1744, comes

LIKE A HOCKEY STICK *A bat of the type used in the 1760s.*

RECORD MAKER
The bat used by Gary Sobers to create a new Test record of 365 in 1957–58.

TYPICAL BAT *used in County Cricket in the 1980s.*

Francis Hayman's *Cricket in Marylebone Fields* – an oil painting which clearly shows the leading players of the day. The two wooden stumps with a single bail are seen, and four bats are featured, one with each batsman and one with each umpire. The bats have a covered black handle and the blades are slightly curved. A red ball is in the bowler's hand. The players are dressed overall in white, with knee breeches and silk stockings, black buckled shoes and dark jockey caps. The batsmen and wicket-keepers do not wear any pads or gloves.

The change to a straight bat came in the 1770s and the law about the regulation size is noted in the section of this book devoted to the Laws. The bat at this stage is still made of a single piece of wood. As bats developed shoulders, there came the natural tendency for the handle to snap off at the shoulder. This led to the spliced bat which came into vogue about 1830, but bats made out of a single piece of wood went on being produced (because they were so much cheaper) until the last years of the nineteenth century. Thomas Nixon, the Nottingham professional,

invented the idea of cane handles. From this development came the next step of inserting a sandwich of rubber, or one of canvas and rubber, held between slices of cane. Rubber handle covers were patented in 1880.

So far as cricket balls are concerned, Duke & Son of Penshurst in Kent were the first manufacturers of cricket balls, it is claimed, from 1760. The best early description of ball manufacture comes from Joseph Farington's diary of 1811, when he visited Duke's factory. Thread was wound round an octagonal piece of cork and then a leather case of bull hide put on the rounded core.

There were also various experiments with stumps. The wood was usually ash and a brass ferrule at the top was common to prevent damage. Several makes of stump also had iron or steel spikes so that it was easier to drive them into the ground. The idea of a stump which would automatically spring back into place when disturbed by the ball was tried out and a number of patents were lodged on the spring gadget required, but these were never used in major matches because of the law which

LITTLE CHANGE *Over the last 125 years there have been remarkably few modifications to the cricket ball.*

STUMPS *have changed in size several times during cricket's history. The topmost in this picture is a typical stump of the 1930s, with its brass ferrule. Below it are the smaller stumps used until 1931.*

entitles a fielder to pull the stump from the ground if the bails are missing. Bails were usually made of ash or boxwood, though in the 1860s iron bails were tried when a fierce wind was blowing.

SILENT WITNESS *This stump saw the cricketing action of the 1946 Tests.*

KEEPING SCORE

The first scoreboards were used in the 1840s, and consisted of a board with hooks on which metal number plates were hung. These boards simply gave the current total, the number of wickets which had fallen and the score of the last batsman. In 1884 came the addition of the scores of both the batsmen at the wicket, so figures on movable rollers replaced the individual tin scoring plates.

The Australian main grounds by 1890 had scoreboards which gave the names of all the batsmen and the score they made, and within 10 years the boards had, in some cases, been extended so that the bowler's name and analyses were displayed. This comprehensive scoreboard was only tried once in England on a permanent basis, at Trent Bridge, Nottingham from 1950 until the 1970s.

Electronic, computerized scoreboards have been gradually phased in during the last 20 years, the Packer World Series Cricket of the late 1970s hastening this process.

As regards the implements of the scorer, the notching of runs on a stick is clearly shown on Hayman's painting of 1744. The switch to written records must

have occurred when it was thought necessary to record individual batsmen's runs, rather than simply the team total. The detailed score for the Kent v England match of 1744 is known, so someone must have written down the details at the time. A few books with scores written in them exist for the first half of the nineteenth century and by the mid-nineteenth century scorebooks were being printed with set grids for batsmen and bowlers in the type of pattern that is still in common use. More sophisticated methods of recording the score have been devised in the twentieth century – Bill Ferguson, for many years Australia's scorer, was foremost in this development.

DRESS CODE

The change in cricketing dress simply followed fashion as breeches gave way to trousers in about 1815. A tall hat replaced the jockey caps.

The first move in the direction of batsmen's pads came with the idea of stitching a lining inside the trouser and inserting rubber between the lining and outer cover, but this was a brief fad

before leg-guards became common. Thomas Nixon, who had introduced cane handles, is credited with inventing cork pads in 1841 and open pads in 1853.

India-rubber padded gloves were advertised for sale in 1844. In 1846, Robert Dark of Lord's was the inventor and manufacturer of Tubular Indian Rubber Gloves,

though another note states that Nicholas Felix, the famous batsman, invented gloves in 1835 with slips of india-rubber glued to each finger. So far as the wicket-keeper was concerned, in 1844 it was recommended that he wear a pair of ordinary gloves, but by 1851 new improved wicket-keeping gloves were being talked about. Lord

TOURING BLAZER *of the MCC. Until 1996, this style was worn by England cricketers overseas.*

TOURING ATTIRE *The MCC touring sleeveless sweater.*

mention the very likely elastic belt with a buckle incorporating a cricketing design and probably brown, or brown and white, boots.

The professional teams of the 1850s wore standard coloured shirts, the All-England shirt being white with red dots. Blazers were first used, it is believed, for the Lady Margaret Boat Club of St John's College, Cambridge, in 1862. The following year the Oxford cricket team wore blue blazers. Striped blazers were in vogue in the 1880s.

Head gear changed from top hats to pot hats and in the 1850s hats often had a club ribbon as a band. Public schools seem to have introduced caps to cricket, Eton, Rugby, Winchester and Harrow all having their own distinctive caps in the 1850s. The I Zingari had a striped forage cap with IZ on the front and elastic to hold the cap on the wearer's head.

The buckled belt gave way to a silk scarf round the waist in the 1880s and brown boots were replaced by white buckskin. The Australian Aborigines each wore a sash of a different colour when playing in England in 1868, which colour was marked on the scorecard, thus enabling spectators to identify the players.

PROTECTING ONE'S PERSON

The first abdominal protectors were noted in 1851, but their design is not known. In 1880, they were known as person protectors and in 1890 as groin protectors.

The idea of an umpire wearing a white coat has an interesting beginning. In the days of underarm and round-arm bowling, umpires wore ordinary black suits, but when over-arm bowling and the idea of bowling over the wicket began batsmen complained that they lost sight of the ball against the umpire's suit. It is believed that the first time an umpire wore a white overcoat was in 1861, when the United Eleven opposed the Free Foresters. At first, some spectators ridiculed white-coated umpires, but the innovation caught on and by the 1870s was common practice. The white coats in many cases reached almost to the ground, but they have gradually had their hems raised, first in Australia, then generally, to the present level.

Cricket pads were worn by most batsmen by the 1880s. Pads had been of brown leather, but white

Harris stated that in his early days (i.e. about 1868) wicket-keeping gloves were made of yellow leather, which used to get so hard that the gloves had to be soaked before being put on.

The use of white clothing during the eighteenth century had given way by the mid-nineteenth century to a bizarre variety which would surprise even today's multi-coloured teams. A description of a fictitious cricketer in 1858 makes interesting reading: "Captain Spangles was attired as follows: cap of harlequin pattern, red neck-cloth with a pin composed of gold stumps and cross bat, the British cricketer shirt, illustrated with portraits of favourite players in attitude, and grey and black zebra flannel trousers." The writer fails to

EARLY PAD *Brown leather was often used in the construction of pads during the late nineteenth century.*

BREAKING WITH TRADITION *In the 1990s coloured pads were introduced in the Sunday League.*

later became the trademark of the England wicket-keeper Bob Taylor. More recently, the West Indian players adopted broad-brimmed hats.

The major change in headgear, though, was the use of the protective helmet. Back in 1933, Patsy Hendren had devised a three-peak cap to guard the temples against the fast bowling of the time, but this did not catch on. Even earlier, in 1870, when the first and only fatality in English first-class cricket occurred through a batsman being hit on the head, the next batsman to come in wore a towel as a turban. So far as the modern helmet is concerned, Mike Brearley, the England captain, devised a sort of helmet which looked like dog flaps hanging out of his cap. Within a year or so Dennis Amiss, the Warwickshire and England batsman, adapted a motor-cycle helmet and quite a number of designs developed with various grilles in front of the face and other protective pieces. By the middle of the 1980s, it was unusual to see a batsman come to the wicket in first-class cricket without a

canvas or leather ones were in use generally by the close of the nineteenth century. Some batsmen wore skeleton pads but they did not last.

In the Edwardian era, cricket dress became standardized, players being dressed uniformly in white shirt and flannels, white boots and white pads. Every club of any pretension had its own colours and these appeared on caps, blazers and as bands on sweaters – the wearing of sweaters had arrived in the late 1890s. In English county cricket, amateurs still appeared in their ordinary club caps, rather than the county cap, and often wore a neckerchief.

This standard dress remained almost unchanged until the 1970s – except that the Australians adopted a baggy cap, as opposed to the close-fitting English style of cap. In the late 1960s, floppy hats began to appear in first-class matches – Greg Chappell, playing for Somerset in 1968 and 1969, was one of the first to sport such a garment in county matches; it helmet. The practice of close-to-the-wicket fielders on the leg side also wearing a helmet followed. Other protection used by batsmen involved thigh pads and forearm protectors. Thigh pads were certainly being worn in first-class cricket in 1947.

The advent of coloured clothing has been an emotive subject among traditional English supporters. The Kerry Packer World Series players in the late 1970s wore different-coloured apparel. The English county players were instructed to wear coloured clothing for Sunday League matches for the first time in 1993; the players had their names on the back and the name of the team on the front of the shirt. Coloured pads were also used and a white ball with black sightscreens, although these games were all played in daylight, unlike overseas where night or day-night games were common practice.

The editor of *Wisden* was happy enough to accept the break with traditional white clothing, but he ended his statement on the matter with the following warning:

"If, however, the counties are

planning to change their colours every year to exploit children and make them buy up-to-date gear at rip-off prices, which is what happens in football, then they are taking the road to hell." It need hardly be added that since 1993 the designs have all been changed!

The major grounds have a new design of sightscreen, which can not only be converted from black to white, but can also be switched to an advertising display. This option is used in alternate overs during televised matches. Also to accommodate television, the middle stump has been hollowed out and a television camera installed to give close-up pictures.

above **SUN HAT** *worn by Clive Rice in the 1980s.*

left **ENGLAND TOURING CAP** *worn during the the 1901–02 visit to Australia.*

below **MCC** *England touring cap of the 1930s.*

right **NOTTINGHAMSHIRE COUNTY CRICKET CLUB** *cap of the 1940s.*

THE CULTURE OF CRICKET

Whether on the field or off it, cricket exerts a powerful influence over the English way of life. The writings of Neville Cardus and John Arlott appeal to a wide audience, as does cricket coverage on radio and television. The sport has also inspired many talented artists, from G. F. Watts onwards.

Strenuous efforts are now being made to promote cricket as a worldwide game, mainly through television. Countries which possess fewer cricket players than any self-respecting Yorkshire town are being given membership of the International Cricket Council, in the belief that official recognition will inspire the inhabitants to adopt cricket wholesale. Test-playing countries are being asked to foster the game on their continent. The scheme is thoroughly commendable, but will nations that have steadfastly turned their backs on cricket, in some cases for as long as 200 years, now be persuaded that cricket is for them?

ENGLISH EXPORT

It is a historical fact, however, that cricket is peculiar to the English and to Anglophiles. Even such near neighbours as the Irish, Scots and Welsh have for the most part ignored the game. It was the English landlords with estates in the rest of the British Isles who played cricket in front of the "big house", usually with guests of the household and against such invited teams as Free Foresters, Incogniti and the like. The tenants and estate workers, for their

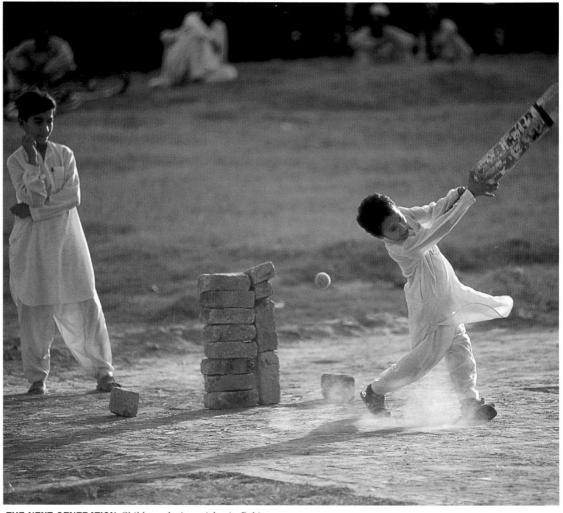

THE NEXT GENERATION *Children playing cricket in Pakistan.*

part, made up annual teams, but rarely took the game back to their villages.

Although the villagers of the Weald can be said to have created the modern game, Wealden folk stayed very much between the North and South Downs and did little or nothing to promulgate the sport beyond their boundaries. Those responsible for spreading cricket were the landed gentry of Surrey, Sussex and Kent – or rather their sons, for those youths took the game to Eton, Harrow, Charterhouse, Westminster and Winchester. When they left those schools, they went to Oxford or Cambridge or to the army or navy. Cricket went with them.

It was an ideal occupation for soldiers with time on their hands. Thus the militia, mustered to ensure that the French Revolution did not spread across the English Channel, played cricket. Meanwhile, the boys at the great schools organized the first inter-schools matches and a little later the undergraduates fixed the first university match.

As early as 1676 there is a record of cricket being played outside Britain – in Aleppo (now in Syria) but then part of the sprawling Ottoman Empire. The players were visitors from a British naval vessel and English residents in Aleppo. No evidence exists, though, that the Turks or the Syrians were wielding cricket bats.

The first description of a cricket match was written, in 1706, by William Goldwin, educated at Eton and Cambridge. In 1721, sailors of the East India Company were reported to be playing cricket on the west coast of India and a few years later the English colonists in America organized games. In 1766, cricket was being played in Paris, but only by Englishmen and some upper-class Frenchmen.

The oldest cricket club outside mainland Britain and still existing today is the Calcutta Club, founded in or before 1792 and then intended exclusively for Europeans. When the first known century was scored in Ireland in 1800, the batsman was Ensign Beckett of the Coldstream

Guards – the first hundred in India, in 1804, was by R. Vansittart of the Old Etonians. A match was recorded in Cape Town, between officers of the Artillery Mess and the Colony in 1808. The officers of the Brigade of Guards played cricket near Brussels on the eve of the Battle of Waterloo. As the British Empire expanded, cricket was played by the army, however outlandish the locale.

The middle of the nineteenth century saw the creation of the modern public school system, one of its tenets being muscular Christianity. Cricket was an integral part of this ethos. "It's not cricket" was a phrase which emanated from the schools – as was the importance of playing the game for the game's sake rather than for winning or losing.

This last point is of interest because in the late twentieth century winning has become all-important in many quarters and this conflicts with the Englishness of cricket. Lord Harris, at one time Governor of Bombay, and for much of his life the most important figure in cricket, expressed great concern that inter-county cricket in the nineteenth century was becoming a sport dominated by trophies, cups and money. He begged county cricketers not to follow such a path.

Until the 1960s, cricket clubs in the South of England stood firm against being forced into league systems, content to play just friendly fixtures. The greatest cricket club of all, the MCC, which played hundreds of fixtures each season, steered clear of competitive games.

In contrast to this, Australian cricket at club level has been organized into competitive leagues since the Victorian era. This is one reason why Australia, with a fraction of the number of active cricketers that could be found in England, has competed on an equal footing at Test level.

In two parts of what was the British Empire cricket has been taken up at a serious level – one being the West Indies, the other the Indian sub-continent. In both cases it was a long slow process – in contrast to the speed with which soccer spread.

As the twenty-first century approaches, the throbbing heartland of cricket can be found in Pakistan, India and Sri Lanka. In those three countries youths play cricket on odd pieces of land using home-made implements, just as used to happen in England. Rowland Bowen, the noted cricket historian, expressed the opinion about 30 years ago that cricket was dying; he was referring only to cricket in England. And though cricket as the cultural experience known to Englishmen is dying, a new variety is blossoming.

GENTLEMEN VERSUS PLAYERS

In the eighteenth century match scores were careful to distinguish between the paid players and the amateurs, the former being shown purely by the surname or sometimes their Christian name and surname, the latter being Mr Blank or Blank Esq.

According to Pycroft's *The Cricket Field*, the Gentlemen (i.e. the amateurs) first opposed the Players in 1798, but the first recognized match in the series between the two classes took place at Lord's in 1806. The Gentlemen won both the games played that year, though they had a professional or two as given men. The match became one of the showpieces of the year and, after the creation of Surrey's ground at the Oval, it was common practice to stage one fixture at each ground each season. A third venue, Scarborough, was used regularly for an end-of-season match from the 1880s onwards. Other venues occasionally staged the match.

The distinction between Gentlemen and Players was maintained even when a county side was made up of a mixture – the two classes having separate dressing rooms, even separate gates to enter the playing area. When playing away they stayed in separate hotels and travelled to their destination in

separate compartments on the train, first-class and third.

The distinction in first-class county cricket did not cease until 1963. Since the Australians did not divide their cricketers into two classes, this caused some problems when they first toured England – the Australians were all paid players. The English authorities got around this, however, by making the Australians "honorary" amateurs!

LITERARY TRADITION

The earliest known publication on the game of cricket is a description of a match, issued in 1706 and written in Latin verse, called *In Certamen Pilae* by William Goldwin. The second, *Cricket: An Heroic Poem* by James Love, describes the Kent v All England match on the Artillery Ground, London, in 1744. Several more pieces of verse in the manner of Love's poem followed.

Aside from these "literary" efforts, cricket's appearances in print until the 1830s were confined to books of instruction, of scores, of the Laws and of regulations for various clubs. This rather staid diet was enlivened in 1833 when a volume entitled *The Young Cricketer's Tutor* made its appearance. The author was named as John Nyren, whose father had captained the famous Hambledon Club side in the 1770s, but the actual writer, described as the "editor", was Charles Cowden Clarke, a well-known literary figure of the day.

The book gives pen portraits of the Hambledon players and their most notable opponents, and the style in which it is written evokes the feel of Hambledon in its heyday. The book has been reprinted numerous times and is still issued at intervals to satisfy the demand of new generations of readers. Thirteen years after the Nyren-Clarke masterpiece, the journalist William Denison wrote *Cricket: Sketches of the Players*, which consisted of long essays on 37 contemporary cricketers. The year before, an amateur cricketer and Blackheath schoolmaster wrote a treatise on batsmanship entitled *Felix on the Bat*. (Felix was the cricketing name of Nicholas Wanostrocht.) An integral part of this well-written book are the illustrations derived from a series of sketches by G. F. Watts.

The end of the 1840s saw the start of the modern cricket annual. Fred Lillywhite, the scorecard printer at the Oval, published *The Young Cricketer's Guide*. This annual, which was made up of potted scores, averages and current players' biographies, ran until 1866 when Fred Lillywhite died – though not before he had also pioneered the cricket tour book. He accompanied George Parr's team to North America in 1859 and wrote and published a book on that first tour. The annual – known to cricket bibliophiles as "Fred's Guide" – had two rivals including John Wisden's *Cricketers' Almanack*. This last-named commenced publication in 1864 and through the 1870s had two more Lillywhite annuals to contend with – James Lillywhite's *Cricketers' Annual* and John Lillywhite's *Cricketers' Companion*. The final Lillywhite production came out in 1900; thereafter *Wisden* was out on its own and earning its sobriquet, the cricketer's bible.

The first worthwhile history of the game had appeared in 1851 – James Pycroft's *The Cricket Field*.

"FRED'S GUIDE" *title-page from 1859.*

Like Nyren's book, this history was to be reissued many times and remained the standard work on the game's early history until the 1890s, although such exhaustive tomes as Charles Box's history – gilt-edged and running to over 500 pages – arrived to fill bookcases.

The first weekly magazine devoted entirely to cricket, simply entitled *Cricket*, appeared in 1882 under the editorship of the most versatile of sporting polymaths, C.W. Alcock.

Cricket biographies, or ghosted autobiographies, commenced inevitably with W.G. Grace in 1890, closely followed by Richard Daft (from the same publisher) .

Arthur Haygarth, that diligent gatherer of scores and biographical notices, persuaded the Lillywhite organization to undertake publication of his life's work, namely the full score of every important cricket match in chronological order, with biographical notes on players, usually when they first appeared at Lord's. The project lost money for everyone connected with it, but the MCC were kind enough to publish 10 volumes even after the initial four had made a loss. They are now regarded as an essential part of a cricket historian's library.

The master of erudite cricket statistics, wrapped in a cloak of history, was F.S. Ashley-Cooper. He assisted Alcock on the weekly magazine and contributed to several of the annuals. He also wrote a goodly number of small cricket booklets.

The newspapers had from the 1830s devoted many column inches, relatively speaking, to cricket reports, but these were very pedestrian – a plodding account of the day's play, in the extreme cases almost over by over. This all changed after the First World War with the emergence of a new style of reporting in the pages of the *Manchester Guardian*. Their correspondent was Neville Cardus. He captured on paper the cricketer's characteristics and the atmosphere of the game, the subtle differences between the county teams and the ambience of the grounds they used.

Cardus never played cricket at a senior level, but one writer of

JOHN ARLOTT *Outstanding broadcaster.*

distinction who did was R.C. Robertson–Glasgow. He followed Cardus's lead, but in his own inimitable way. The period between the wars also produced the best description of a fictitious village match – A.G. Macdonell's chapter entitled "The Cricket Match" in the book *England, their England*.

In Australia, the outstanding journalist of the 1930s was Ray Robinson, who wrote for the *Melbourne Star* and, in the 1940s, for the *Sydney Daily Telegraph* and later other Sydney papers. His first book did not appear until 1945, but was a great success and several more followed. Arthur Mailey, the leg-spinner, was, though in an entirely different vein, Australia's answer to Robertson-Glasgow. Mailey not only wrote but illustrated his pieces with cartoons.

The major West Indian writer whose career began in the interwar period was C.L.R. James. He used cricket to mirror the political problems of the West Indies. *Beyond a Boundary*, which is still in print, is his best-known book.

After the Second World War, two former Test cricketers became noted journalists: Ian Peebles, the Scottish-born Middlesex bowler, and Jack Fingleton, the Australian opening bat. Fingleton wrote the book on the famous "bodyline" tour – *Cricket Crisis*.

The 1940s saw a deluge of tour books, some fairly dire, and the number of ghosted autobiographies rose until scarcely a cricketer of note lacked at least one. By now however the spoken word was vying with the written. Continuous radio commentary on Test Matches became available, and enthusiasts in England woke in the small hours to listen to their wireless sets where voices fought against atmospherics. One man successfully combined the written and spoken word, John Arlott. He was to wireless commentary what Cardus had been to journalism. His Hampshire burr epitomized cricket's roots – was Hambledon calling once more? His extensive vocabulary gave him a head start on most of his fellow commentators.

In total contrast to Arlott, it seemed, was Brian Johnson, a man of jolly wheezes, whose literary diet at Eton must have been mainly *The Magnet* and its contemporaries. His schoolboy humour, centred on cream cakes, made the BBC programme 'Test Match Special' so popular that people only moderately interested in the game switched on.

CRICKET AND THE BOX

Television, however, began to dominate the airwaves. At first TV merely provided commentary with pictures, but that all changed with the Packer Revolution. Kerry Packer, the Australian television mogul, tried to obtain the broadcasting rights for major matches in Australia, but the cricket officials stayed faithful to the national Australian Broadcasting Corporation. Packer reacted in 1977 by buying up almost the entire Australian Test team, the West Indian Test side and sundry Test players from the rest of the world. He then proceeded to stage "Super-Tests" in rivalry with the official games. To promote his venture he abandoned the traditional white clothing for cricketers and gave each side coloured clothing in the manner of soccer. He played matches under floodlight and tried such gimmicks as a camera hidden in the middle stump, logos painted on the turf and many other innovative ploys. Within two or three years, traditional cricket had fallen for his television-based ideas and the advertising firms who wanted exposure on television became more important than the ordinary spectator.

In a curious way all the television razzmatazz has affected one esoteric group who would normally shun such public exposure. Television requires winners – not only teams, but "Man of the Match", "Man of the Series", "Player of the Year". The idea that two or more players could possibly be judged equal appears to be anathema to advertisers and TV moguls, so peculiar statistical analyses have to be devised to ensure a single victor.

The cricket statisticians now come into their own. Cricketing records, which had been the ultra-introverted Ashley-Cooper's province, became important to the commercial cricketing world. Roy Webber, the scorer for BBC television, even had a telephone exchange named after him. The Association of Cricket Statisticians and Historians was formed in 1973 and has a membership of some 1,300. More to the point, it has published about 300 books on statistics over the last 25 years.

Rowland Bowen took it upon himself to investigate the origins of cricket, and indeed to research the "facts" published in many books which touched on cricket history. For eight years he published the findings of the researches made by himself and his coterie in a quarterly magazine. This culminated in his book *Cricket: A History of its Growth and Development Throughout the World*.

In Australia, the study of cricket's history has been pursued in much greater depth than elsewhere and has reached university level, with a number of books on the Australian people and cricket being published.

MEMORABILIA

Before the First World War only a handful of eccentrics collected "memorabilia" related to cricket. Foremost of this small band was Charles Pratt Green. Green wrote to all the famous batsmen of the day asking for one of their worn-out bats, preferably one which had been used to record a notable innings, and in return he bought the batsman a new bat of his own choice. In that way, he amassed over 100 bats.

A. J. Gaston, a Sussex cricket enthusiast, concentrated more on cricket books. Autographs were eagerly sought by schoolboys who in some cases took their hobby on into later life. Between the wars, the millionaire Sir Julien Cahn built up a valuable collection, not only buying Green's historic bats, but also acquiring the library of Ashley-Cooper.

The ultimate aim of cricket book collectors is a complete set of *Wisden*. Demand outstripped supply and prices reflected this. The first three editions of John Wisden's little almanack all command a price at auction exceeding £3,000 – in contrast with the original published price of one shilling (5p). Bookshops specializing in cricket have been founded to cater for the growing market. Dealers operating from their own homes issue lists of stock for sale.

The major auction houses in the UK hold sales of sports items, largely centred on cricket. A society has been established for some 10 years catering for memorabilia collectors. If a cricket motif is present on an otherwise unremarkable piece of pottery or bric-a-brac, the price rises considerably, the aesthetic value counting for little. Professional cricketers hold auctions at which they seem to sell their entire wardrobe – caps and blazers are particularly prized by collectors.

CIGARETTE AND TRADE CARDS

In the popular mind, cricketing cigarette cards will always be associated with John Player & Sons and in particular with the album that firm issued for the 50 cards in the 1938 *Cricketers* series. The cards depict 34 current English county cricketers – those likely to feature

CRICKETING CARDS *A major collectible.*

in the 1938 Tests – and the 16 Australians chosen to tour England that summer. In fact, the first cigarette cards depicting cricket personalities had been issued in the United States and in Australia in the 1880s. Complete sets devoted to cricketers, however, were first issued in the UK by Wills. Taddy & Co in 1908 produced the most extensive range ever attempted: 238 cards in all are believed to have been issued, Taddy having a card for virtually every county player of note.

The ill-fated Triangular Test Tournament of 1912, when England, Australia and South Africa competed during a rain-sodden English summer, produced another surge of cricket cards, a set of 70 being published by F & J Smith.

Some collectors specialize in cigarette and other cricketing trade cards. It is estimated that there are in excess of 12,000 such cards.

After the First World War, the cricket card rivalry did not return

until 1923 when two firms, R & J Hill and Godfrey Phillips, launched sets. John Player produced their first *Ashes* set in 1926. The outbreak of the Second World War saw the end of cigarette cards, but firms such as those producing packets of tea and packets of sweets issued trade cards, some of which featured cricketers. Increasingly, though, soccer players took preference, the market for the latter being that much larger.

POSTAGE STAMPS

Unlike cigarette cards, postage stamps featuring cricketers are an entirely post-Second World War phenomenon. The first cricket stamps were issued in 1962 by the Cape Verde Islands, a Portuguese colony off the west coast of Africa. Later that year Pakistan followed suit.

English philatelists had for many years to be satisfied with a collection of Post Office cancellation marks on the standard British stamp – the major cricket grounds had at some time post offices on site. The first cricket-related British stamp was issued in 1973 and depicted W.G. Grace as drawn by Harry Furniss, the cartoonist. The GPO had intended to celebrate the centenary of the County Championship, but the issue was regarded by historians as a bizarre joke since most considered either 1864 or 1890 as the start of the championship.

Marcus Williams, who at one time wrote many articles on the subject, is considered the expert on cricketing postage stamps.

POSTCARDS

Over the last 10 years the interest in collecting postcards featuring cricket has increased considerably. This hobby of "deltiology" began soon after the legalization of picture postcards in 1894 and enjoyed its original heyday in the days prior to the First World War. Hawkins & Co., a firm of photographers based in Brighton, took photographs of most of the county teams which visited the County Ground at Hove, as well as individual pictures of many players. These are now eagerly sought by collectors.

CONTROVERSIES & SCANDALS

With the exception of apartheid, cricket's controversies have tended to centre on money. Gambling in the eighteenth century led to game rigging. Amateur 'earnings' have upset professionals. The higher rewards given to winning players and teams causes the laws to be bent. Cricket has never been quite the 'gentlemanly' game portrayed by idealists.

As soon as the latest scandal breaks, be it the allegations, and in some cases admissions, of players accepting bribes to fix the results of matches, or suggestions of players tampering with the ball during matches to their sides' advantage, the pundits cry that cricket is going to the dogs. In the old days nothing like this, or that, ever occurred; all cricketers were as pure as the driven snow. Gentlemen would never stoop to such low conduct. All the rose-coloured-spectacles come out in force, and the petty squabbles of the past are lost in the glow.

The very first records of the game are mainly concerned with court cases of some sort. The seventeenth-century players who were brought before the ecclesiastical court for playing cricket on a Sunday no doubt besmirched the good name of cricket. In the civil court in 1718, a judge was asked to make a decision regarding a match. Kent were playing London for half a guinea a man, but when it seemed Kent would lose, three of the Kent team left in order to avoid defeat and thus having to pay. The judge ordered that the match had to be completed, which it duly was – the

"PUBLIC DISSIPATION" *Eighteenth-century commentators were cautious of cricket.*

court costs were reported as £200.

By the 1760s the game had gained a grim reputation, as the following paragraph indicates:

"The game of cricket which requires the utmost exertion of strength and agility, was followed until of late years, for manly exercise, animated by a noble spirit of Emulation. This sport has too long been perverted from diversion and innocent pastime to excessive gaming and public dissipation: Cricket matches are now degenerated into business of importance."

The authorities at London's most celebrated cricket ground, the Artillery Ground, banned public matches from the ground because of the numbers of rogues and vagabonds attracted by the gambling and various criminal activities.

The early 1800s still saw bookmakers at major cricket matches and players being bribed to lose matches. In 1817, William Lambert, the leading professional of the time, was accused of selling a match and banned from Lord's for life. About the same time bookmakers were removed from Lord's. However, betting on matches still continued and was to cause some major problems when the England teams toured Australia.

AMATEURS v PROFESSIONALS

In the 1850s and 1860s, the major quarrels were between various groups of professionals. William Clarke was the manager and captain of the highly successful professional touring side which travelled the British Isles, playing anywhere provided the remuneration for Clarke was sufficient. After several years, about half the players employed by Clarke reckoned that they would do better by breaking away and forming a rival professional side. This was duly created and was financially viable, though Clarke ignored it and would not allow his players to play against the rival team.

After Clarke died in 1856, the

two XIs made up their differences and for some seasons the major showpiece match was between the two sides at Lord's. George Parr succeeded Clarke in managing the professional touring side, but in the 1860s he became embroiled in an argument with the authorities who ran the ground at the Oval. This meant that the professionals employed by Parr refused to play for their counties at the Oval and Nottinghamshire ceased temporarily to play Surrey.

The appearance of W.G. Grace on the cricket field and his incredible batting performances in the 1870s meant that he was the star attraction at any cricket match and added hundreds if not thousands to the numbers who paid to watch a game. The problem was that he played as an amateur, but did not belong to the landed gentry and thus could not afford to spend his summers playing cricket six days a week without payment. He therefore put in very heavy expenses claims for each match appearance. To aggravate the position, the whole of the county team for which Grace played – Gloucestershire – were amateurs, but when they played a county game their expenses were more than if the whole team had been professional. In fact, Grace himself put in expenses which were twice the top professionals' pay.

The Gloucestershire County Cricket Club Committee held a meeting and issued the following statement:

"That only actual expenses shall be paid to members playing for the county, EXCEPT where special arrangements are made, such arrangements to be made from time to time by the Committee."

This resolution seemed to cover all eventualities and helped everyone, but satisfied no one.

The cricket press were upset when the MCC announced that they never paid amateurs more than their bare expenses and asked how the club could reconcile their statement with the acknowledged fact that W.G. Grace made more money from cricket than any professional. The English professionals were upset when the 1878 Australians toured England, supposedly as amateurs, but were paid £20 each for a match appearance whereas the English pros opposing them were only offered £10 per man.

The position of the Australians as paid amateurs came to be accepted by the English pros as a fact of life, but the next problem to erupt came from the leading Nottinghamshire pros. Nottinghamshire at that time was the strongest county and the players felt that they were unfairly treated by the county committee. They put a set of demands to the club which included the guarantee of a benefit after 10 years and a permanent engagement for the season, rather than being paid on a match-by-match basis. The committee refused to budge and the seven principal players went on strike. The strike held solid until mid-July, when the players started to trickle back, though the two ringleaders, Arthur Shrewsbury and Alfred Shaw, did not make peace with the club until the following season.

THROWING ACTION

No sooner had Nottinghamshire settled its differences with its players than cricket encountered trouble from another direction. The actions of some of the current fast bowlers were considered illegal in some quarters – and that of Lancashire's Jack Crossland was particularly suspect. The captain of the 1882 Australian touring team, Billy Murdoch, stated that several English bowlers would be no-balled if they appeared in Australia. It was obvious that the English authorities paid heed to Murdoch for, when selecting the England team for the Test at the Oval, they pointedly ignored Crossland, although in terms of form he was the clear choice to fill a vacancy left when Fred Morley was unfit to take part.

Crossland nonetheless continued to play for Lancashire through 1882 and 1883, even though in the latter season he was no-balled for throwing in local cricket, but never in county games.

Lord Harris met the problem head on, as captain of Kent, when he announced that the county would not play against Lancashire until both Crossland and another Lancashire bowler, Nash, were withdrawn from the side. This hit Lancashire hard since Nottinghamshire had already refused fixtures with them on the grounds that Crossland was not qualified to play for Lancashire (he was Nottinghamshire-born). Middlesex also cancelled their Lancashire fixture. In the middle of 1885, the MCC ruled that

1909 AUSSIE TEAM and Pete McAlister.

Crossland was not qualified for Lancashire; that county therefore dropped him and at the end of the year also finished with Nash.

The throwing row died away for a while. However, 10 years later it surfaced once more. The Australians Jones and McKibbin were both singled out in the press as chuckers. Australian umpire James Phillips no-balled Jones for throwing and the famous Australian bowler of a previous generation, Spofforth, condemned McKibbin's action. In England, a number of bowlers were no-balled for throwing including the famous C.B. Fry, but the epidemic did not end until a list of doubtful bowlers was drawn up and the county captains came to a gentlemen's agreement not to use any of the bowlers on the list. This effectively ended the throwing problem for some 50 years.

AUSSIES BATTLE IT OUT

The next major controversy was entirely an Australian affair. It was a battle for control between the leading Australian players and the Australian Board of Control with regard to teams sent to tour England. The Board was formed in 1905, but not in time to organize the proposed 1905 Australian tour to England. This tour was run by the Melbourne Club in conjunction with the players themselves and Frank Laver of Victoria was appointed by the team as the player-manager. The tour went ahead and nothing untoward occurred. In 1906, however, disputes arose between anyone and everyone in Australian cricket, including the various state associations and their players, particularly in New South Wales. The best way to illustrate the muddle is to quote the cricket press from May 1906:

"It is simply impossible to say what is the latest development of the situation in Australia, for the cablegrams, press and private, differ to a degree which is unusual. Hence it is stated that several players have been suspended, disqualified, excommunicated by the New South Wales Cricketers' Association; that no players have been suspended etc; that time has been given to the recalcitrant players to repent of their misdeed; that the Melbourne Club has sent an invitation to the Marylebone Club to send out a team this autumn, and that the offer has been declined; that no such invitation was ever sent; that a rival Board of Control has been formed by clubs which would not join the original Board; that no rival Board has been formed; that the players who accepted the offer of the Melbourne Club, and were suspended, have gone down on their knees to apologise, and have thrown over the Melbourne Club."

This confusion continued so that, when in 1909 a team was organized to tour England again, the selection committee chosen by the Board was somewhat odd, for it included Peter McAlister rather than either Monty Noble or Victor Trumper, both of whom put their names forward and were far better qualified in terms of experience and expertise. To compound the error, the committee selected McAlister as vice-captain for the tour. McAlister was also appointed treasurer for the tourists, whilst the players independently picked Frank Laver to look after their financial interests. This produced a conflict of interest, and a great deal of mud-slinging when the Board tried to check the details on the team's return to Australia.

The ill-feeling generated bubbled through the next two years and finally blew up during a selectors' meeting convened to pick the players for the fourth Test of the 1911–12 Ashes series v England. McAlister accused Clem Hill, the current Australian captain, of being the worst leader Australia had ever had. Hill punched McAlister and the pair went into a clinch. They were saved from falling through a window to the street 30 feet below by the intervention of the Board's secretary. This was one dramatic incident in a catalogue of rows between the Board and the players and the end result was that most of the major players did not go to England on the 1912 tour. The First World War finally brought the quarrels to an end.

BODYLINE BOWLING

The great controversy between the two World Wars revolved round the 1932–33 bodyline series. In the late 1920s, pitches in Australia specifically were all in favour of the bat; allied to this, two batsmen of extraordinary talent, Don Bradman and Bill Ponsford, emerged. On two occasions, team totals topped 1,000 and both players had innings exceeding 400. When Australia toured England in 1930, Bradman proved almost invincible and among other feats created a new highest score in Test cricket. After the England side had been chosen for the 1932–33 tour to Australia, studies of Bradman's technique revealed that he appeared to be weakest playing fast bowling pitched on the leg stump. England possessed a

CLEM HILL *Australia's 1911–12 captain.*

battery of fine fast bowlers with Harold Larwood as the spearhead. Douglas Jardine, the England captain, decided to use Larwood to attack the leg stump with a half circle of close fielders on the leg side. The tactic proved successful, in that Bradman's batting average all but halved from around 100 to nearer 50. England went on to win the Ashes.

However, in the process, several Australian batsmen were injured, hit by the ball whilst batting against Larwood, and the Australian press named the leg-theory method "bodyline". Larwood and Jardine, in particular, were accused of not playing cricket; the Australian Board threatened to cease playing the Test series and bitter telegrams were dispatched by the Board to the MCC at Lord's. The English authorities were adamant that the English bowlers were not bowling at the batsmen and that the only serious injury caused to an Australian happened when Bert Oldfield ducked into a ball that he thought would rise, was hit on the head and knocked out. This accident was not the result of "bodyline" bowling. The Australian crowds barracked Larwood and Jardine excessively in support of their team and this led to a counter-claim by the MCC that this volume of barracking was unsportsmanlike.

The arguments went on through the English summer of 1933 and, with the Australians touring England in 1934, something had to be done to placate both sides if the 1934 Ashes series was to proceed peacefully. Jardine led the England side in India in the winter of 1933–34, then from India announced he would not play in England in 1934. This removed the architect of leg-theory; the question at the start of the 1934 season, therefore, was whether Larwood and his principal bowling partner, the left-armer Bill Voce, would play for England. Injury had meant that Larwood had missed most of the 1933 summer, but he was now fully fit again. The MCC asked Larwood and Voce to make an apology for the way they had bowled in 1932–33 but both refused. They were of the opinion that they had simply bowled to the orders of the England captain and thus had nothing to apologize for. Several ghosted newspaper articles under Larwood's name put matters a little more forcibly. Larwood and Voce were both Nottinghamshire players and were supported by their county captain, Arthur Carr. Carr employed the bowlers using leg-theory tactics in some championship games. This not only made the situation worse but meant that two counties announced that they would not be playing Nottinghamshire again.

Despite tremendous clamour from the English press, the selectors did not pick Larwood and Voce for the 1934 Ashes series. Australia won the series. Arthur Carr was sacked by Nottinghamshire; Larwood never again played in Test cricket; but Voce returned and was the most successful bowler on the next trip to Australia in 1936–37. Larwood retired from first-class cricket in 1938 and in 1949 emigrated to Australia with his family.

"STOP THE TOUR"

The major cricketing problem of the period between 1960 and 1990 was how to deal with South Africa and apartheid. The situation came to a head in 1968, when the English selectors decided to replace Tom Cartwright, who had reported unfit, with Basil D'Oliveira in the squad to tour South Africa during the winter of 1968–69.

D'Oliveira had great success in local cricket in South Africa, but as a Cape coloured had no prospect of being chosen for first-class cricket. He had emigrated to England and qualified by residence for Worcestershire and for England. he was chosen for England in 1966. However, he was not on the original list to tour South Africa in 1968–69. When he filled a vacancy that arose in mid-September, the South African Prime Minister, Mr Vorster, immediately accused the English authorities of picking D'Oliveira for political reasons and the tour

was cancelled.

A special meeting of the MCC was called to discuss tours to and from South Africa, the Reverend David Sheppard and Mike Brearley being the major figures to suggest that tours should cease. However, those wishing to continue tours won the day, and South Africa were given the green light to visit England in 1970. A young white South African studying in London, Peter Hain, then organized a "Stop the Tour" campaign. After discussions with the British Government and a debate in the House of Commons, the tour was cancelled and the South African Cricket Association were informed that no further Test tours involving South Africa would take place until South African cricket was run on multi-racial lines.

Official Test matches involving South Africa therefore ceased, but the reaction from South Africa was to persuade Test-quality players to come to the country unofficially. Teams from England, Australia, the West Indies and Sri Lanka all toured South Africa in the 1980s. The players who went found themselves facing a variety of bans when, or if, they returned home – both the West Indian and Sri Lankan authorities put a life ban on their rebel players. The problems were not settled until 1991 when the South African Government changed its policy and introduced multi-racial elections.

PACKER'S CIRCUS

The Kerry Packer Affair occupied the cricket officials for several years in the late 1970s. Mr Packer, a media tycoon, put in a bid to broadcast Test matches from his station in 1976 and his bid was higher than that already accepted by the Australian Board. Despite discussions, the Board stayed with its original decision and Packer decided to set up rival super-Tests. In 1977, he signed up virtually the whole of the current Australian

Test squad, almost all the notable West Indian Test players, plus a selection of English, South African, Pakistani and other players. The last group formed The Rest and Packer organized a full programme of Super-Tests and one-day games between the three sides, playing throughout Australia.

The reaction in England was to ban the English players who signed for Packer but, after a famous court case, the English authorities were found guilty of restraint of trade. The trial lasted nearly seven weeks and cost the TCCB dearly. Packer's Circus, as it was called, played two full seasons in Australia and toured the West Indies, after which Packer reached an agreement with the Australian Board and obtained exclusive rights to broadcast official Tests for 10 years. Packer's revolution changed the face of cricket, with the official bodies adopting many of the TV gimmicks used by Packer and the salaries paid to players being massively increased.

MATCH-FIXING

Rumours that had been circulating in cricket for around five years about match-fixing in international matches came to a head in April 2000 with allegations by Indian police authorities that South African players Hansie Cronje, Pieter Strydom, Nicky Boje and Herschelle Gibbs were guilty of "cheating, fraud and criminal conspiracy relating to match-fixing and betting". A businessman, Sanjeev Chawla and a bookmaker Rajesh Kalra, were named. Cronje phoned Ali Bacher, managing director of the United Cricket Board of South Africa at 3 a.m. to admit "dishonesty", and was relieved of the captaincy of his country. Soon other players from South Africa and other countries became involved in rumour and speculation, and it emerged that the South African team held three meetings before rejecting a large sum to fix a one-day international in India in 1996. South African authorities appointed Judge Edwin King to investigate the whole

affair. A report compiled earlier by Judge Qayyum into allegations of match fixing in Pakistan, previously kept secret, was released and was found to recommend life bans for players Salim Malik and Ata-uh-Rehman and sanctions and fines against other well-known players, some for failing to co-operate with the enquiry.

Hansie Cronje submitted a 6,300-word statement to the King Commission in which he admitted to taking four bribes, concerning one-day internationals and Test matches, including one for ensuring a positive result in the Test match between South Africa and England at Centurion Park, Pretoria, when South Africa forfeited their second innings, setting England a generous target to win, which they achieved.

In his statement Cronje implicated former India captain Mohammad Azharuddin as the person who introduced him to a bookmaker, Mukesh Gupta, and Azharuddin and others were investigated by India's Central Bureau of Investigation. Both Cronje and Azharuddin were subsequently banned from cricket.

As more and more accusations were made and more international cricketers were drawn into enquiries, Sir Paul Condon, ex-Commissioner of the Metropolitan Police, was appointed the ICC's first anti-corruption investigator. It is unlikely that the full extent of the corruption which blossomed in the mid-1990s, and extended into the new century, will ever be known, but it is clear that it was widespread and that the huge sums which are bet illegally in India and Pakistan on cricket have in recent years managed to influence the events on the field in a way which has rendered many results, particularly in one-day internationals, suspect.

Sadly, shortly after announcing a wish to embark on a media career, Hanse Cronje himself was killed on 1 June 2002 when a plane carrying him and two pilots crashed into a mountain near his home. Many, including ex-colleagues, still hero-worship him, and overlook his 'one mistake' while others find this distasteful.

CRICKET RECORDS

HIGHEST TEAM TOTALS

Only two totals over 1,000 have been scored in first-class cricket. In both cases, the batsman who led the run glut was W.H. Ponsford – 429 v Tasmania and 352 against New South Wales. The 10 highest team totals are:

1,107	Victoria v New South Wales, Melbourne	1926–27
1,059	Victoria v Tasmania, Melbourne	1922–23
952–6	Sri Lanka v India, Colombo	1997
951–7d	Sind v Baluchistan, Karachi	1973–74
944–6d	Hyderabad v Andhra, Secunderabad	1993–94
918	New South Wales v South Australia, Sydney	1900–01
912–8d	Holkar v Mysore, Indore	1945–46
912–6d	Tamil Nadu v Goa, Panjim	1988–89
910–6d	Railways v Dera Ismail Khan, Lahore	1964–65
903–7d	England v Australia, the Oval	1938
887	Yorkshire v Warwickshire, Edgbaston	1896

LOWEST TEAM TOTALS

The lowest total in any game of cricket is naturally enough 0. The first recorded example was in Norfolk in July 1815 – Fakenham, Walsingham and Hempton were all out 0 against Le cham, Dunham and Brisley. The 10 lowest totals in first-class cricket are:

6	Bs v England, Lord's	1810
12	Oxford University v MCC, Cowley Marsh	1877
12	Northamptonshire v Gloucestershire, Gloucester	1907
13	Auckland v Canterbury, Auckland	1877–78
13	Nottinghamshire v Yorkshire, Trent Bridge	1901
14	Surrey v Essex, Chelmsford	1983
15	MCC v Surrey, Lord's	1983
15	Victoria v MCC, Melbourne	1903–04
15	Northamptonshire v Yorkshire, Northampton	1908
15	Hampshire v Warwickshire, Edgbaston	1922

The last score on the above list is unique in that, batting a second time, Hampshire hit 521, then bowled out Warwickshire to win the game by 155 runs.

The lowest team total in Test cricket:

26	New Zealand v England, Auckland	1954–55

VICTORIES BY THE LARGEST MARGINS

The biggest victory of all occurred when Pakistan Railways – see highest team totals – hit 910–6d and their opponents only managed 59 in their two innings! The five biggest wins are:

Innings and 851 runs	Railways v Dera Ismail Khan, Lahore	1964–65
Innings and 666 runs	Victoria v Tasmania, Melbourne	1922–23
Innings and 656 runs	Victoria v New South Wales, Melbourne	1926–27
Innings and 605 runs	New South Wales v S Australia, Sydney	1900–01
Innings and 579 runs	England v Australia, the Oval	1938

HIGHEST INDIVIDUAL INNINGS

The first recorded innings above 100 was made by John Minshull who hit 107 for the Duke of Dorset's XI v Wrotham in 1769. William Ward hit the first double-century – 278 for MCC v Norfolk – in 1820. The present record score has stood for nearly 100 years. The top 10 highest innings in first-class cricket are:

501*	B.C. Lara, Warwickshire v Durham, Edgbaston	1994
499	Hanif Mohammad, Karachi v Bahawalpur, Karachi	1958–59
452*	D.G. Bradman, New South Wales v Queensland, Sydney	1929–30
443*	B.B. Nimbalkar, Maharashtra v Kathiswar, Poona	1948–49
437	W.H. Ponsford, Victoria v Queensland, Melbourne	1927–28
429	W.H. Ponsford, Victoria v Tasmania, Melbourne	1922–23
428	Aftab Baloch, Sind v Baluchistan, Karachi	1973–74
424	A.C. MacLaren, Lancashire v Somerset, Taunton	1895
405*	G.A. Hick, Worcestershire v Somerset, Taunton	1988
400*	B.C. Lara, West Indies v England, St John's, 2003–04	2003–04

* not out

The best innings in Test cricket are:

400*	B.C. Lara, West Indies v England, St John's	2003–04
380	M. L. Hayden, Australia v Zimbabwe, Perth	2003–04
375	B.C. Lara, West Indies v England, St John's	1993–94

365*	G.St.A. Sobers, West Indies v Pakistan, Kingston	1957–58
364	L. Hutton, England v Australia, the Oval	1938
340	S.T. Jayasuriya, Sri Lanka v India, Colombo	1997
337	Hanif Mohammad, Pakistan v West Indies, Bridgetown	1957–58
336*	W.R. Hammond, England v New Zealand, Auckland	1932–33
334*	M.A. Taylor, Australia v Pakistan, Peshawar	1998–99
334	D.G. Bradman, Australia v England, Headingley	1930

* not out

MOST RUNS IN A SEASON

When Denis Compton and Bill Edrich broke the record in 1947, they each played in 30 first-class matches. The most matches played by anyone in 1996 was 20, so though four-day games in theory might provide an opportunity to beat Compton's record, it is most unlikely. The leading run-scorers in an English first-class season are:

		M	I	NO	Runs	HS	Avge	100s
D.C.S. Compton (Middx)	1947	30	50	8	3,816	246	90.85	18
W.J. Edrich (Middx)	1947	30	52	8	3,539	267*	80.43	12
T.W. Hayward (Surrey)	1906	37	61	8	3,518	219	66.37	13
L Hutton (Yorks)	1949	33	56	6	3,429	269*	68.58	12
F.E. Woolley (Kent)	1928	36	59	4	3,352	198	60.94	12
H. Sutcliffe (Yorks)	1932	35	52	7	3,336	313	74.13	14
W.R. Hammond (Gloucs)	1933	34	54	5	3,323	264	67.81	13
E.H. Hendren (Middx)	1928	35	54	7	3,311	209*	70.44	13
R. Abel (Surrey)	1901	38	68	8	3,309	247	55.15	7
W.R. Hammond (Gloucs)	1937	33	55	5	3,252	217	65.04	13

* not out

Outside England the most runs in the current Test-playing countries in a single season are:

		Runs	Avge	
Australia	D.G. Bradman	1,690	93.88	1928–29
South Africa	J.R. Reid	1,915	68.39	1961–62
West Indies	E.H. Hendren	1,765	135.76	1929–30
New Zealand	M.D. Crowe	1,676	93.11	1986–87
India	C.G. Borde	1,604	64.16	1964–65
Pakistan	Saadat Ali	1,649	63.42	1983–84
Sri Lanka	R.P. Arnold	1,475	70.23	1995–96
Zimbabwe	G.W. Flower	983	57.82	1994–95
Bangladesh	M. Abedin	1,012	72.28	2001–02

MOST RUNS IN A FIRST-CLASS CAREER

As with the most runs in a season, the reduction in the number of first-class matches means that Hobbs' record is unlikely to be broken.

		M	I	NO	Runs	HS	Avge	100s
J.B. Hobbs	1905–34	834	1,325	107	61,760	316*	50.70	199
F.E. Woolley	1906–38	978	1,530	84	58,969	305*	40.77	145
E.H. Hendren	1907–38	833	1,300	166	57,611	301*	50.80	170
C.P. Mead	1905–36	814	1,340	185	55,061	280*	47.67	153
W.G. Grace	1865–08	869	1,478	104	54,211	344	39.45	124
W.R. Hammond	1920–51	634	1,005	104	50,551	336*	56.10	167
H. Sutcliffe	1919–45	754	1,098	124	50,670	313	52.02	151
G. Boycott	1962–86	609	1,014	162	48,426	261*	56.83	151

* not out

The highest career averages by a batsman who reached 10,000 runs are as follows:

D.G. Bradman	1927–48	234	338	43	28,067	452*	95.14	117
V.M. Merchant	1929–51	150	234	46	13,470	359*	71.64	45
Ajay Sharma	1984–2001	129	166	16	10,120	259*	67.47	38
W.H. Ponsford	1920–34	162	235	23	13,819	437	65.18	47

* not out

MOST RUNS IN TEST CAREER FOR EACH COUNTRY

England	G.A. Gooch	118	215	6	8,900	333	42.58	20
Australia	A.R. Border	156	265	44	11,174	205	50.56	27
South Africa	G. Kirsten	73	129	10	4,775	275	40.12	12
West Indies	B. C. Lara	106	187	6	9,657	400*	53.35	25
New Zealand	M.D. Crowe	77	131	11	5,444	299	45.36	17
India	S.M. Gavaskar	125	214	16	10,122	236*	51.12	34
Pakistan	Javed Miandad	124	189	21	8,832	280*	52.57	23
Sri Lanka	P.A. De Silva	93	159	11	6,361	267	42.97	20
Zimbabwe	A. Flower	63	112	19	4,794	232*	51.54	12

* not out

HIGHEST WICKET PARTNERSHIP

The highest in first-class cricket is given, but if that did not take place in a Test match, then a second line giving the highest Test partnership is given.

FIRST
561 Waheed Mirza and Mansoor Akhtar, Karachi Whites v Quetts, Karachi 1976–77
413 V. Mankad and Pankaj Roy, India v New Zealand, Madras 1955
SECOND
576 S.T. Jayasuriya and R. Mahanama, Sri Lanka v India, Colombo 1997
THIRD
467 A.H. Jones and M.D. Crowe, New Zealand v Sri Lanka, Wellington 1990–91
FOURTH
577 V.S. Hazare and Gul Mahomed, Baroda v Holkar, Baroda 1946–47
411 P.B.H. May and M.C. Cowdrey, England v West Indies, Edgbaston 1957
FIFTH
464* M.E. Waugh and S.R. Waugh, New South Wales v W Australia, Perth 1990–91
405 S.G. Barnes and D.G. Bradman, Australia v England, Sydney 1946–47
SIXTH
487* G.A. Headley and C.C. Passailaigue, Jamaica v Lord Tennyson's XI, Kingston 1931–32
346 J.H.W. Fingleton and D.G. Bradman, Australia v England, Melbourne 1936–37
SEVENTH
460 Bhupinder Singh and P. Dharmani, Punjab v Delhi, Delhi 1994–95
347 D.St.E. Atkinson and C.C. Depeiza, West Indies v Australia, Bridgetown 1954–55
EIGHT
433 V.T. Trumper and A. Sims, A. Sims' XI v Canterbury, Christchurch 1913–14
313 Wasim Akram and Saqlain Mushtaq, Pakistan v Zimbabwe, Sheikhupura 1996–97
NINTH
283 J. Chapman and A. Warren, Derbyshire v Warwickshire, Blackwell 1910
195 M.V. Boucher and P.L. Symcox, South Africa v Pakistan, Johannesburg 1997–98
TENTH
307 A.F. Kippax and J.E.H. Hooker, New South Wales v Victoria, Melbourne 1928–29
151 B.F. Hastings and R.O. Collinge, New Zealand v Pakistan 1972–73
151 Azhar Mahmood and Mushtaq Ahmed, Pakistan v South Africa, Rawalpindi 1997–98

BEST BOWLING IN AN INNINGS

The best possible analysis for a bowler in an eleven-a-side match is to take all 10 wickets without allowing a single run. The top 10 analyses in first-class cricket are:

O	M	R	W		
19.4	16	10	10	H. Verity, Yorkshire v Nottinghamshire, Headingley	1932
19	11	20	10	P.M. Chatterjee, Bengal v Assam, Jorhat	1956–57
12	2	26	10	A.E.E. Vogler, E. Province v Griqualand West, Johannesburg	1906–07
21.3	10	28	10	Naeem Akhtar, Rawalpindi B v Peshawar	1995–96
16.2	8	18	10	G. Geary, Leicestershire v Glamorgan, Pontypridd	1929
23.2	14	28	10	W.P. Howell, Australians v Surrey, the Oval	1899
21.3	10	28	10	A.E. Moss, Canterbury v Wellington, Christchurch	1889–90
21.3	10	28	10	Naheed Akhtar, Rawalpindi v Peshawar, Peshawar	1995–96
16	7	30	10	C. Blythe, Kent v Northamptonshire, Northampton	1907
8.5	0	35	10	A. Drake, Yorkshire v Somerset, Weston	1895
27	11	32	10	H. Pickett, Essex v Leicestershire, Leyton	1895

The best analysis in Test cricket is:
51.2 23 53 10 J.C. Laker, England v Australia, Old Trafford 1956

BEST BOWLING IN A MATCH

A number of bowlers have taken all 20 wickets in a match, the first recorded instance being by the F.R. Spofforth, who took 20 for 48 in Bendigo, NSW in 1881–82.

The best records in first-class matches are (the first being the Test record):

19–90 J.C. Laker, England v Australia, Old Trafford 1956
17–48 C. Blythe, Kent v Northamptonshire, Northampton 1907
17–50 C.T.B. Turner, Australians v England XI, Hastings 1888
17–54 W.P. Howell, Australians v W. Province, Cape Town 1902–03
17–56 C.W.L. Parker, Gloucestershire v Essex, Colchester 1925
17–67 A.P. Freeman, Kent v Sussex, Hove 1922
17–89 W.G. Grace, Gloucestershire v Nottinghamshire, Cheltenham 1877
17–89 F.C.L. Matthews, Nottinghamshire v Northamptonshire, Trent Bridge 1923

MOST WICKETS IN ENGLAND IN A SEASON
The contraction in the number of first-class matches means that the records below are unlikely to be beaten. It is now rare for a bowler to reach 100 wickets in a season.

		O	M	R	W	Avge
A.P. Freeman	1928	1,976.1	423	5,489	304	18.05
A.P. Freeman	1933	2,039.0	651	4,549	298	15.26
T. Richardson	1895	1,690.1	463	4,170	290	14.37
C.T.B. Turner	1888	2,427.2	1,127	3,307	283	11.68
A.P. Freeman	1931	1,618.0	360	4,307	276	15.60
A.P. Freeman	1930	1,914.3	472	4,632	275	16.84

To take 100 wickets in a season outside England is most unusual. The following have achieved the feat:

Australia, C.T.B. Turner 106 in 1887–88
South Africa, R. Benaud 106 in 1957–58
India, M.W. Tate 116 in 1926–27; Kabir Khan 113 in 1998–99
Pakistan, Ijaz Faqih 107 in 1985–86; Murtaza Hussain 105 in 1995–96;
  Abdul Qadir 103 in 1982–83
South Africa, S.F. Barnes 104 in 1913–14

MOST WICKETS IN A FIRST-CLASS CAREER

		R	W	Avge	5i	10m	BB
W. Rhodes	1898–30	70,322	4204	16.72	287	68	9–24
A.P. Freeman	1914–36	69,577	3776	18.42	386	140	10–53
C.W.L. Parker	1903–35	63,817	3278	19.46	277	91	10–79
J.T. Hearne	1888–23	54,352	3061	17.75	255	66	9–32
T.W.J. Goddard	1922–52	59,116	2979	19.84	251	86	10–113
A.S. Kennedy	1907–36	61,034	2874	21.23	225	45	10–37
D. Shackleton	1948–69	53,303	2857	18.65	194	38	9–30
G.A.R. Lock	1946–70	54,709	2844	19.23	196	50	10–54
F.J. Titmus	1949–82	63,313	2830	22.37	168	26	9–52
W.G. Grace	1865–08	50,980	2809	18.14	240	64	10–49

MOST WICKETS IN TEST CAREER FOR EACH COUNTRY

England	I.T. Botham	10,878	383	28.4	27	4	8–34
Australia	S.K. Warne	13,145	517	25.42	27	8	8–71
South Africa	A.A. Donald	7,334	330	22.25	20	3	8–71
West Indies	C.A. Walsh	12,688	519	24.44	22	3	7–37
New Zealand	R.J. Hadlee	9,612	431	22.29	36	9	9–52
India	Kapil Dev	12,867	434	29.74	23	2	9–83
Pakistan	Wasim Akram	9,779	414	23.62	25	5	7–119
Sri Lanka	M Muralitharan	11,779	527	22.77	43	13	9–51

ALL-ROUND RECORDS

Until the reduction of first-class matches in England, the standard measurement of an all-rounder was that he scored 1,000 runs in a season and took 100 wickets. The two outstanding all-round feats which go beyond this record are 2,000 runs and 200 wickets in a season – performed only once by G.H. Hirst of Yorkshire in 1906, and 3,000 runs and 100 wickets, again only achieved once, by J.H. Parks of Sussex in 1937. Since the reduction in matches, just two players have managed 1,000 runs and 100 wickets – R.J. Hadlee in 1984 and F.D. Stephenson in 1988 – and both played for Nottinghamshire.

The outstanding all-round career figures are as follows:

	M	R	Avge	W	Avge
W. Rhodes	1,110	39,969	30.81	4,204	16.72
W.G. Grace	869	54,211	39.45	2,809	18.14

The outstanding all-round career figures at Test level are:

I.T. Botham (Eng)	102	5,200	33.54	383	28.40
R. Benaud (Aus)	63	2,201	24.45	248	27.03
G.St.A. Sobers (WI)	93	8,032	57.78	235	34.03
R.J. Hadlee (NZ)	86	3,124	27.16	431	22.29
Kapil Dev (India)	131	5,248	31.05	434	29.64
Imran Khan (Pak)	88	3,807	37.69	362	22.81

Botham and Sobers also took more than 100 catches each.

WICKET-KEEPING

Most dismissals in an English season are 128 (79 ct, 49 st) by L.E.G. Ames for Kent in 1929; in a career, 1,649 (147 ct, 176 st) by R.W. Taylor of Derbyshire.

At Test level, R.W. Marsh holds the record for a single series, 28 (all caught), the record in a career is held by I.A. Healy with 395 (366ct, 29st) – both players are Australian.

FIELDING

Most catches by a fielder in an English season are 78 by W.R. Hammond of Gloucestershire in 1928; the most in a career by F.E. Woolley of Kent with 1,018.
Most catches in a Test series are 15 by J.M. Gregory of Australia, and in a Test career 173 by M.E. Waugh of Australia.

CRICKET CHRONOLOGY

1598 First reference to the game – in a court case in Guildford, Surrey

1646 First recorded cricket match at Coxheath, Kent

1706 A poem in Latin by William Goldwin gives first description of a match

1709 Match between Kent and Surrey at Dartford – first inter-county game

1710 Cricket first mentioned at Cambridge University

1727 Cricket first mentioned at Oxford University

1739 Earliest known pictorial reference showing boys playing cricket.

1744 Kent v All England on the Artillery Ground, London, first major match whose detailed score is preserved

1744 Earliest extant Laws of Cricket

1751 New York oppose London in New York

1767 Charles Powlett takes over the Hambledon Club in Hampshire about this time

1769 First recorded century: John Minshull 107 for Duke of Dorset's XI

1787 Thomas Lord opens his first ground (now Dorset Square) in London

1792 Calcutta Club in India in existence

1794 First recorded public school match: Charterhouse v Westminster

1800 First instructional book published by T. Boxall

1803 First cricket in Australia – Sydney

1806 First Gentlemen v Players Match at Lord's

1814 Present Lord's cricket ground opened

1825 Sussex play Kent in the match from which the county championship originated

1827 First Oxford v Cambridge university match

1828 Round-arm bowling legalized

1835 Nottinghamshire oppose Sussex in the former's first quest for the title of Champion County

1844 United States play Canada for the first time – the oldest international contest in the world

1846 Surrey oppose Kent in the former's first quest for the title of Champion County

1850–51 Tasmania play Victoria at Launceston in the first Australian inter-colonial first-class match

1855–56 New South Wales play Victoria in the former's first first-class match

1857 Cambridgeshire oppose Surrey in the former's first quest for the title Champion County

1859 George Parr leads first England team overseas – to North America

1859 Middlesex oppose Kent in the former's first quest for the title Champion County

1861 Yorkshire oppose Surrey in the former's first quest for the title Champion County

1863–64 Otago play Canterbury in the first first-class match in New Zealand

1864 *Wisden's Cricketers' Almanack* first published

1864–65 Barbados play Demerara (British Guiana) at Bridgetown in the first first-class match in the British West Indies

1864 Over-arm bowling legalized

1864 Hampshire join the County Championship (drop out in 1885 and rejoin in 1895)

1865 Lancashire join the County Championship

1868 Australian Aborigines tour England

1868–69 Trinidad play Demerara (Guyana) in the former's first first-class match

1870 Gloucestershire join the County Championship

1871 W.G. Grace becomes the first batsman to hit 2,000 first-class runs in a season

1871 Derbyshire join County Championship (drop out after 1887 and rejoin in 1895)

1873–74 Auckland and Wellington each play their first first-class match

1876 W.G. Grace becomes the first batsman to score 300 in first-class cricket: 344 for MCC at Canterbury

1876–77 First-ever Test match: England v Australia, Melbourne

1877–78 South Australia play Tasmania in the former's first first-class match

1878 First first-class match in the United States – Philadelphia v Australia at Nicetown

1878 First official Australian tour to England

1880 Kennington Oval stages its first Test, England v Australia

1881–82 Sydney cricket ground stages its first Test, England v Australia

1882 Somerset join County Championship (drop out after 1884 and rejoin in 1891)

1884	Lord's, London, stages its first Test, England v Australia
1884	Old Trafford, Manchester, stages its first Test, England v Australia
1888–89	South Africa's first Test v England at Port Elizabeth
1888–89	Newlands, Cape Town, stages its first Test, England v South Africa
1889–90	Natal, Western Province and Transvaal each play their first first-class match. Currie Cup inaugurated
1889–90	First English team tours India
1890–91	Eastern Province and Griqualand West play their first first-class match
1892–93	Sheffield Shield competition inaugurated this season
1892–93	Queensland play New South Wales in the former's first first-class match
1892–93	First first-class match in India: Parsees v Europeans in Bombay
1892–93	Western Australia play Victoria in the former's first first-class match
1894–95	Jamaica play their first first-class match
1895	Essex, Leicestershire and Warwickshire join the County Championship
1898	Board of Control set up to run Tests in England
1899	Worcestershire join the County Championship
1899	Trent Bridge, Nottingham, stages its first Test, England v Australia
1899	Headingley, Leeds, stages its first Test, England v Australia
1900	Six-ball over introduced into England
1902	Edgbaston, Birmingham, stages its first Test, England v Australia
1902–03	Border play their first first-class match
1903–04	Orange Free State play their first first-class match

1905	Australian Board of Control set up
1905–06	Hindus join the Bombay Tournament
1905	Northamptonshire join the County Championship
1906–07	Plunket Shield presented to Canterbury
1909	ICC (Imperial, now International, Cricket Conference) founded
1909–10	Rhodesia (Zimbabwe) play their first first-class match
1911–12	First first-class match in South America
1912–13	Muslims join the Bombay Tournament
1915–16	First first-class match in Madras Presidency Tournament
1921	Glamorgan join County Championship
1925–26	First first-class match in Ceylon (Sri Lanka): Dr J. Rockwood's Ceylon XI v W.E. Lucas's Bombay XI
1926	English Women's Cricket Association founded
1926	India, New Zealand and the West Indies join England, Australia and South Africa in the ICC
1926–27	Queensland join the Sheffield Shield
1928	West Indies' first Test v England at Lord's
1929–30	New Zealand's first Test v England at Christchurch
1929–30	Queen's Park Oval, Port of Spain, stages its first Test, England v West Indies
1929–30	Basin Reserve, Wellington, stages its first Test, England v New Zealand
1929–30	Kensington Oval, Bridgetown, stages its first Test, England v West Indies
1930–31	First first-class match in the Moin-ud-Dowlah Cup
1931–32	Woolloongabba, Brisbane, stages its first Test, Australia v South Africa
1932	India's first Test v England at Lord's
1932–33	England v Australia bodyline series

1933–34	Eden Gardens, Calcutta, stages its first Test, India v England
1934–35	Ranji Trophy Competition inaugurated
1937–38	Last first-class match in South America: Argentina v Sir T. Brinckman's XI at Belgrano
1947–48	Western Australia join the Sheffield Shield
1947–48	First first-class match in Pakistan: West Punjab Governor's XI v Punjab University
1947	D.C.S. Compton hits 3,816 first-class runs in season – new record and also 18 hundreds
1950–51	Central Districts join Plunket Shield
1952–53	Pakistan's first Test v India at Delhi
1952	Pakistan join the ICC
1953–54	Qaid-I-Azam Tournament for first-class cricket in Pakistan inaugurated
1956–57	Northern Districts join Plunket Shield
1958–59	Leeward Islands play their first first-class match
1959–60	Windward Islands play their first first-class match
1961–62	Duleep Trophy competition inaugurated
1963	Gillette (now NatWest) Cup inaugurated
1965–66	Shell Shield competition inaugurated in the West Indies
1965	Ceylon, Fiji and USA become first Associate ICC members
1968	TCCB replaces English Board of Control
1969–70	First one-day competition in Australia
1969	Players (now AXA Life) Sunday League inaugurated
1970	South African tour to England cancelled due to anti-apartheid campaign
1970–71	BCCP Trophy competition inaugurated (continued as Patron's Trophy)

1970–71	First one-day international, Australia v England, Melbourne
1971–72	NZ Motor Corp Tournament: first one-day competition of major standing in New Zealand inaugurated
1972	Benson & Hedges Cup inaugurated
1972	Prudential (now Texaco) One-Day Trophy inaugurated
1973–74	Deodhar Trophy inaugurated: first one-day competition of major standing in India
1975–76	Gillette Cup for one-day matches in the West Indies inaugurated (now Shell/Sandals Trophy)
1975	First World Cup
1977	Kerry Packer, Australian media magnate, signs up 51 Test players to create World Series Cricket
1977–78	Tasmania join the Sheffield Shield
1979–80	First Benson & Hedges World Series Cup
1980	Present Laws of Cricket published
1981–82	Benson & Hedges Night Series inaugurated in South Africa
1981–82	Sri Lanka's first Test v England in Colombo
1983–84	Asia Cup inaugurated
1988–89	Lakspray Trophy becomes first first-class competition in Sri Lanka
1991–92	Zimbabwe's first Test v India in Harare
1992	Durham join the County Championship
1993	All County Championship matches arranged for four days
1993–94	Logan Cup raised to first-class status in Zimbabwe
1997	England and Wales Cricket Board established
2000	County Championship split into two divisions.
2001	Bangladesh granted Test match status.

INDEX

PICTURE CREDITS

The publishers would like to thank the following sources for their kind permission to reproduce the pictures in this book:

Action Images: /Jason O'Brien 18.

Alpha/Sport and General: 185.

Bridgeman Art Library: /Marylebone Cricket Club/Francis Hayman: 186.

Colorsport: 21, 25, 31, 33t, 55, 57, 58, 64, 65, 66, 67tl, 69, 85, 86, 100, 103, 108, 120t, 121, 123b, 130, 132, 133r, 134b, 135l, 137l, 139, 142, 143c, 143t, 145, 147, 148, 150, 151, 152, 153t, 153b, 156, 157, 158, 159t, 161, 162b, 163t.

Patrick Eagar: 7, 39, 46, 49.

Empics: /Matt Dunham/AP: 6; /Neal Simpson: 3,

5t, 26; /John Walton: 24.

Getty Images: 17, 22, 52bl, 68, 102, 106, 113, 123t, 133, 154b, 164t; /Hulton Archive: 56, 62, 93, 101, 124, 127, 135r, 136, 143b, 144b; /Hamish Blair: 74; /Shaun Botterill: 44, 80, 89, 104, 192; /Simon Bruty: 99; /Graham Chadwick: 176; /Chris Cole: 89, 125t, 162t; /Sue Forster: 38l; /Laurence Griffiths: 55; /Mike Hewitt: 38r, 45, 48, 81, 82, 91, 129t, 166, 175t; /Image Select: /Ann Ronan: 9, 10br, 12, 13, 33b, 54; /Inpho: 43; /Ross Kinnaird: 36, 141t; /Joe Mann: 73, 90; /Clive Mason: 4, 28, 30, 63br, 171; /Indranil Mukherjee/AFP: 35; /Adrian Murrell: 19, 27, 32, 34, 37, 41, 72tr, 75, 79, 87, 88, 91, 94, 95, 105, 107, 109, 120b, 25b, 126, 128, 137r, 141b, 154t, 159b, 163r, 164b, 165, 173, 175b, 199; /Ben Radford: 29, 67r, 70, 72tl, 90, 119, 134t, 174; /Clive Rose: 60; /AFP/Jewel Samad: 5b; /AFP/Dibyangshu Sarkar: 76; /Ben Shaw: 59; /Mark Thompson: 129b.

Ken Kelly: 195.

Mary Evans Picture Library: 11, 50.

M.C.C: 194b, 196.

Popperfoto: 92, 97, 98, 110, 111, 144t, 169, 172, 177, 184; /BTH: 96, 112: /David Joyner: 184.

Topfoto.co.uk: 181, 194t.

Peter Wynne–Thomas: 14, 15.

Every effort has been made to acknowledge correctly and contact the source and/copyright holder of each picture, and Carlton Books Limited apologises for any unintentional errors or omissions which will be corrected in future editions of this book.